THE COLLECTED WORKS OF JEREMY BENTHAM

General Editors
F. Rosen and P. Schofield

ECONOMICS AND SOCIETY

In the essays presented in this volume Bentham lays down the theoretical principles from which he develops his proposals for reform of the English poor laws in response to the perceived crisis in poor relief in the mid-1790s. In 'Essays on the subject of the Poor Laws' Bentham seeks to justify the principles on which entitlement to relief should be grounded, while in 'Pauper Systems Compared' he presents a sustained comparison between home relief and institutional relief. The polemical 'Observations on the Poor Bill' is a lively critique of the Bill introduced into the House of Commons by William Pitt in 1796. The ideas advanced here by Bentham were a significant influence on Edwin Chadwick, and, through his mediation, on the Poor Law Amendment Act of 1834. The essays are based almost entirely on manuscript sources, and published here for the first time in definitive form.

The Collected Works of Jeremy Bentham

The new critical edition of the works and correspondence of Jeremy Bentham (1748–1832) is being prepared and published under the supervision of the Bentham Committee of University College London. In spite of his importance as jurist, philosopher, and social scientist, and leader of the Utilitarian reformers, the only previous edition of his works was a poorly edited and incomplete one brought out within a decade or so of his death. The overall plan and principles of this edition are set out in the General Preface to *The Correspondence of Jeremy Bentham*, vol. 1 (Athlone Press), which was the first volume of the *Collected Works* to be published.

Volumes published by Oxford University Press

Constitutional Code
Volume 1
Edited by F. Rosen and J. H. Burns

Deontology, together with A Table of the Springs of Action and Article on Utilitarianism
Edited by Amnon Goldworth

Chrestomathia
Edited by M. J. Smith and W. H. Burston

First Principles preparatory to Constitutional Code
Edited by Philip Schofield

Securities against Misrule and other Constitutional Writings for Tripoli and Greece
Edited by Philip Schofield

Official Aptitude Maximized; Expense Minimized
Edited by Philip Schofield

Colonies, Commerce, and Constitutional Law: Rid Yourselves of Ultramaria and other writings on Spain and Spanish America
Edited by Philip Schofield

'Legislator of the World': Writings on Codification, Law, and Education
Edited by Philip Schofield and Jonathan Harris

Political Tactics
Edited by Michael James, Cyprian Blamires, and Catherine Pease-Watkin

Correspondence, volume 6: January 1798 to December 1801
Edited by J. R. Dinwiddy

Correspondence, volume 7: January 1802 to December 1808
Edited by J. R. Dinwiddy

Correspondence, volume 8: January 1809 to December 1816
Edited by Stephen Conway

Correspondence, volume 9: January 1817 to June 1820
Edited by Stephen Conway

Correspondence, volume 10: July 1820 to December 1821
Edited by Stephen Conway

Correspondence, volume 11: January 1822 to June 1824
Edited by Catherine Fuller

WRITINGS ON THE POOR LAWS

VOLUME I

edited by
MICHAEL QUINN

CLARENDON PRESS · OXFORD

OXFORD
UNIVERSITY PRESS

Great Clarendon Street, Oxford OX2 6DP

Oxford University Press is a department of the University of Oxford.
It furthers the University's aim of excellence in research, scholarship,
and education by publishing worldwide in

Oxford New York

Athens Auckland Bangkok Bogotá Bombay Buenos Aires Cape Town
Chennai Dar es Salaam Delhi Florence Hong Kong Istanbul Karachi
Kolkata Kuala Lumpur Madrid Melbourne Mexico City Mumbai
Nairobi Paris São Paulo Singapore Taipei Tokyo Toronto Warsaw

and associated companies in Berlin Ibadan

Oxford is a registered trade mark of Oxford University Press
in the UK and certain other countries

Published in the United States
by Oxford University Press Inc., New York

First published 2001

British Library Cataloguing in Publication Data

Data available

Library of Congress Cataloging in Publication Data

Data applied for

ISBN 0-19-924232-1

1 3 5 7 9 10 8 6 4 2

Typeset by Joshua Associates Ltd., Oxford
Printed in Great Britain
on acid-free paper by
Biddles Ltd., Guildford & King's Lynn

PREFACE

This volume is dedicated to the memory of Dr Janet Semple, who commenced the editorial work, but whose untimely death denied to Bentham scholarship the full benefit of her considerable talent. She is sorely missed.

The Bentham Committee wishes to thank the Wellcome Trust whose grant allowing for the appointment of an editor and half-time Research Assistant has made possible the preparation of the present volume. The Committee is indebted to University College London for its considerable and important support, and to the British Academy, the Arts and Humanities Research Board, and the Economic and Social Research Council for continuing financial assistance.

I would like to thank University College London Library, the British Library, University of London Library, Wellcome Institute Library, and the Public Record Office for permission to quote from manuscripts in their possession and for assistance in tracing rare books and other documents. Special thanks are extended to the staff of University College London Library, and in particular to Ms Gillian Furlong and Ms Susan Stead.

I am indebted to the General Editors, Professor Frederick Rosen and Dr Philip Schofield, for their careful reading of, and invaluable comments on, the completed text and Editorial Introduction. Thanks are especially due to Dr Schofield, whose unstinting energy and assistance has shepherded the volume through its final stages. I am grateful to colleagues at the Bentham Project both for specific help and advice in instances too numerous to mention, and for providing a supportive environment in which to work. In particular, thanks are due to Mrs Irena Nicoll, for shouldering the painstaking task of checking the annotation; to Dr Jonathan Harris and Ms Catherine Pease-Watkin, for reading and commenting on the Editorial Introduction, as well as providing illumination on a whole range of points; and to Mrs Kate Barber for general secretarial assistance. My greatest debt is owed to Ms Catherine Fuller, without whose immense contribution, encompassing the greater part of the transcription of the manuscripts and of the research for the annotation, in addition to never-failing assistance and support, the volume simply would not have been completed.

I gratefully acknowledge the help received in the elucidation of references in the text and other assistance from the following scholars: Professor W. F. Bynum, Dr Stephen Conway, Professor Martin Daunton, Dr Anthony Draper, Professor John L. Flood, Mr Peter Griffin, Dr Marco Guidi, Mr Derek Hudson, Mr Jan de bie Leuveling Tjeenk, Mr A. D. E. Lewis, Professor Roy Porter, Dr Edith Schipper, Professor Robert Sharples, Mrs Katja Strahl-Draper, and Professor Giancarlo de Vivo.

M.Q.

CONTENTS

SYMBOLS AND ABBREVIATIONS

Symbols

| |	Space left in manuscript.
[to]	Word(s) editorially supplied.
[?]	Reading doubtful.
[. . . ?]	Word(s) proved illegible.

Abbreviations

Apart from the standard abbreviations the following should be noted:

Bowring	*The Works of Jeremy Bentham*, published under the superintendence of . . . John Bowring, 11 vols., Edinburgh, 1843.
UC	Bentham papers in the Library of University College London. Roman numerals refer to boxes in which the papers are placed, arabic to the leaves within each box.
CW	This edition of *The Collected Works of Jeremy Bentham*.

EDITORIAL INTRODUCTION

The writings contained in the present volume were composed by Bentham in two intense periods of activity. In the first period, lasting from February to late May 1796, Bentham addressed on the one hand the nature and causes of the demand for relief, and on the other the basic principles which should govern its provision, producing 'Table of Cases calling for Relief'[1] and three 'Essays on the subject of the Poor Laws', namely 'Definitions and Distinctions', 'Fundamental Positions in regard to the making provision for the Indigent Poor', and 'Collateral Uses derivable from a system of Industry Houses'.[2] At the end of May 1796, Bentham's intention was to incorporate 'Essays on the subject of the Poor Laws' in a projected major work entitled '*Penetocomia*, or Principles of Legislation and Management relative to the subject matter of the Poor Laws'. In the event, although Bentham drafted considerable additional material for inclusion in this work, it remained radically incomplete.[3]

The themes which Bentham had intended to pursue in '*Penetocomia*', on the basis of the general propositions contained in 'Essays on the subject of the Poor Laws', were developed in the second period of activity, lasting from late December 1796 to mid-February 1797. During this period, he completed both 'Pauper Systems Compared, or a Comparative View of the several systems establishable as well as established in relation to the Poor',[4] and 'Observations on the Poor Bill'.[5] The former work grew out of a preliminary general survey of competing systems of relief with which Bentham had intended to prefix a sustained critique of the particular provisions of the legislative reform of poor relief introduced by William Pitt,[6] while the latter contained the substance of that critique. In addition, Bentham composed both 'Essay on the question, Who are the persons for whom the several bounties provided by this Bill are intended?', which appears in the present volume as an Appendix to 'Observations on the Poor Bill',[7] and the writings which appear as Appendices to the volume as a whole, namely 'Neighbour's-Fare Principle Defended' and 'Farming Defended'.[8]

[1] See pp. xvi–xix below.
[2] See pp. xix–xxxiii below.
[3] See pp. xxv–xxviii below.
[4] See pp. xxxii–xli below.
[5] See pp. xli–xlix below.
[6] William Pitt the Younger (1759–1806), leader of the administration as First Lord of the Treasury and Chancellor of the Exchequer 1783–1801, 1804–6.
[7] See p. xlix below.
[8] See pp. l and li below respectively.

It was only after completing these writings that Bentham undertook the detailed exposition of his specific scheme for the provision of relief to indigence. He again took up themes previously intended for presentation in the now abandoned '*Penetocomia*', and developed the ideas instead in 'Pauper Management Improved', where he advocated the contract management of poor relief. In July 1797, whilst engaged in the drafting of 'Pauper Management Improved' Bentham received an invitation from Sir John Sinclair, President of the Board of Agriculture,[1] which was to issue in the composition of Bentham's only writings on poor relief to be published in his lifetime: 'as I am applying to all the intelligent men of my acquaintance for Papers to be inserted in our transactions I cannot think of overlooking so capital a hand as Mr. Bentham. The object to which I wish you would direct your attention, is the proper Management of the poor'.[2] Bentham replied that Sinclair's request would be fulfilled, and indeed had been anticipated, since he had 'been thinking of nothing else but poverty for these seven or eight months'.[3] After pointing out that the products of his labours were voluminous, Bentham suggested that abstracts might be made.[4]

On 8 September 1797, as a result of Sinclair's invitation, Bentham sent 'Table of Cases calling for Relief' to Arthur Young, editor of the *Annals of Agriculture, and other useful Arts*,[5] together with a 'Pauper Population Table', designed to elicit a flow of statistical information with regard to those in receipt of poor relief. These tables, accompanied with remarks intended to explain 'the importance of the information I am thus labouring to collect',[6] were published under the title 'Situation and Relief of the Poor'.[7] In subsequent issues of the journal, Bentham's abridgement of 'Pauper Management Improved' appeared as 'Outline of a Work entitled Pauper Management Improved'.[8] The

[1] Sir John Sinclair (1754–1835), MP for Caithness 1780–4, 1790–6, 1802–6, 1807–11, Lostwithiel 1784–90, and Petersfield 1797–1802, President of the Board of Agriculture 1793–8, 1806–14.

[2] See Sinclair to Bentham, 5 July 1797, *The Correspondence of Jeremy Bentham*, vol. v, ed. A.T. Milne, London, 1981 (*CW*), p. 369.

[3] See Bentham to Sinclair, 13 July 1797, ibid. 370.

[4] Ibid. 371.

[5] Arthur Young (1741–1820), agriculturist, editor of the *Annals of Agriculture, and other useful Arts* 1784–1809, Secretary of the Board of Agriculture 1793–1811.

[6] Bentham to Young, 8 September 1797, *Correspondence* (*CW*), v. 377.

[7] See *Annals of Agriculture*, xxix (1797), 393–426 (Bowring, viii. 361–8).

[8] See *Annals of Agriculture*, xxx (1798), 89–176, 241–96, 393–424, 457–504, and xxxi (1798), 33–64, 169–200, 273–88 (Bowring, viii. 369–439). 'Outline of a Work entitled Pauper Management Improved' was extracted from the first four of the intended six books which were to constitute 'Pauper Management Improved'. Bentham's decision to abandon this work appears to relate to his recognition of the inadequacy of the actuarial assumptions on which his calculations of birth and mortality rates were based. On 18 May 1800 he confided as follows to Pierre Étienne Louis Dumont (1759–1829), his Genevan translator and editor, who had sent

work was reprinted as a separate pamphlet in 1798, and published in 1812,[1] while a French translation appeared in 1802.[2]

Bentham's discussion of poverty involved much more than the minute exposition of a specific plan of reform: it encompassed an investigation of the basic principles on which provision of relief should be grounded, and a sustained comparison of alternative systems of relief. Of the writings contained in the present volume, only 'Table of Cases calling for Relief' was published in Bentham's lifetime, while only 'Observations on the Poor Bill' was published subsequently.[3]

HISTORY OF THE TEXTS

The details of the history of the separate essays included in the present volume will follow an account of the way in which Bentham's interest in poor relief was first stimulated.

The legislative foundation of poor relief in England had been established in 1601 by 43 Eliz. I c.2, which instructed parishes to relieve the impotent, put the able-bodied to work, and correct the idle. These injunctions were satisfied in differing degrees and by an enormous variety of methods, since responsibility for delivering relief was laid upon some fifteen thousand separate parishes, which developed their own customs and practices concerning its extent and mode of delivery.

At the end of 1795, the English poor law was under severe strain. The price of bread, the staple diet among the poor in southern England, had risen in price to a level which outstripped the wages of the rural poor.[4] Very real hardship was accompanied by increases in expenditure on the poor rates, the local tax on occupied property and

him some statistical research on the poor: 'I forbear discussions and dissertations. They present a dilemma for which no solution strikes me at this instant, and it may be some time before I apply myself again to this subject'. See *The Correspondence of Jeremy Bentham*, vol. vi, ed. J.R. Dinwiddy, Oxford, 1984, (*CW*), p. 297.

[1] *Pauper Management Improved: Particularly By Means Of An Application Of The Panopticon Principle Of Construction*, London, 1812. This edition also included 'Situation and Relief of the Poor'.

[2] *Esquisse d'un ouvrage en faveur des pauvres, adressée a l'éditeur des Annales d'Agriculture, par Jérémie Bentham*, Paris, 1802. This edition also included a French translation of 'Situation and Relief of the Poor'.

[3] See p. xlvii below.

[4] The effect of the disruption of trade attendant upon the outbreak of war with France in February 1793 was exacerbated by poor harvests in 1794 and 1795. In January 1795 the price of corn stood at seven shillings a bushel, its highest level for four years, and by late summer had reached almost fourteen shillings.

land which funded the parochial system of relief. As magistrates and overseers across the country sought to develop local expedients to address the crisis, Samuel Whitbread[1] introduced a Bill in the House of Commons on 9 December 1795 to allow magistrates at Quarter Sessions to set minimum wage rates for agricultural labourers.

In the period before the second reading of the Bill on 12 February 1796, William Pitt, leader of the administration, had, according to his own account, 'paid considerable attention to the subject, and endeavoured to collect information from the best sources to which he had access', with a view to doing 'every thing in his power to bring forward or promote such measures as would conduce to the interests of the country'. In successfully opposing Whitbread's Bill, on the grounds that it endeavoured 'to establish by authority, what would be much better accomplished by the unassisted operation of principles', Pitt indicated his preparedness to bring forward extensive reforms of his own.[2]

Recognizing his own comparative lack of expertise in the field, Pitt sought the advice and assistance of others in drafting his measure. One such adviser was William Wilberforce,[3] a friend and admirer of Bentham since early 1795, and his unfailingly supportive, if somewhat ineffectual, ally in the long campaign to build the panopticon prison house.[4] Early in 1796, Wilberforce seems to have sent to

[1] Samuel Whitbread (1764–1815), MP for Bedford 1790–1815.

[2] See *Parliamentary History* (1795–7), xxxii. 705, 712, 706 respectively.

[3] William Wilberforce (1759–1833), philanthropist, MP for Hull 1780–4, Yorkshire 1784–1812, and Bramber 1812–25. Among Pitt's other likely confidants on the matter, George Rose (1744–1818), MP for Launceston 1784–8, Lymington 1788–90, and Christchurch 1790–1818, Secretary to the Treasury 1782–3, 1783–1801, Vice-President of the Board of Trade 1804–6, 1807–12, Treasurer of the Navy 1807–18, the architect of 33 Geo. III, c.54, which gave legal recognition to Friendly Societies, seems certain to have been involved from the outset. Thomas Ruggles (1737?-1813), writer on the poor laws, became involved in February 1796, as indicated by a letter of 5 February 1797, from Ruggles to William Bray (copied at UC cli. 44), in response to the hostile observations on the Bill made by the committee of the vestry of St Giles and St George, Bloomsbury, in which he states, 'I attended Mr Pitt & the Gentlemen consulted by him at his house at different times, through the month of February last year and left town the end of the month with a Commission from him to explain and recommend the plan the heads of which we had then concluded on in a Pamphlet calculated for popular attention.' Charles Abbot (1757–1829), first Baron Colchester, MP for Helston 1795–1802, Woodstock 1802–6, and Oxford University 1806–17, Bentham's step-brother, appears to have been consulted only at a much later stage in the proceedings: see *The Diary and Correspondence of Charles Abbot, Lord Colchester*, ed. Charles, Lord Colchester, 3 vols., London, 1861, i. 82–3. For discussion of others possibly involved in the drafting of the Bill see J.R. Poynter, *Society and Pauperism: English Ideas on Poor Relief, 1795–1834*, London, 1969, p. 63; and J. Ehrman, *The Younger Pitt: the Reluctant Transition*, London, 1983, p. 473.

[4] For a detailed account of Bentham's panopticon writings, and of his ultimately frustrated attempts to build the prison, see J. Semple, *Bentham's Prison: A Study of the Panopticon Penitentiary*, Oxford, 1993. For Wilberforce's recognition of his own lack of success in expediting the execution of the panopticon project see Wilberforce to Bentham, 21 November 1796, *Correspondence* (*CW*), v. 309–10.

Bentham a draft of a Poor Bill, presumably with a request for comments.[1] By 10 February 1796 Bentham had written and had twice copied a brief critique of one clause of 'Wilberforce's bill', namely that which proposed 'Power to Justices to order Overseers &c to advance a sum of money to any person intitled to relief to enable such a person to purchase a Cow or other animal'.[2] On 8 March 1796, very probably in relation to this critique, Bentham wrote to Wilberforce: 'The more I think of the System, which through your means, is about to be set on foot, in relation to the Poor Laws, the more I am delighted with it. But to one clause a sheet of objections have presented themselves, which I take the liberty of submitting to you.'[3]

Wilberforce, therefore, was primarily responsible for stimulating Bentham to develop his thinking on poverty. On 20 February 1796, Bentham reported to his brother, Samuel:[4] 'I have just seen Wilberforce—what he wants chiefly from us he says is—indications of employment—and of places to be hired for the purpose of working rooms on Rumford's plan.[5] I told him *employment* was a *difficult point* he seemed fully sensible of it. We are to have breakfast on the subject.'[6] As will be seen, Bentham did draft considerable material on the subject of employment,[7] perhaps with a view to responding to Wilberforce's prompting, although even at this early stage he himself was developing a more wide-ranging body of work on poor relief.

Bentham also acknowledged the influence of William Morton Pitt.[8]

[1] In a draft letter to Pitt of 28 February 1796 Bentham refers to 'the excellent Bill which I was favoured with in manuscript by a common friend': see ibid. 188. It is very probable that the 'common friend' was Wilberforce, and that the manuscript draft of the Bill referred to was that which survives at UC cli. 46–61, headed 'Poor Bill, Wilberforce's', and consists of thirty-two sections. This draft is recognizably an early version of the Bill eventually introduced by Pitt, and in particular contains versions of what Bentham would later criticize as the 'Apprenticeship clause' (UC cli. 49), the 'Family-Relief, or Extra-Children clause', the 'Relief-Extension, or Opulence-Relief clause', and the 'Cow-Money clause' (UC cli. 52–3).

[2] UC cli. 52. Bentham's draft of his criticism of the clause is at UC cliii. 365–8. The two copies, both dated 10 February 1796, are at UC cliii. 369, 370 respectively.

[3] Bentham to Wilberforce, 8 March 1796, *Correspondence* (*CW*), v. 193.

[4] Samuel Bentham (1757–1831), Bentham's younger brother, naval architect and engineer.

[5] Sir Benjamin Thompson (1753–1814), Count von Rumford of the Holy Roman Empire, social reformer and inventor, discussed the employment of the poor in 'An account of the establishment for the poor at Munich', and 'Of the fundamental principles on which general establishments for the relief of the poor may be formed in all countries': see Thompson, *Essays, Political, Economical and Philosophical*, 4 vols., London, 1796, i. 1–188.

[6] Bentham to Samuel Bentham, 20 February 1796, *Correspondence* (*CW*), v. 186. In this letter Bentham confided to Samuel that Wilberforce shared Bentham's own opinion of Rumford's work on the poor, which is to say 'there is not much in it'.

[7] See p. xxvi below.

[8] William Morton Pitt (1754–1836), MP for Poole 1780–90 and Dorset 1790–1826, shared with Bentham a concern about the lack of accurate information in relation to the poor. Bentham wrote to him on 1 March 1796, thanking him for 'the Statistical present with which you have honoured

In his letter to Wilberforce of 8 March 1796, Bentham mentioned the possibility of sending his observations on the 'Cow-money clause' to Morton Pitt, 'who, you tell me, is a fellow-labourer in the same vineyard'.[1] In an undated draft dedication to his poor law writings, Bentham addressed both men:

To W.W. & W.M. Pitt Esqs.

My worthy and much respected friends. The commands of one of you, the example of both of you gave occasion to this little work: permitt it to wear the honour of your names. Searching the uttermost depths of the subject, contemplating it in new points of view, as well as reviewing it in the old, if it be good for any thing it will live: and to visit posterity in such company is a pleasing thought.

J.B.[2]

Table of Cases calling for Relief

No manuscript copy of 'Table of Cases calling for Relief' survives,[3] possibly because of Bentham's practice of destroying the manuscripts of his published works. In submitting 'Table of Cases calling for Relief' to Arthur Young, on 8 September 1797, Bentham wrote:

If you print any of these Papers, especially the Table of Cases calling for Relief, do me the favour to apprise me of your determination as soon as formed, that I may apply to your Printer to print off some extra-copies for me to give away. What you do not print return to me. The Table of Cases etc. I am in continual want of and have no correct copy of.[4]

Although Bentham was adding elucidatory comments to 'Table of Cases calling for Relief' as late as December 1797,[5] it had assumed its essential shape by the middle of February 1796.[6] All but one of

me', almost certainly with reference to a population table for the Parish of Corfe Castle in Dorset, which Morton Pitt had compiled: see *Correspondence* (*CW*), v. 189. The table was published as 'Extract from an account of the population of Corfe Castle. *Drawn up by the order of, and communicated by, W. M. Pitt, Esq. M.P.*' in *Annals of Agriculture*, xxvi (1796), 188–93.

[1] Bentham to Wilberforce, 8 March 1796, *Correspondence* (*CW*), v. 194. Whether Wilberforce had referred to any active involvement by Morton Pitt in the drafting of the proposed Poor Bill, rather than to a general interest in poor relief, is unclear, but the former supposition is supported by Bentham's comment on an addition made to the manuscript draft of the Bill sent to him by Wilberforce, 'In another hand—Moreton Pitt's?': see UC cli. 61.

[2] UC cliii. 361. Originally the dedication had been to a single person, presumably Wilberforce, but Bentham then emended the draft to reflect the double dedication.

[3] MSS relating to 'Table of Cases calling for Relief' survive at UC ii. 491, cxxxiii. 4, 91–2, and cliii. 155.

[4] Bentham to Young, 8 September 1797, *Correspondence* (*CW*), v. 375n.

[5] See UC cxxxiii. 91–2.

[6] See 'Explanation of Table of Cases Calling for Relief', dated 12 February 1796, at UC cxxxiii. 4, which is a draft of the explanation of the uses of the Table which appears at its head in the published version, and of 'Observation (a)', regarding the use of the term 'hands' to describe the persons in need of relief: see p. lvii below. Of Bentham's other writings on poor

Bentham's cross-references to 'Table of Cases calling for Relief' contained in his writings in the present volume, which were written between February 1796 and February 1797, accord with the version of 'Table of Cases calling for Relief' published in the *Annals of Agriculture* in November 1797.[1] Further evidence that 'Table of Cases calling for Relief' remained substantially unaltered is to be found in the plans drawn up by Bentham in May 1797 for 'Classes Mustered',[2] the first chapter of Book Two of his projected work 'Pauper Management Improved'. The chapter was to be based upon the categories of indigence enumerated in 'Table of Cases calling for Relief'. Apart from two changes in the order of the categories, and the presence in the 'Classes Mustered' plan of an additional category later subsumed under another head in the published Table, the respective enumerations match perfectly.[3]

'Table of Cases calling for Relief' was published in the *Annals of Agriculture* in 'Situation and Relief of the Poor',[4] which also included 'Pauper Population Table', and an outline of 'Non-Adult Value Table'.[5] Neither of these two works is reproduced in the present volume, and their omission calls for an explanation. The publication together of the other two Tables and 'Table of Cases calling for Relief' was not essential, but to some extent accidental. The composition of both 'Pauper Population Table' and the outline of 'Non-Adult Value Table' post-date that of 'Table of Cases calling for Relief' by over one year. 'Pauper Population Table' was drafted by Bentham in 1797, and copies were circulated privately by him in September of that year, for completion and return.[6] In publishing 'Pauper Population Table' in

relief, only the earliest, the essay 'Definitions and Distinctions', does not make reference to 'Table of Cases calling for Relief'.

[1] The single inconsistency occurs at UC clii. 126, in the text of the third of Bentham's 'Essays on the subject of the Poor Laws', and appears to be an error on his part: see p. 96 & n. below.

[2] See UC clii. 264–7.

[3] At UC clii. 264–5, the categories 'Sick Hands' and 'Unripe Hands' appear as numbers VI and VII, while in the published 'Table of Cases calling for Relief' this order is reversed. At UC clii. 265, the category 'Out of Place Hands' appears as number XI, while in the published 'Table' it is number IX. Finally, at UC clii. 266, category number XVIII is listed as 'Ill-famed Hands', while this category does not appear in the published 'Table'. It appears, from a comment at UC cli. 178, that Bentham may have decided, after drafting the plan of 'Classes Mustered', that the category 'Ill-famed Hands' was equivalent to category number XV, 'Suspected Hands': 'Hands whose want of employ proceeds from badness of character may be distinguished by the name of *Suspected* or Ill-famed hands.'

[4] See *Annals of Agriculture*, xxix (1797), between pp. 410 and 411 (Bowring, viii. between pp. 360 and 361).

[5] See *Annals of Agriculture*, xxix (1797), between pp. 392 and 393 (Bowring, viii. between pp. 362 and 363), and 413–26 (Bowring, viii. 365–8) respectively.

[6] Bentham sent copies of the 'Tables' to Caroline Fox (1767–1845), George Rose, and Samuel Parr (1747–1825) between 5 and 7 September 1797: see *Correspondence* (*CW*), v. 373–4. A list of some sixty-five people to whom Bentham sent or planned to send either his 'Poor Project as printed in Young's *Annals* or only the blank Tables' is at UC cxxxiii. 74.

the *Annals of Agriculture*, Bentham hoped to generate a flow of statistical information which would assist in the formation of the financial projections that he intended to include in 'Pauper Management Improved'. Bentham himself expressed the difference between 'Pauper Population Table' and 'Table of Cases calling for Relief' as follows: 'The *Pauper-Population-Table*, being contrived for a particular purpose—that of collecting information—such classes, and such only, were inserted in it, as afforded a hope, that the numbers of each might be found capable of being collected. . . . in the *Table of Cases calling for Relief* are designed to be comprised *every* class, and every individual that can ever enter into the composition of the general mass'.[1] His efforts, like those of others, reflect the paucity of accurate information available.[2] The purpose of 'Pauper Population Table' clearly relates to the completion of Bentham's projected work 'Pauper Management Improved', and not to the works contained in the present volume, which were substantially complete by the time it was devised. Bentham, indeed, indicated in his succeeding contribution to the *Annals of Agriculture* that 'Pauper Management Improved' was '*To be filled up, and the work published in one volume octavo, as soon as a sufficient number of the communications solicited in* Vol. xxix. No. 167, *of the Annals of Agriculture have been obtained.*'[3]

'Non-Adult Value Table' was also specifically focused towards 'Pauper Management Improved', and was designed to elicit information concerning the expense and earnings of pauper children. The foundation of Bentham's contention that the National Charity Company, a central feature of which was the pauper panopticon, would be profitable, and thereby attractive to both government and to potential investors, was his belief that the economic value of children might be rendered positive. In short, the connection between 'Table of Cases calling for Relief' and the works in the present volume is much closer, both historically and thematically, than the connection between it and either 'Pauper Population Table' or 'Non-Adult Value Table'. None of the works included in the present volume presuppose the existence of, or make reference to, the other two Tables.

[1] *Annals of Agriculture*, xxix (1797), 411 (Bowring, viii. 365). Although headed 'Observations on the Table of Cases calling for Relief', this short section in fact explains the relation between 'Table of Cases calling for Relief' and 'Pauper Population Table'.

[2] Private efforts to collect information regarding the poor were not uncommon. For instance, early in 1796, in the course of working on the poor laws, Wilberforce had distributed a questionnaire with twenty-three headings relevant to the state of the poor in various parts of the country: see R.I. and S. Wilberforce, *The Life of William Wilberforce*, 5 vols., London, 1838, ii. 414–16.

[3] *Annals of Agriculture*, xxx (1798), 89 (Bowring, viii. 369).

Since 'Table of Cases calling for Relief' itself contains the proposition that the demand for relief is created not by poverty but by indigence, a proposition which is central to 'Definitions and Distinctions', the first of Bentham's 'Essays on the subject of the Poor Laws', it is possible either that the 'Table' dates from after the completion of the essay, or that both were drafted during the same period in early 1796. Whatever the precise chronology, both works illustrate the nature of Bentham's approach to the subject of poor relief. His initial investigation concerned the nature of the origins and causes of the demand for relief.

Essays on the subject of the Poor Laws[1]

Bentham never published 'Essays on the subject of the Poor Laws', and appears to have planned at various points to incorporate part or all of them in other writings on poor relief.[2] However, in the subsequent writings contained in the present volume, Bentham makes numerous cross-references to 'Essays on the subject of the Poor Laws', whilst in terms of intellectual consistency, they not only stand independently, but logically precede his other writings on poor relief.

Essay I: Definitions and Distinctions

While none of the manuscripts associated with the essay 'Definitions and Distinctions' are dated,[3] there is no doubt that it was composed early in 1796, at the same time as, if not slightly earlier than, 'Table of Cases calling for Relief'. Bentham had the essay copied at least twice,[4] and it is very likely to have been among the poor law papers which he circulated privately during 1796. In a note recording the number of copies made of 'Essays on the subject of the Poor Laws', 'Definitions and Distinctions' is referred to simply as 'Introduction'.[5] The text as presented includes both the final sentence of Bentham's draft, which for some reason was omitted from the copyists' texts of the essay, although there is no indication of cancellation in the manuscript, as well as a sentence added at the copying stage, presumably by Bentham.

The essay was certainly drawn upon by Patrick Colquhoun in his *Treatise on Indigence*, published some ten years later, in which he

[1] This title appears at UC clii. 59. Two variants, 'Essays relative to the subject of the Poor Laws' and 'Essays on the Poor Laws', appear on copies of the first essay at UC clii. 57 and cliii. 21b respectively.

[2] See pp. xxv & n., xxix, and xxxv & n. below.

[3] The draft of the essay is at UC cliii. 1–8b.

[4] The two surviving copies of the essay are at UC cliii. 21–4 and clii. 57–8 respectively.

[5] See UC clii. 60.

rehearses almost verbatim Bentham's distinctions between poverty and indigence, and his four-fold division of degrees of ability.[1] Colquhoun contacted Bentham on 4 December 1796, offering his good offices in the matter of the panopticon penitentiary, and on 31 December 1796 he acknowledged receipt of 'valuable MS', one of which was 'Table of Cases calling for Relief', of which Colquhoun intended to make a copy, and another of which was almost certainly 'Essays on the subject of the Poor Laws'.[2]

Essay II: Fundamental Positions in regard to the making provision for the Indigent Poor

On 24 February 1796 Bentham wrote to his brother: '*Poor Provision* goes on swimmingly, rich in *sens* and bidding fairer for engaging attention than even *Safeguard*, to which it cannot be refused the preference.'[3] The work to which Bentham referred as '*Poor Provision*' can be identified with some certainty as 'Fundamental Positions in regard to the making provision for the Indigent Poor',[4] the second of the 'Essays on the subject of the Poor Laws', despite the fact that none of the manuscripts containing plans or text for this work are headed 'Poor Provision'. Bentham's intention was to produce a work setting out the principles upon which poor relief should be based, encapsulated in a series of 'positions', each of which would be accompanied by supporting reasons.

By 18 March 1796 Bentham had completed a first draft of the essay, which, as its title 'Fundamental Positions with Reasons' indicates, combined the positions themselves and the reasons

[1] Patrick Colquhoun (1745–1820), Lord Provost of Glasgow 1782–4, stipendiary magistrate at Worship Street, Shoreditch 1792–7, and Queen Square, Westminster 1797–1818. See *A Treatise on Indigence; exhibiting a general view of the national resources for productive labour; with Propositions for ameliorating the Condition of the Poor, and Improving the moral Habits and increasing the Comforts of the Labouring People, particularly the Rising Generation*, London, 1806, pp. 7–9; and Colquhoun to Bentham, 23 January 1807, *The Correspondence of Jeremy Bentham*, vol. vii, ed. J.R. Dinwiddy, Oxford, 1988 (*CW*), p. 405, where Colquhoun acknowledges his intellectual debt to Bentham.

[2] See Colquhoun to Bentham, 4 December 1796, *Correspondence* (*CW*), v. 325, and Colquhoun to Bentham, 31 December 1796, ibid., 349. Colquhoun subsequently sent Bentham a statement of his own thinking on the poor laws, a copy of which, headed by Bentham 'Colquhoun's Plan', is at UC cli. 40–3.

[3] Bentham to Samuel Bentham, 24 February 1796, *Correspondence* (*CW*), v. 187. It is unclear with which work or projected work *Safeguard* is properly identified.

[4] This title appears at UC clii. 59 and cliii. 21, both of which are Title and Contents pages for the essay. The former also bears the variant 'Fundamental Positions relative to the providing for the Indigent Poor'. Bentham's draft bears the title 'Fundamental Positions in regard to the providing for the Indigent' (UC cliii. 55), reproduced at the beginning of one of the two copies (cliii. 25), while a further variant, 'Fundamental Positions in regard to the providing for the Indigent Poor', appears as the title of the other copy (clii. 61).

grounding them.[1] The plan of contents for this draft, complete with page references,[2] includes ten sections as follows: I. Relief—Object; II. Relief—Means; III. Relief—Conditions; IV. Ability—Degree; V. Charge; V. Minors; VI. Security; VII. Healthiness; VIII. Beggars; and IX. Extra Relief.[3] The draft corresponding to this plan of contents was preceded by an introduction, and succeeded by an eleventh section of positions with attendant reasons entitled 'Reform', neither of which are referred to in the contents sheet, and presumably post-date its composition.

During the composition of the first draft, Bentham produced a further body of manuscripts relating specifically to the justification of the public provision of relief, the subject of § I of the essay. This material grew until it occupied some forty-six manuscript pages, for which he compiled three marginal contents sheets, headed 'Poor Relief Necessary', on 17–18 March 1796.[4] At around the same period, although the exact date is unknown, Bentham drafted a third discrete series of manuscripts headed '*Quantum Adversaria*',[5] which provided the reasons supporting the fundamental positions contained in §II of his first draft, that relief should be limited to the 'necessaries of life'.

By 28 April 1796 Bentham had produced a second draft of the

[1] The marginal contents sheet is at UC cli. 4, while the text sheets to which it relates are at clii. 225–56, and are headed 'Poor I. Effects'.

[2] Bentham often produced plans of projected works or sections of works headed 'Contents' which were prospective, indicating the themes with which he intended to deal under a particular head. The existence of such 'Contents' is by no means a guarantee that the text itself was ever written. Conversely, Bentham also produced 'Contents' sheets for already-existing drafts, assembled using the marginal summaries of material which he had written, and which included page references. To avoid confusion, the latter are referred to throughout this introduction as 'marginal contents sheets'. For the relationship between the text, marginal summary paragraphs, and marginal contents sheets, see pp. li–lii below.

[3] See UC cli. 4. All these sections, occasionally with modified titles, featured in Bentham's second draft of the essay.

A *brouillon* of 17 March 1796 (UC cxxxiii. 11), headed 'Poor', contains the earliest draft contents of the essay, entitled 'Fundamental Positions Heads'. In this *brouillon*, thirteen sections are enumerated as follows: I. Relief—Necessity to which it should apply; II. Relief—Quantum in which it should be applied; III. Relief—at whose expence it should be administered; III. Conditions; IV. Work—how to be adjusted to ability; V. Work—proportion; V. Work—Healthiness—regard due to it; VII. Work—quantum of it how to be adjusted[?] to that of relief; VIII. Work—performance of it how to be secured; IX. Beggars—how to be dealt with; X. Extra relief—at whose expence; XI. Minors—how to be dealt with; XII. Reform—how to be conducted.

The marginal contents sheet at UC cli. 4 also bears a pencilled list of contents which gives further indication of the development of the organization of the essay. In this list of contents the section 'Work—Healthiness' is listed as § V, where it appears in Bentham's second draft of the essay. Bentham also changed the title and position of the section 'Charge', which appears both in the pencilled list of contents and in the second draft of the essay as § VI 'Account between relief and work'. Finally, the section 'Minors' is listed as § X, while it appears as § IX in Bentham's second draft of the essay.

[4] UC cli. 1–3. The text is at UC clii. 8–53.

[5] UC clii. 1–6.

fundamental positions, but without their supporting reasons. He substantially revised the fundamental positions contained in §§I and II, and settled on the final ordering of his text, which now included the additional §XI. Reform, and a conclusion. He had this new text copied at least twice.[1] Bentham circulated these copies, presumably together with those of the first essay on the subject of the poor laws. On 21 May 1796, for instance, Thomas Powys[2] returned to Bentham his 'interesting Papers', almost certainly a reference to 'Definitions and Distinctions' and 'Fundamental Positions in regard to the making provision for the Indigent Poor'.[3] Bentham also sent copies of the essays to Baron St Helens and Count Rumford.[4]

It was not Bentham's intention, in the event of publication, to leave the positions standing bare without their supporting reasons. This is indicated by the title page of the second draft privately circulated by Bentham: 'The propositions here submitted in the character of fundamental positions, were originally accompanied with *reasons*, *illustrations*, and *remarks*, which are intended to be subjoined (when in print) in the form of *Notes*.'[5] The present volume fulfils Bentham's intention, insofar as it has proved possible, of printing the positions together with their supporting reasons.[6]

The text as it appears in the present volume is reconstructed from the sources described above. The introduction is taken from Bentham's first draft of the essay, and is followed by the fundamental positions as they appear in the second draft. Where possible, the positions are each followed by their reasons, which are drawn from three sources. The first of these sources is the above-mentioned first

[1] The draft is at UC cliii. 55–77, clii. 68, 191–5, while the copies are at cliii. 25–31 and clii. 61–7 respectively. Both copies include the text of UC clii. 263, a folio from Bentham's first draft of the essay, as fundamental position 60, the final one of the essay. The present volume similarly includes the text of this folio, although as position 54, where it appears to be most coherently placed. The Title and Contents pages for the essay at UC cliii. 21 and clii. 59 respectively are dated 28 April 1796.

[2] Thomas Powys (1743–1800), MP for Northamptonshire 1774–97, created Baron Lilford 1797.

[3] The letter is docketed '1796 May 21. Poor. Powys Albermarle Street to J.B. Q.S.P. Returning *Poor* Papers 1st parcel': see *Correspondence* (*CW*), v. 203n. Whilst Bentham was in a position to circulate versions of the first two 'Essays on the subject of the Poor Laws' by this date, it is unclear whether the third essay had yet been completed and copied.

[4] On 1 June 1796, Alleyne Fitzherbert (1753–1839), Baron St Helens, diplomat and friend of Bentham, returned his 'valuable cahiers' on the poor, which contained 'Fundamental Positions in regard to the making provision for the Indigent Poor' (St Helens makes textual reference to it in his letter): see *Correspondence* (*CW*), v. 213. Rumford wrote to Bentham on 10 July 1796, thanking him for the chance to peruse his 'Essays on the Poor-Laws': see *Correspondence* (*CW*), v. 227.

[5] See UC cliii. 21a.

[6] The reasons, however, are presented as part of the main text, rather than in the form of notes.

draft, 'Fundamental Positions with Reasons'. As the positions contained in §§IV–XI changed very little between the first and second drafts,[1] it has been possible to reunite the fundamental positions as contained in Bentham's second draft, with the reasons which ground them from his first draft. The lack of surviving manuscripts for the first draft of §III. Relief—Conditions, presents no problems in this regard since the indications from the marginal contents sheet are that Bentham did not draft any reasons specifically in support of the positions contained therein.[2]

Bentham did, however, make significant revisions to §§I and II. In addition to giving each section a new title, he increased the number of positions contained in them, and made some revisions to their ordering. Thus the first draft of §I. Relief—Object, contained four positions: '1. No immediate death for want of relief. 2. Nor lingering death. 3. No certain relief but at the public charge. 4. No one ought to be left destitute of proper guardianship.' In the second draft of this section, now entitled Necessity of Relief, the first two positions reappear unaltered, but are followed by three new positions (positions 3–5) which argue the need for a certain fund for relief, and therefore reject the limitation of that fund. Two further positions, 6 and 7, which reject private provision and endorse provision at the public charge, are substantively equivalent to position 3 of the first draft. Finally, positions 8–10 of the second draft deal with the issue of guardianship and are a reiteration and expansion of position 4 as contained in the first draft.

The first draft of §II. Relief—Means, contained three positions: '5. Relief ought not to be such as to put receivers into a better plight than givers. 6. Nor therefore to exceed necessaries. 7.—of the cheapest quality.' In the second draft of this section, now entitled Quantum of Relief, Bentham provided seven new positions (11–17) which developed and reiterated the content of position 5 of his first draft, whilst positions 18–19 of the second draft are essentially reiterations of positions 6 and 7 of the first draft. Since the only manuscript source for the reasons grounding the positions is derived from the first draft, Bentham's cross-references in these two sections do not always correspond to the positions as rearranged in the second draft. To avoid confusion, explanatory editorial footnotes have been supplied where appropriate.

The texts of three further series of manuscripts are incorporated at

[1] Bentham's most significant revision in the second draft in these sections was to omit six positions dealing with the education of minors, although he does refer to them later in his poor law writings. The text of these positions is supplied in an editorial footnote: see p. 55n. below.

[2] See UC cli. 4.

the appropriate points in the text. The first is the large body of material corresponding to the marginal contents sheets headed 'Poor Relief Necessary', which was clearly intended for inclusion in the essay, and is here included in § I as 'Observations' on position 7.[1] In the latter part of this series of manuscripts, having made the case for public provision, Bentham went on to discuss objections to it, and in particular objections to the form of public provision which involved the use of industry houses. It is possible that in the event of the publication of the essay Bentham would have revised and perhaps abbreviated this material. It is certainly true that many of the points he made here in defence of industry houses were dealt with again at greater length in 'Pauper Systems Compared'. However, in the absence of any clear indication of Bentham's intentions, the text is reproduced in full.

In the present volume, the above sequence of manuscripts is immediately followed by a second short sequence, which deals with the objection to industry houses on the ground of their denial of liberty.[2] At the end of the 'Poor Relief Necessary' contents sheets, Bentham added the following note: 'Addenda 6. Uncomfortable by being shut up. 7.—by being banished from their connections.'[3] The contents of this second sequence of manuscripts corresponds exactly to this note. Although its composition post-dates the rest of the essay,[4] and appears to have been drafted with a different projected work on the poor, namely '*Penetocomia*, or Principles of legislation and management relative to the subject matter of the Poor Laws',[5] in mind, its inclusion fulfils Bentham's intention to add such a discussion to his text at this point. A third series of manuscripts, those headed '*Quantum Adversaria*', provide the reasons grounding the positions contained in § II of the essay, and are included at that point.[6]

By the late spring of 1796, Bentham's first two 'Essays on the subject of the Poor Laws' having been completed, he began to plan and execute the next stage of his writing on poor relief. While

[1] See the earlier discussion of this material at p. xxi above. The material is prefaced in the present volume by the text of a sheet of observations taken from Bentham's first draft of the essay (UC clii. 227), and also that of a single folio (clii. 55), headed 'Relief Necessary' and numbered 'p. 1', which is not referred to in any contents sheet but which fits the sense of Bentham's text at this point.

[2] UC clii. 382–7.

[3] See UC cli. 3.

[4] The heading of these MSS, 'Poor Management—Place Where' indicates that they were probably drafted in early May 1796: see p. xxvii & n. below. The first page of the sequence (UC clii. 382) bears a note in pencil in Bentham's hand, 'Old supposed to be now[?] superseded', probably added after the drafting of 'Pauper Systems Compared', the central theme of which is the place where poor relief should be given.

[5] For a discussion of '*Penetocomia*', which never achieved more than fragmentary status, see pp. xxv–xxviii below.

[6] See p. xxi above.

working on 'Fundamental Positions', Bentham had, on 17 March 1796, compiled a 'Poor *Brouillon*',[1] where he set out a series of subjects which he intended to discuss, most of which were addressed in one or another of his subsequent writings on the poor. However, the themes and ideas sketched out here are not integrated in any organized fashion. Among the areas touched upon, both the idea of a 'charitable loan office' and that of a 'poor man's bank' were elaborated in the third essay on the subject of the poor laws, 'Collateral Uses derivable from a system of Industry Houses',[2] while his remarks on 'Pauper Comforts' foreshadow the intended content of Book IV of 'Pauper Management Improved'. The demerits of out-allowances, of which seven are listed, and the responses to objections to industry-house provision, together with the discussion of the advantages of large-scale houses, are pursued in 'Pauper Systems Compared'. Brief remarks on the problem of economic stagnation, and its effect on the independent poor, indicate that Bentham intended to investigate this issue more thoroughly.

By 31 May 1796, however, Bentham had begun to draw themes together.[3] After listing the sections of the now completed 'Fundamental Positions', he made two attempts to plan the contents of a major work. At this stage he does not appear to have given the work a title less generic than 'Poor', but the sketched contents accord with a title referred to elsewhere in the poor law manuscripts, namely '*Penetocomia* or Principles of legislation and management relative to the subject matter of the Poor Laws'.[4]

According to both plans contained in 'Poor *Ordo*', the first section of this proposed work was to be entitled 'Fundamental Principles'. This section would have contained the second essay on the subject of the poor laws, namely 'Fundamental Positions in regard to the making provision for the Indigent Poor',[5] and possibly the first

[1] UC cxxxiii. 11.

[2] For a discussion of this *brouillon* in relation to the third essay see p. xxix below.

[3] UC cxxxiii. 10, headed 'Poor *Ordo*'.

[4] This title appears at UC cliii. 356 (6 January 1797), in a *brouillon* for 'Observations on the Poor Bill'. In a fragmentary draft of an advertisement for the poor law writings at UC cli. 105, undated but probably also composed around the same time, the following variant appears: 'Principles of Legislation and Administration in relation to the concerns of the Poor: including a compleat plan of education for the proposed Inspection Industry House Establishments: with disquisitions applicable to the superior classes.' The connection between '*Penetocomia*' and the *Ordo* of 31 May 1796 was suggested by W. Roberts, 'Bentham's Poor Law Proposals', *Bentham Newsletter*, iii (1979), 31.

[5] The assertion of the identity between the essay 'Fundamental Positions' and the projected §I 'Fundamental Principles' is supported by the fact that Bentham proposed that both be enacted by the legislature. In Bentham's introduction to 'Fundamental Positions' he proposed that the positions be 'adopted in substance and sanctioned and promulgated (for example in the shape of Resolutions) by the authority of the legislature' (see p. 8 below). Similarly, a fragment

essay, 'Definitions and Distinctions'. At this stage Bentham had evidently not made up his mind concerning the form in which the essays would be published, and indeed there are later indications that he considered publishing at least the second and third as appendices to 'Pauper Systems Compared'.[1]

In Bentham's first draft plan, the second section of the proposed work was entitled 'Plan of Management or Modes of carrying these principles into practice', and was organized under eleven sub-headings. However, in Bentham's second draft plan, this section was reorganized into four separate sections, namely § II. Management 1. Employment; § III. Management 2. Supply; § IV. Management 3. Place; and § V. Management 4. Official Establishment. In May 1796 Bentham wrote and revised a considerable body of manuscripts for the first of these sections, dealing with employment, the subject on which Wilberforce had earlier asked him for help.[2] These manuscripts survive almost intact, as do the marginal contents sheets associated with them.[3] They were, however, never incorporated into

of text, headed 'Plan—Parliamentary Sanction' (UC cli. 107), concludes, 'Resolved that it is the opinion of this House that', while a marginal note reads, 'So go on from Fundamental Principles'. The absence of any MS headed 'Fundamental Principles' also implies that the two titles refer to the same body of material.

[1] See p. xxxv & n. below. [2] See p. xv above.

[3] The marginal contents sheet at UC cxxxiii. 5 (8 May 1796), headed 'Employ—Contents', contains a series of twenty-six marginal summaries, the first twenty-five of which correspond to the text sheets at cliv. 295–304. UC cxxxiii. 6 (13 May 1796), headed 'Employ—Contents Old', is a copy of cxxxiii. 5.

UC cxxxiii. 7 (13 May 1796), headed 'Employ—Contents New—Works Improper', contains three distinct series of marginal summaries. The first, headed 'Works Improper', contains twenty-three summaries. The corresponding text sheets for summaries 1–3 are at UC cliv. 354; for summaries 6–7 at cliv. 352; for summary 8 at cli. 174–5; for summary 10 at cli. 222; for summaries 11–14 at cliv. 353; and for summaries 18–23 at cliv. 355–9. The corresponding text sheets for the second series of five summaries, headed 'Works Predeterminable', and for the third series of seventeen summaries, headed 'Works Proper—Own Supply', are at UC cliv. 314–19 and 335–47 respectively.

UC cxxxiii. 8 (15 May 1796), headed 'Employ (New)—Contents', contains two distinct series of summaries. The corresponding text sheets for the first, headed 'Employ Peacock', and containing seven summaries, are at UC cliv. 320–6. The second, headed 'Employ After Peacock', contains twenty-four summaries. The corresponding text sheets for summaries 1–3 are at UC cliv. 333–4; for summaries 4–13 at cli. 229–38; for summaries 14–16 at cli. 241–2; and for summaries 18–24 at cliv. 327–32. The text sheets corresponding to summaries 4–13 and 14–16, regarding the employment of the insane and the deaf and dumb respectively, were later transferred by Bentham to his chapter on Appropriate Establishments in 'Pauper Management Improved'. Bentham's mention of Peacock refers to James Peacock (1738?-1814), architect, and in particular to his *Outlines of a Scheme for the General Relief, Instruction, Employment, and Maintenance of the Poor*, London, 1777.

UC cxxxiii. 9 (25 May 1796), headed 'Employ Contents—Employ Improper', contains a series of seventeen marginal summaries for which the corresponding text sheets are at cliv. 348–51, cli. 191–217.

Finally, a series of text sheets headed 'Employment Proper—Rules' at UC cliv. 305–12, which sets out seventeen rules governing the choice of employments, does not correspond to any of the above marginal contents sheets, although almost certainly composed at the same time.

any finished text, and when Bentham returned to the subject of employment in the following year while drafting 'Pauper Management Improved', he appears to have made a fresh start, rather than seeking to rework the already existing material.

Bentham also made some progress in drafting material for § IV. Management 3. Place.[1] Much of this material was superseded by § Pauper Systems Compared', where Bentham undertook a similar comparative analysis of out-allowances, parochial workhouses, and large-scale industry houses as modes of relief.[2] There is no evidence that Bentham drafted any material at this stage for § III. Management 2. Supply or § V. Management 4. Official Establishment.

§ VI. Management 5. Collateral Uses, was entitled 'Collateral Uses derivable from a system of industry houses' in Bentham's first draft contents on 'Poor *Ordo*'. The appearance of this title suggests that Bentham may have intended to use the third essay on the poor laws for this section, and thus had presumably drafted it by this time.[3] Certainly none of the manuscripts headed 'Collateral Uses derivable from a system of Industry Houses' show any indication of having been originally drafted for inclusion in a larger work on the poor. Bentham also drafted material relating to § VII. Independent Poor—Assistances Proper, and § VIII. Independent Poor—Assistances Improper, but this material fails to form a coherent text.[4] There is

[1] A marginal contents sheet headed 'Poor—Place *Where*' is at UC cliii. 78 (4 May 1796), and contains a series of marginal summaries divided into four sections, with page references to thirty-one text sheets. Only five of these sheets survive at UC clii. 377–81. At the top of the first of these Bentham has written in pencil: 'Old—to be examined whether superseded.' Many of the arguments which Bentham intended to include in this section, concerning the comparative demerits of home provision under the heads of 'universality', 'employment', and 'economy of relief', were developed in 'Pauper Systems Compared', which did indeed supersede much of this earlier material.

[2] A further sequence headed 'Poor—Place Where' is at UC clii. 382–7. The text does not correspond to the marginal contents sheet bearing this heading, but does correspond to *addenda* to one of the marginal contents sheets for the essay 'Fundamental Positions', in which it has been included in the present edition: see p. xxiv above. A related fragment at UC cxxxiii. 13, headed 'Poor Place Where', consists in a series of pencilled comments briefly listing objections to industry houses, and criticizing the provision of 'schools for work without boarding'.

[3] See p. xxix below.

[4] Two plans for the materials on the independent poor survive at UC cxxxiii. 12 (May 1796), headed 'Poor Independent', and at cliii. 214 (24 May 1796), headed 'Poor Independent, Davies, Facienda JB'. Neither plan features page references, for both were composed before Bentham had drafted any corresponding text. In the fragments of text which do survive, Bentham drew the distinction referred to in the titles of § VII and § VIII between proper and improper assistance to the independent poor. The types of gradual and immediate assistance proper to be given to labourers in husbandry are discussed at UC cliii. 243–7, 219; occasional relief at cli. 289; sick relief at cliii. 218; and proper responses to the case of a general stagnation in manufacturing at cli. 219–21. In terms of 'false' or improper assistances, bounties to production are discussed at UC cliii. 221, 220, 226, 225; keeping down prices at cliii. 222; the rating of wages at cliii. 237–42; and the raising of wages at cliii. 223–4. The wages of the independent poor were further

no evidence that Bentham drafted any material at this stage for § IX. Fund. Finally, there is a single folio headed 'Overseers' which rehearses briefly the arguments Bentham intended to make in § X. Existing System, Its Defects, although the correspondence may be coincidental.[1]

In the event, Bentham did not proceed to the completion of a work as planned in this *Ordo*. It appears that he still intended to complete and publish such a work in January 1797,[2] even though the discussion of § IV. Management 3. Place was largely superseded by that of 'Pauper Systems Compared', which he was drafting at that time. By early February 1797 Bentham had begun drafting material under the heading 'Poor Plan' for the work which he entitled 'Pauper Management Improved', in which the subject matter of several further sections set out in the '*Ordo*' was to be addressed in the context of Bentham's proposal for the formation of a National Charity Company to manage poor relief in England and Wales. Thereafter no further mention is made of '*Penetocomia*', and by the time of the submission of 'Situation and Relief of the Poor' to the *Annals of Agriculture* in September 1797, he was referring to his writings on poor relief as contained in 'Pauper Systems Compared' and 'Pauper Management Improved', which were 'two independent, though connected, volumes'.[3]

discussed at UC cli. 20–4. Bentham also responded specifically to the work and proposals of David Davies (d.1819?), a pioneer in the collection of statistics on the income and expenditure of agricultural labourers, especially in *The Case of Labourers in Husbandry Stated and Considered, in Three Parts*, London and Bath, 1795, at UC cliii. 248–9, and, with reference to the restraint of luxury, at cliii. 235–6. Bentham attacked out-allowances, and discussed the mortgaging of the property of the independent poor seeking relief, at UC cliii. 215–17. Moreover, also under the heading of the independent poor, Bentham conducted a discussion concerning varieties of political rhetoric, which he termed 'carping', 'croaking', and 'puffing', at UC cliii. 227–34. A fragment at UC cli. 288, headed 'independent', contains a discussion of possible retrenchment of Overseers' expenses under a reformed system of poor relief.

[1] UC cli. 11. Criticism of the injustice of the existing system was also the theme of a sequence of text to which this folio appears related, and for which no plan survives. This sequence is divided into the following segments: UC cli. 7–8, headed 'Introduction—Poor's Cry', where Bentham argued that the interests of the poor were those of the vast majority of the population, while rejecting any policy of equalization of wealth; cli. 9–10, '*Onus Ubi*', where he rejected the simple increase in the size of the districts responsible for the finance and administration of poor relief as a solution to the inequities of a variable poor rate; cli. 12–18, 'Settlement', where he attacked the laws of settlement as a restraint on the liberty of the poor; and cli. 19, 'Settlement—Title to Relief', where he repeated his contention that the proper title to relief is given by indigence. One indication that the composition of this sequence may date from the period at which the 'Poor *Ordo*' was composed is given by a cross-reference at UC cli. 18 to '§. Collateral Uses'.

[2] See p. xxvn. above.

[3] See *Annals of Agriculture*, xxix (1797), 396 (Bowring, viii. 361–2).

Essay III: Collateral Uses derivable from a system of Industry Houses

The exact period during which Bentham composed his third essay on the poor laws remains uncertain. At one point in the text he referred to 'the extraordinarily high prices . . . of the present winter',[1] which would indicate a date in the early months of 1796. In addition, Bentham twice referred in the text of Essay II, 'Fundamental Positions in regard to the making provision for the Indigent Poor', which was completed by 18 April 1796, to the essay 'hereunto annexed, Collateral uses of a system of industry houses'.[2] These two references, however, are not necessarily reliable indicators that 'Collateral Uses' had also been completed by this date, since both are additions to the text made subsequent to its original drafting. The first was a marginal addition to Bentham's draft in his own hand, while the second was added in the form of a marginal note to a fair copy of the essay. Nevertheless, in the *brouillon* of 17 March 1796, Bentham listed eight points to be made with reference to a 'Charitable loan office',[3] all of which appear in § I, in the context of a discussion of the 'Poor Man's Loan Office'.[4] Also in the *brouillon*, under the heading 'Collateral Uses Topics', Bentham enumerated 'Poor Man's Bank Topics' which correspond closely to the discussion of the 'Poor Man's Bank' in the essay. Finally, on 20 April 1796 Bentham received a letter from Charles Bunbury,[5] replying to a request for information regarding the Veterinary College, a subject discussed in § III of the essay, which may indicate that Bentham was working on this section at this time.

It appears likely that Bentham had substantially drafted the essay by the time he prepared the 'Poor *Ordo*' of 31 May 1796, where, in his first sketch of the contents, 'Collateral Uses derivable from a system of Industry Houses' appears as the title of § III.[6] The fact that none of the text sheets for the essay are headed 'Poor', and do not contain any indication that they were intended for any other work, implies that Bentham had already drafted the essay by this date. He then considered including it as a section in the larger work, '*Penetocomia*', which he was then planning, just as he

[1] See p. 92 below.
[2] See UC cliii. 28 and clii. 68 respectively, and pp. 51 and 63 below.
[3] See UC cxxxiii. 11: this section of the *brouillon*, which contains page references albeit to a single folio, at least indicates that Bentham had begun to draft material used in the essay by this date.
[4] See UC clii. 77, cliii. 11, clii. 87, 77, 88–9, 77–9, 90–1, 79–80, 92–3: see pp. 69–78 below.
[5] Sir Thomas Charles Bunbury (1740–1821), MP for Suffolk 1761–84, 1790–1812.
[6] For a discussion of this 'Poor *Ordo*' see pp. xxv–xxviii above.

considered including his first two 'Essays on the subject of the Poor Laws' in the same work.[1]

The conclusion that Bentham had drafted 'Collateral Uses' by the end of May 1796 is further supported by a marginal contents sheet headed 'Poor—Non-Adults', compiled in June 1796, which contains the marginal summaries corresponding to the text sheets for 'National Musical Seminary', the sixteenth and last collateral use discussed in the essay as it appears in the present volume.[2] These text sheets appear to have been excluded from the fair copy of the essay, although it is clear from the running headings and the text of the draft that they were originally intended for inclusion therein.[3] It seems likely that in June 1796 Bentham intended to separate discussion of this collateral use from the rest of the essay, and to incorporate it elsewhere in '*Penetocomia*'. In the event, the execution of this plan was frustrated by his decision to abandon '*Penetocomia*'. In 1797, however, Bentham considered including his discussion of the 'National Musical Seminary' in the chapter of his proposed work, 'Pauper Management Improved', which dealt with pauper education.[4] Since he published neither the essay 'Collateral Uses', nor 'Pauper

[1] See p. xxv & n. above. The implication of a reference of a later date, made by Bentham during the drafting of 'Pauper Systems Compared', is that early in 1797 he was considering publishing 'Collateral Uses derivable from a system of Industry Houses' as an appendix to that work: see p. xxxv n. below.

[2] UC cxxxiii. 106 (12? June 1796), with corresponding text sheets at cxlix. 54–5, 64–5, 55–63, cliii. 14–17, 20, 18–19.

[3] All the MS pages are headed 'Collateral Uses, Musical Seminary', although the title 'Collateral Use the fifteenth and last', which appears at the beginning of the text (UC cxlix. 54), has been cancelled in pencil.

[4] i.e. Bk. II, Ch. XII, of which Bentham's précis was published in 'Outline of a Work entitled Pauper Management Improved', *Annals of Agriculture*, xxx (1798), 266–76 (Bowring, viii. 395–7), but included no reference to musical education. Bentham did compile four marginal contents sheets headed 'Pauper Education' (UC clxxxiii. 102–5) from materials drafted for this chapter, for which corresponding text sheets survive. He began by arguing that the education of poor children was of paramount importance because of their large number and the urgency of their need, and that its object should be happiness (UC cliii. 84–9). After comparing the guardianship of parents with that of the industry house (UC cliii. 90–5), he discussed physical 'Occupations' and recommended laborious exercise, specifically walking, running, and swimming, as profit-yielding and healthy (cxlix. 93–100; cliii. 96–107). He then indicated that pauper children should receive 'Intellectual education' (UC cliii. 108–13), but distinguished between 'Studies inadmissible' (cliii. 114–19) and 'Studies admissible' (cliii. 120–41).

It appears from UC clxxxiii. 100, headed 'Pauper Education Contents V. Musick', and a copy of the marginal contents corresponding to the text for 'National Musical Seminary', that Bentham intended to include music as an admissible study in 'Pauper Management Improved'. UC cxxxiii. 101 (24 February 1798), headed 'Poor Plan. Heads. Pauper Education', contains Bentham's plan for his précis of Bk. II, Ch. XII, to be included in 'Outline of a Work entitled Pauper Management Improved'. MSS at UC cliii. 81–3, and cxlix. 70–100, 103–6, 109–11 bear the heading 'Heads, Education', and appear to have been scrutinized, heavily emended, and for the most part cancelled, by Bentham, in the process of preparing this précis. Further material relating specifically to musical education is at UC cxlix. 105–6.

Management Improved', his final intentions regarding these manuscripts must remain uncertain.

The essay itself survives as both a draft and a fair copy.[1] A memorandum by Bentham indicates that the whole text was copied twice, and that a third copy was made of collateral uses 11 and 12, 'Female Midwifery Lecture Establishment' and 'Veterinary Lecture Establishment'.[2]

When Bentham moved on to the drafting of 'Pauper Management Improved' in 1797, he intended to make considerable use of the text of 'Collateral Uses' in composing Book III of that work, 'Collateral Benefits'. Of the sixteen collateral uses discussed in the essay as it appears in the present volume, thirteen are discussed at greater or lesser length in Book III of the published 'Outline of a Work entitled Pauper Management Improved'.[3] There seems no obvious reason for Bentham's decision to exclude discussion of the three remaining collateral uses, namely uses 10, 'Lying-in Dispensary', 11, 'Female Midwifery Lecture Establishment', and 16, 'National Musical Seminary', from 'Outline of a Work entitled Pauper Management Improved', and it may be that the last at least would have been included under the heading of 'Pauper Education'.[4] The omission of the two uses relating to childbirth is the more surprising in that Bentham devoted a chapter in the 'Outline of a Work entitled Pauper

[1] See UC clii. 60. The draft is at UC clii. 71–7, cliii. 11, clii. 87, 77, 88–9, 77–9, 90–1, 79–80, 92–3, 81–6, cliii. 9–10, clii. 98–103, cxxxiii. 38, 40, clii. 104–20, 94–7, 121, 122, 121, 123–9, 164–75, 182–3, 176–7, 178, 177, 179–81, 131–43, 146, 143–5, 147–63, 184–8, 190, 189, cliii. 12–13, cxlix. 54–5, 64–5, 55–63, cliii. 14–17, 20, 18–19, and the copy at clii. 196–7, cliii. 32–54, clii. 206–18.

[2] See UC clii. 198–200 and 201–5 respectively.

[3] In the instance of eleven of the collateral uses discussed in the essay, the text of Book III of the 'Outline' contains a discussion which either closely corresponds to, or is inclusive of, but more extensive than, the text of the essay. Bk. III, Ch. IV of 'Outline of a Work entitled Pauper Management Improved', entitled Temporary Indigence Relieved, in *Annals of Agriculture*, xxx (1798), 410–14 (Bowring, viii. 406–7) is closely related to the discussion of collateral use 1, 'Poor Man's Loan Office'. Bk. III, Ch. V. Frugality Assisted, *Annals of Agriculture*, xxx (1798), 414–24, 457–88 (Bowring, viii. 407–17), contains a more extensive discussion of uses 2, 'Poor Man's Bank', and 4, 'Friendly Society Bank'. Bk. III, Ch. VI. Pecuniary Remittance facilitated to the Poor, *Annals of Agriculture*, xxx (1798), 488–90 (Bowring, viii. 417), is closely related to the discussion of use 3, 'Poor Man's Bank of Remittance'. Bk. III, Ch. VII. Distant Conveyance facilitated to the Poor, *Annals of Agriculture*, xxx (1798), 490–4 (Bowring, viii. 417–18), is closely related to the discussion of uses 5–8, 'Poor Man's Inns', 'Poor Man's Carriage Stages', 'Pass Stages for the passing of Delinquents or supposed Delinquents', and 'Pass Stages for the conveyance of poor Debtors to Prison under arrest', respectively. Bk. III, Ch. X. National Force strengthened without Expense, *Annals of Agriculture*, xxx (1798), 502–4, and xxxi (1798), 33–7 (Bowring, viii. 420–1), contains text closely related to the discussion of uses 13–15, 'Militia Nursery', 'Marine School Establishment', and 'Shipwreck Relief' respectively, as well as additional material concerning the supply of naval timber. In addition, Bk. III, Ch. XII. Useful Knowledge augmented and disseminated, *Annals of Agriculture*, xxxi (1798), 51–64, 169–70 (Bowring, viii. 424–8), contains brief discussions of the epidemiological aspects of uses 9, 'Medical Dispensaries', and 12, 'Veterinary Lecture Establishment'.

[4] See p. xxxn. above.

Management Improved' to the subject of 'Rate of Infant Mortality Diminished',[1] which, nevertheless, makes no mention of them.

Little manuscript material dealing with collateral uses, and written specifically for 'Pauper Management Improved', appears to have been written.[2] It was clearly Bentham's intention in 1797 to publish an unabridged version of 'Pauper Management Improved', and to this end a great deal of manuscript material was drafted, of which a considerable amount survives.[3] It appears likely that he drew on the existing text of 'Collateral Uses' when preparing Book III of 'Outline of a Work entitled Pauper Management Improved',[4] but did not go on to complete a new draft of the Book for the full draft of 'Pauper Management Improved', which, had it been drafted, would presumably have superseded 'Collateral Uses'.

Pauper Systems Compared, or a Comparative View of the several systems establishable as well as established in relation to the Poor

Even taking into consideration the relative paucity of dated manuscripts relating to the poor laws, the period between early June 1796 and early January 1797 is notable for the complete lack both of such manuscripts,[5] and of any mention by Bentham in correspondence of his continuing to work in this field.[6] It may be that Bentham simply ceased to write on poor relief in the second half of 1796. It is certainly true that several other matters were claiming his attention during this period. In July 1796, Bentham recognized that the opposition of Earl Spencer[7] to the sale of part of his estate in Battersea for the erection of the panopticon penitentiary was insurmountable, and that he therefore required a new site for his projected prison.[8] Throughout

[1] i.e. Bk. III, Ch. XI, *Annals of Agriculture*, xxxi (1798), 37–51 (Bowring, viii. 421–4).

[2] Fragments discussing the 'Poor Man's Bank' are at UC cliv. 138–40, 158–64, while a *brouillon* headed 'Frugality Bank' is at cliv. 157 (6 April 1798). A further fragment relating to 'Medical Dispensaries' is at UC cliv. 155–6.

[3] For instance, complete drafts of Bk. III, Ch. II. Mendicity Extirpated, and Bk. III, Ch. III. Habitual Depredation Extirpated, are at UC cliv. 168–222 and 226–77 respectively.

[4] It was Bentham's practice to destroy the manuscripts from which a published text had been produced, so very few manuscripts which correspond to the text of 'Outline of a Work entitled Pauper Management Improved' survive.

[5] In addition to a *brouillon* of 4 June 1796 relating to Pitt's Poor Bill (see p. xli below), three further folios can be identified as having been composed in the early part of June 1796: UC cli. 401 (4 June 1796) contains a series of questions regarding the expense of maintenance in workhouses; cxxxiii. 56 (7 June 1796) is a collection of statistics relating the level of the poor rate to the use of workhouses; and cxxxiii. 106 (12? June 1796) is a marginal contents sheet headed 'Poor—Non-Adults', associated with Bentham's intended work '*Penetocomia*'. The next subsequent date which appears in the poor law MSS is 1 January 1797 at UC cli. 171.

[6] Bentham did continue to circulate 'Essays on the subject of the Poor Laws' during the latter half of 1796: see p. xx n. above.

[7] George John Spencer (1758–1834), second Earl Spencer.

[8] See Bentham to Samuel Bentham, 2 July 1796, *Correspondence* (*CW*), v. 222.

July and August 1796 Bentham was investigating the possibility of acquiring Hanging Wood near Woolwich, but this proposal also ran into formidable opposition,[1] and by early September 1796 he had moved on to yet another possible site, namely Tothill Fields in Westminster.[2] For the remainder of the year he was busy 'intriguing like Lucifer'[3] in the ultimately doomed attempt to acquire this new site. However, Bentham's continuing attention to the panopticon project would not necessarily have left him no time in which to write. After all, 'Essays on the subject of the Poor Laws' had been drafted while the effort to get the prison built had occupied a considerable proportion of his time and energy, and that effort would hardly slacken when he threw himself back into writing on the poor at the end of 1796.[4]

The likeliest explanation is that the lack of dispatch shown by Pitt's administration in introducing the Poor Bill was reflected by a decline in Bentham's own interest in pursuing his writings in the same area. Despite the apparent urgency of Pitt's intentions in February 1796, the 'Heads of the Bill' were not printed until the beginning of May 1796. Parliament was dissolved on 20 May 1796, and did not meet again until 27 September 1796. It was not until 22 December 1796 that Pitt sought leave to bring in a 'Bill for the better support and Maintenance of the Poor'. However, the introduction of Pitt's Bill into Parliament appears to have stimulated Bentham into a particularly frenetic period of work.

The genesis of 'Pauper Systems Compared' seems to lie in Bentham's intention to provide a context for his critique of the specific provisions of Pitt's Bill[5] by means of an introductory general survey of systems of provision for the poor. Hence, the text which grew into 'Pauper Systems Compared' was initially intended by Bentham to preface his specific work on Pitt's Bill. In a *brouillon* of 6 January 1797,[6] Bentham gave the title of his work on Pitt's Bill as 'View of the Poor Bill—with critical observations and ulterior suggestions'. Many of the text sheets for 'Pauper Systems Compared' bear the headings

[1] Bentham's hopes of acquiring Hanging Wood were dashed by the opposition of Charles George Perceval (1756–1840), second Baron Arden, son-in-law of the proprietor, Sir Thomas Spencer Wilson (1726–98): see Arden to Bentham, 10 August 1796, ibid. 241; and Bentham to Charles Long, 14 August 1796, ibid. 243–4.

[2] See Bentham to Long, 5 September 1796, ibid. 259–61.

[3] Bentham to Samuel Bentham, 15 November 1796, ibid. 300.

[4] In addition to the demands of the panopticon project, a further portion of Bentham's time was occupied with plans for the 'Advertiser', a newspaper which would reprint précis of advertisements found in other papers, for which *brouillons* dating from June 1796 survive at UC cviii. 17–20. No evidence has been discovered to indicate that Bentham was working on any other significant project in the second half of 1796.

[5] See pp. xlii–xliii below.

[6] UC cliii. 356.

'View', 'Poor View', or 'Poor Bill', which are clearly abbreviations of this title, often in conjunction with 'Systems Compared'.[1] It appears that around this time Bentham twice began a preface to 'View of the Poor Bill', in which he made reference to the reception given to *A View of the Hard Labour Bill*[2] by the authors of the Bill, and discussed his brother's initial development of the panopticon idea in Russia. However, the surviving material is fragmentary.[3]

Bentham at some stage decided to produce two discrete works rather than one. It was as a consequence of this decision that he presumably cancelled the following passage in the draft of 'Pauper Systems Compared', having realized that in the event of its separate publication the passage was no longer appropriate:[4]

Of the three systems thus discriminated, the Home-Provision system, the Small-Establishment system, and the Large-Establishment system, the system embraced by the present Bill before us appears to be a compound of the two first. Unfortunately for my wishes, the Large-Establishment system, to the exclusion of both the others, is the system, and the only system, that has presented itself to my view as suitable to the purpose. Such being my misfortune, as a preliminary to the examination of the Bill in detail, I shall exhibit a comparative statement of the advantages and disadvantages that appear attendant on the three systems considered in a general point of view. I shall then examine in detail the particular course taken by the Bill [in] pursuit of the system which it has adopted.[5]

The text of 'Pauper Systems Compared' exists only in draft, and is the least developed of the texts which appear in the present

[1] The variation in headings does not appear to be of significance. For instance, the discussion of the 'Limited-Provision System' begins with a folio marking the beginning of a new chapter, blank except for the title 'Poor View—Limited Provision' (UC clii. 439). This folio is followed by four text sheets bearing the heading 'Systems Compared' (UC clii. 440–3), and a final text sheet bearing the heading 'View' (clii. 444). By far the most common form of heading amongst the text sheets for 'Pauper Systems Compared' consists of 'Poor Bill' at the top of the page above the text, combined with 'Systems Compared' at the top of the right hand margin: see, for instance, UC clii. 453–7, 458b-66, 468–85, 489–96, 499–511, 513–15, 517–20, 522–8, 531–43.

[2] *A View of the Hard-Labour Bill; being an abstract of a pamphlet, intituled, 'Draught of a Bill, to punish by Imprisonment and Hard-Labour, certain Offenders; and to establish proper Places for their Reception.' Interspersed with Observations relative to the subject of the above draught in particular, and to Penal Jurisprudence in general*, London, 1778.

[3] See UC clii. 412, 415–18; 414, 419; 420–1, 413; cxxxiii. 28.

[4] The composition of 'Pauper Systems Compared' and 'Observations on the Poor Bill' overlapped chronologically, but it is unclear exactly when Bentham decided to produce two discrete works. The text sheets which compose 'Pauper Systems Compared' contain only one date, that being no more specific than 'January 1797' (UC clii. 472), whilst the last of five marginal contents sheets for the work (cli. 6), composed after the text had been drafted, is dated 10 February 1797. By the latter date, Bentham had already sent for copying a large portion of the text of 'Observations on the Poor Bill': see William Robertson to Bentham, 10 February 1797, *Correspondence* (*CW*), v. 356.

[5] UC clii. 438.

volume.[1] There is ample evidence that its intended scope and structure underwent considerable alteration during its composition, with the result that the final organization of the text remains conjectural. For instance, in a marginal contents sheet Bentham indicates that the essay 'Fundamental Positions in regard to the making provision for the Indigent Poor' was at one stage intended to appear as an appendix to the work,[2] while a fragmentary piece of text implies that the essay 'Collateral Uses derivable from a system of Industry Houses' was also to be appended to it.[3] Further, there is strong evidence that at one point Bentham intended to subjoin the substance of his specific plan for the establishment by subscription of a National Charity Company to assume responsibility for relief of the poor in England and Wales, which was later to emerge as the subject of his projected work 'Pauper Management Improved'. Thus the title of 'Pauper Systems Compared', as given in Bentham's first marginal contents sheet of the work, was 'Comparative View of the several systems establishable as well as established in relation to the Poor. To which is added A Proposal for a new system calculated to effect a gradual reduction of the Poor Rates without diminution of necessary relief or advance of national expence.'[4] Moreover, in an undated draft of an advertisement for subscriptions to the National Charity Company, in which he confusingly asserted that 'Pauper Systems Compared' had already been published, Bentham gave the work the following title: 'A Comparative view of the several systems establishable as well as established in relation to the poor: to which is annexed A Plan &c, being the present plan with the addition of sections containing arguments in vindication of sundry of the principles contained in it.'[5]

[1] A very few folios in a copyist's hand survive at UC cli. 62, cliii. 479, 485–6. These three last, however, are to be found in the midst of material in Chadwick's hand. Since UC cliii. 485 bears a watermark '1830', it seems likely that these extracts were copied on Chadwick's instructions many years after their composition. Edwin Chadwick (1800–90), sanitary reformer and Secretary of the Poor Law Commission 1834–46, first met Bentham in 1829.

[2] See UC cliv. 75, a marginal contents sheet for 'Pauper Systems Compared'.

[3] See UC clii. 368–9, part of a fragment (clii. 368–71) which criticizes the provisions in Pitt's Poor Bill establishing a system of parochial schools of industry open to children of families not in receipt of poor relief, on the ground that they addressed not the central problem, the effective relief of indigence, but 'a corollary to the problem', the promotion of industry. The passage contains what appears to be a reference to 'Collateral Uses derivable from a system of Industry Houses': 'in the Appendix I do a good deal of this sort of corollary work: and the reason of my doing it is, that having got my national system of Industry Houses, a system paid for by the still more pressing object, I do it, as it seems to me, without expence. Having got up my Large-Scale Industry Houses, provided for that which is most pressing, . . . then, as it seems to me, would be the time, to propagate it, and take offsets from it.'

[4] See UC cliv. 75.

[5] See UC cli. 105. The draft advertisement also refers to the proposed publication of 'Principles of Legislation and Administration in relation to the concerns of the Poor: including

The work in the present volume has been organized with reference to the internal evidence of the manuscripts, to the surviving marginal contents sheets, and to a brief plan of the work. Five marginal contents sheets for the body of the text survive,[1] and have been heavily relied upon in its reconstruction. The title of the work is taken from an undated sheet, headed 'Pauper Systems Compared—Title and Contents', containing a brief plan of the work. This plan indicates Bentham's decision to separate his 'Poor Plan' from the body of 'Pauper Systems Compared', since it also contains a title for the work which was to become 'Pauper Management Improved'.[2]

In this plan, the work is divided into ten chapters: § I. Systems enumerated; II. No-provision System; III. Limited or Inadequate-Provision system; IV. Home and Community Provision compared; V. Large and Small-Community Provision compared; VI. Community Provision compared with Community and Home Provision mixt, for Non-Adults; VII. Farming System examined; VIII. Establishments for the *prevention* of Indigence examined; IX. Various projects for the reduction of the Poor Rates; X. Establishments for Extra Provision in favour of Adults.' Bentham's subsequent additions to the plan indicated that Chs. II–III were to deal with the quantum or amount of provision, and that Chs. IV–VII were to deal with the place where provision is made. He also indicated his intention to insert two new chapters, under the generic heading 'Fund', between Chs. VII and VIII. These new chapters were respectively entitled 'Old Rateables'

a compleat plan of education for the proposed Inspection Industry Establishments: with disquisitions applicable to the superior classes'. This was a work which Bentham was planning to compose in May 1796, but on which he made only very limited progress (see p. xxviii above), and which appears to have been abandoned early in 1797 in consequence of the decision to write 'Pauper Management Improved'.

[1] UC cliv. 75–8, cli. 6. Only the last of these is dated, namely 10 February 1797.

[2] See UC cxxxiii. 2. The full title of Bentham's 'Poor Plan' is given here as 'Pauper Economy improved: or A new Scheme of Provision for the Poor: calculated to satisfy all just claims—repel all unjust ones—wind up Industry to its highest pitch—preserve the perishing part of the Population—and immediately to reduce, and at length annihilate the burthen of the Poor-Rates, without either risk or expenditure at the public charge: To which is added Proposal for the formation of a Subscription Fund by authority of Parliament for the carrying of the above purposes into effect.' The proposal itself is as follows: 'Proposal for the formation of a Subscription Company, for the management of the concerns of the Poor: under the name of The National Charity Company: in whom the existing Poor Rates shall be vested, on their subscribing a Capital adequate to the purpose: Shewing how the amount of the Rates may be immediately limited—speedily and considerably reduced—finally abolished—all just claims to relief satisfied—all unjust ones repelled—industry screwed up to its highest pitch—the condition of the burthensome Poor meliorated—population preserved and encreased—morals improved—mendicity and habitual depredation extirpated—frugality assisted—employment insured—and all other proper helps afforded to the self-maintaining Poor, as well as various new advantages to the community in general—at the hazard, but to the probable profit, of the Subscribers, without expence or hazard to Government or the Public at Large.'

and 'New Rateables', while the latter was itself divided into § 1. Paupers at a non-Pauper period—Prevention. 2. Others'.

While Bentham essentially completed the text with regard to the topics of quantum and place, he failed to draft fully the text corresponding to the latter portion of this plan. No manuscripts have been discovered which relate to the additional chapters dealing with the question of the fund from which expenditure on poor relief was to be drawn, and it may be that Bentham never composed any material on this subject for inclusion in 'Pauper Systems Compared'. Small fragments of text survive for Chs. VIII[1] and IX,[2] but none corresponding to the final chapter.[3]

The marginal contents sheets for 'Pauper Systems Compared' indicate that Bentham's draft began with a brief introductory passage, which set out five 'topics of distinction' between systems. Three of these topics, namely quantum, place, and fund, also occur in the plan, while two further topics, quality, or the degree of comfort, and management of the fund, appear to have been introduced by Bentham during the process of drafting. The text of this introductory passage[4] is reproduced in the present volume.[5] The original draft continued with a single folio, which has not been identified, but which quickly dismissed the 'No-provision' and 'Limited-provision' systems, that is the subjects of Chs. II and III according to the plan.[6] There followed a second folio, also missing, which introduced the three modifications of the 'Adequate-Provision system', that is the Home-Provision, Small-Establishment, and Large-Establishment systems.[7] However, the summaries corresponding to these two folios were cancelled by Bentham on the marginal contents sheet, while the succeeding uncancelled summaries introduce the Small-Establishment and Large-Establishment Systems. The draft text corresponding to these summaries[8] is headed 'Systems enumerated', which is the title of Ch. I according to the plan. This ordering has

[1] See UC clii. 366–7, where Bentham discussed preventive measures advocated by David Davies; and clii. 372–3, where he discussed sick-relief and superannuation annuities.

[2] See UC clii. 402–3, 407–8, 405–6, 410, 404, 409, where Bentham discussed the transformation of the poor rates into a subscription, and its replacement by a poll tax.

[3] However, according to the plan (UC cxxxiii. 2), Bentham intended to discuss the following subjects: 1. Sick Hospitals; 2. Lying-in Hospitals; 3. Alms Houses; 4. Charity Schools; and 5. Free Schools.

[4] i.e. UC clii. 431–2.

[5] See pp. 143–4 below.

[6] See UC cliv. 75. The marginal summaries are as follows: 'Systems relative to the provision for the Poor. 1. No-provision. 2. Limited or inadequate provision. 3. Unlimited or adequate. No-provision and Inadequate-provision systems dismissed with reprobation.'

[7] See ibid. The marginal summary is as follows: 'Adequate-provision system its three modifications 1. Home-Provision. 2. Small-Establishment. 3. Large-Establishment.'

[8] See UC clii. 433–6, 438.

been followed in the present volume, while extended drafts of Chs. II and III have been identified,[1] and incorporated according to the plan.

The marginal contents sheets correspond to the plan with regard to Chs. IV and V, while Bentham's draft for these chapters is complete.[2] At this point, the marginal contents sheets contain an additional chapter, not found in the plan, dealing with objections to Industry Houses, including those advanced on the grounds of the quality of relief, or the degree of comfort to be discovered therein.[3] The corresponding text is reproduced in the present volume as Ch. VI.[4]

One of the 'Pauper Systems Compared' marginal contents sheets, relating to management rules, indicates that Bentham intended at one time to include at this point a discussion of 'Points of good management stated with reference to the subject in hand, to show that they have never hitherto been completely observed'.[5] A pencil note immediately following the above summary reads 'Not written', and indeed only one page reference appears in this section of marginal contents. However, the existence of manuscripts, headed 'Systems Compared', which do deal with this subject,[6] indicates that Bentham did in fact make some progress in drafting this material. In the marginal contents sheet, twenty-one such rules are enumerated. However, this particular sheet is very heavily amended, and it appears that Bentham's discussion of the principles of management went through several revisions. His final decision appears to have been to hold over the discussion for inclusion in 'Pauper Management Improved'. Indeed, a revised version appears in 'Outline of a Work entitled Pauper Management Improved' at Bk. II, Ch. IV, where thirty-two management 'principles' are enumerated.[7] The surviving manuscripts comprise twenty-seven rules or principles, and contain internal references to the text of 'Pauper Management Improved'.[8] Although Bentham began the discussion of management

[1] See UC clii. 424–9 and 440–4 respectively.

[2] See UC clii. 453–4, 455–7, 454, 458a, 458b, 458a, 459, 460, 459, 461–2a, 462b, 462a, 463, 464–5, 463, 465, 466–8, 469–77, 479–93, 500, 497–9, 512, 501–7, 494–6, 508–11, 513–15, and clii. 517–20, cliv. 585, clii. 521–8 respectively.

[3] See UC cliv. 77–8.

[4] See UC clii. 447–52, 530–43, 547–63.

[5] See UC cliv. 78.

[6] See, for instance, UC cliii. 154, 172.

[7] See *Annals of Agriculture*, xxx (1798), 137–62 (Bowring, viii. 380–6).

[8] The surviving MSS relating to principles of management are as follows: Introductory Observations, UC cliii. 143; Rule 1. Inspection architecture principle, UC cliii. 144; Rule 2. Appropriate assortment principle, clii. 357; Rule 3. Ample Scale principle, clii. 358; Rule 4. Comparison and selection principle, clii. 359; Rule 5. Tabular statement principle, clii. 360–2; Rule 6. Uniform management principle, clii. 363; Rule 7. Local consideration principle, clii. 364; Rule 8. Interest-and-duty-junction principle, cli. 473, cliii. 145; Rule 9. Life and health assurance principle, cliii. 146–52; Rule 10. Transparent management principle, cliii. 154, 153; Rule 11. Universal industry principle, cli. 474; Rule 12. Employment appropriation principle,

rules with the intention of including it in 'Pauper Systems Compared', he eventually reserved it for 'Pauper Management Improved'. Hence, this material has been excluded from the present volume. In drafting the material on management, Bentham composed an extended defence of the Neighbour's-Fare Principle, which he decided to present as a separate discussion. The text is reproduced as Appendix A.[1]

The marginal contents sheets conclude with material corresponding to Ch. VI of the plan,'Community Provision compared with Community and Home Provision Mixt, for non-adults'. The corresponding manuscripts are headed 'Minors *Schola*',[2] and are reproduced in the present volume as Ch. VII. This Chapter contains the earliest explicit references in Bentham's poor law writings to the proposed National Charity Company. The exact point at which Bentham formed the intention to propose the creation of such a joint stock company, to which the existing poor rates would be paid, and which would assume responsibility for the administration of poor relief in England and Wales, is unclear. No mention of such an institution is made in 'Essays on the subject of the Poor Laws'. The undated plan of 'Pauper Systems Compared', however, appears on a folio alongside a proposal for the launch of such a company by subscription.[3] On 20 January 1797 Patrick Colquhoun wrote to Bentham with reference to his own proposals for reform, 'I trust however you will understand by it what I mean, and particularly that I do not mean *that a Joint Stock Company shall manage the poor*',[4] which may imply that Bentham had floated the idea with Colquhoun before this date.

Whenever the idea was firmly adopted by Bentham, he only began to incorporate references to the National Charity Company in his writings in early 1797. By this time he had decided that the organization, capitalization, and responsibilities of the company would provide a major theme of the projected work 'Pauper Management

cli. 475–6; Rule 13. Labour division principle, cli. 477; Rule 14. Employment mixing principle, cli. 478; Rule 15. Self-supply principle, cli. 479–81; Rule 16. Piece work principle, cliii. 160; Rule 17. Peculiar premium principle, cliii. 163, 161–2; Rule 18. Honorary reward principle, cliii. 164; Rule 19. Separate work principle, cliii. 165–7, 157, cliv. 591, cliii. 158–9; Rule 20. Earn-first principle, cliii. 173, 168–71; Rule 21. Self-liberation principle, cliii. 172; Rule 22. Neighbour's-fare principle, cliii. 189–90, 174–88; Rule 23. No fermented liquor principle, cliii. 191; Rule 24. Habit respecting principle, cliii. 192; Rule 25. Wholesale purchase principle, cliii. 193; Rule 26. Save-all principle, cliii. 198–200; and Rule 27. Polychrest principle, cliii. 194, 196, 195, 197. A fragment at UC clii. 564, headed 'Progress of society through the systems', appears to be abandoned.

[1] See pp. 267–75 below.

[2] See UC clii. 389–90, cxlix. 107–8, clii. 391–401.

[3] See UC cxxxiii. 2.

[4] See Colquhoun to Bentham, 20 January 1797, *Correspondence* (*CW*), v. 354.

Improved', for which he began to draft material in January 1797.[1] The fact that the surviving references in the final chapter of 'Pauper Systems Compared' appear to assume the reader's familiarity with the company and its structure may indicate simply that having begun drafting materials for 'Pauper Management Improved', in which reference to the company is ubiquitous, Bentham simply mistakenly assumed such a familiarity on their part. Alternatively, it may be the case that Bentham envisaged that 'Pauper Management Improved' would be published together with 'Pauper Systems Compared', and that in revising 'Pauper Systems Compared' for publication he would have been much more explicit regarding his support for such a company.

A related uncertainty concerns the placing of Bentham's discussion of farming, or contract management, of the poor.[2] In the plan of 'Pauper Systems Compared', referred to above, Ch. VII is entitled 'Farming system examined',[3] while early in the text itself, Bentham includes the following reference: 'To *farm* the Poor, as the phrase is, is to vest the management of the concerns of the Poor in interested hands. This introduces the discussion relative to the eligibility of the Farming System—for which see Ch. | |.'[4] Clearly, at this stage he intended to include a discussion of contract management in the text, even if he was uncertain of its final location. On the marginal contents sheet, he added a note to the effect that discussion of the farming system had been 'posted off to §. Parallel between L[arge] and S[mall] systems',[5] although no discussion of the farming system is contained in that chapter.[6]

It appears that Bentham finally decided to omit the examination of the farming system from 'Pauper Systems Compared', which would help to explain the dearth of references in that text to his proposal for the creation of a National Charity Company, intended, of course, to

[1] See UC cliv. 68 (15 February 1797), a marginal contents sheet headed 'Poor Plan Contents', which indicates that Bentham had already drafted a considerable amount of material concerning the organization and constitution of the Company for 'Part I' of the plan.

[2] Bentham had envisaged undertaking some discussion of the farming system from an early stage in his writing on poor relief. In his *brouillon* of 17 March 1796 (UC cxxxiii. 11), one of the reasons he listed in favour of large-scale houses of industry was 'Manager being *good* may be interested'. Again, on 4 May 1796, in his marginal contents sheet for the section 'Management—Place Where' of the projected work '*Penetocomia*' (UC cliii. 78), Bentham argued that one advantage possessed by large-scale industry houses, in contrast to parochial workhouses, lay in the 'facility of engaging a good manager', and continued: 'Advantage derivable from the facility of giving the Manager when good an interest in the success of the management. The interest is at the highest pitch when the management is *farmed*.—Cause of the complaints against the farming system: 1. Managers uneducated. 2. No means of profitable employ—parsimony therefore the sole resource.'

[3] See UC cxxxiii. 2.

[4] See p. 144 n. below (UC clii. 432).

[5] See UC cliv. 76.

[6] See pp. 184–90 below.

operate upon the principles of contract management. The text of Bentham's defence of farming the poor is reproduced as Appendix B.[1]

Observations on the Poor Bill

Bentham directed his attention to Pitt's Poor Bill during three distinct periods. During the first period, in February 1796, he wrote a brief critique of one clause of the manuscript draft of the Bill which had been given to him by Wilberforce.[2] The printing of the 'Heads' of the Poor Bill at the beginning of May 1796 prompted a second consideration. On 4 May 1796, Bentham, writing to Charles Abbot, reported that he had just received the 'Heads' from George Rose, and commented, 'what stuff!'[3] One month later, on 4 June 1796, Bentham produced a *brouillon* for a criticism of the Bill.[4] His criticisms encompassed both the substance and the drafting of the 'Heads', as is shown by his listing of Matter, Method, Form, and Expression, as 'Heads of Defect'. Bentham's substantive criticisms of the 'Heads' centred on eight 'Sources of Profusion', originating in seven specific clauses. The detailed criticism of five of these sources would form the core of 'Observations on the Poor Bill', when Bentham drafted the work in January and February 1797. The absence from 'Observations on the Poor Bill' of any discussion of two of the remaining three sources of profusion, as identified by Bentham in June 1796, is explained by the omission of the provisions giving rise to them from the Bill as amended by committee.[5] Although the provision giving rise to the third source of profusion survived in the text of the Bill as amended by

[1] See pp. 276–89 below.

[2] See pp. xiv–xv above.

[3] Bentham to Abbot, 4 May 1796, *Correspondence* (*CW*), v. 203.

[4] UC cliii. 352. Two printed copies of the 'Heads', entitled 'Heads of a Bill for the better Support and Maintenance of the Poor' and 'Heads of a Bill for Amending and Enforcing the Laws for the Relief Instruction and Employment of the Poor', survive in Pitt's papers (see Chatham Papers, PRO 30/8/307). The latter appears to be a revision and extension of the former, and it is to the latter that Bentham's references to the 'Heads' correspond. By the time of the Bill's introduction into the House of Commons in December 1796 the earlier title had been readopted.

[5] The first source of profusion identified by Bentham in the 'Heads' of the Bill but omitted from the Bill as amended by committee, namely 'Place of real settlement charged with expence of relief granted by place of provisional settlement', referred to § 12 of the 'Heads', which provided that the expense of relief given to persons without a settlement in a particular parish should be reclaimed from the parish where the relieved person did possess a settlement. The second source of profusion, 'Litigation on appeal from allowance', referred to § 3 of the 'Heads', which provided that the level of allowance for extra children would be set locally by parish overseers, and that an appeal against that level might be made to two Justices of the Peace. In the Bill as amended by committee, the level of such allowance was set at 'not less than One shilling for each such child': see *House of Commons Sessional Papers of the Eighteenth Century*, ed. S. Lambert, 145 vols., Wilmington, Delaware, 1975, ciii. 164.

committee, Bentham did not discuss it at length.[1] At this stage, it appears that Bentham intended to accompany his critique of the substance of the Bill with an extensive critique of its drafting. In particular, he objected to the Bill's obscurity and ambiguity.[2] It is unlikely that Bentham drafted any corresponding text at this time, except a short manuscript sequence headed 'Poor Bill—Stile. Conclusion'.[3]

The introduction of the Bill into the House of Commons prompted Bentham to return to the Bill for a third time, and to undertake a detailed study of the measure. The Bill received its first and second readings on 29 December 1796 and was transferred to a Committee of the whole House. On 31 December 1796 it was ordered, 'That such a Number of Copies of the said Bill, as amended by the Committee, be printed, as shall be sufficient for the Use of the Members of the House', and further consideration of the Bill was set for 17 February 1797.[4] The House of Commons was then adjourned until 14 February 1797. By 5 January 1797, Bentham had come into possession of the text of the printed Bill as amended by committee, and had précised its contents on two folios, of which only the second survives.[5] Bentham's references in 'Observations on the Poor Bill', which was written in January and February 1797, correspond to the text of the Bill as amended by committee.[6]

It is appropriate to attempt a brief description of the substance of Pitt's measure before discussing the development of Bentham's comments upon it.[7] The provisions of the 'Heads', and of the Bill based upon them, were complex and numerous. Pitt's plan combined the introduction of a system of workhouses with several new

[1] The third source of profusion, 'Interest acting as a check to profusion diminished by enlargement of districts', referred to § 10 of the 'Heads', which provided that where parishes united for the purposes of the Bill, persons would acquire a settlement in the parishes collectively, rather than in the specific parish in which they resided. This provision survived as § 6 of the Bill as amended by committee. In the event, Bentham decided not to criticize this section of the Bill. Indeed, his comments on the effect of the Bill on the law of settlements tended to be favourable rather than critical: see p. 248 n. below.

[2] UC cli. 468–72. This sequence, which contains explicit reference to the 'Heads' at UC cli. 471, may date from as early as June 1796, and was certainly drafted before 5 January 1797, by which date Bentham was referring to the text of the Bill as amended by committee.

[3] Writing in pencil, Bentham began a 'Concluding Proposal', which consisted in a tribute to the qualities of Count Rumford: 'The talents, probity and benevolence of Count Rumford are well known in higher circles, but the fame as well as the benefit of his talents has been spread by the press through all ranks of the community' (UC cliii. 352). The text was abandoned at this point.

[4] See *Commons Journals*, lii (1796–7), 263.

[5] UC cliii. 355 (5 January 1797).

[6] For the text of the Bill as amended by committee see *Commons Sessional Papers of the Eighteenth Century*, ciii. 163–94.

[7] For more detailed discussion of the contents of Pitt's proposals for reform of the poor laws see Poynter, *Society and Pauperism*, pp. 62–5.

entitlements to relief at home. Thus, on the one hand, Pitt sought to provide work for those seeking relief. To this end, 'Schools of Industry' were to be established in every parish or union thereof, to be overseen by a new administrative structure which gave increased powers to local magistrates.[1] These 'Schools of Industry' would provide employment and, if necessary, maintenance, to persons seeking relief who could not be employed at home. Refusal of employment, either at home or in a 'School of Industry', would disqualify the refuser from relief.[2] On the other hand, outdoor relief was to be extended in several ways. In the first place, extra allowances were to be paid to families containing large numbers of children.[3] In addition, it was proposed that the parish make up the wages of private employees to 'the full rate', in the event that they were paid less.[4] The possession of property was not to be a disqualification from receiving relief,[5] while parishes were required to arrange apprenticeships for children who had been employed in the 'Schools of Industry'.[6] Finally, parishes were empowered to relieve by providing purchase money for a cow.[7] The Bill also proposed the establishment of parochial subscription funds, which would provide benefits in sickness or old age, although neither the source of contributions to the fund nor the benefits payable from it were explained.[8] Finally, the Bill sought to ease the effects of the law of settlement, which connected each individual to a particular parish where they had their settlement, and which gave rise to enormous litigation between parishes, and 'removals' of persons seeking relief to their parish of settlement.[9]

On 5 January 1797, having précised the Bill as amended by Committee, Bentham drafted a *brouillon* for his work on it.[10] He made several criticisms under the heading of 'form', addressing the 'riddle' presented by the notion of the 'benefit of the act', and the Bill's 'disorder', describing its arrangement as 'hotchpotch'. Finally, he berated the failure to publish a pamphlet explaining the reasons grounding the several clauses, and argued that the Bill's shortcomings in this area might have been reduced 'had the planner of it imposed upon himself the task of explaining and justifying the contents'.[11] In substantive terms, Bentham attacked the omission of

[1] See *Commons Sessional Papers of the Eighteenth Century*, ciii. 167–89. [2] See ibid. 174. [3] See ibid. 164. [4] See ibid. [5] See ibid. 165. [6] See ibid. 174. [7] See ibid. 164–5. [8] See ibid. 165–7.

[9] In particular, the Bill forbade the removal from a parish of any person because of expenses incurred for relief granted under its provisions: see ibid. 165.

[10] UC cliii. 354.

[11] In fact, Thomas Ruggles had been commissioned by Pitt in February 1796 to write just such a pamphlet, and does seem to have produced a draft. However, Ruggles's draft appears to

specific provision for 'the dishonest among the indigent', since, 'Whatever be the demand [for relief] in the case of the honest exists in double force in the case of the dishonest. It is in the one case for the sake of the indigent only, in the other case for the sake of the indigent and everybody else besides.' Under the heading 'Concluding faciendum', Bentham proposed the following:

Penitentiary Panopticon Experiment to be tried for a year. J.B. if then found deserving of confidence to undertake a Poor Panopticon on public account—accounting on oath for the fidelity of the expenditure—Managing on the principles published. Somebody else at the same time on own account—Emulation between them.

Although by February 1797 at the latest, Bentham was preparing to argue that the affairs of the poor would be better managed by a national joint stock company,[1] he seems to have been prepared in early January 1797 to entertain the idea that he should manage a single panopticon poor house at the expense of government. Contrary to Bentham's firm expectations at this time, the plan for a penitentiary panopticon was never executed, and so did not pave the way for the building of a panopticon poor house.

On 6 January 1797 Bentham drafted a further *brouillon*,[2] in which he again criticized the Bill for its obscurity, with particular reference to the notion of 'benefit'. Under the heading 'Topics of Praise', he recognized the 'general Humanity' and 'particular attachment to the interests of the lowest ranks in life' displayed by the authors of the Bill. He further indicated that 'the inconveniences pointed out in the Bill will be found to be the inseparable result of the Home-Provision system'. The system itself, rather than this particular Bill, was to blame: 'any other provisions that could have been inserted in it would have been productive of the same or equal inconveniences'.

On 13 January 1797, Bentham reported that, 'every moment I can command is occupied at present by a pursuit which will admitt of no adjournment, I mean the thorough discussion of the Poor Bill'.[3] In a *brouillon* of the same date,[4] Bentham criticized the 'Cow-money Clause' in terms reproduced quite closely in his final text.[5] The

have been superseded by Pitt's later revisions to his plan, which rendered, according to Ruggles, 'the whole objectionable, if not impracticable'. See UC cli. 44 and p. xiv n. above.

[1] See pp. xxxix–xl above.

[2] UC cliii. 356.

[3] See Bentham to William Baldwin, 13 January 1797, *Correspondence* (*CW*), v. 352.

[4] UC cliii. 353.

[5] For the 'Cow-money Clause' see *Commons Sessional Papers of the Eighteenth Century*, ciii. 164–5.

brouillon contains fragmentary material for an intended preface, in which Bentham described himself as 'not only Counsel against this Bill, but . . . Counsel for another system'.[1] He also defended his critical attitude to the Bill in terms of the 'invitation' to propose measures of reform, presumably a reference to the fact that Wilberforce had sought his views on an early draft of the Bill nearly a year earlier.[2] The *brouillon* concludes with draft material on 'stile', which appears to confirm that as late as 13 January 1797 Bentham still intended to discuss both the substance and the form of the Bill at some length in the body of the text. In the event, Bentham decided to present criticism of the perceived infelicities of the Bill, in terms of the ambiguity and opacity of its form and style, in a discrete 'Essay on the question, Who are the persons for whom the several bounties provided by this Bill are intended?'.[3] In 'Observations on the Poor Bill', substantive criticisms of the system of out-allowances as presented in the Bill occupied all his attention, and criticism of the form of the Bill was confined to a single footnote.

No marginal contents sheets for 'Observations on the Poor Bill' have been discovered, but Bentham's autograph draft, divided into eight Chapters, survives intact. Ch. 1 provides an introduction to the work,[4] and is followed by five Chapters each dealing with a specific clause of the Bill.[5] Ch. 7. attacks the proposed timetable for the establishment of the rights, duties, and institutions envisaged by the Bill,[6] while Ch. 8 is the conclusion to the work.[7] There are three fair copies of substantial portions of Bentham's text, all dated February 1797. For ease of reference, these copies will be referred to as A, B, and C.[8] Bentham sent his draft of the work to the office of William Robertson, an attorney, for copying. On 10 February 1797 Robertson returned one fair copy to Bentham, reporting that he had himself copied the principal part of the manuscript.[9] All three copies omit the first paragraph of Bentham's draft, which refers to 'Pauper Systems

[1] The other system to which Bentham referred was the 'Large-Establishment system', as distinguished from the 'Home-Provision system' in 'Pauper Systems Compared'. As indicated above (p. xxxiii), Bentham's original intention was to preface his detailed criticisms of the Bill with the general survey of possible systems of poor relief which developed into 'Pauper Systems Compared'.

[2] See pp. xiv–xv above.

[3] See p. xlix below.

[4] The draft is at UC cliii. 371–2, 373, 372, 374–6.

[5] The draft of Ch. 2 is at UC cliii. 377–87; Ch. 3 at cliii. 388–94; Ch. 4 at cliii. 395–406; Ch. 5 at cliii. 407–15; and Ch. 6 at cliii. 416–27.

[6] The draft is at UC cliii. 429–36.

[7] The draft is at UC cliii. 437–40.

[8] Copy A is at UC cliii. 441–54; Copy B at cliii. 455–65; and Copy C at cliii. 466–78.

[9] See William Robertson to Bentham, 10 February 1797, *Correspondence* (*CW*), v. 356–7. Robertson indicated that he had received the draft on 9 February 1797.

Compared',[1] but include the remainder of Chs. 1–5 of the present text. Copy B, which bears comments and corrections in Bentham's hand, includes the Conclusion as it appears in the present text. Copy C includes the Conclusion except for the final paragraph, while Copy A lacks the Conclusion altogether. All three copies lack Chs. 6 and 7, although a pencil note by Bentham to a recipient of Copy A does refer to Ch. 6, offering to send it on if required.[2]

In his letter of 10 February 1797, Robertson expressed his 'doubt whether the *public* will ever have the benefit of [Bentham's] invaluable and convincing arguments', and stated that, 'though they may convince the Minister (a most desirable matter) I should very much regret the not seeing the whole thereof in print'.[3] Whilst there is no evidence that Bentham communicated 'Observations on the Poor Bill' directly to Pitt, there is evidence that he may have given the work, or at least shown it, to George Rose. In fact, Rose wrote to Bentham on 11 February 1797, presumably in response to a request for a meeting, to arrange an appointment with Bentham for the following morning.[4] On 11 February 1797 Herbert Robertson[5] asked Alexander Peter Buchan to forward to Bentham two pamphlets critical of the Bill, one written by Robertson himself, together with a copy of a letter from Thomas Ruggles to the Joint Vestry of St Giles and St George, Bloomsbury, which also found fault with the Bill.[6] Buchan forwarded these materials on the same day, together with a note from Robertson which cautioned, 'I do not see any objection to Mr B's seeing Mr Ruggles's Letter, but confide in his not shewing it to any other person or mentioning it to Mr Rose'.[7] There would seem little reason to debar Rose specifically from access to Ruggles's letter unless Robertson had reason to believe that Bentham was about to discuss matters bearing on the Poor Bill with Rose, and therefore

[1] For a discussion of the relationship between 'Pauper Systems Compared' and 'Observations on the Poor Bill' see p. xxxiii above. [2] UC cliii 464.

[3] William Robertson to Bentham, 10 February 1797, *Correspondence* (*CW*), v. 357.

[4] Rose to Bentham, 11 February 1797, ibid. 358.

[5] Herbert Robertson, brother of William and also an attorney, was vestry clerk to the united parishes of St Giles in the Fields and St George, Bloomsbury.

[6] See Buchan to Bentham, 11 February 1797, ibid. 357 & n. The pamphlets forwarded by Buchan (1764–1824), physician, were Herbert Robertson, *An Abstract of some important Parts of a Bill, now depending in Parliament, intituled, 'A Bill for the better Support and Maintenance of the Poor;' with some Practical Observations on the Effects that will probably be experienced in many Parishes, particularly those that are large and populous, if the said Bill is passed into a Law. Prepared by a Committee of the Joint Vestry of the United Parishes of St. Giles in the Fields, and St. George, Bloomsbury*, London, 1797; and Isaac Wood (1735–1801), *A Letter to Sir William Pulteney, Bart. Representative in Parliament for the Borough of Shrewsbury, containing Some Observations on the Bill for the better Support and Maintenance of the Poor, presented to the House of Commons, by the Right Hon. William Pitt*, Shrewsbury, 1797. A copy of Ruggles's letter is at UC cli. 44.

[7] See Buchan to Bentham, 11 February 1797, *Correspondence* (*CW*), v. 357n.

might have occasion to show him the letter. Since Rose was also the source from which Bentham had received the 'Heads' of the Bill nine months earlier, it might have seemed appropriate to Bentham that Rose should be the representative of the administration to which his critique of the Bill should be delivered.

In fact, any intention Bentham might have had to publish 'Observations on the Poor Bill' was swiftly overtaken by events in Parliament. On 17 February 1797 the further consideration of the Bill was deferred until 27 February, when it was again deferred, ostensibly until 9 March, but in the event indefinitely.[1] In the face of opposition from many quarters, the Bill was shelved. To what extent Bentham circulated the text of 'Observations on the Poor Bill' before the abandonment of the Bill must remain a matter of conjecture. Certainly, his opinion that the provision made by the Bill was potentially ruinous in its liberality was shared by many of the local administrators who would have been responsible for its implementation.[2]

'Observations on the Poor Bill' was edited by Edwin Chadwick in 1838, and printed for private circulation, with the title 'Observations on the Poor Bill, introduced by the Right Honourable William Pitt'.[3] Chadwick's text, with its title, was reproduced, with minor alterations, in the Bowring edition of Bentham's *Works*.[4] Bentham himself

[1] See *Commons Journals* (1796–7) lii. 288, 349, 383.

[2] Criticism of the Bill was widespread and vigorous, although the reasons advanced in opposition to it were varied and by no means mutually consistent. Between 15 February and 27 March 1797 the House of Commons received some thirty petitions, one of them from fifty-six parishes in and around London, demanding the defeat of, or local exemption from the terms of, the Bill. Opposition arose both from urban parishes, particularly in London, which were apprehensive about the increase in costs which the Bill would involve, and from incorporated districts which had established functioning workhouses, and which feared that the investment made in such institutions would be lost or needlessly duplicated in consequence of the Bill's provisions for the establishment of local schools of industry. The vestry of Kensington adopted the expedient followed by that of St Giles and St George, publishing a hostile pamphlet, *Some Observations on the Bill now pending in Parliament, for the Better Support and Maintenance of the Poor. Prepared for the use of the Trustees of the Poor of the Parish of Kensington*, London, 1797.

Besides Isaac Wood, other critical commentators included Sir Frederick Morton Eden (1766–1809), *The State of the Poor; or, an History of the Labouring Classes in England, from the Conquest to the Present Period; In which are particularly considered, their Domestic Economy, with respect to Diet, Dress, Fuel, and Habitation; And the various Plans which, from time to time, have been proposed, and adopted, for the Relief of the Poor: together with Parochial Reports Relative to the Administration of Work-houses, and Houses of Industry; the State of Friendly Societies; and other Public Institutions; in Several Agricultural, Commercial and Manufacturing, Districts*, 3 vols., London, 1797, i. 478–84; and Sir William Young (1749–1815), *Considerations on the Subject of Poor-Houses and Work-Houses, their Pernicious Tendency, And their Obstruction to the Proposed Plan for the Amendment of the Poor Laws; in a letter to the Rt. Hon. W. Pitt*, London, 1796.

[3] A copy of Chadwick's edition of the text, forty-eight pages in length, dated 7 May 1838, and printed by William Clowes and Sons of Stamford Street, is preserved in the British Library, shelf-mark C.T. 208 (10). The first sixteen pages of a proof copy are at UC clv. 120.

[4] Bowring, viii. 440–61.

never included any reference to the author of the Bill in his title for the work. In the *brouillon* of 6 January 1797, Bentham gave the title of the work as 'View of the Poor Bill with critical observations, and ulterior suggestions'.[1] In his autograph draft, Bentham used the heading 'Poor Bill', while the copyists' texts are headed 'Observations on the Poor Bill'. The latter title has been adopted in the present edition for two reasons. In the first place, the earlier, longer title refers to a projected work which Bentham did not in fact write, since the text did not in the end include the extensive criticisms of the style and presentation of legislation which were at one time envisaged. In the second place, the fact that it post-dates the longer title may indicate that it represents Bentham's final thoughts on the matter.

Chadwick's edition of 'Observations on the Poor Bill' departed from Bentham's intentions in several respects. First, in Ch. 4 Chadwick included a paragraph written by Bentham in February 1796, in criticism of an early version of the 'cow money clause', although there is no indication that Bentham himself intended its inclusion.[2] Second, Chadwick placed the Conclusion of 'Observations on the Poor Bill', without any heading, at the end of Ch. 5, where it does indeed appear in the copyists' texts, but for the simple reason that when Bentham sent his draft for copying, Chs. 6 and 7 remained either unwritten or incomplete. Following Copy B of the work, Chadwick also omits the final paragraph of the Conclusion. In the present edition, the Conclusion appears complete and in its proper place as Ch. 8. Third, Chadwick decided to present Ch. 7 not as a discrete chapter, but, under the title 'General Remarks on Home Provision', as one of two supplemental essays which follow Ch. 6, and thus conclude the work. The second supplemental essay was 'Essay on the question, Who are the persons for whom the several bounties provided by this Bill are intended?', overlooking Bentham's decision to limit the focus of 'Observations on the Poor Bill' to the substantive revisions made by the Bill to the system of out-allowances or 'Home Provision'. Fourth, Chadwick confusingly prefaced Bentham's discussions of particular sections of the Bill with the text of those sections of the Bill as published in Eden's *State of the Poor*.[3] Since Bentham quoted from the text of the Bill as

[1] UC cliii. 356.

[2] See UC cliii. 368 and Chadwick's edition of 'Observations on the Poor Bill', p. 20 (Bowring, viii. 449).

[3] See 'Heads of a Bill for the better Support and Maintenance of the Poor', in Eden, *The State of The Poor*, iii. pp.cccxiii–cccxxxviii. This version of the 'Heads', which contains 130 clauses, and differs from the earlier versions preserved in Pitt's papers, appears to be the text of the Bill as introduced in the House of Commons on 29 December 1796, before its amendment by committee.

amended by Committee, neither the numbers of the clauses as indicated by Chadwick, nor, in some cases, their wording, correspond to the numeration and wording cited by Bentham. In the present edition, Bentham's specific discussions are accompanied by editorial footnotes containing the text of the relevant clauses in the version of the Bill from which he actually worked.

Appendix to Observations on the Poor Bill: Essay on the question, Who are the persons for whom the several bounties provided by this Bill are intended?

The precise period at which 'Essay on the question, Who are the persons for whom the several bounties provided by this Bill are intended?' was composed is unclear. However, given that in the *brouillons* of 5 and 6 January 1797 Bentham indicated his intention of analysing the obscurity arising from the use of the term 'benefit' in the Bill,[1] and that as late as 13 January 1797 he was still intending to discuss both the substance and the 'stile' of the Bill in that text,[2] the drafting of the essay presumably did not begin until after this latter date. One further indication is given by a pencilled footnote to Bentham's draft of Ch. 2 of 'Observations on the Poor Bill': 'I have by me a dissertation of 15 or 16 pages, the result of which is that the discovery [of who the persons are that are entitled to the benefit of the Act] is impossible.'[3] The note might be taken to imply that the essay was written before Bentham began drafting the text of 'Observations on the Poor Bill', but the fact that the note itself was in the form of a marginal comment, written in pencil, and added at some time subsequent to the original composition of the text, renders any inference less than certain.

'Essay on the question, Who are the persons for whom the several bounties provided by this Bill are intended?' was included in Chadwick's edition of 'Observations on the Poor Bill'.[4] Chadwick introduced into the text of the essay a draft conclusion to a projected discussion of the Bill's 'stile', possibly written as early as June 1796, although there is no indication that Bentham himself had any intention of including this material.[5]

[1] See pp. xliii–xliv above.

[2] See p. xlv above.

[3] UC cliii. 377. The note, in the form of a pencilled marginal comment in Bentham's hand, also appears in Copy B of 'Observations on the Poor Bill' (UC cliii. 456b), but is absent from Copies A and C.

[4] See pp. 38–45 (Bowring, 457–60).

[5] See p. xlii & n. above. The material is inserted in Chadwick's edition of 'Observations on the Poor Bill' at pp. 45–7 (Bowring, viii. 460–1).

Appendix A
Neighbour's-Fare Principle Defended

The material which forms the text of the present Appendix[1] was originally composed as a commentary on 'Rule 22. Neighbour's-Fare Principle', one of the management rules proposed to be included in 'Pauper Systems Compared'. Bentham then seems to have decided to include the material in 'Pauper Management Improved'. On 15 February 1797, he drafted a marginal contents sheet for Part I of his 'Poor Plan'.[2] Alongside the detailed marginal contents for Part I of the 'Poor Plan', Bentham listed the sections to be contained in Part II. The title of Part II, § 14, added in red ink at some time subsequent to the first drafting of the contents page, was given as 'Neighbour's-Fare Principle Defended'.

The identity between the text which formed the commentary on 'Rule 22. Neighbour's-Fare Principle' and the material envisaged by Bentham as constituting 'Neighbour's-Fare Principle Defended' is confirmed by a marginal contents sheet of 21 February 1797, headed 'Poor Plan Contents'.[3] This marginal contents sheet contains the summaries of the texts of two proposed sections of the 'Poor Plan', one of which is 'Neighbour's-Fare Principle Defended'. The summaries of 'Neighbour's-Fare Principle Defended' correspond exactly to those which appear in the margin of the text sheets which constitute the commentary on Rule 22.

By 21 February 1797, then, Bentham had decided to incorporate his defence of the Neighbour's-Fare Principle in 'Poor Plan', soon afterwards to be entitled 'Pauper Management Improved'. However, no reference to this defence appears in the 'Outline' of 'Pauper Management Improved' published in the *Annals of Agriculture* in 1798, and it may be that Bentham had decided to omit it altogether. The discussion is relatively complete and coherent, and it is, therefore, included as an Appendix to the present volume.

Appendix B
Farming Defended

The history of the material which forms the text of 'Farming Defended'[4] replicates to some extent that of 'Neighbour's-Fare Principle Defended'. As with 'Neighbour's-Fare Principle Defended', Bentham at one stage planned to include an examination of the 'Farming system' in 'Pauper Systems Compared', but in the event

[1] See UC cliii. 175–88.
[2] UC cliv. 68, headed 'Poor Plan Contents I'.
[3] UC cli. 5.
[4] UC clii. 331–7, 340–1, 338–9, 342–56.

failed to do so.[1] Again as with 'Neighbour's-Fare Principle Defended', Bentham then seems to have decided to include the material in 'Pauper Management Improved'. 'Farming defended' appears as Part II, § 15 of the work on the marginal contents sheet of 15 February 1797,[2] and as § 13 on a second marginal contents sheet.[3]

By 21 February 1797, Bentham had drafted his defence of farming the poor for inclusion in 'Poor Plan'.[4] It seems that he remained uncertain about the appropriate place for the discussion within his poor law writings, and may have decided not to publish the material. As is the case with its companion piece 'Neighbour's-Fare Principle Defended', 'Farming Defended' does not appear in 'Outline of a Work entitled Pauper Management Improved' as published in the *Annals of Agriculture*. In the face of uncertainty concerning Bentham's final intention with regard to this material, and in view of the fact that the discussion itself is to a large extent coherent and complete, the text is included as an Appendix to the present volume.

TEXT

The Manuscripts

With the exception of 'Table of Cases calling for Relief', all the essays in the present volume have been reconstructed from manuscript. Bentham's original drafts form the basis of the texts, except where Bentham himself has corrected the copyists' texts. Significant differences between Bentham's drafts and the copies are indicated in editorial footnotes. The text is written on single sheets of foolscap ruled with a wide margin. Many of the text sheets contain numerous additions (either interlinear or marginal), deletions, and emendations. At this time Bentham was not in the habit of dating his text sheets. Having revised his text, Bentham wrote marginal summaries in the form of short paragraphs which he numbered consecutively. Once he had drafted a body of material corresponding to an intended work, or sometimes to a specific section or subsection thereof, he transferred the marginal summaries, with the appropriate page

[1] See p. xl above.
[2] UC cliv. 68.
[3] UC cliv. 69, headed 'Poor Plan Contents'.
[4] See UC cli. 5. The text sheets themselves are headed 'Plan—Objection farming'. The appearance together of the two defences on the marginal contents sheet of 21 February 1797 indicates that by this time Bentham viewed them as closely connected. Moreover, see the comment at UC cliii. 188 appended to Bentham's draft discussion of the 'Neighbour's-Fare Principle': 'Introduce this *first* or *last* after the Farming defence.'

numbers of the text sheets, to double sheets of foolscap, ruled into several columns, and headed 'Contents'. These marginal contents sheets were frequently dated, and often contain additions, deletions, and emendations, indicating that Bentham moved back and forth between text and contents sheets as he developed the essay in question.

Before beginning to draft an essay, Bentham would sometimes compose *brouillons*, containing notes, draft passages, and ideas or examples for development, written on double sheets of foolscap ruled into columns, and usually dated. Also on such sheets, either before beginning to draft a text, or in parallel with it, he would produce plans, entitled '*Ordo*' or 'Contents', which typically contain the titles of potential chapters or sections, thus indicating the intended organization of the text in question. Whilst providing an insight into Bentham's intentions with regard to the content of a work at a particular, usually early, stage of its conception, such sheets can be misleading. For instance, he often failed to fulfil part or all these plans, so that often no text for particular sections was ever written. On occasion Bentham would draft 'Contents' sheets which combined a plan of the essay, consisting of the titles of its chapters and sections, with marginal contents of the specific part of the essay on which he had just been working.

Some general points with regard to the organization of the texts presented in this volume should be made. Since Bentham did not publish any of the works contained in this volume, with the exception of 'Table of Cases calling for Relief', their organization remains to some extent conjectural. The paucity of dated material only increases the degree of uncertainty. However, Bentham's manuscript drafts of the texts are generally well organized. Moreover, the reconstruction of the texts is facilitated by the fact that Bentham did not produce a multiplicity of drafts for particular chapters, sections, or pages of his poor law writings. For instance, 'Pauper Systems Compared' consists in a single manuscript draft in Bentham's hand, which largely corresponds to the five marginal contents sheets which he compiled for the work. Where difficulties have arisen, reliance has been placed on internal evidence, such as the headings, pagination, the numbering of marginal contents, and finally, of course, the sense.

The location and, where possible, the date of related manuscripts not included in the text has been indicated in the Editorial Introduction above or, where appropriate, in editorial footnotes accompanying the text. For the manuscripts used in the present edition reference should be made to the Table of Manuscripts below.

Table of Manuscripts

Essays on the subject of the Poor Laws

Essay I: Definitions and Distinctions

	MSS (UC)
	cliii. 1–8[1]

Essay II: Fundamental Positions in regard to the making provision for the Indigent Poor

	MSS (UC)
Introduction	clii. 221–4
§I.	cliii. 55; clii. 225; cliii. 55; clii. 230; cliii. 56; clii. 227, 55, 8–53, 382–7; cliii. 56[2]
§II.	cliii. 57–9;[3] clii. 1–6
§III.	cliii. 60[4]
§IV.	cliii. 61; clii. 232; cliii. 61–3; clii. 235; cliii. 63; clii. 234; cliii. 64;[5] clii. 236
§V.	cliii. 65;[6] clii. 237–8
§VI.	cliii. 66–7;[7] clii. 241
§VII.	cliii. 68–9;[8] clii. 244
§VIII.	cliii. 70; clii. 245; cliii. 70; clii. 246–7; cliii. 70;[9] clii. 248
§IX.	cliii. 71; clii. 250–1; cliii. 72[10]
§X.	cliii. 73; clii. 255–6; cliii. 73–4[11]
§XI.	cliii. 75; clii. 263; cliii. 75; clii. 257; cliii. 75–7; clii. 258–62[12]
Conclusion	clii. 68, 191–5[13]

Essay III: Collateral Uses derivable from a system of Industry Houses

	MSS (UC)
Introduction	clii. 71–2, 196,[14] 73–6[15]

[1] Copied at UC cliii. 21b-24, and again at clii. 57–8.
[2] UC cliii. 55–6 are copied at cliii. 25, and again at clii. 61.
[3] Copied at UC cliii. 25–6, and again at clii. 61–2.
[4] Copied at UC cliii. 26, and again at clii. 62.
[5] UC cliii. 61–4 are copied at cliii. 26–7, and again at clii. 62–3.
[6] Copied at UC cliii. 27, and again at clii. 63.
[7] Copied at UC cliii. 27, and again at clii. 63.
[8] Copied at UC cliii. 27–8, and again at clii. 63–4.
[9] UC cliii. 70 is copied at cliii. 28, and again at clii. 64.
[10] UC cliii. 71–2 are copied at cliii. 28, and again at clii. 64.
[11] UC cliii. 73–4 are copied at cliii. 28–9, and again at clii. 64–5.
[12] UC cliii. 75–7, clii. 263 are copied at cliii. 29–30, and again at clii. 65.
[13] Copied at UC cliii. 30–1, and again at clii. 66–7.
[14] There is a folio missing from Bentham's original draft at this point. The deficiency is supplied from the corresponding copy at UC clii. 196.
[15] This section is copied at UC clii. 196–7.

§I.	clii. 77; cliii. 11; clii. 87, 77, 88–9, 77–9, 90–1; cliii. 33;[1] clii. 79–80, 92–3, 81–6; cliii. 9–10; clii. 98–103; cxxxiii. 38, 40; clii. 104–20, 94–7[2]
§II.	clii. 121, 122, 121, 123–9[3]
§III.	clii. 164–75, 182–3, 176–7, 178, 177, 179–81, 131–43, 146, 143–5, 147–63[4]
§IV.	clii. 184–8, 190, 189; cliii. 12–13;[5] cxlix. 54–5, 64–5, 55–63; cliii. 14–17, 20, 18–19

Pauper Systems Compared, or a Comparative View of the several systems establishable as well as established in relation to the Poor

	MSS (UC)
Introduction	clii. 431–2
Chapter I.	clii. 433–6, 438
Chapter II.	clii. 424–9
Chapter III.	clii. 440–4
Chapter IV.	
Introduction	clii. 453
§1.	clii. 454, 455–7, 454
§2.	clii. 458a, 458b, 458a, 459, 460, 459, 461–62a, 462b, 462a, 463, 464–5, 463
§3.	clii. 466–77, 479–82, 483, 482, 484
§4.	clii. 485–8
§5.	clii. 489–91, 492, 491, 492
§6.	clii. 493
§7.	clii. 500, 497–9, 512, 501–7, 494–6, 508
§8.	clii. 509–11, 513–15
Chapter V.	clii. 517–20; cliv. 585; clii. 521–8
Chapter VI.	
§1.	clii. 447–52, 530–43, 547–52
§2.	clii. 553–7
§3.	clii. 558–63
Chapter VII.	clii. 389–90, cxlix. 107–8, clii. 391–401

[1] There is a folio missing from Bentham's original draft at this point. The deficiency is supplied from the corresponding copy at UC cliii. 33.

[2] With the exception of UC cxxxiii. 38 and 40, the material in this section is copied at cliii. 32–42.

[3] The whole section is copied at UC cliii. 43–5.

[4] The whole section is copied at UC cliii. 46–54, clii. 206–14. UC clii. 132–63 are also copied at clii. 198–205.

[5] Copied at UC clii. 215–18.

Observations on the Poor Bill

	MSS (UC)
Chapter 1.	cliii. 371–2, 373, 372, 374–6[1]
Chapter 2.	cliii. 377–87[2]
Chapter 3.	cliii. 388–94[3]
Chapter 4.	cliii. 395–406[4]
Chapter 5.	cliii. 407–15[5]
Chapter 6.	cliii. 416–27
Chapter 7.	cliii. 429–36
Chapter 8.	cliii. 437–40[6]

Appendix to Observations on the Poor Bill: Essay on the question, Who are the persons for whom the several bounties provided by this Bill are intended?

MSS (UC)
cliii. 363–4; cli. 454–7
- - - - - - - - - [7]
cli. 458–67

Appendix A: Neighbour's-Fare Principle Defended

MSS (UC)
cliii. 175–88

Appendix B: Farming Defended

MSS (UC)
clii. 331–7, 340–1, 338–9, 342–56

Presentation of the Text

It has been editorial policy to reflect as far as possible the manuscript sources on which the essays in this volume are based, but without sacrifice thereby of clarity and sense. Bentham's spelling and capitalization have been retained in most instances, although editorial discretion has been exercised with regard to his punctuation, which is often inconsistent and sparse. Punctuation marks have been adjusted and supplied where clearly indicated by the sense, or

[1] There are three copies of UC cliii. 372–6 at cliii. 441–2, 455–6, and 466 respectively.
[2] Copied three times at UC cliii. 442–5, 456–8, and 467–70 respectively.
[3] Copied three times at UC cliii. 446–7, 458–60, and 471–2 respectively.
[4] Copied three times at UC cliii. 448–50, 460–2, and 473–5 respectively.
[5] Copied three times at UC cliii. 451–3, 463–4, and 476–7.
[6] Copied at UC cliii. 465, and again at 478, though the latter lacks the final paragraph.
[7] A text sheet is missing at this point. The deficiency is supplied by the corresponding text from Bowring, viii. 458–9.

required for the sake of clarity, but not in cases where this might involve a dubious interpretation of the meaning. The words and phrases underlined by Bentham for emphasis have been rendered in italics, as have all foreign words and phrases, some of which Bentham underlined and some of which he did not. In general, standard abbreviations have been retained, though some abbreviated words have been expanded to their full form.

The manuscripts contain many deletions, additions, and emendations which represent Bentham's later corrections to the text. The final alternative reading is usually given in the text. Original readings have not usually been indicated. Where there is no text corresponding to some part of a marginal contents sheet, the appropriate marginal summary is reproduced in an editorial footnote. Square brackets in the text are reserved for editorially inserted words, while Bentham's original is, where appropriate, given in an editorial footnote. Bentham's square brackets are replaced by braces. Round brackets are those supplied by Bentham. Vertical strokes indicate a gap or blank space in the manuscript.

Bentham's own footnotes are indicated by superscript letters, and editorial footnotes by superscript numerals, with a separate sequence for each page of text.

The only part of the present edition based on a text published during Bentham's lifetime is 'Table of Cases calling for Relief'. The present edition corresponds as closely as possible with the style and conventions, including spelling, capitalization, punctuation, the use of italics, and other devices, of the printed text published in 1797. Editorial apparatus is confined to the use of square brackets to indicate editorially inserted words: in these cases, the original reading is indicated in an editorial footnote.

ESSAYS ON THE SUBJECT OF THE POOR LAWS

ESSAY I
DEFINITIONS AND DISTINCTIONS

The definitions and distinctions which form the matter of this first Essay may, in conjunction with the positions which occupy the succeeding one, serve to fix our notions relative to several points of leading importance in relation to the subject of the Poor Laws: and where they fail of putting an end to differences of opinion, they may still be of use, in placing in a clear light the point on which the difference turns. In a practical view, besides pointing out the most advantageous, if not only, means, they may preserve both time and money from being wasted, in pursuit of ends, either separately unattainable, or collectively repugnant and incompatible.

The proper object of the system of laws, known in this country by the name of the *Poor Laws*, is to make provision for the relief not of *poverty*, but of *indigence.*

The distinction between poverty and indigence is an article of fundamental and primary importance.

Poverty is the state of everyone who, in order to obtain subsistence, is forced to have recourse to labour.

Indigence is the state of him who, being destitute of property (or at least destitute of the species of property necessary to the immediate satisfaction of the particular want by which he happens to be pressed),[a] is at the same time either unable to labour, or unable, even for labour, to procure the supply of which he happens thus to be in want.

Poverty as above defined is the natural, the primitive, the general, and the unchangeable, lot of man. The condition of persons whose property has placed them in what are termed *opulent* or *easy circumstances*, that is, who live upon the permanently recurring produce of labour already in store, is but an *exception*, which, under the most equal distribution of the stock thus laid up, could never, for any length of time, be very extensive.

As labour is the source of wealth, so is poverty of labour. Banish poverty, you banish wealth: banish all those who, (in the words of the English law of Settlements) are *liable to become chargeable*, you banish all those who are either *disposed* or *qualified* to become

[a] A man may be proprietor, for example, of the house he lives in, to the value of thirty or forty pounds, besides furniture, cloaths, and tools &c., and yet be at the point of starving, and in that respect in a state of utter indigence.

serviceable. If *labour* is liable to *cease*, so is *property* to be *destroyed* or *spent*: so that, to clear a district of persons liable to become chargeable, there is *one* way, and *but* one, which is to clear it of inhabitants.[a]

Indigence, therefore, and not *poverty* (I must repeat it), is the evil,

[a] The law of Settlements, as it stands in England, (the law giving each man a right to be maintained in case of indigence, *in* and at the expence of some particular Parish or Parish-like District in which he is said to have his *settlement*) wears the *appearance* of having been dictated by the inconsiderate aims above alluded to: but it is only the *appearance*. The option it had was a perplexing one: to expose itself to this imputation, or to expose every parish in the kingdom to be devoured by vagabonds pouring in upon it in swarms. The efficient causes of title with regard to settlement might perhaps have been better chosen: but such as they were, they produced the effect they aimed at, and that a good one, the giving *limits* to a burthen which otherwise would have had *none*.[1]

Meantime, comes a dictum of Common Law and says, (what Common Law in company with common humanity could hardly avoid saying,) *no* man, *settlement or no settlement, shall be left to starve*.[2] Between Statute Law and Common Law what follows?—that a man who *has* a settlement has but one: but that a man who has *no* settlement, has as many as he pleases. An Englishman is confined to his parish: though the bounds of it be narrower than the Rules of the King's Bench Prison.[3] But a Scotchman, an Irishman, a foreigner, an enemy, has the whole country at his command. Were 50,000 French to land at Dover (leaving their provisions at Calais) and apply to the Overseers of Dover parish, the Overseers would be bound to victual them: at least untill the Magistrates of Kent should please, if such should be their pleasure in aid of the Parish, to press the County into the service.

There was needed another option, which was to *spread* the burthen:—making the whole kingdom, or some large part of it, each man's parish, but how to manage the

[1] The notion that each person 'belonged' to a certain parish from which he should seek relief at need was of several centuries standing. As early as 1388 (12 Ric. II, c.7) beggars were directed to return to their parish of birth to be relieved. The Act of 1662 (13 & 14 Car. II, c.12) which established the basis of the law of settlements was an attempt to clarify the question of responsibility to provide relief, and to prevent generous parishes being swamped by itinerant paupers. The Act established forty days' residence in a parish as the criterion of a settlement there, after which the parish became liable to provide relief in case of need, and legalized the removal of potentially chargeable immigrants, with certain exceptions, on complaint from parish officials to Justices of the Peace. Subsequent legislation enacted that the forty-day qualification period did not begin until the immigrant had given written notice to the parish officers of their place of abode, and such notice had been published in the parish church. An Act of 1795 (35 Geo. III, c.101) made removal illegal until a person actually required relief, although 'rogues, vagabonds and other idle and disorderly persons', as well as unmarried pregnant women, were excluded from this protection.

[2] The question of responsibility for the maintenance of persons who required relief in parishes other than those where they had their settlement, during a period in which they could not speedily be removed to those parishes, had been addressed directly by 22 Geo. III, c.83, § 38 (1782). This enacted that it was the responsibility of every parish to administer such relief as the demand for it arose, regardless of settlement, and that the costs of such relief should be recoverable subsequently from the parish where the person concerned was possessed of a settlement.

[3] The King's Bench Prison took its name from the gaols attached to the Court of King's Bench. Affluent prisoners were able to purchase 'freedom of the Rules', that is liberty to come and go unhindered, provided that they remained within three square miles of the prison.

the removal of which constitutes the proper object of the Poor Laws. To banish poverty, is an attempt founded in inadvertence, and which, in the nature of things, must have either no effect or a bad one. *Indigence* may be *provided for*: *mendicity* may be extirpated: but to extirpate *poverty* would be to extirpate *man*.

The natural, and only natural, source of the subsistence of every man who has it not in the shape of property in store, is obviously his *own* labour, at least in so far as it is adequate to the purpose. Whether in any and what respect this natural and primitive order of things ought, from views of general utility, to be broken in upon, is a question that will meet us in its proper place.

In respect to the degree of ability with regard to labour, compared with the necessary quantum of subsistence, the condition of man is susceptible of four very material distinctions: viz:

1. Utter inability.[a]
2. Inadequate ability.[b]
3. Adequate (meaning *simply* adequate) ability.
4. Extra-ability.

The *sum* of the labour that has been exerted is the source of the *whole stock* of the *matter of wealth*[c] (including that of *subsistence*) that either *exists* or ever *did* exist in the world, land in its unimproved state (covered or not covered with water) excepted.

The sum of Extra-ability with regard to labour (viz: so much of it as hath been employed) is the source of so much of that matter as hath been consumed over and above what has been consumed in the shape of necessaries, added to so much of it as remains in store.

Since, after all that has been wasted and destroyed, besides what has been used, of the matter of wealth, after all that has been unproductively employed of the sum of labour, and after all that has been suffered to lie unemployed of the sum of ability with regard to labour, there remains so large a mass of the matter of wealth in store, it follows, that *extra-ability* is the *natural* and *general* state of

spreading is another difficulty, for the solution of which, matters at that time of day[1] were not ripe. Are they at present?—to try whether they are or no, is among the objects of the present papers.

[a] Synonymous expressions: Total or absolute inability: utter, total, or absolute want of ability.

[b] Deficient or defective or insufficient ability: partial inability or want of ability.

[c] Instead of saying wealth, it becomes necessary to say *the matter of wealth*, since the use of the word *wealth*, standing by itself, is confined to the case where a *large* quantity of any of the matter of which wealth is composed, is considered as being lodged in the *same hand*.

---

[1] i.e. in 1662, when the law of settlements was enacted.

man: and that even *simply adequate* ability, much more *inadequate* ability and *utter* inability, form but so many exceptions to the general rule.

The cause of inability may be *personal* to a man, or *exterior* to him: it may be *within* or *without* him. A man may be able to do work if he had it, but he may be unable to obtain it, or (to come to the point at once) unable to procure what he stands in need of in return for it.

Considered with reference to any particular *species* of work, inability, when of the *personal* kind, may result either from want of *strength*, or from want of *skill*.

The poor may be stiled *independent* or *dependent*, according as they depend or not for their subsistence upon public contributions. When the *independent* Poor become *dependent*, it can only be on the score of *indigence*, real or supposed.

Relief may be distinguished into *simple* relief and *extra-relief*. Whatever is over and above the amount of the demand created by *indigence* may be stiled *extra-relief*.

The demand created by indigence, can never be said to extend beyond the absolute *necessaries* of life. For generally speaking the ability of those who are maintained by their *own* labour, does little more than pass this limit: and beyond it there are no bounds.[a]

Neither by *good* nor by *ill desert*, can any thing be added to, or taken from, the quantum of the demand on the score of indigence.

By good desert, nothing is added. Good desert, to constitute a claim, whether it be upon the public or upon an individual, must exist in the shape of special *service*: and in that case whatever is administered in consequence is not *relief*, but *reward*.

By *ill* desert, nothing is taken away. The demand on the score of indigence, extends not (as hath been just observed, and will be made still more manifest) beyond bare subsistence. If, on the ground of ill desert, any thing be taken from the quantum of relief, such reduction

[a] The Kings of the earth, despoiled like Lear of their regalities, command our pity:[1] but it is not in the power of parishes to give kingdoms.

[a] [*opposite*] One man may be *a very worthy, good sort of man*: but so ought we all to be: and if every man who is so were to bring in his bill for being so, who would there be to pay it?

Another man may be *a very worthless fellow*: but if he is really so, and can be made out to be so, it must be on account of this or that act of worthlessness, that he has committed. If it be a crime, he will be punished according to the crime: if it be less than a crime, it will be too much to punish him more than a man is ever punished for

[1] Lear was a legendary King of Britain who, according to Shakespeare's version of the story, in his old age divided his kingdom between his daughters Goneril and Regan, only to be subsequently rejected by them, and harrassed to the point of madness.

has the effect of *punishment*: and the exercise of it ought to be governed by the same rules as the infliction of punishment.[a]

a crime, even for the highest crime, that is to starve him, to leave him to perish by a slow death.

To both these opposite characters, the text will not be the less applicable, although neither the one be pensioned nor the other starved, *Verily, verily, ye have your reward.*[1]

[1] Matthew 6: 16.

ESSAY II
FUNDAMENTAL POSITIONS IN REGARD TO THE MAKING PROVISION FOR THE INDIGENT POOR

Introduction

The following positions which are submitted to the reader in the character of fundamental positions may, if just, be of use to two different descriptions of persons and in a double point of view—to legislators as standards of propriety serving for the guidance of the Draughtsman in the framing of the provisions of detail: to the Agents of the executive power, in the character not only of standards of propriety serving for their guidance in the exercise of whatever latitude of discretion they may find themselves intrusted with by the legislature, but also in the quality of warrants serving to justify them in the eyes of the public in respect of the course they take in the exercise of that discretion.

In this latter character of warrants the principles in question might be not altogether without their use, although presented by the hand of an uncommissioned individual: serving them as a screen from the imputation of blame originating in themselves. If there be any deficiency in respect of humanity, of justice, of frugality, of good economy, in any of these rules, the origin of it is to be found not in our own hands, not in our own heads, not in any sinister affections or prejudices of our own: they come to us not from our own bosoms, but from a disinterested at least, and not incautious, howsoever misguided hand.

This much may be done even by private, unadopted and unencouraged industry. But it is manifest enough that the value of the benefit to the public agents in question could not but be greatly enhanced, as well in respect of the ease to the mind in the way of guidance as in regard to the protection against obloquy, were the rules in question to be adopted in substance and sanctioned and promulgated (for example in the shape of Resolutions) by the authority of the legislature.

Should these positions stand the test of examination, no small progress will be found to have been made: the only question remaining will be that which has regard to the application of these rules: the ascertaining whether a proposed measure of detail stands really approved by the rules thus set up as standards.

By any one step little or nothing will appear to be done: but at the last step every thing will be found to be done. Taken separately they will seem scarce worth setting down: and the more evidently just, the less worth laying down. But taken collectively, they are so modified and put together as to be consistent with each other: whereas among all the notions that have hitherto been advanced on this subject there reigns a perpetual inconsistency: and that not only as between writer and writer, but as between notion and notion of the same writer.

In this, as in other branches of political economy, nothing more easy than to find arguments, nothing more difficult than to frame just conclusions: every body sees more or less on some side, nobody sees every thing on both sides: much less is capable of assigning to every thing its due weight.

Almost every body has his favourite object, which in his view eclipses all the rest.

Should any of the positions in question prove false in point of principle, it may still have its use: a clear statement of a question may have its use, whether the answer given to it be true or false.—If I am not right, I trust it will be seen with tolerable clearness in regard to what points, and how far, I am wrong. It will come to the same thing to the public whether I am right myself, or only the cause of rectitude in other men.

I have accordingly set myself to distinguish, and place in as a clear a point of view as possible, on the one hand propositions of opinion in relation to the several points that call for determination, on the other hand the reasons producible in support of the affirmative or negative side of each proposition.

No inconsistency will be found, every rule having been compared with, and adjusted to, and *ground* down as it were, by every other: a degree of conformity which was not brought about without sacrificing the first and many a succeeding draught in a multitude of instances.

These positions thus laid down, should disputes still continue, it may be known at least, and that with perfect distinctness, what is in each instance the subject of the dispute.

§I. *Necessity of Relief*

[Position][1] 1. In a civilized political community, it is neither consistent with common humanity, nor public security, that any individual should, for want of any of the necessaries of life, be left to perish *outright*—[a]

Reasons

1. Regard to common humanity.
2. Regard to public security. Certain death being the lot of innocence, and only a chance of punishment, capital or not capital, the lot of criminality, [is it][2] not to be expected that in such an exigency a man should seek to relieve himself by whatever means, whether by fraud or force?

[Position] 2.—Or *gradually*, to wit through infirmity or disease.

[Position] 3. In every extensive political community, there will, at every given moment, be a multitude of individuals, of various descriptions, in whose instance the misfortune of perishing, through want of the necessaries of life, either outright or gradually, can not, to any sufficient degree of certainty, be prevented, but by means of a *certain* fund of relief, appropriated to the purpose. (For the list of the cases of the several descriptions of individuals so circumstanced, see the annexed *Table of Cases calling for Relief.*)[3]

[Position] 4. In every such community, as well the number of the indigent, as above described ([position][4] 3), as the degree of

[a] The tendency of the four first of these rules is to *establish* the demand on the public on the score of indigence: that of the three following ones, to *limit* it.[5] The four first have humanity for their motive and public security for their object: the three others, justice for their motive and frugality for their object. The two objects, like certain muscles in the human body, are antagonists to each other and draw opposite ways. Either, exclusively pursued, must lead to error: of the dictates of both, duly regulated by each other, perfection would be the result.

[1] In order to distinguish the fundamental positions from the reasons and observations which relate to them, they are preceded by the editorial insertion '[Position]'.

[2] MS 'it is' contradicts the evident sense of the passage.

[3] See p. lvii above.

[4] MS 'art.' In cross references, Bentham often referred to the 'positions' as 'articles'. For the sake of consistency and clarity, 'position' has been substituted for 'article' where appropriate.

[5] In Bentham's original draft, in which this note appears, the number and ordering of the 'positions' differed somewhat from the final form as presented here. In the original draft, Bentham's 'four first' rules correspond to positions 1–10, concerning the necessity of relief; the 'three following' to positions 11–19, concerning the quantum of relief. For further details see the Editorial Introduction, pp. xxii–xxiii above.

indigence on the part of each, is essentially and incessantly liable to change. (See the Table.)

[Position] 5. No *fixed* sum therefore, allotted out of any fund, public or private, for the relief of indigence, can, unless it be excessive, be for two days together, unless by accident, adequate to the purpose.

Observations

If the sum be fixed, the chances are infinity to one, against its being properly adjusted to the demand: it will either be beyond the exigence, and there it stands exposed to the objections in point of economy and justice which form the basis in point of reason of the three [succeeding][1] rules; or it will fall short of the exigence, and there by the supposition a proportionable number of the individuals intitled to relief must necessarily perish, unless supported by private charity, the necessary precariousness of which has been already stated,[2] or maintained by acts of fraud or force, in a word, by all those offences against property which the law punishes as crimes.[a]

The annexed *Table of Cases calling for Relief* exhibits a view of the several descriptions of persons who by an abolition or fixation of the supply afforded at the public charge would be left to perish by famine, or driven to acts of desperation, justifiable by necessity though punishable by law.

[Position] 6. No private fund, that is no fund, depending on the uncompulsory contributions of individuals, can, to any sufficient degree of certainty, be so much as kept up to any certain standard, as adjusted to precedent demand, much less predetermined to encrease in exactly the same degree, and at exactly the same time, with every encrease in the demand.[3]

[Position] 7. No fund therefore, but a public fund, can ever be permanently adequate to the purpose.

[a] See Observations on Position 1.[4]

---

[1] MS 'preceding'. The three rules here referred to by Bentham correspond to positions 11–19 of the final draft of the essay, concerning the quantum of relief: see pp. 38–40 below.

[2] In Bentham's original draft, the discussion of the necessity of a public fund for indigence relief appeared before that of the rejection of the limitation of the sum available for indigence relief. According to the ordering of the present text, what appears here as a reference back to a discussion of the 'precariousness of private charity', should be read as a reference forward, specifically to 'Observations' on position 7: see pp. 12–15 below.

[3] In the margin, Bentham has noted in pencil at this point: 'P[rinciple] of Public Charity.'

[4] See p. 10 above.

Observations

When administered at the public expence, and by the agents of the public, the supply may keep pace with the demand: there is every requisite to enable it so to do, nothing to prevent it from so doing.

When the inclination, and the power necessary to the production of any effect, exist at the same time and exist in the same agent, the effect takes place: so long as either of these requisites is wanting, the effect fails of being produced. With regard to the effect in question, on the part of the public the power can not fail: the inclination may be given and is given, in this as in other cases, by the expedients employ'd to bind the persons in question to the observance of their duty: knowledge of the individuals standing in need of relief, and of the quantity and quality of the relief they respectively stand in need of, can not be wanting to those who are predisposed to receive it, so long as there are individuals whose indigence creates the demand for it. Accordingly the great complaint under the existing system in England, the system of public charity, and therefore of forced charity, is not that the quantity of relief supplied is too scanty upon the whole, but that it is too ample.

Some have maintained that there should be no provision at the expence of government by law for the poor, or at least that whatever the existing provision be any where, it should not be permitted to encrease.

Ask the reason, it turns ultimately upon nothing but the magnitude of the present expence: for as to the idleness on one part, it is no otherwise an evil than in as far as it necessitates expence on the other.

But the evil of the expence of relief has its limits; and the evil resulting from the negative of relief would have none.

On the part of individuals, acting without concern, the chances against equality as between the quantum of the demand and the quantum of the supply are as infinity to one. In the country, where vicinity makes acquaintance, knowledge of distress will seldom enough be wanting: none can perish without observation, but either inclination or power, or both, will be very apt to fail. The persons under whose observation the poor chiefly fall, the only persons under whose observation they are sure to fall, are their fellow-poor. Of the Labourers in Husbandry, the great bulk of the inhabitants of this country, it has been proved that [of] those who have more than two children, their utmost means are inadequate to their own maintenance. The Farmers and independent handicrafts-men within whose circle of observation the distress may lie may be but few: of those, some may be hardhearted in general, others inimical or indifferent to the particular individuals applying for relief, others struggling with their own indigence, though in a superior sphere. With regard to proprietors, the most ordinary state of Parishes is to have but one, under the denomination of the Squire. The Squire may be in a state of comparative indigence in his sphere, and to such a degree as not to be able to do any thing; though this indeed is certainly not the most common case. In general he might do more or less if he thought fit, and if he knew of the demand. But he is perhaps a minor and at school, or at college, or abroad, or he is not resident on the spot: and if he were, it is a thousand to one against his doing exactly and constantly as much as he is now obliged to do by law, and that not too much for the demand.

Resident or non-resident, the supply afforded by the rich proprietor would be proportional not to the demand of the necessities, but to his own conception of his own superfluities: he would give as much as decency in his estimation prescribed, or which in his estimate would be the same thing, humanity demanded: but as to the distribution of it among the necessitous individuals, or the sufficiency of it upon the whole, that would be left to agents, it would be no concern of his: he has given a great deal, as much as ever he could spare: if it failed of being sufficient he is sorry for it, but he can do no more.

Sometimes a whole tract of country becomes a prey at once to some sweeping calamity: fire, inundation, tempest, bad season, vermin among the crops, mortality among the cattle, and then what must be the lot of the most indigent class?

In towns, ability comparatively speaking will not very often be deficient, inclination, to a certain degree, may not be wanting: but there knowledge of the sort and degree which is necessary to proportion the supply to the exigencies of the individuals whose necessities call of it, will be extremely apt to be deficient: for there, vicinity as between the indigent class and the wealthy is comparatively in a very slight degree productive of acquaintance.

What is every body's business is nobody's business: each, uncertain in what degree others will think fit to share with him in the burthen, grudges to bestow under that uncertainty, what, were he sure of a proportionable contribution on the part of others, he would give without grudging.

Of this state of things, the universally probable result is that many for want of the requisite supply would perish: the best possible result is that those who are able to contribute, should come to an understanding amongst themselves and contribute in the proportion of their several faculties: in short, do precisely that which is done by law.

But though an agreement of this sort were entered into in any particular district, and as punctually observed as if the observance were enforced by law, this would not put matters upon as good a footing, even in that particular district, as if the whole business of the maintenance of the indigent were arranged by law: for the steady charity of this district would have a perpetual tendency to attract the distressed from the fluctuating and unsteady charity of the circumjacent districts and overwhelm it.

The union of the two inconveniences of excess and defect is inseparable from the state of things which abandons the relief of the indigent to the chance medley of private charity. If the spectacle of indigence [does][1] not come across a man, and wretchedness does not present itself, few indeed will set themselves to hunt it out. Street begging, and that in the most public manner, is a matter of absolute necessity: pain is there the engine, and the only engine, by which relief can be extracted, and the beggar who by any means whatever can contrive to produce most pain will fare the best. The dole of the passenger will accordingly be the prey of the best actor, or of him who can contrive to inspire most disgust, [if] compassion be not excluded by it, not to him whose necessities are most urgent. By this means meantime, the inordinate success of those who are most expert in the trade will operate as a lure, and draw many into it who are not driven into it by indigence: and in this as in other professions which afford high prizes, the felicity of the few will augment the multitude and the misery of the many.

Numerous are the descriptions of individuals who are altogether incapable of maintaining themselves: the efficient cause of their inability is in some instances permanent, in others only temporary in its duration: but how short-lived soever, while it lasts, the exigency it creates is as pressing as if it were eternal. In some instances it exists within themselves, in others it comes upon them from without: in some instances it is because ability with regard to work is not yet formed: in others because it is extinct: in some instances it is accompanied with blame on their part, either on the score of probity or prudence: in others, altogether unaccompanied with blame. A table exhibiting these diversities in their principal features is annexed, under the title of *Table of Cases requiring Relief*.[2]

Of all these a very large proportion, there is no saying how large a proportion, must in the nature of things be left to perish if their chance for relief be placed upon the uncertain and unequal footing of private and casual charity.

[1] MS 'do'. [2] See p. lvii above.

The experience of our own as well as other nations, and in the most recent instances, testifies the insufficiency of voluntary contributions and separate exertions to supply upon a large scale and to purposes which are considered as coming under the denomination of necessary: the *dons patriotiques* in France, the contributions from County meetings to the expences of national defence, and the association for the lessening the consumption of bread, are cases in point.[1] Objects of supererogation may be provided for by works of supererogation: but what would the condition of this country, or any considerable country, be, if the maintenance of government in all its other branches were committed to the casual exertions of individuals?

The case is that there are those in whose estimation the preservation of the indigent from starving, of whatever age or sex, is not considered as ranking among works of necessity: it is on the contrary regarded as a less evil than the cost of paying their share to the contributions imposed by government for this purpose. In their estimation, could their shoulders but be eased of this burthen, any state of things which has in other countries taken place, or which could in this country eventually take place, would meet their wishes.

Publications accordingly are not wanting, in which even in this country, and as matters now stand and have stood for these 200 years,[2] it has been expressly recommended to take away the public

[1] The expression *Dons Patriotiques* was first used in 1789, although the concept of a voluntary offering to the nation was much older. The first *Dons Patriotiques* were the subscriptions to a fund opened by the National Guard of Versailles, into which subscribers were to pay a year's income, with the aim of liquidating the national debt. The province of Touraine also opened a patriotic subscription, and the example was followed in other places. Although considerable sums were raised, the National Assembly, faced with spiralling debt, approved in September 1789 the levy of a compulsory *Contribution Patriotique*, under which all taxpayers were to declare their revenue and contribute one quarter of it to the exchequer.

On 14 March 1794, Henry Dundas (1742–1811), first Viscount Melville, Home Secretary 1791–4, Secretary for War 1794–1801, First Lord of the Admiralty 1804–5, sent a circular to Lords Lieutenants containing a 'Plan of Augmentation of the Forces for Internal Defence' by the raising of volunteer forces (see *House of Commons Sessional Papers of the Eighteenth Century*, ed. S. Lambert, 145 vols., Wilmington, Delaware, 1975, xciii. 49–58). In response, subscriptions were opened in many counties to support local volunteer corps. At their greatest extent, the paper strength of these volunteer forces exceeded 300,000 men, although after the initial flush of enthusiasm it proved difficult to raise fresh subscriptions, and increasingly the corps were forced to apply to central government for financial assistance.

In the summer of 1795, the high price of wheat and the consequent scarcity of bread led to the establishment of several associations, particularly in London, for the purposes of raising subscriptions for distribution among the poor, of reducing the subscribers' consumption of wheaten bread, and of encouraging the consumption of 'mixed' bread, in which the proportion of wheat was reduced. By 11 December 1795 a committee of the House of Commons had drawn up an agreement, the subscribers to which undertook to reduce consumption of bread in their households by one third. The price of wheat did fall in 1796, but rather because of an increase in the supply of imported grain than through the reduction of demand.

[2] i.e. since the consolidation of the Elizabethan poor laws by 39 Eliz. I, c.3 (1597), re-enacted by 43 Eliz. I, c.2 (1601).

supply altogether, and to leave everything to the casual charity of individuals.[1]

In these publications it is stated, and stated in the same breath—

That the voluntary supply would always be sufficient.

That it never would be sufficient—and that accordingly numbers would perish for want of sustenance.

1. That accordingly, among adults, the superfluous hands would be starved off every where, till numbers were reduced to that for whose labour there is a demand, and who would consequently be able to get a living for themselves and families without assistance from other people.

This result in a multitude of instances could scarce fail of taking place: as any one may be satisfied by looking over the Cases requiring relief exhibited in the table.[a]

2. That among adults again the improvident, that is, those who out of their weekly earnings had not as soon as they began to earn any thing laid up a stock of wealth adequate to the provision against all possible contingencies, would also perish.

3. That this would *a fortiori* be the case with all those whose indolence, the effect of drunkenness or disease entailed upon them by their own imprudence, had disqualified for productive labour.

4. That nine out of ten of the infants brought into the world by the wives of the poorer class of labourers would perish in their infancy: or at least some such considerable proportion, that being the proportion which, according to Adam Smith, it is observed perishes in Scotland, a country where the preservation of the poor from starving is left to private charity.[2]

5. That marriages would accordingly be checked: in that a large proportion of those who repair with alacrity to the marriage bed

[a] Accordingly in Scotland, where there is no relief for the Poor by law, in the reign of King William,[3] 80,000 persons of all ages died by famine in the compass of one year: at least $\frac{1}{15}$ part of the then existing number of the people.[4]

[1] See in particular Joseph Townsend (1739–1816), Rector of Pewsey in Wiltshire 1763–1816, *A Dissertation on the Poor Laws, by a Well-Wisher to Mankind*, London 1786, especially pp. 87–8.

[2] See Adam Smith (1723–90), political economist and moral philosopher, *An Inquiry into the Nature and Causes of the Wealth of Nations* (first published in 1776), ed. R.H. Campbell, A.S. Skinner, and W.B. Todd, 2 vols., Oxford, 1976, i. 97: 'It is not uncommon, I have been frequently told, in the Highlands of Scotland for a mother who has borne twenty children not to have two alive.'

[3] William III (1650–1702), King of England, Scotland, and Ireland from 1689.

[4] Bentham's source was Sir John Dalrymple (1726–1810), *Memoirs of Great Britain and Ireland; from the Dissolution of the last Parliament of Charles II. till the Capture of the French and Spanish fleets at Vigo*, new edn., 3 vols., London, 1790, Pt. III, Bk. V, iii. 109. Bentham uses the same information, citing Dalrymple explicitly, in 'Pauper Systems Compared', p. 148 n. below.

through a certainty of a maintenance for the produce of it, would then abstain from it.

6. What is not added, but what might have been added, is that among a people accustomed as those of the southern part of the island are, prompted by climate and habit, to a more free indulgence of every appetite than those of the northern, in proportion as marriage was thus checked, a loose would be given to fornication, to prostitution, to child murder, to wilful abortion, and to whatsoever impurities should be found more probable than forced continence. To take away an encouragement from the [lawful][1] mode of satisfying the desires in question is certainly to give it to the other.[a]

Among these effects, that marriage should be checked is stated as a desirable one: that the mortality among the infants and among such adults as happened not to have a sufficiency in store against casualties, and among those whose indigence was the result of misconduct, is stated as not to be lamented, as being no more than what must take place in the natural course of things.

But with these sentiments, even in the instance of the most improvident and most dissolute, it is not in my power to agree.

In many instances an irresistible propensity to drunkenness, an irresistible propensity to debauchery, an utter incapacity of taking thought for the morrow,[2] may like idiocy and other specie of insanity, of which they may be regarded as modifications, be considered as constitutional infirmities: and even where this ground of extenuation does not exist, a penalty severer than felony without benefit of clergy, a lingering death instead of an instantaneous one, seems rather too severe a punishment for imprudence. In other instances, the infirmity is the result of bad education: and then the punishment proposed is the punishment of one individual for the delinquency of another.

A man, it may be said, *ought* to be prudent—But will he?—If he will not, if it is clear that he will not, whether he ought or no is a question scarcely worth the asking. If, in any one case, the existence of a duty

[a] If it were fit policy to check marriage among the Poor, for the purpose of checking population, it must be allowed that whatever may be the other reasons for seeking to restrain the enormities alluded to, nothing could be more inconsistent and absurd than the punishing them on account of any tendency real or supposed on the part of such enormities to operate as checks to population. If a defalcation from the population of a country be any detriment to it in point of opulence and prosperity, it can only be in as far as it applies to the most productive, that is to the hardest working, the poorest class of the people. Defalcation from the class of consumers in a country is no defalcation from its absolute wealth, and is an actual accession to the sum of relative wealth.

[1] MS 'unlawful' contradicts the evident sense of the passage.

[2] Matthew 6: 34.

were a sufficient reason for refusing to make provision for the breach of it, so would it be in every other case: if the existence of that class of duties which are comprehended under the head of *prudence* were a sufficient warrant for refusing to save a transgressor himself from the consequences of his transgression, the existence of the duties comprized under the head of *probity* would be a warrant equally sufficient for refusing to save the rest of the community from the consequences of transgression on the part of its respective members. If it be good reasoning to say men ought to live prudently, *therefore there ought to be no hospitals*, it would hardly be bad reasoning to say men ought to live honestly, therefore there ought to be no gallows.[a]

In administering to imprudence, at the expence of the public, relief from disease, from famine and from slow death, it certainly concerns the public not to administer it upon such terms as, by rendering what otherwise would be imprudence eligible upon the whole, shall change its nature, converting [it] into prudence in one point of view and into improbity on the other, shifting the evil consequences

[a] Better ten guilty criminals escape, says a maxim of I forget what law or law-writer, converted by this time into a proverb—better ten guilty criminals escape, than one innocent person be punished.[1] In the auction for the praise of humanity, some have squared the number, and cried 100: others have cubed it, and cried 1000. I have great doubts even about the ten: because punishment, in proportion as it sinks in certainty, must to be effectual be raised in magnitude, so that it is to the propensity to favour the guilty, which is one feature of the existing system of law, that the extravagant and ineffectual severity, which is another feature of it, appears to be indebted for its existence. Hence it is that in the account as between the criminal and the innocent, I have great doubts whether it would be better that ten criminals should escape punishing, than one innocent be made to perish, supposing the necessity of the sort of punishment by which people are made to perish, and of the non-necessity of which I have never for these 25 years entertained the smallest doubt.[2] But in the account as between two classes of persons both equally innocent, the poor and those in easy circumstances, when the question is whether one should perish for want of necessary relief, or a greater number get more relief than would have been necessary, I can never look upon the proportion of ten to one as too great.

[1] Bentham's immediate source may have been Sir William Blackstone (1723–80), first Vinerian Professor of English Law at Oxford University 1758–66, Justice of Common Pleas 1770, 1770–80, Justice of King's Bench 1770, *Commentaries on the Laws of England*, 4 vols., Oxford, 1765–9, iv. 352. Blackstone in turn refers to Sir Matthew Hale (1609–76), Lord Chief Baron of the Exchequer 1660–71, Chief Justice of King's Bench 1671–6, *Historia Placitorum Coronæ*, 2 vols., London, 1736, ii. 289, which in fact states, 'it is better five guilty persons should escape unpunished, than one innocent person should die'.

[2] For Bentham's early writing on capital punishment see *Théorie des peines et des récompenses*, ed. Étienne Dumont, 2 vols., London, 1811, i. 269–316; *The Rationale of Punishment*, ed. Richard Smith, London, 1830, pp. 168–97; and 'Principles of Penal Law', Bowring, i. 441–50. Dumont states that he based the text on manuscripts written by Bentham in 1775: see *Théorie des peines et des récompenses*, i. p.vi. Pierre Étienne Louis Dumont (1759–1829) produced five recensions of Bentham's works, of which *Traités de législation civile et pénale*, 3 vols., Paris, 1802, was the first.

of transgression from the transgressor to other people. But administering relief on these terms is a very different sort of policy from withholding it.

If compassion for the indigent themselves were not sufficient warrant for the continuing the provision made for their relief on the steady basis of public contribution, regard for the security of the affluent would of itself be sufficient to forbid the abolition of it. When a man has no other option than to rob or starve, the choice can hardly be regarded as an uncertain one: it can seldom be a matter of much doubt which side of the alternative will be embraced: and if between stranger and stranger it were come to a question of life against life, I am sure I see on which side probability lies, nor, were it worth the enquiry, is it by any means clear that duty lies on the opposite side. Bacon puts the case between a weaker man who in a shipwreck has got part possession of a plank, and a stronger man who beats him off and takes his place. He is against hanging the strong man, and with reason: since if you hang him, you will lose *two* men, and if you let him alone, you will save *one*.[1]

When the indigent are moreover totally helpless and equally unable to destroy others as to save themselves, here the argument fails, it must be confessed, on the score of public prudence. But how far the picking out for the purpose of saving them those who if not saved might do mischief, from those from whom no mischief is to be apprehended, would be reconcileable either to justice or to humanity, is a matter which I leave to be considered by the proper judges.

To those who were able to murder, rob or steal, relief might be administered, while infants, in consideration of their inability to committ such crimes, might be left to starve. But if any such expedient be preferable, I would beg leave to stand excused from being the proposer.

Those who contend for the abolition of the public provision for the indigent, and state the starving of the indigent as the necessary consequence, insist not the less that the abolition would be a beneficial measure, full of benefit even to the indigent themselves.[2] For the mortality amongst the indigent, though owing in a certain

[1] See Francis Bacon (1561–1626), first Baron of Verulam and first Viscount Saint Alban, Lord Chancellor 1618–21, statesman and philosopher, 'Maxims of the Law', in *The Works of Francis Bacon*, ed. J. Spedding, R.L. Ellis, and D.D. Heath, 14 vols., London, 1857–74, vii. 344. Bacon defends the action of the man who beats the other from the plank on the ground that the action is necessary to the preservation of his life, and argues that the man should not be punished since his action is justifiable, but does not rely on the particular argument advanced here by Bentham.

[2] For examples of this argument see Townsend, *A Dissertation on the Poor Laws*, pp. 13–15; and John McFarlan, *Inquiries concerning the Poor*, Edinburgh, 1782, p. 34.

degree to the unchangeable doom of nature, is owing in a still greater degree to the exertions thus made by art and policy to counteract the intentions of nature. For the case is, continue they, that what is intended to be administered, or at least ought to be administered to none but those whose indigence is inevitable, is actually given to those on whose part indigence might have been, and but for the donation would have been, avoided; that is to the prodigal and the unthrifty: and thence has the effect of adding to the sum of indigence all that mass which would not have existed but by the existence of that part which has for its efficient cause the unthriftiness and prodigality thus produced. Take away then this factitious addition thus made to the mass of indigence, and upon the whole after the abolition, there will in process of time be less indigence, and consequently less of the mortality and other evils that are the consequence of indigence, than before.

But in this argument, to which I have endeavoured to do the fullest justice, two positions are expressly or tacitly assumed: 1. That it is an inseparable property of public charity to be misapplied in a greater proportion than it is well applied: to be bestowed on avoidable indigence in greater proportion than upon unavoidable: to be bestowed, in the instance of those whose indigence has the mere want of work, not of the inability to perform it, for its efficient cause, upon such terms as shall render it the more apparent interest of the poor upon the whole rather to expose themselves to indigence than to avoid it: and [2.] That if voluntary indigence is not thus fostered by public charity, it will not be equally fostered by private. But these positions, which at least are not of the class of self-evident propositions, are either assumed without so much as the pretence of enquiry, or after a sort of enquiry than which nothing can well be conceived to be more loose. And yet where so strong a measure as the immediate consignment of vast multitudes to a lingering death is proposed as the sole means of keeping down the growth of the same calamity in future, the foundation for such measure, in point of necessity, might one should have thought have warranted a degree of scrutiny a little closer and more attentive.

Another matter that may be worth consideration is whether, howsoever the matter might have stood originally before any public provision had been established, whether, I say, now that such a provision is established and has been established these two hundred years, the claim to it does not rest at present on the footing of right, on the same footing with the claim of every man of property to be maintained in the possession of his estate. In the case of an individual, sixty years possession gives security to a title originally bad:[1] more than thrice this duration belongs to the possession of the indigent considered as a body, and the title to that possession originally a good one—as good an one as any can be, the express appointment of the legislature. As among men of landed estates every remainder man under a settlement is born with the rightful expectation of coming into the enjoyment of the settled property upon the contingency of his surviving, so in the labouring class every man is born with the equally rightful expectation of coming into the enjoyment of a maintenance, charged upon the estates of proprietors, upon the contingency of his falling into indigence. In this point of view, and as *against*, or rather to avoid falling into, the track of anarchy, as *towards* the legislature, the title of the indigent to their subsistence, seems to stand upon as strong ground at least as that of any man of property to his estate—as that of the most opulent to his opulence.[a]

If it be maintained, as we have seen it maintained, that the indigent class would at the long run not be the worse for the abolition of their existing fund of subsistence, it will of course be contended, and certainly with much greater appearance of reason, that the opulent class, the class at whose expence that fund is formed, would at any rate be much the better.

They would be better, it has been said, in more respect[s] than one:

[a] Between the two cases there is, it is true, this difference, that in the one the subject matter of the title is commonly an individual thing, a thing certain as lawyers call it, in the other always a thing uncertain, a thing that remains to be liquidated. But to the purpose of the argument, that distinction makes no difference. If a title to value unliquidated were a bad title, perilous indeed would be the condition of all the movable property in the kingdom: since when an article of that description is out of a man's possession, all that the law gives a man against those who choose to dispute it with him, is—not the thing itself, but money under the name of damages in lieu of it.

Maintain the right of the indigent to sustenance, fixing it upon a proper basis, the interests of subsistence, of equality, and those of security with regard to property are thus reconciled, as far as the matter in question is concerned, and as far as they are reconcilable. Each supports the other, and all these blessings stand. Sacrifice the interests of subsistence and of practicable equality to those of existing property, those of property itself would be shaken, if it be in the power of any thing to shake them, by the concussion that would follow. The abolition of what is more particularly meant by the public debt would be a less dangerous as well as less mischievous injustice.

---

[1] At Common Law a claim to prescription of title rested upon a presumption of a lost grant. To set up his claim, the 'demandant' was required to show that he had exercised the right in question either in his own person or in that of an ancestor. By 32 Hen. VIII, c.2 (1540), the possession of the ancestor had to be shown to have been within the previous sixty years. The implication of Bentham's remark is that the statute, whilst explicitly excluding claims over sixty years old, was held effectively to protect a title once that period had elapsed.

they would be all the better for it not only by money in pocket: but they would also be the better for it in point of moral character: since what is now the produce of compulsion would then be the effusion of benevolence, and it is the nature of benevolence, as of most other moral virtues and affections, to gain strength from exercise.[1]

That of the unindigent class those individuals who being forced to it contribute at present their share, and if no longer forced to it would give nothing, or less than their share, would be proportionably in pocket by the abolition of the legal duty is not to be disputed. But whether the whole of the unindigent class taken together would be the better for it even in this respect, and whether there would even be the advantage of an alleviation in the quantum of the public burthen to set against the mass of misery of which such an abolition would be productive, is a very different question, and not quite so clear an one. It is neither the expectation nor, if I understand right, the wish of those who contend for the abolition of the legal contribution that no relief at all, no uncompelled relief, should be administered: they speak of the uncompelled donations of individuals as a resource which would be always open, which it would not be their wish, and, what is more material, were it their wish it certainly would not be in their power, to close. So much, if anything, as the sum total of the uncompelled contributions, in the state of things contended for, wanted of being equal to that of the sum total of the present contributions, uncompulsory and compulsory taken together, by so much would the expence be reduced by the abolition, it must be confessed. But whatever were the relative amount of the produce of the tax in the two cases, that the supply of a given sum would be collected with less burthen upon the whole upon the proposed plan of what is called voluntary contribution, than upon the existing plan of what is called involuntary contribution,[a] is what I am unable to admitt.

[a] The more common terms voluntary and involuntary make sad confusion when thus applied: as if an act produced by fear operating upon the will were less the result of the will than an act produced by hope.

To regard it as uncompulsory is a mistake, resulting from the ambiguity of terms. It is extorted by painful sensations, not elicited by pleasurable ones. There is a pleasure attending the relieving one's self from these sensations—true—and so is there in relieving one's self from the tooth ache: but this does not make it better for a man to catch a tooth ache than to be free from it. It is uncompulsory as against a particular set of pains: the pains held out by the law: but against pain in general it is not uncompulsory. If I give a penny for sweetmeats for my own or my child's eating, this giving is truly voluntary: for it is to obtain pleasure that I give it: if I give it for bread to give to a starving beggar, or, what comes to the same thing

[1] For examples of this view see Townsend, *A Dissertation on the Poor Laws*, pp. 98–9; and McFarlan, *Inquiries concerning the Poor*, pp. 180, 182.

The contribution of a given sum would in that case be attended with much more pain than now. If I gave money to save the indigent from perishing it would be because I had the affliction of seeing them, or at least believing them, to be on the point of perishing: this affliction, a constantly recurring affliction, is now all saved to me.

Be the case as it may with the system of uncompulsive charity as to profit and loss in regard to hard money, there is an article of expence in which it would be under an undeniable disadvantage, I mean the article of *time*.

It is a property incident to many taxes, and which in the instance of those to which it is incident, is apt to enhance, in a greater proportion than would readily be conceived, the burthensomeness of the tax, the being attended with a loss of time, the being a tax not only upon solid property but upon *time*. The enhancement which the money tax would receive by the tax upon time is greater perhaps in the instance in question than in any other: the labour of conveying the produce to its *proper* ultimate destination is greater in this instance than in any other: this labour, in the present instance, falls exclusively upon the shoulders of the contributor, and its doing so has even, by those who contend for this mode of supply, been numbered amongst its advantages. To convey to its proper destination the contribution destined for the defence of the country against its foreign enemies I have but to leave it out in readiness for the agent of the public when he calls for it at my house; *and* to convey to its appointed and more or less proper destination the contribution destined upon the present plan for the relief of the indigent against death, disease and famine, the same simple operation is now sufficient as in the former case. But to convey to its proper destination an equal sum upon the proposed plan of uncompulsive charity, I must add to the inconvenience of giving the much greater inconvenience of finding out who are the proper and most proper objects to receive. I must expose my sympathetic feelings to the spectacle of misery in all its forms: my senses to the assaults of stench and filthiness: and my health and life to the danger of contagion. I must be careful to give neither too little nor too much. I must witness the wretchedness and hear the tales of woe of all that wear the appearance of misery, I must employ my industry to find out which are the most miserable, that my contribution may not be yielded to a weaker claim in preference to a stronger. I must observe in what degree my fellow contributors have contributed their share, that the effect of my own pittance may not, like a

one who I fear would otherwise starve, the giving is voluntary but in name: it is only to relieve myself from pain that I give it; and if I had not felt pain, I should not have given it.

drop in the ocean, be thrown away. I must scrutinize the amount of their respective contributions to the respective claimants, that no one may have his own supply doubled by his own fraud, while a fellow claimant for want of his portion is left to perish. In a word, to apply my contribution with any tolerable degree of propriety in comparison of what it is applied with at present, I must be a Parish Officer, an Overseer of the Poor,[1] with many times the quantity of trouble that now lies on the shoulders of such a Parish Officer, and that for life.

How it may be with others it is for others to say.—For my own part, this I know, that at present whatever may be the contribution allotted to me I pay it with the utmost cheerfulness, and should do to the utmost extent in point of rate, to which it can any where be found to reach: because I am spared the trouble of applying it, because I am satisfied of its being applied to its destination, with that rough degree of equality and propriety at least, which I believe indeed to be susceptible of improvement, but which I believe in the mean time to be upon a par or nearly upon a par with many if not all the other branches of the public service, and because others contribute as well as myself, and in a tolerably correct proportion with myself. Were the tax to be abolished, an event which, even were my views confined to my own personal interest, I should regard as one of the heaviest calamities that could befall me, my first care would be, after the abolition of the tax, to find out what would have been my proportion under the tax: and for the application and distribution of it, my next care would be to find out somebody who on receiving an additional contribution for his trouble would be content to take that part of my duty off my hands.

Taken in both its branches, a tax upon money and a tax upon time, the burthensomeness of it would be enhanced by its inequality. The present tax, though not so equal in the mode of levying it as a tax upon consumption, laid upon superfluities, a tax in which every man pays according to his own estimate of his means, is, for a direct tax upon property, as equal an one as perhaps most that are any where to be found: it bears upon every householder according to the estimate of his means, grounded on the annual value of the property he holds in his occupation: the hardhearted as well as the humane are pressed into the service of humanity. On the proposed footing, nothing could exceed the inequality of the tax: it would leave the hardhearted

[1] The Overseers of the Poor were unpaid officers of the parish, and were charged by 43 Eliz. I, c.2 (1601) with the administration of poor relief. Churchwardens were Overseers *ex officio*, and were joined by a small number of laymen, usually two, appointed annually by Justices of the Peace on the recommendation of the vestry.

untouched, whatever were their opulence: it would bear exclusively on the humane, and that with a degree of severity in exact proportion to their humanity.

The inequality of it would be still further enhanced by another part of its tendency. It would not only fall exclusively on the humane, but among the humane themselves it would have a particular tendency to fall in larger proportion upon the poor than upon the rich.

It is an observation that has been frequently made, and which I have seen made by those who in the same breath were for giving this direction to the pressure of the burthen, that the classes the least elevated above actual indigence are proportionally more liberal in their contributions, and that in a reasonable degree, than the most elevated.[1] It is natural they should be so. Natural Temper being the same, a man's sympathy is more strongly exerted by the spectacle of suffering, the more exposed he feels himself to be to the danger of experiencing similar suffering, and the nearer the similitude which the suffering he witnesses appears to bear to the suffering of which he has had experience.

Poor and rich, humane and hard-hearted together, one grievance would press upon them in common, the inordinate encrease of public begging with its attendant mischiefs. This, under the present system of legal provision, ought to be, and under such alterations as might be made in it, as certainly might be, perfectly suppressed. But under the proposed system, the natural encrease of it would be enormous, while neither the suppression nor so much as the checking of it would be either desirable or possible. At present if a passenger chooses not to make this worse than no use of his money, his answer to the Beggar is easy and admitts not of a reply: 'Get you gone to the Parish.' But if in this sense there were no Parish, what answer could a man find to give to a naked and starving cripple? Those who would committ the famished poor to the effusions of unbidden charity as the sole fund would not surely prohibit the miserable indigent from the faculty of putting in their claim to it. They would not, as often as they see a famished mendicant begging his life, give him a whipping instead of it. If they did, it would be in vain: for without food, death is certain and comes unbidden: whereas happily the whips do not lash of themselves, nor would the hands necessary to keep them going in proportion to the demand be easy to be found.

With us in England, in London and the other great towns, the practice of begging is, it must be confessed, but too prevalent, because the coercive measures established for the prevention of it

[1] See, for example, McFarlan, *Inquiries concerning the Poor*, pp. 160–3.

are essentially incapable of answering the purpose.[1] In the high roads the same practice is again but too prevalent, partly from the incongruity of the coercive regulations, partly from the want of a mode of supply adapted to the exigencies to which such situations are liable to give rise. But the plague of mendicity in England, where it is at its worst, is nothing in comparison of what it is in countries which afford no regular legal provision for the relief of indigence. Spain,[2] Italy, France, when France was accessible,[3] may be cited as examples.[a]

But in return for all this inconvenience, the class of contributors would, it is said, receive an inestimable benefit: a benefit which would be reaped by the better part of a man's frame, his moral sensibilities. By calling forth so much more frequently and forcibly than at present the benevolent affections of his nature, it would give a proportionable degree of force to that which, like most other affections, is strengthened from exercise, and as often administer to his sensibilities those exquisite sensations which [accompany][4] the exercise of that best of human faculties.

The disposition to insist upon this advantage (supposing that any

[a] In England no Inn, no Coffeehouse, no house of entertainment ever suffers a beggar to enter the Yard, much less the house, to make his experiments upon the humanity of customers. In France I have been assailed by mendicants introduced at meal times by the Innkeeper, and making the circuit of the table. In Leghorn, in Genoa, I have seen Beggars in knots of three or four together open the door with as little ceremony as if they had been customers, and address themselves successively to every box, and maintain their station with as much perseverance as any of the company: beggars whose condition was such as rather to operate in the way of annoyance by its filthiness, than in the way of compassion by its nakedness.[5]

[1] Coercive measures for the prevention of begging had been laid down in 17 Geo. II, c.5 (1744), which consolidated a series of statutes dating back to the fourteenth century. The statute was not consistently enforced, and the readiness of magistrates to redirect beggars to their parish of settlement, and to provide passes to facilitate their travel, without the prior infliction of punishment in the form of incarceration in a house of correction or whipping, led to the enactment of 32 Geo. III, c.45 (1792), by which no passes were to be issued before the vagrant in question had been punished in one or other of these ways. For Bentham's views on the best means of eradicating mendicity see §X, pp. 56–7 below. For Bentham's discussion of the inefficacy of 17 Geo. II, c.5 see 'Outline of a Work entitled Pauper Management Improved', Bk. III, Ch. II, in *Annals of Agriculture, and other useful Arts*, xxx (1798), 292–6, 393–9 (Bowring, viii. 401–3).

[2] For indications regarding the prevalence of beggars in Spain see, for example, Joseph Townsend, *A Journey Through Spain in the Years 1786 and 1787; with particular attention to the Agriculture, Manufactures, Commerce, Population, Taxes, and Revenue of that country; and Remarks in passing through a part of France*, 3 vols., London, 1791, ii. 8, 84; iii. 17.

[3] France had not been 'accessible' since the declaration of war on Great Britain on 1 February 1793.

[4] MS 'accompanies'.

[5] Bentham travelled via France, Genoa, and Leghorn in August and September 1785 to join his brother Samuel Bentham (1757–1831) in Russia.

advantage in the way in question would really be among the results of such a system), the insisting upon this advantage as if it were capable in any degree of making up for the mischief necessary to give birth to it, is a delusion that results from a sort of inversion unhappily but too common among men in respect of the order of preference as between ends and means. The use, the sole real and ultimate use of benevolence, excepting of course the correspondent effect of producing pleasure, which is not to the present purpose, is the prevention of pain: and it is only in proportion as pain is actually prevented in any instance that in that instance benevolence is of any value. Here, misery is to be purposely produced, and why? In the hope of giving birth and vigour to benevolence. To every species of virtue, whether moral or intellectual, belongs a class of mischiefs which it has a tendency to avert, a tendency to which alone it stands indebted for its title to the appellation of a virtue. According to this policy the mischiefs in each case are to be let in for the sake of finding occupation to the virtue, lest peradventure it should become languid for want of exercise. By the same rule, dangers of all kinds are to be embraced: foreign wars should be kept up for the sake of keeping up courage: civil wars, insurrections and seditions, to keep alive the sacred flame of patriotism: disease propagated for the advancement of medicine: and in a word the field of misery enlarged in all its dimensions, for the sake of affording business and stage-room for the exhibitions of benevolence. By the same rule, gin ought to be made as cheap as possible to promote the habit of sobriety: brothels with apt signs planted at the corner of every street, to afford exercise to continence.

Not that even this advantage, slight and preposterous as it is, would come in to help atone for the mischiefs of the measure. Whatever exercise can be of any use in the way of giving strength to the benevolent affections is afforded at present, and will continue to be afforded in but too [ample][1] abundance under every improvement which the nature of things can ever admitt of in the condition of the human race. Whatever enjoyment can be reaped from the satisfaction of those propensities may be reaped under the system of legal provision in its present [form], and may continue to be reaped in as high perfection under the utmost improvement of which that system is susceptible. Indeed, the farther this branch of improvement can be carried in this line, and the less of necessity there is for the exercise of benevolence, the purer and more valuable will be the mass of enjoyments resulting from the exercise of benevolence.

[1] MS 'amble'.

Pleasure of the positive kind, pleasure without alloy, will succeed that negative pleasure which has a dash of precedent pain for its inseparable accompaniment. The pleasure of relieving comparative want in friends will succeed to the necessity of relieving absolute want in strangers. The pleasure of raising men from subsistence to affluence will take the place of the pleasure of raising them from famine to subsistence. The benevolence which has more of pain than of pleasure in its company will have less and less call to exercise itself.

The proposing to render beneficence precarious instead of certain, to transfer the operations of beneficence from a certain and steady ground to a fluctuating precarious one, does appear to me I must confess, rather a singular way of promoting the interests of benevolence. If it be serving the interests of benevolence to contend for the liberty of not paying a man's quota to the relief of indigence, it may be serving the interests of justice to contend for the liberty of not keeping one's engagements.[a]

[a] If this mode of propagating virtue be a good one in the instance of benevolence, try it upon the other virtues—try it upon another branch of justice, that which is peculiar to the situation of a Judge.—The administration of justice in England, it may be said, is, as far as probity is concerned, upon a bad footing. No instance ever exists, or is so much as suspected to exist, of a Judge's taking a bribe. But in this negative and as it were instinctive sort of virtue there is no merit, nor any room for merit, on the part of any Judge: because under the existing order of things, from one cause or other so matters are constituted that a man in that situation can hardly be said to have the option whether he will take bribes or no. So compleatly hopeless is the prospect of success on the part of any offer of that sort, that no such attempt is ever made. But where there is no temptation there can be no trial, no emulation, no excellence,—in a word, no virtue. This was not the case in the good old times. This was not the case in those halcyon days when the Bench was filled with men bred under the wing of the great and good Elizabeth.[1] In those days probity in a Judge was not as now, a vulgar and mechanical virtue, common to the whole tribe. In those days virtue was virtue; and a man might rise superior even to a Bacon by refusing bribes.[2]

To restore the virtue of probity in a Judge to its primaeval splendor, throw the veil of perpetual secrecy over the whole face of judicial proceedings—Administer justice as it is administered in general upon the Continent—in Spain, in Germany, in Russia. Suffer no publication of Reports—no accounts of proceedings in newspapers, admitt no advocates at the hearing of a cause but the four or five who are concerned in it.

Introduce by law the wholesome exercise of listening to sollicitations as avowedly practised by the members of the French Parliaments. To every Judge's chamber annex a closet, where separately and secretly, rank, opulence and beauty may lay themselves at his feet. Judicial Probity, like gold, will thus rise the brighter from the

[1] Elizabeth I (1533–1603), Queen of England and Ireland from 1558.

[2] Having been accused of taking bribes, Francis Bacon, then Lord Chancellor, was impeached in 1621. He pleaded guilty and was deprived of office, imprisoned in the Tower, fined £40,000, and barred from holding office or sitting in Parliament. James VI (1566–1625), King of Scotland from 1567, and as James I, King of England and Ireland from 1603, pardoned him and effectively revoked the fine, but never employed him again in state affairs.

If the notion that the system of legal provision is radically incapable of effecting a diminution in the mass of evil attendant on indigence be given up, the only position remaining on that side will be the notion that the collateral evils of whatever remedy can be applied to lighten the weight of mischief are essentially more than equivalent to the utmost benefit of the alleviation.

To judge of the proportion between these quantities an estimate must be taken of the several modes of relief which have been or can be employ'd under the system of legal provision, together with an estimate of the inconveniences respectively ascribed to them.

The modes of relief employ'd are:

1. Out-allowances—administering the relief whether in money or in kind at each man's home.

2. Maintenance in Parish Work-houses: that is in Establishments of very uncertain and unequal magnitude, but in most instances comparatively inconsiderable.

3. Maintenance in Houses of Industry: that is in Establishments of considerable and tolerably uniform magnitude, formed by a junction affected to this purpose amongst a number of Parishes.

In each of these, administration is either carried on in the ordinary way, or by contract in the way of *farming*: the expence is either unlimited with regard to the contributors, being determined by the discretion of their Agents, or limited with relation to the contributors, being unlimited only with relation to a Contractor or Farmer, who for a fixt sum, and in consideration of the savings he hopes to make out of that fixed sum, agrees to take the burthen upon him, subject to every degree of uncertainty with regard to its amount.

Of maintenance by out-allowances, and in Parish Workhouses, nothing need upon the present occasion be observed. I have nothing to say in defence of them, having stated in another place[1] the objections which appear to apply to those modes of maintenance, and which appear to me conclusive against both of them as compared to the mode of maintenance in which Houses of industry [are][2] employed.

The general heads of objections urged against the mode of maintenance in which Houses of Industry are employed are:

1. That it is unfrugally expensive: and here it is assumed, expressly or tacitly, that whatever be the present rate of expence is

furnace: and those who are uncorrupted because they are incorruptible will stand distinguished from the vulgar herd who know nothing of corruption, only because they have never happened to fall in the way of it.

[1] See 'Pauper Systems Compared', pp. 154–83 below.

[2] MS 'is'.

incapable of diminution, but open to encrease and likely to be encreased to an indefinite amount.

2. That it is uncomfortable to those whose welfare it more particularly has in view.

3. That it is prejudicial to them in point of health.

4. That it is prejudicial to them in point of morals.

And that thus it is prejudicial to the interests of both parties: as well of those on whom the burthen of affording the relief is imposed, as of those for whom the benefit of it is intended.

One head of objection to Houses of Industry is that the management is unfrugal.—The obvious conclusion is render it more frugal.—No such thing—the conclusion is, abolish these Houses.

This head of objection branches naturally into a number of subordinate ones.[a]

1. One is that the supplies furnished are too good—that is too expensive. In point of fact the objection is, I believe, very generally not to say universally true. What is the inference? that it ought to be made less expensive: it ought to be reduced to the scantling given in the fundamental positions above laid down.[1]—No such idea occurrs to the objector—the only inference is—Down with the Houses.

2. Another objection is—that besides being too expensive in quality, they are too abundant in quantity, and the superfluity thrown away or supposed to be thrown away.—Natural remedy—'Gather up the fragments that nothing be lost.'[2]—Proposed remedy—Down with the Houses.[3]

But it is insisted that if there were nothing thrown away, still under this head the supply would be unreasonably expensive. For in the House the dependent poor have enough: and out of the House the independent poor have not half enough. Is that so?—then neither can the independent Poor be made to work so much, or earn so much by half, as the dependent Poor may be made to work. The remedy is—starve none that do not choose to starve—feed none but in proportion as he works.—No such idea occurs: but this and this one only—Down with the Houses.

3. Another is, that too little work is done—very little indeed.

[a] Macfarlane §III, p. 94.[4]

[1] See p. 10 above.

[2] John 6: 12.

[3] In the margin, Bentham has noted at this point: 'If you do not feed men with the fragments, you may still employ them without loss by feeding hogs with it. Apply this to potatoes cooked by baking.'

[4] i.e. *Inquiries concerning the Poor,* pp. 93–4, where McFarlan objects to 'the profuse allowance made to the poor in England', and complains that 'the provision made for them is in general better than is due to them', and that 'little or no work [is] done in poor houses'.

Natural remedy—*cause more work to be done.*—Proposed remedy—*Down with the Houses.*

In the same breath, and by way of confirming as well as illustrating the objection, accounts are given all this while, of different establishments of this kind in which different proportions of work are done. What might at least [have][1] occurred, in the shape of a partial remedy at least, is the causing as much to be done in the several, more uneconomical houses, as in the least uneconomical of the whole. For if a child of such an age, or a man or woman of such habit of body does so much work in any one house, what should hinder his doing as much in every other?—No such thing—the shorter remedy is—Down with the Houses.

But it is insisted that the extraction of work to any superior value, to any value worth reckoning is, in such a situation, morally impossible: for here the motives employ'd are solely of the compulsive class: and by motives of the compulsive class no work to a value worth reckoning, in comparison of what is performed by the independent Poor, can ever be extracted. Instead of saying simply of the compulsive kind, the terms employed are probably terms of rhetoric—pressure, force, violence, slavery and so forth. Are these the sort of motives employ'd, and no others?—But why so? Whatever sort of motive is best calculated to produce the desired effect, what should hinder its being employ'd in such a situation more than in another? Natural remedy—employ whatever motives not being otherwise objectionable are of a nature most effectual.—Proposed remedy—Down with the Houses.

Just as well might it be said, in three instances at least out of four, that no labour worth reckoning is ever extracted from the independent poor. Of what nature is the motive for working in any instance where the pay rate of wages is fixed, not rising with the amount of work: in a word in every case in which the workman is paid according to time, and not by the piece? It is fully as much compulsion, force, slavery and so forth out of a house as it can be in a house. If a man is thought not to have done enough he may be punished for his idleness by being turned off: if he does ever so much work in the time, he gets no reward for it. Has the loss of employ, and with it of subsistence for an indefinite time till another employer can be found (which may not be perhaps for several days or weeks), has so unlimited a forfeiture less of punishment in it, than the loss of a particular meal's meat, or even than a few stripes, if stripes were necessary?

The truth is, that wherever pay does not rise with the value of the work done the efficient cause of the work is of a compulsive, a penal

[1] MS 'of'.

nature: wherever it does rise with the value of the work, it is of a remuneratory nature, the force of reward being substituted, or at least added, to that of punishment. Where the work is done, whether in such a house or not in such a house, under a master who acts on his own account, or an inspector who acts on the account of others, makes no sort of difference.

Where, in a house where no food can be obtained which is not administered by, or by order of, a master, the administering of a meal's meat is postponed till the work in consideration of which it is administered is done, whether the motive employ'd in this case be of the nature of punishment or of the nature of reward, or of both together, is a question of words, not worth insisting on for the present purpose. To whatever class the expedient be referred, the efficacy of it is too assured to admitt dispute. The use of it is consonant to reason. What is more, it is consonant not only to the meaning, but to the very words of scripture, letter as well as spirit. 'Even when we were with you,' says S[t] Paul to the Thessalonians,[a] 'even when we were with you, this we commanded you, that if any would not work, neither should he eat.' Is there any other place in which the expedient is more certain in point of efficacy or more practicable, than in a House of Industry? This expedient, the suggestion of simple reason and sound sense, what should hinder it being employed in a House of Industry? Where can there be greater facility for employing it?

Another objection is that Houses of this kind are full of nastiness.[b]—Natural remedy—clean them.—Proposed remedy, pull them down.

Another objection is that Houses of Industry are scenes of contention, and scolding. At the same time, so it is observed and admitted in the same breath, are private families. Where then lies the difference? That in the Industry Houses there is a common umpire to appeal to and a common ruler, who whether appealed to or not has it in his power to put an end to all such mischiefs. In private families, at least where man and wife are equally matched, or where the quarrel is between one head of a family and another, there is no such opportunity of mediation, no such power.

But in establishments so numerous the occasions of such disturbances are proportionally more numerous.—What matters it,

[a] III. 10.[1]

[b] Towns[d.], p. 71.[2]

[1] i.e. 2 Thessalonians 3: 10.

[2] i.e. Townsend, *A Dissertation on the Poor Laws*, p. 71: 'The quiet and the cleanly dread the noise and nastiness, even more than the confinement of a work house.'

when the means of quelling them are at hand. Where is there likely to be least disturbance? A place in which the occasions of raising disturbance are [more][1] numerous, at the same time that there are means of quelling them all, or a place in which the occasions of raising disturbances are fewer, but no means of quelling any of them?

Regulations, it is admitted on the other hand, may be made on this view, but it is roundly asserted that neither are they nor will they be observed. Why not? Why not as well as in manufactories? With still more reason might it be contended that there ought to be no such establishments suffered as manufactories. Has the Master of a Manufactory more power over his free independent workman than the Master of a House of Industry over his dependent inmates?

But in these houses, it is added, there are always scolders, who by their faculty of creating annoyance by scolding, tyrannize over and always will tyrannize over the meek and well-behaved, so as to render their lives uncomfortable.—And will they so? What, in spite of the Governor? If he takes no heed of it, because it does not reach him, place him in the midst of it, and then surely he will, even if only for his own sake. Place the Chaplain, and the Surgeon there along with him, and see whether all three will submitt to this vocal tyranny of tongues.

Oh, but if they will not suffer themselves as well as those committed to their charge to be thus tyrannized over, so much the worse: for then they are not fit to be where they are. To be fit for their offices they must be men of 'discretion and humanity: their duty being to take particular care of the infirm, the diseased and helpless. Persons of this character are ill qualified to execute severe laws on pitiable wretches, however much they may deserve punishment.'[a] Such is the proposition—whoever is a man of discretion and humanity will suffer those under his care to make as much noise in their quarrelling as they please. In a prison, among felons, among the most hardened of felons, the reputation of humanity may be maintained by a man qualified to keep them, and actually keeping them, in the best order, and the freest from disturbance. In Newgate it was actually maintained by Akerman. Would Akerman have suffered himself, would Howard have suffered himself, to have been tyrannized by a parcel of scolders in a Poorhouse?[2]

[a] p. 99.[3]

---

[1] MS 'less' contradicts the evident sense of the passage.

[2] Richard Akerman (1722?-92) was Keeper of Newgate Prison from 1754 until his death. John Howard (1726?-90), philanthropist and penal reformer, had investigated conditions in practically every gaol in England and Wales in the course of his researches. Both men attracted plaudits for their humanity and benevolence.

[3] i.e. McFarlan, *Inquiries concerning the Poor*, p. 99.

Oh but the worthless poor, if not suffered thus to tyrannize in and over a Poor house would not live there: so that if 'a master be found to exercise rigorous discipline, it would not answer the end'.[1]

Not live there?—What would they do then? Die there? Is the only alternative thus *tyranny or death*? Not so, for they would escape—they would return to beggary and idleness—and why? Because 'they would think themselves justified in it.'[2]—All this while, by the supposition, they can not live out of the house, for if they can, how came they in the house? And yet forsooth they will go and live out of the house because they think themselves justified in it: as if a man's own opinion of his justification, and an opinion so founded, would fill his belly.[3] One of two things: either it is meant they should be at liberty to come and go as they think proper, or it is not: if it is, let them go, if they will there is no harm done: if it is not, means will probably be provided for preventing them from making their escape. Oh but if such means are provided, they will be ineffectual. In the same way you may prove that there ought to be no prisons. In arguing with this reasoner one thing you must allow him all along: that whatever measures you take for any purpose it is impossible they should succeed.

By the same argument, it may be proved that they will be receptacles of vice. Regulate as you please, your regulations are of course sure to be ineffectual. Those who agree in nothing else, and whose enmity no power can subdue, will continue to transgress with impunity the rules of the house and to abuse without discovery the bounty they receive.[a] Place them then so that they may be for ever either naturally under your eye, or in such a situation as not to know but that they are so. This I suppose would be inhumanity and injustice: punishing the well-behaved for the offences of the ill-behaved. Make the distinction then: and expose to view such only as are ill-behaved.—Oh—but the discrimination is impossible: it is impossible to know the one from the other—such is the hypocrisy and artifice that reign inseperable from this abode. To prevent vice among a set of people when they are all living together under your

[a] p. 98.[4]

[1] See McFarlan, *Inquiries concerning the Poor*, p. 99.

[2] See ibid., p. 100, which in fact reads as follows: 'they would think themselves justified in making their escape'.

[3] There is no text corresponding to the following marginal summary, which belongs here: 'A little before this the great grievance was that the ill-disposed would flock to the House and only the well-disposed fly from it. Now the evil is that the ill-disposed will escape out of the House. They are neither to go nor to stay: and which ever they do, it is always the fault of the Houses.'

[4] i.e. McFarlan, *Inquiries concerning the Poor*, p. 98.

eye is [a thing][1] out of the bounds of possibility. To make sure of them, you must send each of them to live wherever he will, and how he will, without the controul or so much as the knowledge of any superintending power, of any authority which if vice were to make its appearance would be disposed to check it.

If the evils which respectively form the matter of these objections either do not exist in the degree in which it is necessary they should exist to answer the purpose of the argument, or if existing in that degree, they are entirely accidental, capable of being remedied and likely to be remedied under the continuance of the establishment, in either case they form no just ground of objection to the establishment: and the just inference from them would have been not that the establishment ought to be abolished, but that the evils ought to be corrected. Instead of that no sooner is the objection started, and produced in the slightest form, than a jump is taken in favour of the abolition as a matter of course. Whatever inconvenience or shadow of an inconvenience is found, or supposed to exist in any degree, in any one establishment, upon any one occasion, is concluded to exist in the highest degree upon all occasions, in all such establishments, existing or possible, to be of such a magnitude as to form a clear overbalance for all possible advantages derived or derivable from any such establishments, and to be essentially incapable of all remedy. Against such objections, and so urged, were they admitted to be conclusive, no human institution, public or private, political or domestic, existing or possible, could ever maintain its ground in point of expediency for two minutes together. It would follow that there ought to be no such thing as government, administration, trust, agency, servitude, guardianship, partnership or marriage.

One objection—injury to liberty—inhuman to deprive them of their liberty—to confine them within walls—within a walled space—still worse if within the four walls of a house—to shut them up &c.

Another objection—injury to liberty in another shape—banishment—banishment from their native soil—from their native parishes—banishment from their friends—from the friends of their youth—from their dearest relatives.

That these are so many restraints upon liberty, so many deprivations of a certain portion of liberty, and that there is a degree of inconvenience attached to each of these several privations, is beyond dispute. To these inconveniences correspond so many objections against Industry House[s]: but so are they against government, not

[1] MS 'nothing'.

against corrupt and tyrannical government only, but against government in the best and purest form of it, whatever that form may be, and not only against government, but against society itself, against every condition of life you can name.

To a man's doing work in any place, to a man's receiving maintenance in any place, an indispensable condition is, his being there. In this sense therefore, true it is that those who are maintained in a house are so far confined in it. Moreover, in as far as a man is confined in one place, he is banished from another, and indeed from all others. If this circumstance be a reason for reprobating Industry Houses, it is a reason for reprobating almost every thing else: for reprobating the existence of a navy, the existence of an army, the existence of a militia, the existence of every branch of navigation and distant commerce, the existence of almost everything that can be brought under the name of a manufactory—the existence, in short, of every species of domestic service. Who would ever pay or take a servant who should reserve to himself the liberty of staying in the house or quitting it whenever he pleased.

There is a Jest-book story of a conscientious Preacher, a zealot against non-residence, who, to repress his zeal being confined by his superiors to particular texts, contrived to draw an argument in behalf of his favourite tenet from that part of Genesis which is exclusively occupied in genealogies. Abraham begat Isaac: a plain example of the necessity of residence: for how would the elder Patriarch have begot the younger, wherever it was, if he had not been resident there?[1] In the same way, in the spirit of this argument against Industry Houses, he might have alledged that the act of generation was an evidence of confinement, and the exercise of it a hardship upon the patriarch exercising it.

That punishments unmerited are grievances, and that confinement and banishment may be punishments, and very severe ones, is not to be disputed. To know in any particular case whether the obligation to abide in any particular place does or does not come with propriety under any such invidious denomination, ask the question how the obligation came to be imposed. With a man's consent, or without it? Without cause, or in the way of a condition annexed to the grant of a benefit? If without consent, and without benefit, it may then afford a ground for regret at least, if not for censure: it may then bear the name of a punishment, which is unjust, if either without delinquency or beyond delinquency, or of a tax, which is unjust, if without necessity, or beyond a man's ability of endurance. But what becomes

[1] For the genealogies see Genesis 4: 17–26, 5: 1–32, 10: 1–32, and 11: 10–29. The begetting of Isaac, however, is related at Genesis 21: 2–3.

of the hardship when the obligation is never imposed but with consent, and in the way [of] a condition annexed to a favour by which part of the community is saved from perishing by the labour, and at the expence of, another.

To persons of every other description, to the opulent of every description, to the industrious of every description, life is a chequered scene, made up of white and dark spots, of pleasant and unpleasant circumstances. In a Poor House of all places, in a House where a set of persons without property are to be supported by the Industry of another, the brilliant part is expected to be without spot, and if a spot be found there it is laid hold of as a matter of reproach to the whole plan of maintenance. Of exemptions which the nature of things allows not to any Palace, the absence is proclaimed as a grievance peculiar to Poor Houses. Not having a home to go to, the giving them a home is considered as a hardship, because the giving them a common home is banishing them from their friends and connections—that is, maintaining them at a few miles distance. A new world would require to be created, impossibilities would require to be realized, incompatibilities brought together, before the tenderness of these adversaries of Industry Houses could receive any degree of satisfaction. What if a man has two friends equally dear to him, one at one place, another at another, and both immoveable, at least by him? What is the legislator to do with him in order to save himself from the infamy of setting up such a sink of oppression? Is he to be put to live in both places at once? Or is he to have a carriage kept for him, that he may go backwards and forwards, according as he is [in] the humour? The army, the navy, the members of the Civil Establishments in the several Colonies and other distant dependencies, the Diplomatic body, the members of the first families in the Kingdom, the members of the Royal Family itself, are bandied to and fro upon the earth, and banished from their connections without scruple: the indigent of all descriptions, are they either to be maintained in idleness among their relations, as some would have it, or left to starve for want of maintenance, as others would have it, rather than expose them to the inconvenience of being stationed at the distance of a few miles from some place which in some instances, it is presumed, would have obtained their preference.

The language of all this tenderness, contrasted with its object, its professed object, is curious enough. To be confined to any scene of industry, not to be provided for unless a man will submitt to be provided for at a certain place, is a hardship: but it is no hardship to be starved. Not to be able to see his friends, all of them at all times, is a hardship—but it is no hardship to be starved. Every thing in short is a hardship but a lingering death, the panacea by which all these grievances are to be cured.[a]

[Position] 8. In the instance of every individual, rendered by nonage, or whatever other cause, to such a degree incapable of governing his own conduct as to remain exposed, at every step, to the imminent danger of trespassing, either against his own security, or that of other individuals in general, the sort and degree of governance, or *guardianship*, necessary to save him from falling into such trespasses, is comprehended in the catalogue of the necessaries of life.[b] (For the several sorts of persons in whose instance such guardianship is necessary, see the Table, Cols. I, II, & III.)[1]

[Position] 9. In every class of persons so circumstanced, there will always be a multitude of individuals, in whose instance no suitable private guardian exists, or can be found.

[Position] 10. In the instance of every such individual, it is necessary therefore, that a guardian or set of guardians, should be provided, by public authority, and at the public charge.

§II. *Quantum of Relief*

[Position] 11. (1) In the instance of a considerable proportion of the inhabitants of this country (England, Wales being included), labouring for themselves, the circumstances of families are such, that according to the cheapest and most frugal mode of living generally known, the utmost earnings of such members of the family upon whose earnings the other members necessarily depend, are not upon an average, in such instances in which the number of children is greater than a certain ordinary number (two for instance), sufficient to afford, to the whole family together, such a stock of the neces-

[a] Townsend, Dissert., p. 72. D°. in Sir W. Young, p. 43.[2]
[b] As per [Position] 1.[3]

---

[1] See p. lvii above.

[2] Bentham's first reference is mistaken, in that Joseph Townsend attacks workhouses 'not only as holding out the terror of confinement, but as adding banishment from all their friends to loss of liberty', not in *A Dissertation on the Poor Laws,* but in *Observations on Various Plans Offered to the Public, for the Relief of the Poor,* London, 1788, p. 20. Bentham's second reference is to Sir William Young (1749–1815), *Considerations on the Subject of Poor-Houses and Work-Houses, their Pernicious Tendency, And their Obstruction to the Proposed Plan for Amendment of the Poor Laws; in a letter to the Rt. Hon. W. Pitt,* London, 1796, p. 43, where Townsend's remark is cited with approval.

[3] See p. 10 above.

saries of life, as (according to [positions][1] [1 & 2])[2] is requisite for the support of life.

[Position] 12. (2) In the above case are the families of labourers in husbandry, composing, according to probability, a majority of the whole number of inhabitants.

[Position] 13. (3) In every country, the whole stock of existing wealth (land, dry or covered with water, with its rude produce in each case, being excepted) is the *product* of the labour of individuals, deriving their subsistence from their own labour.

[Position] 14. (4) In every country, the whole stock of wealth, existing at any period, is therefore (except as excepted) either the *property* of individuals labouring for themselves, or property derived from the labour of individuals labouring for themselves.

[Position] 15. (5) Maintenance afforded at the public charge to indigent individuals, in consideration of their inability, or supposed inability, to provide, by their own labour, for their own maintenance, is therefore afforded at the expence partly of those who labour for themselves, partly of those whose property is derived from the labour of those who labour for themselves.

[Position] 16. (6) If the condition of individuals, maintained without property of their own, by the labour of others, were rendered more eligible than that of persons maintained by their own labour, then, in proportion as the existence of this state of things were ascertained, individuals destitute of property would be continually withdrawing themselves from the class of persons maintained by their own labour, to the class of persons maintained by the labour of others; and the sort of idleness which at present is more or less confined to persons of independent fortunes, would thus extend itself, sooner or later, to every individual of the number of those on whose labour the perpetual reproduction of the perpetually consuming stock of subsistence depends: till at last there would be nobody left to labour at all, for any body.

[Position] 17. (7) The destruction of society would therefore be the inevitable consequence, if the condition of persons maintained at the public charge were *in general* rendered more eligible, upon the whole, than that of persons maintained at their own charge, those of the latter not excepted, whose condition is least eligible.

[1] MS 'art.' [2] MS '2 & 3'. See p. 10 above.

[Position] 18. (8) It follows that (as far at least as concerns persons who have not as yet been in the habit of receiving public bounty, see Tit. *Reform.* §XI [position 6]),[1] the supplies afforded to persons maintained on the score of indigence, at the public charge, ought not to extend to any *species* of article, not included in the list of the absolute necessaries of life, as characterized by the two first rules.[2]

[Position] 19. (9) Nor, in the instance of any species of article, to be more expensive in *quality*, than the least expensive of those in use amongst persons maintained at their own charge.[3]

Quantum Adversaria[4]

Nothing seems more incontestible than the propriety of this position. It is so obvious that it seems scarce worth mentioning: and in practice one would expect to see it universally adopted. On the contrary, if we were to enquire all over the kingdom for instances of its adoption, we should not find it adopted in any single instance.

Amongst the best managed, upon the whole, of the existing Industry Houses, is that of Shrewsbury. But the annual expence per head is there demonstrably at least as much again as it need to be, and therefore as it ought to be. The expence is there £8. 17. 0. a head: at Edinburgh it is but £4. 7. 0. a head: not half so much:[a] even in the Isle of Wight it is not above £5 a head.[b] In the Shrewsbury House, the Poor have three meals a day, and meat every day for one of them, while the bulk of the independent Poor, the labourers in husbandry, are glad if they can [have] meat one day out of the seven. The Author

[a] The medium between £4. 4. 0. and £4. 10. 0., Macfarlane, p. 113.[5]

[b] Wood, *Shrewsbury House*, p. 114.[6]

---

[1] MS 'art. 5', i.e. Position 58, p. 59 below.

[2] i.e. Positions 1 and 2, p. 10 above.

[3] Beside this paragraph, Bentham has noted in pencil: 'P[rinciple] of frugality.'

[4] i.e. 'the arguments in opposition to the extent (of relief)'.

[5] i.e. McFarlan, *Inquiries concerning the Poor*, p. 113, which, in relation to the workhouses in Edinburgh, states: 'At an average, the whole annual expence of each individual in these houses does not exceed from L.4:4:0 to L.4:10:0 per annum'.

[6] See Isaac Wood (1735–1801), *Some Account of the Shrewsbury House of Industry, its Establishment and Regulations; with Hints to Those Who May Have Similar Institutions in View. . . . The Second Edition. To Which is Added, the Third Edition of the Bye-Laws, Rules, and Ordinances, of the said House. Also an Appendix; Containing a Correspondence with the Rev. J. Howlett, Vicar of Great Dunmow, Essex, Author of several Essays on Population, and of an Enquiry ito the Mortality of Country Houses of Industry, &c.*, 2nd edn., Shrewsbury, 1791, p. 114, where the figure for expenditure per head in the Isle of Wight is given in the letter addressed to the author from John Howlett (1731–1804), political economist, reproduced in the Appendix. Howlett asserts that expenditures at Shrewsbury are 'higher than those of the House in the Isle of Wight by nearly 3*l*. a head; double those of the Edinburgh workhouses'. The figure of £8. 17. 0. for expense per head at Shrewsbury is given at p. 107.

of the well-written and instructive account of that House, being attacked upon the ground of this excess, says that 'the expense, after a variety of experiments, could not be curtailed without a reduction of the quantity which the Directors' (adds he) 'do not wish—and I trust never will—to diminish.'[1] Could not, that is they did not choose it. That they were wrong in their choice, all circumstances considered, is more than I wish, or can take upon me, to aver: but as to the possibility and even the practicability—whatever is actual is not only possible but practicable.

'What claims more particularly the public notice' says the Rev[d] Mr Howlett, with great justice, on the subject of this expence, is that it is 'double what at least a million of poor in this kingdom maintain themselves for in their own cottages.'[a] To this it is answered that this alledged amount of the expence of the independent poor is 'inferred from incomplete data and the result of course not to be relied on.'[2] But the data have since been rendered compleat, at least compleat enough for the purpose, by the Rev. Mr Davies:[3] and from thence it should seem that the expence of the Poor as above stated is set down by Mr Howlett somewhat indeed, but not much too low.[b]

Look on one side only of the argument, it is impossible the condition of this or any part of mankind can be too eligible: accordingly, in one of the best managed of the existing Industry Houses it is mentioned with pride and exultation that the poor maintained have their allowance for pocket-money, and their dependents and pensioners: and [upon] this occasion a pretty story is told, which demonstrates, with equal force of evidence, the excellent moral principles of the individual who is the subject of it, and the

[a] p. 114.

[b] Give the calculation in note.[4]

---

[1] See ibid., p. 114n. There are some minor inaccuracies in the rendering of this and the following passages.

[2] See ibid.

[3] See David Davies (d.1819?), Rector of Barkham, Berkshire, *The Case of Labourers in Husbandry Stated and Considered, in Three Parts*, London and Bath, 1795, Pt. I, §II, pp. 5–19, entitled 'An enquiry into the state of the Poor, necessary, previous to a reform of the Poor-Laws. The manner in which the *accounts* here given of the earnings and expences of labouring families were obtained. Accounts of six families in the parish of *Barkham*, with an abstract of the same.' Davies, who earned recognition as a pioneer in the gathering of accurate information on the budgets of labouring families, gives detailed weekly income and expenditure figures for six such families during a period around Easter, 1787.

[4] Bentham does not appear to have made such a calculation. Davies, however, at ibid., p. 23, gives a figure of '[£]26 very nearly for the whole yearly expence of a family of five persons', which, allowing for the difficulty involved in deriving an annual expense per head from statistics relating to families containing small children, would indicate the expense of maintenance per head per year to have been somewhat over £5, in comparison with Howlett's implied assertion that one million independent poor subsisted on £4. 8. 6. (i.e. one half of £8. 17. 0., the annual expenditure per head in the Shrewsbury House of Industry).

bad economical principles of the House.[1] A sixth part of the earnings is given to these dependent Poor, who are fed, at other people's expence, twice as well as people in general are fed at their own, twopence in every shilling, without distinction of age or condition, to those who have never seen any other days than what they have seen in the establishment, as well as to those who have seen better days in the world at large, two pence in the shilling upon all their earnings. And to what purpose?—'to enable them to furnish themselves with those little superfluities which custom endears, and almost converts into necessaries'. It is therefore according to an avowed principle that in this house the distinction between superfluities and necessaries is to be obliterated. There would be something to be said, there would be something of an excuse to be given, though that an insufficient one, if the customs in view had been customs formed under the sunshine of past prosperity out of the house, in the world at large: but the custom here pleaded, is a custom formed in the house and by the contrivance and authority of the House. A child of ten year[s] old is spoken of as taking the benefit of it: and his pocket money for the week is in consequence stated as amounting to four pence. Four pence pocket money to a child of ten years old, maintained, without reckoning the pocket money, twice as well and as expensively as he would have been in another of these houses, at least twice as well and as expensively as he would have been maintained, if he had been maintained at home. Four pence a week pocket money for a child of ten years old, maintained at the expence of the parents of other children, because his own are unable to give him maintenance: more than is given on this score to the child of many a gentleman of large and independent fortune. Three pence a week and no more was the allowance made for pocket money in many instances to boarders at the great School at Westminster, the great receptacle for the children of the most opulent families in the kingdom, at the time that I was there.[2] I speak from the most perfect recollection of the quantum of the allowance: to boys of a certain standing it was the ordinary allowance of the House: and there were times, I remember equally well, when I should have been glad of it: the House of Industry boy with his fourpence a week would have been an object of envy to me.

He who has money at command may buy merit with it as well as any thing else and get praise into the bargain. The boy who was the hero of this tale made a most admirable bargain in this way for himself it must be confessed. He got the satisfaction of assisting a

[1] The story on which Bentham proceeds to comment is related in Wood, *Some Account of the Shrewsbury House of Industry*, p. 25.

[2] Bentham attended Westminster School between 1755 and 1760.

sick mother, and a stock of literary immortality into the bargain. When I call it a good bargain, I mean for the boy himself: but for the public at large and for the establishment in question it was a most destructive one; better in a public view that this child, this truly amiable and most deservedly commended child, had cut his sick mother's throat than given her, that is, than had to give to her, the four pence. It sows broadcast the seeds of prodigality and injustice. It would establish the maxim, if any thing could establish it as a universal law throughout the realm of England, that every poor child of ten years old, maintained by taxes imposed on other people and their children, ought to have an allowance of 0–17^{s}–4^{d} a year for pocket money. It saddles the country with a perpetual annuity of several score thousands a year for this one article. It invites parents all over the country to turn their children out of doors, to cut without necessity the parental tie, that, instead of bare subsistence without a farthing of pocket money, they may have double subsistence with 17^{s} 4^{d} a year for pocket money. Had the boy picked any body's pocket of a shilling's worth of the public money, the law would have sentenced him to die for it: he picks the pocket of the managers of [the] Industry House of a million or two of public money, and becomes a hero for it.

Let me not be mistaken, I do not take upon me to say that this allowance of a share of earnings is in itself an indefensible one. All I mean to say, upon the present occasion at least, [is] that it is indefensible upon the grounds on which it is justified and commended: viz: that of furnishing to the persons in question, and in particular to children as young as ten years old, children whose customs [and] habits are formed by, and depend on, the will and pleasure of these trustees for the public, superfluities, under the notion that custom endears them, and almost converts them into necessaries. If more labour could be extracted by the allowance of this share of earnings than by a less allowance, or without any such allowance at all, the allowance is on the score of economy perfectly justified. Is an allowance and an allowance to such an amount necessary to the extraction of as much labour as possible? To this question, it being a foreign one to the present subject, I shall not pretend to give an answer. Mean time be it remembered, that in the instance of the great mass of labour in the country, day labour, no such allowance, nor any part of it, has any existence.

Let it not be imagined that in stating in such strong, though genuine, colours, the error I have held up to view, it enters into my intention or my wishes to reflect any particular mark of censure upon the individuals whose practice and doctrines gave occasion to these observations. The error is not of the individual, but of the public at large. Of those who have given into this delusion I can not be supposed to think very harshly, for none have given deeper into it than myself: the respectable man of whom I have been speaking[1] not so deep by a good deal.

§III. *Conditions of Relief*

[Position] 20. (1) In administering relief at the public charge, Government is warranted in exacting in the way of return, by a condition annexed to the grant of such relief, all such compliances on the part of the individual relieved, as, in its own judgment, are conducive to the benefit, either of the individual himself or of the community at large, at whose expence he is to be relieved.

[Position] 21. (2) Among these compliances may be the following: viz:

1. Working, up to the extent of his ability, and in any manner not inconsistent with the regard due to health and life, as determined by the two first rules.[2]

2. Submission to the rules laid down by Government, in relation to:

i.[3] The *place*, where the *relief* is to be administered.

ii. The *place*, where the *work*, required in return for the relief, is to be performed.

iii. The *mode* of *living* in each place.

§IV. *Ability as to Work*

[Position] 22. (1) To a person labouring under *total* and *absolute* want of ability with regard to work, relief must be administered, without any condition in respect of work, since otherwise he must be left to perish. (For the different classes of persons thus circumstanced see the *Table of Cases calling for Relief*, Cols. I, II, III, IV.)[4]

[1] Isaac Wood.

[2] See Positions 1 and 2, p. 10 above.

[3] For the sake of clarity, Bentham's Arabic numerals in this series have been rendered as Roman.

[4] See p. lvii above. In the original draft (UC clii. 231), Bentham inserted in the text the following list of the classes of persons characterized by utter inability: '1. Sick and hurt: the sickness or hurt extending to this degree. 2. Women lately delivered—up to a certain period after delivery. 3. Minors from birth up to a certain age. 4. Maniacs and Idiots—the insanity extending to this degree.'

[Position] 23. (2) To a person possessed of *adequate ability*, no relief ought to be administered, but on condition of his performing work: to wit such a measure of work as, if employed to an ordinary degree of advantage, will yield a return in value, adequate to the expence of the relief.[1]

Reasons

1. Regard to justice.—The administering relief to persons of that description on any other condition would be an unnecessary invasion of property—an unnecessary defalcation from that portion of security which has property for its object. For the expence of the relief thus to be administered by Government there is no other source of supply but what is produced by taxes: i.e. by labour, or the produce of labour, extracted by force. The benefit of the relief would thus be enjoy'd by one set of men, while the burthen of it was cast upon another.

2. Regard to economy.—Such an arrangement would be prejudicial to the national stock of opulence. Scarce any man will work, if he can obtain the same subsistence without working as he can by working: and many there are, who so long as they can obtain any subsistence at all without working, will decline working, how much soever they might be able to increase their subsistence by it.

3. Regard to the welfare, the lasting welfare, of the individual himself.—The habit of industry is a source of plenty and happiness. The habit of idleness in one who has property is a cause of uneasiness, and, in one who has no property, of indigence and wretchedness.

[Position] 24. (3) The *quantum* of work thus exacted, ought not to be more than adequate to such expence, since the excess, falling upon a person whose ability of payment is at the lowest pitch, has the effect of a hard and unequal tax.

[Position] 25. (4) To a person possessed of a certain degree of ability, *short* of being *adequate*, relief ought not to be administered, but on condition of his paying for it in work, according to the measure of his ability, in [the] manner above described.

Reasons

The same as in the former case.

[Position] 26. (5) To a person who, although at the time of the application for relief not possessed of adequate ability, appears likely

[1] Beside this paragraph, Bentham has noted in pencil: 'P[rinciple] of Industry.'

to become, at a future period, possessed of a degree of *extra-ability*, sufficient to compensate for the temporary inadequacy, relief ought not to be administered, but upon condition of his engaging, to make up for the *deficiency* of the former period, by the *exceedings* of the latter.

Reasons

The same as in the two former cases.

[Position] 27. (6) Ability in relation to any particular species of work, includes not only *strength*, but *skill*. Deficiency in relation to such ability may accordingly exist, either in respect of strength, or in respect of skill.

[Position] 28. (7) To a person who, in consequence of an application made for relief at a period of inadequate ability, stands *engaged*, as above,[a] to work during a period exceeding the continuance of the benefit of the relief, that species of work ought to be presented, which, with reference to his particular ability in point of skill, promises him the speediest *deliverance*.

[Position] 29. (8) *Infirmity*, whether of body or mind, affords not any ground of *exemption* from the conditions respecting work, any otherwise than in as far as it is attended with *inability*.

[Position] 30. (9) Infirmities which destroy or diminish ability, with reference to *one* species of work, leave it more or less unimpaired, with reference to *another*. (For the list of infirmities of mind and body considered in this point of view, see the *Table of Cases calling for Relief*, Cols. I & II.)[1]

[*Observations*]

A table should be formed of the several modes and degrees of infirmity to which human nature is liable with correspondent lists of profitable occupations with reference to which they respectively leave ability undestroy'd.[2]

Examples

1. A person deprived of all his limbs, or of the use of all his limbs, may still possess ability sufficient to the purpose of serving as inspector to most kinds of work, so long as mental faculties, and

[a] [Position][3] 26.

---

[1] See p. lvii above.

[2] No such table has been discovered.

[3] MS 'art.'

sight for observing, and voice for questioning are possessed by him in sufficient vigour.

2. There are few cases of insanity that destroy ability with reference to all kinds of work, or that do not leave it but little impaired with reference to many kinds of work: and whatever work lies within the competency of a person so circumstanced would commonly be of use to him not only as an occupation, and in the way of general health, but in the particular way of diverting his attention from the ideas on which the derangement of his mind depends.

[Position] 31. (10) In every system of provision for the relief of Indigence, different species of work ought accordingly to be provided, corresponding to the different modifications of *ability* left more or less *unimpaired* by the several modifications of *infirmity*. See the table.[1]

[Position] 32. (11) Conditions requiring work ought not to be dispensed with, even though no advantage could be made from the produce of the work, which however, under ordinarily good management, can scarce ever be the case, even for a moment, nor ever for a continuance.

Reasons

1. To prevent the public from being burthened by persons quitting their employments for the benefit of being maintained in idleness.
2. To keep up the habit of exertion and industry.

[Position] 33. (12) An establishment, instituted at the public charge, for the relief of persons labouring under infirmity, without providing works corresponding to their several modes of remaining ability, is absolutely speaking good, in as far as it saves them from perishing who otherwise might have perished, but comparatively bad, with reference to establishments in which such employment is provided.

Reasons

1. Such institutions are unconformable to the dictates of economy: by depriving the public of the produce of so much profitable labour as the persons in question might be engaged to bestow.
2. In another way: by tempting men to counterfeit infirmity, to sink under it, or even purposely contract it, for the benefit of being maintained in idleness.
3. They are more unconformable to the dictates of humanity,

[1] See p. 46 n. above.

meaning enlightened humanity, in respect of the persons themselves to whom relief is thus gratuitously and unthriftily bestowed: since by the want of occupation, they leave them perpetually exposed to the unpleasant state of mind which is the result of inactivity. Even those to whom, at the first commencement of a course of labour, idleness would present itself to the feelings of the moment as preferable, would ultimately find themselves the happier as well as the public the richer, for the habit of occupation.[a]

§V. *Healthiness of Work*

[Position] 34. (1) Work, exacted from persons maintained at the public charge, whether adults or minors, in return for necessary relief, ought not to be of a nature in any degree prejudicial to *health*: how customary soever such work may be, among individuals working on their own account in a state of liberty.

Reasons

1. Whether a man be left to perish for want of subsistence, or made to perish by the labour exacted of him in return for subsistence, comes much to the same thing: with this difference, that the pains and uneasinesses attendant on employments of a nature prejudicial to health, are generally such as appear of a more afflictive kind than the uneasiness attendant on a mere deficiency in point of necessaries.

2. It is no sufficient answer to say, that employments of the nature in question must be carried on by some body: that if not carried on by the persons in question they will by others: and that it makes no difference to the community in general whether they are carried on by the persons in question, or by others. When carried on by persons in an independent state, such persons are free to stipulate for their own recompense, and do obtain such recompense as in their estimation is more than equivalent to the disadvantageous circumstances attached to the employment, otherwise they would not accept it: whereas the paupers in question, if employ'd at all in the

[a] Examples of the application of these positions may be found in the economy of Chelsea and Greenwich Hospitals, and in almost all Parochial Poor-Houses.[1]

[1] Chelsea Hospital was founded in 1682 by Charles II (1630–85), King of England, Scotland, and Ireland from 1660, for the relief of aged and infirm veteran soldiers, and admitted its first pensioners in 1689. The Royal Hospital for Seamen, Greenwich was founded in 1694 by Mary II (1662–94), Queen of England, Scotland, and Ireland from 1689, to provide relief for disabled seamen, and admitted its first pensioners in 1705.

unwholesome employment in question, must be employ'd for pay not affording in their estimation an equivalent for the disadvantages in question.

To a person giving free and full informed consent, no injury, it is true, is done. But here, either consent is altogether wanting, or, if given, is not free, being extorted by the fear of death, speedy or lingering, for want of sustenance.

In the case of minors, it is still more evidently unfree.

§VI. *Account as between Relief and Work*

[Position] 35. (1) The estimate taken, of the value of the relief, in return for which work is exacted of this or that individual, is not compleat, unless to the immediate and separate expence of the occasional supply afforded to him at the time, there be added a proportionable share of the necessary expence, of such part of the establishment, in and by means of which the supply is afforded, as is of a *standing* nature, and of which the benefit is reaped by him in common with the generality of the individuals to whom the establishment affords relief.

[Position] 36. (2) Of this latter description, are the expences respectively required on account of the several articles following: viz:

1. Lodging—comprising the rent of the ground, or interest of the money expended in the purchase of the ground, and in the erecting, fitting up, and furnishing of the Buildings.
2. Wear and tear of the above articles.
3. Lighting.
4. Warming.
5. Medical inspection and attendance.
6. Religious inspection and instruction.
7. Civil inspection and instruction in respect of work.
8. General Management of the particular local establishment in question.
9. General Superintendence of the general system of local establishments.

[Position] 37. (3) To the total expence of relief as above stated, any addition may, without injustice or hardship, be made by government in its charge, so that the sum total of such charge do not exceed that which would be accounted *ordinary profit*, in dealings between *individual* and *individual*.

[Position] 38. (4) But to such ordinary rate of profit no addition ought, in the instance of *adults*, to be made: since the surplus would have the effect of a hard and unequal tax.

[Position] 39. (5) Among adults, therefore, to the charge against an individual possessed of extra-ability, no addition ought to be made in the view of making up for any deficiency of supply, resulting from a deficiency in point of ability on the part of other individuals.

Observations

If the pay of a person thus engaged till what is deemed a compensation shall have been exacted of him be set down at a lower rate than what a person not under engagement would have required for the same work, or the supply is charged upon him at a price exceeding the free market price as above described, an extra profit might thus be exacted from persons endowed[?] with extra ability, applicable as far as it went to defray the expence incurred on account of persons labouring under perpetual inability, or deficiency in point of ability. Such extra-charge does not present any thing contrary to justice or humanity upon the face of it, since the public, being at liberty to annex its own conditions to the relief it administers, may annex any conditions which do not put the party applying for such relief in a worse plight than if he were not to receive it. But in such an arrangement there would be the appearance of hardship and exaction; nor would any supply that could be drawn from it operate any considerable saving to the rateable part of the community, without stretching the term of the engagement in each instance to a duration, which in many instances must be so great as to appear excessive, and give the engagement the appearance of punishment.

§ VII. *Security for the Performance of Work*

[Position] 40. (1) To a person possessing, or appearing capable of being made to possess, *extra-ability*, relief ought not to be advanced, without taking such *security* as shall be adequate to the purpose of insuring, to the public, the performance of the work prescribed in the way of compensation for the relief.

[Position] 41. (2) Such security may be provided, according to the nature and pressure of the exigency, by any of the four modes of arrangement following: viz:

1. Requiring the work to be finished, *before* any relief has been administered.

2. Administering the relief in the first instance, but detaining the party, till the value has been *worked out*, charges of detention, and of fresh and fresh relief during detention, included.

3. In lieu of the *personal* security afforded by the detention, taking *real* security, by goods of adequate value, received and detained in the footing of a *pledge*.[a]

4. Taking such *real* security from any *third* person consenting to afford it.

[Position] 42. (3) For the above purpose, that species of security, being adequate, ought in each instance to be taken, which is least burthensome to the individual.

[Position] 43. (4) But no relief ought ever to be administered *without* security, or with *inadequate* security, or on the merely *personal* security of a *third* person.

Reasons

1. Regard to Economy, to Justice, and to good morals. Any indulgence on this score would leave the door constantly open to profusion to an indefinite extent: to partialities, and to the encouragement of idleness.

§VIII. *Extra-Relief*

[Position] 44. (1) *Extra-relief*, on the ground of wants resulting from past *prosperity*, and not coming, with reference to the person in question, under the head of necessaries of life,[b] ought not to be administered in any instance at the public charge.

Reasons

1. Regard to Economy, to Justice and to good morals. Any indulgence on this score would, in this as in a former instance, open an indefinite door to profusion, to partialities, and to the encouragement of idleness. Whatever reasons plead against affording necessaries without work, plead with greatly augmented force against the affording of superfluities without work.

[a] See essay (hereunto annexed) on the *Collateral Uses* derivable from the system of Industry Houses.[1]

[b] See above §I, [Positions][2] 1, 2.[3]

[1] See pp. 69–77 below.

[2] MS 'Art.'

[3] See p. 10 above.

2. Regard to economy in another point of view. Indulgences of this nature would operate in discouragement of frugality and industry on the part of individuals, by ensuring to them without care or labour a measure of superfluity which nothing but labour can produce.

Observations

This position is in fact included in a preceding one—to wit the 6th as explained by the 7th.[1]

[Position] 45. (2) But the right of administering such extra-relief, may, and ought to be, left to the *charity* of *individuals*.

Reasons

The reasons which forbid the administering such Relief in the former case do not extend to this. The length to which the expence can run in this case can never be excessive.

Partiality in this case is no evil, except in as far as, by engaging a person to bestow his charity where the claim is less strong, it disables him from bestowing it where there is a stronger one. But of this inconvenience there is less danger in the present case than in the other, the individuals, at whose expence relief is in this case afforded, having so much more time for inquiring, and so much greater interest in ascertaining the title to relief, than any Agent of the public, dealing out largesses at the expence of the public, can have.

The objections which forbid public begging, apply not to the present case. The persons in question, do not, like beggars, obtrude themselves upon the presence of all persons indiscriminately, willing or not willing to afford relief, able or not able: and they are supposed ready to execute, according to the measure of their ability, such work as shall be assigned to them, though the produce of it be not sufficient for the relief of their extra-wants.

It is pleasure in this instance, not pain as in the other, the pleasure of exercising benevolence, not the pain of witnessing the demand for it, that gives motive to the charitable hand. It is pleasure, for if it were not, a man would not throw himself in the way of it: and physical wants being already provided for by the general establishment, the operation is that of raising from life to comfort, not that of rescuing from death.

[Position] 46. (3) Things may, and ought to be, so arranged, as that assistance shall be afforded, by the agents of the public, to charitably disposed individuals, in respect of the administration of *extra-relief*, to

[1] i.e. §§ VI and VII, pp. 49–51 above.

wit, by affording facilities of access with respect to the means of ascertaining such facts as constitute the claim to charity on this score.

Observations

The claim to charity on this score is grounded on two circumstances: past prosperity, and past and present good behaviour.

Proportioned to the greatness of the former prosperity is the magnitude of the present suffering: and in proportion to the deficiency of any thing that constitutes a departure from the general habit of good behaviour, is the incapacity of the suffering with regard to the being productive in any way of the beneficial consequences of a punishment—either in the way of reformation or example.

The agents of the public in each establishment might, if the whole number of persons composed in it were sufficiently under their eye, collect the history of the several individuals thus circumstanced, together with an intimation of the particular wants the supply of which would afford them the greatest quantity of gratification. These notices, together with the account of the donations, might be entered upon the books of the establishment, and these books lie open to the inspection of every visitor whose humanity might lead him to apply for it. The collection of these documents would be an occupation altogether suited to the office of the Ecclesiastical Minister whom I suppose resident in the House.[1]

§IX. *Minors*

[Position] 47. (1) From the labour of a *Minor*, brought up and educated at the public charge, the public may, without injustice, hardship, or even deviation from established law or usage, reap the utmost profit that such labour can be made to yield, consistently with the regard due, as above, to the health and permanent welfare of the individual, and that, from the period, whatever it be, of his being taken under the public care, untill the expiration of his minority: to wit, in the same manner as a Master reaps the utmost profit that can be reaped from the labour of his Apprentice: the public taking consequently whatever surplus profit can be reaped from the extra-ability of the minor during his period of extra-ability, and that, even notwithstanding [that] the whole of the expence, bestowed upon him

[1] See 'Collateral Uses derivable from a system of Industry Houses', p. 68 below.

during his periods of inability and inadequate ability, shall have been reimbursed.

Reasons

1. As far as the produce of their labour is concerned, the greater the quantity of labour extracted from them (which depends upon the quantity of labour exerted and the degree of dexterity by which the exertion of it is guided) during their minority, the better their condition will have been rendered at the expiration of that period, when the benefit of their labour will be their own. Labour, so long as it is neither by its immediate, nor in its remote effects, prejudicial to health, can never be too severe.

2. As far as frugality in regard to the expence of their maintenance is concerned, whatever privations they may be subjected to in respect to superfluities, with which, in the course of their period of extra-ability, they might have been able to supply themselves, had they been permitted to receive on their own account the full value of their own labour, will not in this instance produce the sense of hardship which similar privations would be apt to produce in the instance of persons of full age: since their inexperience of the comfort will exempt them from the sensation of regret that accompanies the comparison between the time when it was in possession, and the time when it is no longer at command.

3. In proportion as their habit of privation has been strict during minority, the faculty of enjoyment will be the more valuable, and the source of happiness thus derived more copious, on their arrival at the age of independence.

4. The good education which the minors in question might and ought to be made to receive, over and above their maintenance, is a benefit which they receive over and above whatever maintenance is given to the poor of full age in return for their labours.

5. On the general terms and conditions of Apprenticeship, the Master has the full benefit of whatever labour he can extract from the Apprentice: and the engagement seldom ends before the apprentice is of full age. No hardship is considered as attending an engagement contracted upon these terms. But the condition of persons serving in this way, under and for the benefit of the public, will have the advantage over the condition of apprentices serving under a private master, inasmuch as the service being performed under the public eye, and under a system of inspection not having more in view the service of the master than the comfort of the apprentice, will receive constant protection against all those hardships to which service under a private master is exposed, nor can be otherwise than

exposed in a considerable degree, after every thing that can be done by law for subjecting the exercise of the master's power to the occasional scrutiny of justice.[1]

[Position] 48. (2) The charge against a minor for the relief afforded by the public during his minority, is however not compleat, nor consequently the reimbursement of such charge, unless, to the articles composing the charge against an adult (as above §VI.)[2] be added the two following, viz:

1. His share of the loss, by such *deaths* as *have* taken place among his *fellows*, previously to their respective attainment of the period of adequate ability.

2. An equivalent, for the probable amount of the contingent expence, attending his *own future* maintenance, during the respective periods of inadequate ability, and total inability, to which he is exposed by diseases, casualties, and old age.[3]

[1] Entry to and terms of apprenticeship were regulated by the Statute of Artificers of 1562 (5 Eliz. I, c.4), which set the term of the apprenticeship at 'seven Years at the least, so as the Term and Years of such Apprentice do not expire or determine afore such Apprentice shall be of the Age of twenty-four Years at the least', during which period the apprentice was bound to service in a particular trade, for the pecuniary benefit of his master, upon condition that he was taught the trade in question. Traditionally, the apprentice was considered to have left his own family and joined that of his master, so that he would normally be subject to the will of the latter with regard to working conditions and domestic discipline.

[2] See pp. 49–50 above.

[3] In his original draft (UC clii. 253–4), Bentham included the following seven further 'positions' relating to the education of minors at this point: '3. In the education of children maintained in this manner at the public expence, it should not be an object of endeavour to enable them, or any of them, to acquire a superiority in any respect in relation to children maintained at the expence of their parents.

'4. But if, in the course of such education, opportunities should present themselves of bringing into existence, or into notice, any talent of which the public would not otherwise have had the benefit, without prejudice to any body, such opportunity ought not to be neglected, much less purposely rejected.

'5. Nor, if there be any acquirement, which, at times of necessary or appointed rest from labour, promises to afford them an innocent, and useful or amusing means of filling up their time, should the opportunity of putting them in possession of such qualification be purposely rejected, merely because the possession of it would place them in a situation of superiority in that respect, with reference to the independent part of their fellow-subjects.

'6. Every opportunity not inconsistent with their general welfare ought to be embraced of giving the public the benefit of their services in the way of national defence.

'7. In the instance of both sexes, the work ought to be so ordered, by mixture of employments or otherwise, as that as well after as during their continuance under the public care, they need never remain without employment, in any state of the season or the weather.

'8. In the instance of the female sex, care ought to be taken to mix with the employments meant as sources of subsistence, the exercise of the occupations common to the sex, in the several capacities of the mother, the mistress of a family, and the nurse.

'9. In the choice of employments for the male sex, care ought to be taken not to endanger the want of hands in regard to the employment on which the community depends for its subsistence.'

In relation to position 5, the following innocent and useful acquirements are listed by Bentham on the corresponding marginal contents sheet (UC cli. 4): '1. Reading. 2. Music.'

§X. *Beggars*

[Position] 49. (1) When a plan of *general relief* has been set on foot, by means of which every individual, on application made by him or on his behalf, may be assured of maintenance, on condition of performing work according to the measure of his ability, then, and not till then, every individual who, stationing himself in any place of *public* resort, shall presume either to *ask* or to *accept* of relief, on the score of *charity*, may be, and ought to be, *convey'd*, with or without his consent, to the place of *relief* and *employment* belonging to the district in which he is found.

Reasons

1. Regard to Economy. The community at large is thereby deprived of the benefit of so much labour as might have been extracted from the persons thus gratuitously relieved, had the relief administered to them been subjected to the conditions imposed on their companions in indigence.

2. Regard to good morals. Whatever is given to a beggar who declines work, is a premium, an encouragement, given to idleness.

3. Regard to good morals on a more remote account. Whatever subsistence happens to be derived from private charity is essentially precarious; and, under the pressure of necessity, the aversion to honest industry which gave rise to the practice of begging, and is confirmed and encreased by it, will be apt to suggest dishonest courses in preference.

4. Regard to humanity on the score of other poor, considered as exposed to the temptation of taking up the trade of begging. In a trade [so][1] favourable to indolence, every man who succeeds draws in, by the example of his success, a multitude of others, who can not all meet with equal success, and of whom a great part will find it as ineligible on their personal account, as on that of the public.

5. Regard to humanity on the score of the charitably disposed part of the community.[2]

[Position] 50. (2) At such House of relief and employment, in addition to the *food* and other articles of *immediate* consumption, necessary for the daily maintenance of such apprehended Beggar,

[1] MS 'to'.

[2] At this point, Bentham has noted in the text, 'Continue this', but no material appears to have been written. Bentham, however, discusses the effect of begging on the charitably-disposed part of the community as one of the reasons grounding the necessity of public relief: see §I, pp. 25–8 above.

decent *apparel* should be furnished to him, together with such other articles of *gradual* consumption as may be adapted to his case: and, to the cost of such articles of immediate and articles of gradual consumption, being added the cost of apprehending him, and conveying him to the House, including a competent reward for the persons by whom such apprehension and conveyance shall have been performed, he should then and there be detained, untill the aforesaid accumulated charge were worked out (according to §§ VI, VII)[1] and no longer.

[Position] 51. (3) Upon any subsequent apprehension and conveyance, as aforesaid, of a Beggar, who, after having worked out a former charge against him, as above, shall betake himself afresh to begging, the charge may be doubled or otherwise encreased—and so *toties quoties*.[2]

[Position] 52. (4) To preserve the provision thus made for the extirpation of mendicity from being evaded, on the part of opulent beggars (beggars who have laid up money earnt by begging), work only, and not money, should be accepted, in discharge of the sum charged against the beggar on each occasion, as aforesaid.

§XI. *Reform in regard to Relief and Work*

[Position] 53. (1) The established practice not being anywhere in exact conformity, at present, to the above positions, it follows, that if they were any where to be carried in any degree into execution, it might be necessary that a proportionable *reform*, in respect of the present practice, should take place.

[Position] 54.[3] (2) The Reforms and Improvements of which the mode of providing for the relief of the indigent, in this or any other country, are susceptible, seem all reducible to the following heads, viz:

1. Reducing the quantum of the relief from extra-relief to simple relief: in other words, lopping off what is excessive.
2. Gathering together the fragments of ability with regard to labour in all its degrees, wherever they are to be found.
3. Rendering the connection between relief and labour inseparable, according to this rule:—Nothing ought to be given for nothing, where labour can be had for it.

[1] See pp. 49–51 above.
[2] i.e. 'as often as the occasion demands'.
[3] In both copies of the essay, this 'position' is the final one. The coherence of the text, however, requires its insertion at this point.

4. Employing the collective stock of labour to the most advantage, in respect of the species of work to which it is applied.

5. Providing the stock of supply in the cheapest mode:[a] i.e. according to the cheapest plan of *management*.

[Position] 55. (3) As far as concerns the execution of *work* (to wit an ordinary measure of work) in return for relief, reform may be carried into execution, in respect to *all* persons thus relieved, without exception or reserve: since no individual can look upon the obligation of making an adequate return for the relief he stands in need of as either unjust or hard in itself, or as not comprized in the number of those obligations, for which he as well as every body else, is constantly prepared in point of expectation, by generally established opinions and generally known practice.

Observations

Those who at present do no work may at any time be set to work, and the work of those whose work is not at present adequate to their ability may be raised to that pitch at any time without scruple. This is no more than they are prepared for by general opinion, and by the prescriptions of the existing laws.[1]

[Position] 56. (4) So likewise as far as concerns the confining the administration of the relief, in point of *place*, to *Houses* instituted by the *public* for that purpose, in contradistinction to the *abode* of the *individual* in question: to wit, in cases where either no *work* capable of producing a compensation adequate to the growing demand for relief, or no adequate *security* for the performance of such work, could be provided *elsewhere* than in such House: since, for a change

[a] The provision made for the Poor in England, under the existing law, will be found defective in every one of these points of view.

The new system at present on the carpet will, I fear, in its present state at least, be found still more so:[2] opening no new source of frugality, and opening several new and pregnant sources of expence, which either [do][3] not so much as aim at being profitable, or on many accounts [seem][4] incapable of being rendered so.

---

[1] The notion that the able-bodied poor should be required to work as a condition of their relief was enshrined in 43 Eliz. I, c.5 (1601), the statutory basis for English poor law administration.

[2] In the House of Commons on 16 February 1796 William Pitt the Younger (1759–1806), leader of the administration as First Lord of the Treasury and Chancellor of the Exchequer 1783–1801, 1804–6, announced his intention to bring in a Bill dealing with poor relief (*Parliamentary Register*, 2nd ser. (1796), xliv. 55), although the Bill was not introduced until 29 December 1796. For a discussion of the history of the Bill, and of Bentham's knowledge of it, see the Editorial Introduction, pp. xli–xlvii above. For Bentham's detailed critique of the measure see 'Observations on the Poor Bill', pp. 219–54 below.

[3] MS 'does'.

[4] MS 'seems'.

of this sort, every poor person throughout the kingdom is sufficiently prepared, in point of expectation, by examples of such changes going on every where before his eyes.

[Position] 57. (5) Moreover, in regard to the article of *diet*, in respect of the following classes of persons, such reforms as are indicated by the above positions, may be carried on without scruple or reserve:

1. All *children*, of an age *beneath* that at which the *habits* of the individual, in respect to practice and expectation with reference to this head, may be considered as being formed.

2. All persons, whose *demand* for relief is only *casual* and *temporary*, they not having before had experience of relief in this respect at the public charge, or at least not upon any footing more eligible.

[Position] 58. (6) The classes of persons, in whose instance a reform, grounded on the above principles in respect to *diet*, would bear *hardest*, are all such *adults*, and all such minors *above* the age just above described, as have already had experience of the diet administered in Parish Work-houses, and District-Industry-Houses, that is to say, in the instance of such of the said Houses in which a more expensive and luxurious system of diet has prevailed. In these instances, great *caution* in the introduction of this branch of the system of reform would be necessary, in so far, if at all, as the introduction of it should be deemed eligible.

[Position] 59. (7) Next to the persons habituated to the *experience* of such *extra-expensive* diet, stand those who have been habituated to the *expectation* of it, by being settled in the respective districts, in which it has habitually been administered.

[Position] 60. (8) In the cases *not* appearing to call for any particular degree of caution with regard to reform, the introduction may be effected according to an uniform plan, prescribed by the legislature: in the cases that appear to *demand* such caution, it may be requisite, that the degree and mode of such introduction should be committed to the discretion of the *local authorities*.

Observations

We have spoken of Extra-Relief on the score of past prosperity.[1] The present is a case of Extra-Relief on the score of habitual profusion in the article of relief.

The great mischief of profuse allowance in every shape, and in

[1] See §VIII, pp. 51–3 above.

every branch of public service, is that when once become habitual and reckoned upon as permanent, retrenchment, to the prejudice of the individuals already in possession of the benefit of it, is not only difficult, but can scarcely be looked upon as attended with any advantage. The cessation of that benefit would be attended with the sensation of a loss: a sensation the same in kind, and scarcely if at all distinguishable in degree, from that which would accompany the loss of what was acknowledged to be a man's own property, his own estate. This loss, falling with its undiminished weight on a comparatively small number of individuals, would be felt in its utmost severity: while the benefit of the retrenchment, being distributed among so many, and, in the instance of each person, altogether unliquidated and unmanifested in regard to quantity, and in regard to time, produces no sensation, and in point of effect has scarcely any existence. It is so much taken from Peter for the benefit of Paul: and unfortunately Paul never profits, or at least can never be seen to profit, in point of happiness, so much as Peter suffers, and is seen to suffer, by such a change. Hence the death of those who are in the habit of profiting, and expecting to profit, by public profusion, is the only period at which the abuse can universally be abolished with advantage.

If the objections to retrenchment are thus strong, in the instance of that sort of profusion of which the benefit is reaped by the distinguished few (as in the case of useless or overpaid places and groundless pensions), they are still stronger in the case of that sort of profusion of which the benefit is reaped by the vast and unruly multitude. In the former case, hardship is but hardship: in the latter, it is liable to be attended with the utmost danger. The dignified pensioners would neither have sufficient power, nor, in general, the inclination to rise against the hand that plunged them into distress: on the part of the undignified, power is infinitely greater, nor would the existence of inclination be looked upon as otherwise than probable. On the disposition of men of education calculations may be grounded, dependence may be placed; but from the disposition of the uneducated among mankind in any country, nothing but the worst, especially in a case like the present, ought in prudence to be expected. For benefits conferred, indignation rather than gratitude ought ever to be looked for: for hardships imposed, with whatever reluctance, every thing that can be apprehended from resentment and violence ought to be regarded as certain. As objects of tenderness and beneficence they ought to be treated as children: but as beings whose ignorance, caprice and violence is a perpetual source of danger, instruments ever in readiness for the hand [of] mischief, they ought to be guarded against as enemies. Should what is amiss in the character of the lower orders be regarded as imputable, more or less, to the higher, it would not the less require to be guarded against, so long as it has existence.[a]

[a] According to the observations and calculations made by D[r] Macfarlane (p. 96), 'the deserving poor of good dispositions do not compose a third, perhaps not a fifth part of the general number.'[1] D[r] Macfarlane had, 'for upwards of 15 years, been either an actual Director, or had access to be acquainted with the management, of almost every charitable foundation in Edinburgh and its neighbourhood.'[a] This in Scotland, where the disposition of the lower classes is generally understood to be much more orderly than in England.

In a pamphlet quoted by D[r] Macfarlane, it is stated, as a matter of applause and exultation, that in a House of Industry there mentioned the wheat, 'the beef and every other article is of the best kind'.[2] By whom then are articles of inferior quality to be consumed? 'Not one little Farmer out of ten', it is added, 'can afford to live near so well in their own houses.'[3]—This being the case, were the management of the house as good in point of comfort and good order, where expence is not concerned, as it is profuse in point of expence, nine out of ten of the little Farmers, to say nothing of their labourers, would give up their businesses, and throw themselves into these houses. No foreign invasion and conquest, no national bankruptcy, no revolution in the French stile, could be more compleatly ruinous to a country, than a system of provision for the Poor spread over a country and conducted upon such principles.

In the conceptions of men who write thus (and how many are there who write thus!), wheat and oxen must be dropping regularly from the clouds throughout the land as copiously as manna and quails did once by miracle.[4]

The work of the country would not find a hand, and famine would be the certain and universal consequence, if those by whom none of it is done are crammed with meat, or the quintessence of it, every day in the week, while those by whom the whole of it is done, as far as subsistence is concerned, cannot get their fill of bread and water.

Shall profusion like this cover the face of the whole land? It would be physically impossible. Shall it be suffered to go any where unretrenched, while in other places a provision is established upon just and practicable principles? Yet to retrench it any where, and in any degree, would be a business full of hardship, and full of difficulty. Legislation can scarce venture to trace a line—every thing must be committed to the prudence and felicity of administration in each district, to the circumstances of the moment, to the disposition of individuals, to the degree of fortitude, and the powers of persuasion on the one part, and to the degree of tractability on the other.

a Preface.[5]

---

1 See McFarlan, *Inquiries concerning the Poor*, p. 96. There are minor inaccuracies in the rendering of this and subsequent passages.

2 See ibid., p. 120, where McFarlan cites *Considerations On The Present State Of The Poor In Great-Britain with proposals for making the most effectual provision for them. Which will be attended with this great advantage, the present enormous poor's rates must of course be greatly reduced, and that in a very short time. The whole most respectfully submitted to the consideration of the Parliament*, London, 1773. The author is identified only as 'Humanus'.

3 See ibid.

4 Exodus 16: 13–15.

5 See McFarlan, *Inquiries concerning the Poor*, p. v.

It is in the order of things that men at the head of affairs should be sufficiently aware of all dangers of this kind. The sort of prudence which consists in the being aware, forming a due estimate of the danger in matters of this kind, is not apt to be deficient in men actually at the head of affairs; but it is not unapt to be deficient in the part of those who, at a distance from office, take upon them to be advisers.

Conclusion

Supposing the system of Industry Houses to be universally adopted all over England, and the Houses uniformly distributed, then, by pursuing the lights afforded by Count Rumford's experiments, with regard to the necessary expence of maintenance,[1] and collecting the whole stock of ability on the parts of the persons to be maintained, according to the above rules, I see no reason to doubt but that mendicity might be utterly extirpated, and the labour of the indigent Poor, maintained at the public charge, and under the public management (*adults* and *minors* taken together), might, in time (viz: in the course of 21 years from the opening of the Industry Houses), be made to defray at least the whole of the *annual* expence. Nor does it seem to be despaired of, but that, at the end of a further period of time, savings might be made, sufficient even to reimburse the expence, which at the outset could not but be very great, of the purchase of the ground, together with the erection, fitting up, and stocking of so great a multitude of such capacious Buildings.

The considerations on which these favourable expectations have been grounded, will, as soon as this can be put into form, be stated at large. I am fully apprized of all the objections that have been made (or I believe can be made), and fully prepared to answer them.[2]

But to this economy, as well as to any degree of economy much exceeding that of the existing system, it seems an indispensable condition that the system of *Out-allowances* should not be so much as

[1] Sir Benjamin Thompson (1753–1814), Count von Rumford of the Holy Roman Empire, American-born loyalist in the War of Independence, social reformer and inventor, supplied varying figures for the necessary expense of maintenance, several of which are cited by Bentham at different points in his poor law writings. Rumford recorded that the daily expense of feeding the poor at Munich, on the basis of their receiving one meal a day, amounted to two farthings per head, which he calculated to be the equivalent of $1\frac{1}{2}^{\mathrm{d}}$ at London prices of late 1795. He then indicated that the poor in Great Britain could be fed for $2\frac{3}{4}^{\mathrm{d}}$ per head per day, on the basis of receiving two additional meals per day. See Benjamin Thompson, *Essays, Political, Economical and Philosophical*, 4 vols., London, 1796–1802, i. 242–5.

[2] Bentham's reference is to his projected work 'Pauper Management Improved', which was never published, although an abridgement appeared in serial form under the title 'Outline of a Work entitled Pauper Management Improved' in *Annals of Agriculture*, xxx (1798), 89–176, 241–96, 393–424, 457–504; xxxi (1798), 33–64, 169–200, 273–88 (Bowring, viii. 369–439).

preserved in any instance, much less extended, and least of all extended to the case of *children*; but that all persons maintained at the public expence, should be maintained under the public care.

Of the *Collateral Uses* which I have ventured to suggest (in separate papers) as capable of being made of a compleat system of Industry Houses,[1] I am likewise inclined to flatter myself, that the pecuniary profit, taking them all together, might be made to defray the expence.

It has long appeared to me, and was five or six years ago advanced in print, that, by proper management, the *extra*-ability of *one* part of the dependent Poor, might be made to compensate for whatever want of ability may be found existing among the rest, insomuch that the whole burthen of the Poor Rates might in time be done away.[2] The experiments made by Count Rumford in a situation that invested him with the requisite powers, in a country more favourably circumstanced than England for the institution of political experiments, seem to have already placed this out of doubt.[3]

With regard to the prospect of success, an observation presents itself, of a tendency as encouraging as it is important. The most *successful example* that can be produced of the practice, in relation to any head of management, is, in truth, the *fairest sample*, not only of what *may* be done, but of what, under any tolerable system of general superintendence, is *likely* to be done: except always, in as far as any particular circumstance, of a local or otherwise incommunicable nature, can be pointed out as the course to which the management was, in that instance, indebted for its success. For, the practicability of such best management being demonstrated by experiment, though it were but by a single experiment, what should hinder it from becoming universal? With the good and the bad before them, equally practicable and equally practised, what should lead men to

[1] See Essay III, 'Collateral Uses derivable from a system of Industry Houses', pp. 66–140 below.

[2] Bentham's allusion may be to his writings on the panopticon penitentiary, although no such assertion appears therein: see *Panopticon: or The Inspection-House. Containing the Idea of a New Principle of Construction applicable to any Sort of Establishment, in which Persons of any Description are to be kept under Inspection*, 3 vols., Dublin and London, 1791, and reissued at London in 1812 (Bowring, iv. 37–172).

[3] Rumford was employed by Karl Teodor (1724–99), Elector of Bavaria 1777–99, between 1784 and 1795 in various public services, with special reference to military affairs. Having decided to utilise the army to clear the country of beggars, on 1 January 1790 Rumford organized the rounding up and detention in a military workhouse of all the beggars in Munich. Over the ensuing four years some 10,000 beggars were arrested and detained. In the workhouse the able-bodied were put to work, chiefly in the production of clothing for the army. Unconditional relief was provided to persons unable to work, and Rumford indicates that the system produced a net profit of 100,000 florins during its first six years. See Thompson, *Essays, Political, Economical and Philosophical*, i. 1–112.

choose the bad? While some were taking the good course, others, it is true, were taking a bad one—but how happened it? For want of their knowing *that* others were taking, and *how* others were taking, a *better*.—I suppose all the while (what can not but be supposed), that the operations of every part of the establishment will regularly be made public, and the statement of them digested into such a form, as shall present them, in the most instructive manner, to the observation of all those who are concerned to turn the information to account. Emulation will by that means naturally incline, and authority may, if necessary, engage each local branch of the establishment to pursue, in relation to each branch of the management, that mode of practice the superiority of which in point of advantage has been demonstrated by experience.

The mode of calculation by *averages*, would, on such an occasion, be equally discouraging and delusive. In a certain Poor house, the daily expence of diet has amounted (say) to 9^{d} a day: be it so: be it the same in a hundred Poor houses. But under Count Rumford's plan of management the diet of an equal number of persons, having equal wants, and maintained in an equal degree of health and strength, amounted but to 2^{d} a day.[1] Would 9^{d} be the fair sample of the expence? Would even $5\frac{1}{2}^{d}$ (the average) be a fair sample?—By no means: 2^{d}, and no more than 2^{d}, is the true mark.

In a certain Poor house, the earnings of the inhabitants (such of them included as were employ'd in spinning) never amounted to so much (say) as 1^{d} a day, upon an average: be it so: and be it the same in a hundred Poor houses. But in the year 1790, in the District of Lindsey in Lincolnshire, 112 children, chiefly females, being all that were tried, their ages not exceeding upon an average 11 years and 11 months, earned for two months together, at spinning the sort of worsted called Jersey, each of them, upon an average, $5\frac{1}{2}^{[d]}$ a day: and as the rate had, for five years that the experiment had been tried, been upon the encrease, beginning at 4^{d}, and this last of the five years had encreased from 5^{d} to $5\frac{1}{2}^{[d]}$, the average age being the same, call it then, in round numbers, for children of 12 year[s] old, 6^{d}.[2]

[1] Rumford does not appear to mention a figure of 2^{d} for daily maintenance of the poor under his management. Bentham may have taken this figure from Rumford's discussion of the maintenance of Bavarian soldiers, in comparison with whom, Rumford stresses, the poor could be fed very cheaply: see ibid., i. 229, 242–4, and p. 62 n. above.

[2] See *An Account of the Origin, Proceedings, and Intentions of the Society for the Promotion of Industry, in the Southern District of the Parts of Lindsey, in the County of Lincoln*, 3rd edn., London, [1789], p. 89. The Society for the Promotion of Industry was established in 1783, with the aim of raising funds by subscription for the establishment of schools to teach knitting and the spinning of jersey to children, particularly those of the dependent poor. For two months of every year, 'candidates' would have their output measured, and 'premiums' of clothing were distributed to 'such children, of certain ages and descriptions, within the said district, as in a

Under these circumstances, would 1^{d} a day be a fair sample of the rate of earnings that may be expected to be made by children of that age? Would even $3\frac{1}{2}^{d}$ (the average between 1^{d} and 6^{d})?—No surely: 6^{d}, and not less than 6^{d}, is what ought to be set down as the least amount that may reasonably be expected, as far as the demand for that sort of work extends, from children of that age.

given time shall have produced the greatest quantity of work of different kinds, and of the best quality'. Cash premiums were made available to consistent winners, to be paid over in case of apprenticeship or marriage (ibid., pp. 5–6).

ESSAY III
COLLATERAL USES DERIVABLE FROM A SYSTEM OF INDUSTRY HOUSES

Introduction

When a service is fixed upon, for the sake of which the expence of an establishment, edificial and official, is thought fit to be incurred, a door is oftentimes opened to a provision for a multitude of other services, which, not being separately capable of paying for the expence, could not with propriety have received a separate establishment. The art of multiplying establishments, with or without service, has been cultivated (it has been frequently said) with no inconsiderable degree of attention and success: to speak in the same strain, the opposite art, the art of multiplying services, of grafting many services upon one establishment, may one day perhaps be thought to have a claim to notice.

In point of principle at least, whatsoever may become of practice, it will hardly be denied, that wherever the burthen of an establishment is imposed upon a nation, it ought to be turned to as good an account as possible in the way of use, and as great a body of service as possible extracted from it in all shapes.

Such is the principle, which has suggested a variety of collateral uses, as being capable of being derived from a regular system of Industry Houses, spread over the face of the Country with tolerable regularity, in form of a piece of *net-work*, if the expression may be allowed (the semblance of a *chain* being inadequate), none of them too small to be susceptible of the best management,[a] nor yet so large as to be separated, any of them, from that which is next to it, by too great a distance.[b]

[a] The advantages possessed by management upon a large scale, in comparison of management upon a small scale, are stated in another place.[1]

[b] What distance would be the most commodious, all circumstances considered, and within what limits a variation in point of distance may be reconcilable with the general plan of convenience, are questions considered in another place.[2]

Say, in round numbers:

Counties in England and Wales (52)	50
Parishes and Parish-like rateable districts (14,649)	15,000
Parishes to an Industry House	75
Industry Houses for England and Wales	200

[1] See pp. 187–90 below.

[2] See p. 145 n. below.

The list of these uses may, for the greater facility of conception, be distributed in the first place into four groups, distinguished according to the nature of the additional benefit which the principal institution may in each case be made to yield: the first, *pecuniary*, having respect to the money concerns of the Poor: the second, *itinerary*, having respect to the need they may have, either of their own choice, or by appointment of law, to migrate from place to place: the third, *medical*, having respect to the aids of different sorts that might be grafted with advantage upon the provision which in every establishment for the relief of the Poor must be made for medical assistance: the fourth, *institutional*, having respect to the provision that in every district must be made in the way of *education* for such of the Poor who, through non-age standing in need of guardianship, and through misfortune finding themselves destitute of *natural* Guardians, are placed by necessity under the guardianship of the state.

For the purpose of these several collateral uses, I suppose the plan of management for each Industry House adequate in all points to its professed and principal object. This I require, and this is all that I require: for in what degree soever it is adapted to such principal object, in the same degree it will be found to be well adapted to every one of the collateral objects which I shall propose to graft upon it.

I suppose, in consequence, the existence of a *central Office*, situated of course in the Metropolis, to and from which, communications of all kinds shall be made, from and to the several Industry Houses all over the Kingdom: an Office that shall receive from the several local establishments periodical, and frequent (suppose weekly), Accounts of all pecuniary transactions, and Reports, equally regular and frequent, of all other transactions from which practical inferences with a view to political practice, legislative or administrative, may appear deducible: to the end that abstracts of such Accounts and Reports may be periodically published (annually suppose), for the information of the legislature, and the public at large. This office (merely because, in order to be spoken of, a thing must have a name, and without attaching any importance to the name) I stile for the occasion, the office of *General Inspection* in relation to the Poor, and the Chief person in it, the *Inspector-General* of the Poor.

I suppose in consequence in every such Industry House a regular set of *Books* of both kinds, kept every where upon one and the same plan, in which accounts shall be kept, and entries of transactions made under a set of heads furnished from the Office.

I suppose moreover, in every Industry House, some one person, intrusted with the management in chief, to whom (under the necessity of finding a name by which to speak of him, and, though it be not unconformable to usage, without meaning to attach any importance to the name) I give the appellation of *Governor*.

This Governor, I suppose invested with the requisite degree of trust-worthiness in general, and pecuniary trust-worthiness in particular, by means of the known and approved expedients commonly employ'd for such purposes, to wit one, or more, or all of them, as shall be deemed advisable. I mean proper *nomination*, pecuniary *security*, principal or collateral or both, and, if necessary, pecuniary qualification: and the state of the money committed to his charge so regulated, as that the sum total of those moneys at any one time in his hands, shall never exceed, or never exceed more than in a certain proportion, or never equal, but at the utmost want so much at least of equalling, the amount of the sum for which he shall have given security, as aforesaid.

And moreover that, whatever be the sum thought necessary to be lodged or left in his hands at the commencement of any given period, on the presumption of its equalling the utmost probable amount of the demands (as well fixed as contingent) expectable during that period, the hands of the Governor shall be regularly emptied of all moneys above such fixed sum, by periodical remittances (suppose *weekly* according to the practice in other cases) made to the central office.

Lastly, I suppose, attached to each Industry House, two other Officers, the one for *spiritual*, the other for *medical* assistance, in all its branches, stiled respectively the *Chaplain* and the *Surgeon*, whose whole time shall be considered as devoted to the discharge of their respective Duties.[a]

I now proceed to the statement of the several collateral uses proposed as derivable from the system of principal establishments, beginning with those of a pecuniary nature.

[a] It is among the imperfections of the language, not to possess any denomination, comprized in the compass of a single word, capable of expressing without ambiguity the profession of him who undertakes to render medical assistance in all its branches, viz: the branches respectively professed by the Physician, the Surgeon, the Apothecary and the Midwife, and who, by using a compound appellative, might be stiled the *Medical Curator*. On board a ship, the official name of the Medical Curator is the Surgeon: and he is expected to exercise, besides the functions which his name imports, those of the Physician and the Apothecary, since there is nobody else to execute them. So in country places, the general name of the Medical Curator who embraces the profession in all its branches is the *Surgeon*, stiled frequently, perhaps most frequently, among the lower classes, the *Doctor*, as if his business were to *teach*.

§ I. *First Division of the Collateral Uses that might be made of the system of Industry Houses: Uses Pecuniary*

1. *Collateral use the 1st*—Poor Man's Loan Office.

The governor of each Industry House, with the privity and assistance of the Chaplain, might be empowered and required to lend money upon pledges, to the Independent Poor[a] of the descriptions meant to be favoured in this particular (Labourers in husbandry for example) at rates inferior to those allowed to be taken by private Pawnbrokers. Preventing indigence is still better than relieving it: especially where, as here, the prevention may be altogether unattended by expence.

That an establishment of this nature would be of great use where there happens to be no Pawnbroker already established at the place where the Industry House comes to be erected, is evident at first sight.

But perhaps the same opportunity might afford a means of trying whether a branch of business, of so much importance to the Poor, might not be conducted every where on terms of less burthen to them than those on which it is carried on at present by private Pawnbrokers.[b] In this way of business the rate of profit is very

[a] By the Independent Poor, I mean, on this occasion, the Poor not provided for in any Industry House, nor otherwise maintained at the public charge.

[b] In the early part of the present century, an establishment for similar purposes, professing charity and aiming at profit, was set up by a Joint-Stock Company, who got themselves incorporated, under the name of the *Charitable Corporation*. One Office only was set up, and that in London: it took pledges of the highest value, and consequently from the most opulent class of borrowers. Gold and diamonds poured into it in profusion. Property was collected, in masses capable of furnishing an adequate temptation to the highest class of plunderers. It was trusted to bad hands, and without security, or with insufficient security, and embezzled. The history of the business is extant among the Reports of the House of Commons.[1] Thus expired the system of secure and unexpensive charity in this country, and has never since been attempted to be revived.

The circumstances to which this experiment owed its failure had no more to do with the nature of the subject matter, or the object, real or professed, than water had, or fire. Had the office and the goods been burnt, or swept away by an inundation, the water or the fire would have afforded as good a proof of the incompetency of the

[1] The Charitable Corporation for the relief of industrious poor by assisting them with small sums upon pledges at legal interest was established in 1699 and incorporated by Charter in 1707 with a capital of £20,000, a sum which by 1730 had increased to £600,000. In February 1731 the proprietors and creditors of the company separately petitioned the House of Commons to investigate alleged fraud in its management, both the warehouse-keeper and the cashier having absconded. The investigation revealed a loss of £453,745. 1s. 9¼d. See *Commons Sessional Papers of the Eighteenth Century*, xiv. 1–581.

high:[a] and the fixation by law, designed, as it may have been, in part, to prevent it from being raised (to wit in an arbitrary manner in proportion to the pressure of the exigency),[b] seems also to have

establishment, as is to be drawn from the embezzlement of the stock contained in it. Were the possible embezzlement of the fund destined for the service an objection to any one service, it would be an objection against every other: it would be an objection to the whole of government. Against embezzlement on the part of the lowest class, on the part of those who have neither property nor character to lose, there are no remedies but eyes and doors. Against embezzlement on the part of persons who have either property, or character sufficient to find responsible securities, there are remedies, which, though of a more refined nature, are sufficiently well known and sufficiently effectual, where it is thought proper to turn them to account.

[a] 20 per cent per annum: and nothing less than a month's interest accepted, although the money should not have been outlying for a day.[1]

[b] I say '*may have been*', and '*in part*': for the interests of the Pawnbrokers are the interests, and the only interests, which it is the professed object of the Act of the 24th of the King, Ch. 42 (the Act which forms the groundwork of the existing system of regulations with regard to Pawnbrokers, and the only Act of the reign which enters into any explanation of its views) to protect: viz: against a species of oppression that it seems had been exercised upon them by Judges and Juries, at the instance of the borrowers. 'And whereas several tenders of money,' (says the Act) 'for principal and interest of money lent, and warehouse room of goods pledged, lately made for the redemption of goods pledged to Pawnbrokers, the amount of which interest and charges for warehouse room, so tendered, hath been much below the amount of the usual and customary interest and charges for Warehouse room taken by Pawnbrokers in the said Trade, and at a rate much below the necessary expences thereof, have lately been considered to be sufficient, and verdicts have been obtained by persons making such Tenders as aforesaid, against the Pawnbrokers; and if the said business should be carried on agreeably to such Verdicts, the profits arising thereform would be so much reduced as to be insufficient to afford an adequate maintenance to the Pawnbroker.'[2] So far the preamble—then follows the enacting part.

Compare now the English Laws in favour of *Pawnbroking* with the Laws against the offence of imaginary malignity called *usury*.—From the man of opulence, whose sole motive for borrowing is the prospect, perhaps the certainty, of adding to his opulence, and who offers no security but *personal*, you must not take so much as six per cent. From the man of misery, who borrows but to save himself from starving, and who gives *real* security, of the best and surest kind, into your own hands, and, according to your own estimates, to much more than the value, you may take as far as 20 per cent, and nobody takes less. See the *Defence of Usury*.[3]

---

[1] See 24 Geo. III, c.42, §I (1784), where regulations prescribing the interest chargeable by pawnbrokers are set out, the minimum rate being equal to twenty per cent per year.

[2] See 24 Geo. III, c.42, preamble. There are some minor inaccuracies in Bentham's rendering of this passage.

[3] See *Defence of Usury; shewing the Impolicy of the Present Legal Restraints on the Terms of Pecuniary Bargains*, London, 1787 (Bowring, iii. 1–29), especially 'Letter VIII. Virtual Usury Allowed' (Bowring, iii. 12–14). Instead of the twenty per cent mentioned here, however, Bentham, writing from Russia, indicated that he could not remember the rate commonly charged by pawnbrokers in England, and estimated it at 'a good deal more' than twelve per cent.

operated, with or without the concurrence of other causes, to the effect of preventing it from being depressed so low as the competition might otherwise have depressed it.

In such a situation at least, six per cent by the year, half per cent by the Calendar Month, promises to be a rate quite sufficient to cover all charges.

Taken by itself the principal, if not only, objection, though that perhaps a conclusive one, against the setting up an institution of this kind on the public account, would be the necessity of an establishment, edificial and official, set on foot at the public expence, and consequently upon a scale of less frugality than that which is naturally adopted by private undertakers, and that too, before any assurance of advantage could be obtained. But, on the present supposition, almost all the expence that is necessary would already have been incurred for other purposes—Under-Agents, Presiding Agent, a system of economy, and a system of general superintendence: House-room, if it could not be provided altogether without expence (for instance by applying occasionally to this use a portion of room which might otherwise have been provided with a view to other uses, with which it would not interfere), might at any rate be provided for by an inconsiderable addition to the mass of building that would otherwise have been erected. As to Under-Agents, they might be found equal to such a business among such of the Inmates whose infirmities rendered them less fit for employments of a more active nature. And, where a particular Industry House happened not to afford a person possessed of the requisite qualifications, such a person might be obtained from some other Industry House, and, by means of slight improvement in his situation, with his own consent.

Under these advantages at least, six per cent per annum is the rate of interest which I have ventured to state as the rate at which, in such a situation, a branch of business that, with a view to the object in question, relief to indigence, might perhaps even warrant some expence, might however be conducted without any expence. Five per cent is the rate which people are content to take without any real security. The same rate people would naturally be still more content to take with the benefit of real security, and that of the best and surest kind: and where other charges, as we see, are struck off, it seems hard to say that one per cent, or indeed much less, would not be enough to pay the interest of money laid out in warehouse-room.

At an inferior rate of interest, if I am not much misinformed, the business is carried on, and that without expence, although without the benefit of any such advantages as above mentioned, in foreign countries.[a] Meantime, at whatever rate of interest money is lent in any foreign country, unless Holland be an exception, it seems not easy to say that it might not be but at a rate equally low in this country. I know of no country, Holland excepted, in which capital is

[a] At Paris, while France was France, money (I have been assured) used to be lent upon pledges, under a government establishment, at the rate of 5 per Cent per annum, and no more, in certain cases, with the addition of $\frac{1}{2}$ per Cent, and no more, in other cases. This $\frac{1}{2}$ per Cent, and no more, served to defray the expence of management, House and Warehouse room included. The capital was supplied by government, and though without profit, since 5 per Cent was but little if any thing more than the common rate of interest which might be made without any trouble of management, yet without loss.[1]

At Rome, and other towns in Italy, I have heard it frequently said by Travellers who received their information on the spot, and have even read as much in books which I know not at present how to refer to, the business is conducted upon terms still more favourable.[2]

At Hamburgh, (if we may depend upon a work, now not very modern, but in its day of some account, having been compiled by government and printed for the sole use of government in France) in Hamburgh, Pawnlending, though performed at so low a rate of interest as 6 per cent, is reckoned among the sources of revenue: producing to the government an annual profit amounting in those days to 150,000 *ecus*, whatever may have been meant by *ecus*. Before government took this branch of trade into its own hands, the common rate of profit made by private dealers had been (it is there stated), between 60 and 80 per cent. See *Memoirs concernant les Impositions et Droits en Europe*, 4 Vol. in 4to à Paris Imprimerie Royale, 1768, Vol. 1, Art. —*Hambourg*.[3]

Enquiring of persons connected with Hamburgh, I am told that the establishment still continues, and upon these same terms.

At *Petersburgh*, money is lent, in the same way, on government account, on terms *nominally* the *same* as at Hamburgh, but still *lower* in *effect*: for at Petersburgh, *6* per cent is the *common* rate. The pledges being *forfeitable*, as with us, a *profit* is afforded, *even* at that *common* rate: and for the sake of this profit, individuals join with government and take shares.[4]

---

[1] Bentham is probably referring to the *Mont-de-Piété*, the pawn shop established in Paris by Royal Patent on 9 December 1777. However, while this institution paid interest at five per cent to depositors, it charged interest on loans advanced on pledges at ten per cent.

[2] Bentham's source may have been the work of Antonio Genovesi (1713–69), philosopher and political economist, and in particular *Lezioni di Commercio o sia d'Economia Civile* (first published at Naples in 1766–7), 2 vols., Bassano, 1769. According to *Lezioni di Commercio*, ii. 166, the rate of interest charged by the pawnshops, *Monti di pietà*, established by the Franciscan order towards the close of the fifteenth century, had settled at three per cent. The work had been recommended to Bentham by John Symonds (1730–1807), Professor of Modern History at Cambridge from 1771, who had lived in Italy, and to whom Bentham had written in 1785 asking for advice on literature about Italian political economy: see *The Correspondence of Jeremy Bentham*, vol. iii, ed. I.R. Christie, London, 1971 (*CW*), p. 324.

[3] See Jean-Louis Moreau de Beaumont, *Mémoires concernant les impositions et droits en Europe*, 4 vols., Paris, 1768, i. 73. Adam Smith indicates that the sum of 150,000 ecus was equivalent to £33,750: see *The Wealth of Nations*, ii. 820.

[4] Bentham's reference is to the Loan Fund (*Ssudnaia kazna*), or pawn shop, of the State Orphanage (*Vospitatel'nye doma*) in St Petersburg, which made loans of up to 1,000 roubles on pledges of jewellery and precious metals at 6 per cent interest.

ordinarily more plentiful, or the general rate of interest paid for it lower, than it is here.

Whether, in other places, the business might, in the nature of it, be conducted with advantage to the customers by private Pawnbrokers, on any and what lower terms than the 20 per cent they are allowed to take at present, is a question I pass by as foreign to the subject.

The rate here proposed as an experimental rate might be adopted with the less hesitation since, should the choice prove to be founded on error, nothing can be easier, or speedier, or attended with less inconvenience, than the correction might be. In a word, whatever were the terms pitched upon by government as the properest terms on which to deal with the indigent in this way, the mode of dealing might, at all times, and without difficulty, be adjusted to those terms. Let the determination, for example, be neither to take profit, nor to be at any expence. Then, supposing it to turn out upon experience that six per cent, the rate here proposed, should be attended with a profit of 1 per cent, an abatement of the 1 per cent might, at any time, be made. So, on the other hand, if that rate were found to be attended with a loss, and the amount of the loss ascertained, then the rate might be raised to the exact amount of the loss, without being screwed up to any higher pitch.[a]

The same species of unexpensive charity might be extended to the

After this, think of the *English* Pawnbrokers, and the *impossibility* they are under of '*continuing their business*'[1] without 20 per Cent.

[a] Pawnbroking on public account has been proposed as an expedient of Finance. In that character there appear to be few expedients less competent. As far as it is a resource it is a tax: and as far as it is a tax, it is a tax upon distress. It seems to stand next in the order of incompetency to taxes upon Medical Drugs, and taxes upon Justice (See *Protest against Law-Taxes*, 1796).[2] But, as an appendage to the system of

---

[1] Bentham appears to be paraphrasing the conclusion of his quotation from the preamble to 24 Geo. III, c.42, to the effect that interest charges below twenty per cent would be 'insufficient to afford an adequate Maintenance for the Pawnbroker'.

[2] 'A Protest against Law Taxes' was printed in Dublin in 1793, but was not published as a discrete work during Bentham's lifetime. It was first published together with 'Supply without Burthen' in 1795, not 1796 as Bentham states: see *Supply without Burthen; or Escheat vice Taxation: being a Proposal for a Saving in Taxes by an Extension of the Law of Escheat: including Strictures on the Taxes on Collateral Succession, comprized in the Budget of 7th Dec. 1795. To which is prefixed, (Printed in 1793, and now first published,) A Protest against Law Taxes: Shewing the Peculiar Mischievousness of all such Impositions as add to the Expense of An Appeal to Justice*, London, 1795 (Bowring, ii. 573–83). The taxes on medical drugs which Bentham has in mind are probably the stamp duties imposed by 25 Geo. III, c.79, §II (1785), 'upon every Packet, Box, Bottle, Phial or other Inclosure containing any Drugs, Oils, Waters, Essences, Tinctures, Powders, or other Preparation or Composition whatsoever, used or applied, or to be used or applied, externally or internally, as Medicines or Medicaments for the Prevention, Cure, or Relief of any Disorder or Complaint incident to, or in any wise affecting the Human Body, which shall be uttered or vended in *Great Britain*'. The duty varied according to the cost of the medicine, and could be in excess of twenty per cent.

case of Mortgages. A man can neither eat his House, nor carry it to market. He may be owner of the Cottage he lives in, or of property to a much superior amount, and yet be in a state of extreme distress for want of the necessaries of life. A few pounds, or even a few shillings, advanced in time, might set him at his ease, but the hand to advance them is not always to be found. Indeed upon such security, in the present state of things, it never is or can be to be found: for into the value of an estate of 20[s], 30[s] or 40[s] a year, the law charges attending a single act of incumbrance would cut so deep, and the repetition of the process, besides being scarcely practicable in such an instance, would be so compleatly ruinous, that where an estate of any such dimensions is once broke in upon, the best economy is to borrow as much upon it at once as is to be had, or, what would be still better, part with it outright.[a]

Industry Houses, I see nothing that should hinder its being made use of as an instrument in the hand of Charity.

Nor yet does it follow, that because a profit thus levied upon a distress would, in the hands of government, or in any hands, be, in itself, a bad species of profit, therefore the institution of a system of loan offices on public account, even independently of the Industry Houses in question, would, with reference to the *existing* order of things, be a bad measure. The rate of profit taken by individuals, as above stated, is 20 per cent. Suppose Government, or a Company, could carry on the business without loss at 5 per cent, but for the sake of a profit, took 5 per cent more. This taking of this extra 5 per cent would be bad, with reference to the *best possible* order of things in this behalf, that, by the supposition, *might* be established: but it would be a prodigious improvement, with reference to the order of things actually established. To exaggerate nothing, to look perpetually on both sides, on both with equal impartiality, and on both sides to be sure to take the whole list of influencing considerations into the account, such is the memento which the legislator ought on every occasion to have present to his view, and which, in no part of his field of action, has a stronger claim to attention, or is more apt to be unattended to, than that of political economy.

[a] Suppose a man's Cottage to be worth 30[s] a year, and that he wants a guinea upon it, which is more (suppose) than his remaining stock of moveables could be sold for. He has therefore, no means of securing the repayment of it, except his house: but were he to execute a mortgage of his house, drawn up by an Attorney in the usual stile, and borrow the guinea upon it, and no more, payable in a year, it would be a dearer business to him, than if, on personal security, he had paid interest for the same sum at the rate of some hundred per cent. For, under the existing structure of the laws, it is not one of the least misfortunes attending the condition of the poor, that the burthen of law-charges of all sorts, as well as so many other legal burthens, having a ***minimum*** below which it can never fall, presses upon the individual in a *ratio* increasing more and more in the direct ratio of his poverty, that is in the inverse ratio of his ability to bear the burthen. See *Protest against Law Taxes* (by the Author), 1796.[1] Were a man who had occasion for £10,000 upon a mortgage obliged to pay

---

[1] See 'A Protest against Law Taxes', pp. 7–8 (Bowring, ii. 573): 'Were a three-penny stamp to be put upon every three-penny loaf, a man who had but three-pence to spend in bread, could no

When a Cottager applies to an Attorney to raise a pittance upon his Cottage, the part of the business to which the principal regard is paid must, in the nature of things, be the emolument of the Attorney, and the result, the converting the scratch made in the little property by misfortune, or mismanagement, into a fatal gangrene. Were the Governor of a House of Industry, under the controul of his superiors in office, empowered to administer the relief on the footing of charity, it would of course be administered only in as far as it were wanted, and in as small sums, and those, within the limits of the value, repeated as often as it were wanted. Were the burthen of the Stamp duties taken off, in the instance of money not exceeding a certain sum in the whole thus advanced, to a person of a description intended to be thus favoured (suppose a labourer in Husbandry), and intelligible forms, gutted of learned garbage, provided by the Act, the exigencies

[£1,000][1] to his lawyer, or a tenth part of the money, the hardship would be deemed intolerable. A Cottager in the like circumstances is actually obliged to pay in much larger proportion to the same quarter, and nobody has stated the grievance as worth remedying.

I have, in the publication already referred to, had occasion to show how the poor of this country, that is to say, by many times the greater number of the inhabitants of this, as of every other country, are kept in most respects in a state of perpetual outlawry,[2] partly for the supposed benefit of the public, by the insensibility of the man of finance, partly by the insensibility, or incapacity, or policy, or all together, of the man of law, and at any rate for the real benefit of the misery-making and nonsense-manufacturing profession, whose most valuable property consists in the unintelligibility and worthlessness of its own works. Happy the man of humanity, who, on any occasion, or on any pretence, can, in favour of any class of subjects, however inconsiderable, succeed in procuring this outlawry to be reversed! By the enlightened humanity of men now in office, it has already been reversed to certain purposes, in favour of the contributors to the Societies called *Friendly Societies*.[3]

longer indeed get a three-penny loaf, but an obliging baker could cut him out the half of one. A tax on justice admits of no such retrenchment. The most obliging stationer could not cut a man out half a *latitat* nor half a *declaration*. Half justice, where it is to be had, is better than no justice: but without buying the whole weight of paper, there is no getting a grain of justice.'

[1] MS '£10,000'.

[2] See 'A Protest against Law Taxes', pp. 12–13 (Bowring, ii. 574).

[3] Bentham's reference is to William Pitt, and especially to George Rose (1744–1818), statesman, MP for Launceston 1784–8, Lymington 1788–90, and Christchurch 1790–1818, Secretary to the Treasury 1782–3, 1783–1801, Vice-President of the Board of Trade 1804–6, 1807–12, Treasurer of the Navy 1807–18. Rose was the architect of 33 Geo. III, c.54 (1793), which gave legal recognition to Friendly Societies, and included several provisions in favour of their members with regard to legal charges. By § IV, the sureties required to be lodged by their officers with the Clerk of the Peace were exempted from stamp duty; § IX laid down that any legal proceedings arising from neglect or corruption on the part of those officers would be exempted from stamp duty, and that no legal fees should be charged in relation to any such proceedings; and § XVII exempted persons holding certificates of membership of Friendly Societies from removal under the laws of settlement until they actually became chargeable.

of this description of the Poor might thus be relieved by shillings at a time, as alms would be given, but without expence to the founders of a charity thus unsusceptible of abuse.

As to the *title*, in these minute concerns it will of course be *comparatively* short and simple: and there are probably few counties in England that would not furnish more than one man of legal education, retired from 'the indiscriminate defence of right and wrong',[1] to the honourable condition of a country gentleman, who would be equally able and willing to bestow the assistance of his science to this branch of the national charity, upon congenial terms.

The small capital, which, in each District, would be necessary for this purpose, might be furnished either out of the public treasury, or out of the same fund out of which the rest of the expence of the Industry System came to be provided for; the parish rates for example, as at present.

But before any application were made of the produce of compulsory taxation to this purpose, the mode of voluntary subscription might, it should seem, as well be tried. Five per cent, when regarded as well secured, is, even when money is at the scarcest, looked upon as sufficient interest for money lent by individuals to a local division of the public, as in the case of Roads, Canals, Bridges, and the like. The expectation of a dividend in any the smallest degree exceeding this rate of interest would add the inducement of profit to that of charity, and the completion of a set of subscriptions for this purpose, in extent covering the whole kingdom, and in quantity adequate to the purpose, might, morally speaking, be regarded as infallible. But the principle of pure, though unexpensive, charity, might, it should seem, as well be tried in the first instance, partly as being unexpensive to the public, partly lest those to whom considerations of pure charity would have afforded an adequate inducement should be excluded from the service by the imputation of the less honourable motive. If, in any particular district, the circumstances and dispositions of the inhabitants happened not to afford a stock of superfluous capital altogether adequate, the deficiency might easily be supplied by the contributions from other quarters, where capital was more abundant and disposition more favourable.

The business of Pawnbroking thus ennobled by its object, thus purified of all those accidental concomitants, which have had the

[1] The expression is taken from a letter by Junius, a pseudonymous polemical writer, addressed to William Murray Mansfield (1705–93), Chief Justice of King's Bench 1756–88, and first published in the *Public Advertiser* on 21 January, 1772. See *The Letters of Junius*, ed. J. Cannon, Oxford, 1978, p. 323: 'The indiscriminate Defence of Right and Wrong contracts the Understanding, while it corrupts the Heart.'

effect of attaching to it the idea of disrepute, there would remain nothing in it but the exercise of one of the noblest functions of man, the distribution of charity, and that upon terms of the clearest and most unexceptionable beneficence. It would be an office fit for the cleanest and best respected hands. The Chaplain of the House, with or without an Assistant of his own order, might undertake for that part of the duty in the discharge of which the powers of the head and of the heart were concerned: subordinate hands, I have already ventured to pronounce,[1] and hands which, though fit for this purpose, would for almost any other be almost useless, could never be wanting in such a House.

The whole expence of this part of the institution, whatever it amounted to, might be predetermined and foreknown. Whatever were the quantum of salary pitched upon in the first instance as likely to be sufficient, experiment would shew whether, as such, it found persons deemed competent to the trust to accept it.[a]

Still more might even be done for the relief of the indigent in the way of loan, taking the necessary precautions. Cases may exist, where misfortune may have left a man nothing to pledge, or nothing that he could spare, without plunging still deeper into distress, at the same time that his character might, in the estimation of those to whom the opportunities of being acquainted with it have presented themselves, warrant the trusting him without pledge to the amount of his demand. To trust the stewards of the public money with the power of disposing of it upon such grounds would, however, be a confidence too pregnant with abuse, and, as such, reprobated by the positions already laid down as fundamental ones.[b] But, if any individuals, to save themselves the trouble of being the dispensers of

[a] Suppose £2,000 to be, in a given District, the quantum of capital thought proper to be received in the way of subscription for this purpose. One per cent upon this capital would amount to a hundred a year:[2] an income which, when added to the advantage of Lodging, and other inexpensive perquisites, would, to many a respectable Clergyman, be, in comparison of his present situation, opulence. This one per cent, added to the 5 per cent paid as interest to the Subscribers, makes 6 per cent: which being deducted from the present rate of Pawnbroker's profit, 20 per cent, leaves the saving to the indigent, 14 per cent, more in all cases than $\frac{2}{3}$ of the present charge, and where the money is wanted for less than a month, perhaps some numbers of times more.

[b] See B.1., Ch. 1., §VII.[3]

[1] See p. 71 above.

[2] Bentham is mistaken in his calculation: 1 per cent upon a capital of £2,000 would provide an income of only £20 a year.

[3] i.e. §VII of 'Fundamental Positions with regard to the making provision for the Indigent Poor': see pp. 50–1 above.

their own charity, should think fit to intrust, each of them, what he thought fit to allot to such purposes, with the Governor of the House, the Chaplain, or other Manager of the Loan fund, it should seem that, to the adoption of a mode of relief so clear of all danger of profusion and abuse, there could be no objection.

The use of the intervention of public authority in the business would be this. The title to relief, on the part of the person applying for it, might thus be made a subject of official, and regulated investigation: the enquiry would be performed by hands practised, and known to be practised, in the business: the knowledge of the difficulty of passing a false tale would serve to keep off impostors. The registration of the loan upon the books of the House, and of the observance or breach of the conditions of it, on the part of the Borrower, would be a check upon unpunctuality, and such a check as the nature of the case does not afford in the instance of a similar transaction between an indigent borrower and a private lender. In a word, the effect of this part of the Charitable-loan plan, would be the enabling a man who has a character, and nothing else, *to pledge his character*.

Of sums thus meant to be considered as *lent*, not *given*, the repayment would naturally be stipulated for in the way of *instalments*, according to the notion formed of the probable resources of the borrower. Printed Forms for this purpose would of course be provided: and the instruments exempted from stamp-duties.[a]

2. *Collateral use the second—Applying each Industry House to the purpose of what might be termed a* Poor Man's Bank.

The Governor to keep a Bank of receipt and deposit, receiving money in small sums from all persons of certain descriptions (Labourers in Husbandry, for example), coming with money in their hands, desiring him to receive and keep it for them.

The money to be returned to the depositor or his order, upon demand, but subject to certain conditions and restrictions, just

[a] For, of him who has nothing, nothing can be had: charity, especially so well directed, is not so abundant a commodity as to be a fit object of taxation: and, by such an exemption, nothing would be lost to the revenue; since if this unexpensive species of security were not allowed of, no security would be taken at all. Indeed the transaction, as thus described, would naturally be exempt from stamp duties, even without the appointment of the legislature. For, from a man who has nothing but character to pledge, the security afforded by the powers of legal process would not often be worth taking: and if it were, the books of the House, though unstamped, and thence unreceivable as evidence of themselves, would serve to fix the memory of whoever was privy to the transaction entered on them, and thus, in most cases at least, give sufficient stability to oral evidence.

sufficient to prevent the privilege from being employ'd as an instrument of vexation, out of wantonness or spite.[a]

Were an interest to be allowed for the money so received, the inducement to deposit it would be so much the stronger: and were the rate of interest in a small degree inferior to the rate of the interest paid by government, the difference might defray the charges of management, which, in transactions of such minuteness, bear (in as far as concerns the quantity of time consumed) the greater ratio to the amount. But of the time thus employ'd, a great part, if not the whole, might, in such a Banking House, be a sort of time, which, if not so employ'd, would have possessed no value.[b]

The Public would of course stand as collateral security for its agents, the Governors, to the customers of this system of petty Banks. It need not grudge to do so, reaping on its own terms the benefit of the receipts, upon the principle of regular remittance presupposed in the Introductory Observations.[1]

The most beneficial application perhaps that could be made of an opportunity of this kind, as well as one of those which would be most likely to be made of it, is that of affording a means of laying up a capital for the purpose of facilitating the entrance [to], and providing with comfort for the exigencies of, the married state. The facility of forming a fund for this purpose, in the instance of even the very poorest class of labourers in this country, and that sufficient to place them in a state of comfortable and hitherto unexampled affluence, will appear from the following considerations. From the time a man marries, suppose at 25 (I speak always of the class of labourers in husbandry), or at any rate from the birth of the first child, a certain portion of his accustomed earnings must inevitably be turned aside from the business of administering to his own personal gratifications,

[a] A deduction, for example, to the amount of the smallest species of coin extant, as a half-penny, or a farthing. A farthing would pay for all the trouble, in as much as it is much more than the profit upon many a little shopping transaction that puts the shopkeeper to more trouble.

Were it required, as a further condition, that two successive applications should be made at not less than—say a week's distance—this condition would be attended with a different use, that of affording time for reflection, of which farther on.[2]

[b] A plan might be produced, were it worth while, by means of which the business might, in such a place, be carried on with perfect regularity, and without risk, by the most ignorant and even dishonest hands; one person only, capable of writing, and setting down sums in the roughest way, being employ'd, with the addition of an hour or two of the Chaplain's time at the end of the week, to look over the books. But a detail thus minute would probably, in this stage of the proposal, appear premature.

[1] See p. 67 above.

[2] See p. 85 & n. below.

to that of yielding the necessary support for his wife and family. At eighteen, let us say, he had begun to look towards marriage. From 18 to 25, is a period of 7 years. Had he, during that period, been possessed of the means of securing, and turning to account, what savings he might have found inducement to make, half the amount of the savings which, from the commencement of the matrimonial engagement or a year after, he finds himself obliged by necessity to make, would be sufficient to place him at that wished-for period in a state of comparative affluence.[a]

In process of time, under favour of the facility thus afforded to this species of thrift, a notion that may not unreasonably be expected to form itself, among persons of the class in question, is that of some certain sum, as a sum that a young couple, in that way of life, *ought* to be in possession of, before they engage in marriage. It may come to be disreputable, it may come to be regarded as a mark of improvidence, to set out with less: and the prudent virgin will say to her impatient suitor, ***no: but when you have saved up so much (mentioning***

[a] The following calculation may help to fix our conceptions with regard to the effect producible by the proposed institution in the present instance of the application of it.

	£ s d
Weekly earnings of a labourer in husbandry, upon an average of the year, according to the observations and calculations of the Rev[d] Mr. Davies in his *Case of the labourers in husbandry* (p. 8)	0. 8. 0
Weekly expences of a whole family consisting of Man, Wife, and 3 children (No. 4. p. 11) 6.11$\frac{1}{4}$, say	0. 7. 0
Deduct weekly expences of the Wife and 3 children together, which can not hardly be set at less than those of the Husband alone	0. 3. 6
Remains, for the weekly expences of the Husband alone	0. 3. 6
Add the weekly amount of the Husband's share of the annual expences (say £3.18) (ib. p. 15)[1]	0. 1. 6
Total weekly expence of a Man alone	0. 5. 0
Which, being deducted from his weekly earnings, leaves clear surplus	0. 3. 0
But the above supposed weekly amount of the Man's annual expences is, in the present case, too large, in as much as it supposes a Man, when single, to have a whole cottage to himself at £1.18[s], when, for Man Wife and children together, the rent is but £2: and that the single Man's yearly expence for fewel is as much as the whole expence of the family, 10[s]. On both these accounts together, add 4[s] a year, and, for the yearly amount of the saving of 3[s] a week, instead of £7–16[s] say, for the sake of round numbers	8. 0. 0
Half of that is	4. 0. 0
Which half, if saved up for 5 years amounts (exclusive of interest) to	20. 0. 0

[1] Davies estimates the annual expenses of a family, consisting of the cost of rent, fuel, clothing, lying-in, sickness, and burial, to be £7: see *Case of Labourers in Husbandry*, pp. 15–16. In the British Library copy (shelf-mark 8285. ff. 12. (1).), Bentham has noted in pencil: 'Man's share of maybe £4.'

the sum), then, and not till then, I am yours.—To surrender before the term will be a sort of confession of imprudence: an acknowledgement of the weakness of reason and the strength of appetite: a weakness similar in kind, however inferior in degree, to that which yields to the sollicitations of unhallowed love. To avoid it will become a point of honour: analogous to that which retards the impatient widow in her *flight* (as the Roman law phrases it)[1] towards succeeding marriage: and which, amongst our German ancestors, even in the enterprizing sex, restrained men from obeying the calls of desire for many years after power had attained its growth.[2]

The magnitude of the proportion which the suitor can prevail upon

Respective total amounts of $\frac{1}{8}$ and so on to $\frac{8}{8}$ of such weekly surplus, if accumulated during the respective periods of one, and so on to 7 years, commencing at 18, 19, or 20 years of age.[3]

Without Interest.

Proportions of Savings

Years	$\frac{1}{8}$	$\frac{2}{8}$	$\frac{3}{8}$	$\frac{4}{8}$	$\frac{5}{8}$	$\frac{6}{8}$	$\frac{7}{8}$	$\frac{8}{8}$
1	1	2	3	4	5	6	7	8
2	2	4	6	8	10	12	14	16
3	3	6	9	12	15	18	21	24
4	4	8	12	16	20	24	28	32
5	5	10	15	20	25	30	35	40
6	6	12	18	24	30	36	42	48
7	7	14	21	28	35	42	49	56

With Interest (Simple) at 3p$^{r.}$ cent.

Proportions of Savings

Years	$\frac{1}{8}$	$\frac{2}{8}$	$\frac{3}{8}$	$\frac{4}{8}$	$\frac{5}{8}$	$\frac{6}{8}$	$\frac{7}{8}$	$\frac{8}{8}$
1	d 7$\frac{1}{5}$	s d 1 .. 2$\frac{2}{5}$	s d 1 .. 9$\frac{3}{5}$	s d 2 .. 4$\frac{4}{5}$	s 3	s d 3 .. 7$\frac{1}{5}$	s d 4 .. 2$\frac{2}{5}$	s d 4 .. 9$\frac{3}{5}$
2	s d 1 .. 2$\frac{2}{5}$	s d 2 .. 4$\frac{4}{5}$	s d 3 .. 7$\frac{1}{5}$	s d 4 .. 9$\frac{3}{5}$	s 6	s d 7 .. 2$\frac{2}{5}$	s d 8 .. 4$\frac{4}{5}$	s d 9 .. 7$\frac{1}{5}$
3	s d 1 .. 9$\frac{3}{5}$	s d 3 .. 7$\frac{1}{5}$	s d 5 .. 4$\frac{4}{5}$	s d 7 .. 2$\frac{2}{5}$	s 9	s d 10 .. 9$\frac{3}{5}$	s d 12 .. 7$\frac{1}{5}$	s d 14 .. 4$\frac{4}{5}$
4	s d 2 .. 4$\frac{4}{5}$	s d 4 .. 9$\frac{3}{5}$	s d 7 .. 2$\frac{2}{5}$	s d 9 .. 7$\frac{1}{5}$	s 12	s d 14 .. 4$\frac{4}{5}$	s d 16 .. 9$\frac{3}{5}$	s d 19 .. 2$\frac{2}{5}$
5	s 3	s 6	s 9	s 12	s 15	s 18	£ s 1 .. 1	£ s 1 .. 4
6	s d 3 .. 7$\frac{1}{5}$	s d 7 .. 2$\frac{2}{5}$	s d 10 .. 9$\frac{3}{5}$	s d 14 .. 4$\frac{4}{5}$	s 18	£ s d 1 .. 1 .. 7$\frac{1}{5}$	£ s d 1 .. 5 .. 2$\frac{2}{5}$	£ s d 1 .. 8 .. 9$\frac{3}{5}$
7	s d 4 .. 2$\frac{2}{5}$	s d 8 .. 4$\frac{4}{5}$	s d 12 .. 7$\frac{1}{5}$	s d 16 .. 9$\frac{3}{5}$	s 21	£ s d 1 .. 5 .. 2$\frac{2}{5}$	£ s d 1 .. 9 .. 4$\frac{4}{5}$	£ s d 1 .. 13 .. 7$\frac{1}{5}$

[1] In late Roman law the term for a woman's remarrying is *convolare ad secundas nuptias*, i.e. 'to fly to a second marriage': see *Codex Justinianus*, v. xvii. 9.

[2] See Tacitus, *Germania*, xx. 3: *sera iuvenum venus, eoque inexhausta pubertas*, i.e. 'young men are slow to mate and their powers therefore are never exhausted'.

[3] The following tables have been collated from Bentham's drafts at UC cxxxiii. 38 and 40.

himself to devote, out of his earnings, to this object, for the purpose either of augmenting the comforts of the social state, or accelerating the approach of it, will be, and will be seen to be, a test and measure of his affection: it will be a sacrifice of selfish appetite upon the altar of virtuous love. An emulation of rivalship will thus take place between the suitors of the same woman, and of honour even between the suitors of different women: a contest analogous indeed, but analogous in the way of contrast, to those trials of brutal strength in which the degree of attachment to a mistress is measured by the quantity of liquor swallowed in her praise. It will be a wager which can drink least: which can show himself most frugal and most temperate, as well as most enamoured: and the willing fair will be the prize.

When, by this means, on his marriage, a man finds himself in possession of the sum necessary and sufficient, in his estimation, to provide with comfort for the exigencies attendant on that wished for

With Interest (Simple) at 4p[r.] cent.

Proportions of Savings

Years	$\frac{1}{8}$	$\frac{2}{8}$	$\frac{3}{8}$	$\frac{4}{8}$	$\frac{5}{8}$	$\frac{6}{8}$	$\frac{7}{8}$	$\frac{8}{8}$
1	d 9$\frac{3}{5}$	s d 1 .. 7$\frac{1}{5}$	s d 2 .. 4$\frac{4}{5}$	s d 3 .. 2$\frac{2}{5}$	s 4	s d 4 .. 9$\frac{3}{5}$	s d 5 .. 7$\frac{1}{5}$	s d 6 .. 4$\frac{4}{5}$
2	s d 1 .. 7$\frac{1}{5}$	s d 3 .. 2$\frac{2}{5}$	s d 4 .. 9$\frac{3}{5}$	s d 6 .. 4$\frac{4}{5}$	s 8	s d 9 .. 7$\frac{1}{5}$	s d 11 .. 2$\frac{2}{5}$	s d 12 .. 9$\frac{3}{5}$
3	s d 2 .. 4$\frac{4}{5}$	s d 4 .. 9$\frac{3}{5}$	s d 7 .. 2$\frac{2}{5}$	s d 9 .. 7$\frac{1}{5}$	s 12	s d 14 .. 4$\frac{4}{5}$	s d 16 .. 9$\frac{3}{5}$	s d 19 .. 2$\frac{2}{5}$
4	s d 3 .. 2$\frac{2}{5}$	s d 6 .. 4$\frac{4}{5}$	s d 9 .. 7$\frac{1}{5}$	s d 12 .. 9$\frac{3}{5}$	s 16	s d 19 .. 2$\frac{2}{5}$	£ s d 1 .. 2 .. 4$\frac{4}{5}$	£ s d 1 .. 5 .. 7$\frac{1}{5}$
5	s 4	s 8	s 12	s 16	s 20	£ s 1 .. 4	£ s 1 .. 8	£ s 1 .. 12
6	s d 4 .. 9$\frac{3}{5}$	s d 9 .. 7$\frac{1}{5}$	s d 14 .. 4$\frac{4}{5}$	s d 19 .. 2$\frac{2}{5}$	£ s 1 .. 4	£ s d 1 .. 8 .. 9$\frac{3}{5}$	£ s d 1 .. 13 .. 7$\frac{1}{5}$	£ s d 1 .. 18 .. 4$\frac{4}{5}$
7	s d 5 .. 7$\frac{1}{5}$	s d 11 .. 2$\frac{2}{5}$	s d 16 .. 9$\frac{3}{5}$	£ s d 1 .. 2 .. 4$\frac{4}{5}$	£ s 1 .. 8	£ s d 1 .. 13 .. 7$\frac{1}{5}$	£ s d 1 .. 19 .. 2$\frac{2}{5}$	£ s d 2 .. 4 .. 9$\frac{3}{5}$

With Interest (Simple) at 5p[r.] cent.

Proportions of Savings

Years	$\frac{1}{8}$	$\frac{2}{8}$	$\frac{3}{8}$	$\frac{4}{8}$	$\frac{5}{8}$	$\frac{6}{8}$	$\frac{7}{8}$	$\frac{8}{8}$
1	s 1	s 2	s 3	s 4	s 5	s 6	s 7	s 8
2	s 2	s 4	s 6	s 8	s 10	s 12	s 14	s 16
3	s 3	s 6	s 9	s 12	s 15	s 18	£ s 1 .. 1	£ s 1 .. 4
4	s 4	s 8	s 12	s 16	s 20	£ s 1 .. 4	£ s 1 .. 8	£ s 1 .. 12
5	s 5	s 10	s 15	s 20	£ s 1 .. 5	£ s 1 ..10	£ s 1 .. 15	£ 2
6	s 6	s 12	s 18	£ s 1 .. 4	£ s 1 .. 10	£ s 1 .. 16	£ s 2 .. 2	£ s 2 .. 8
7	s 7	s 14	£ s 1 .. 1	£ s 1 .. 8	£ s 1 .. 15	£ s 2 .. 2	£ s 2 .. 9	£ s 2 .. 16

state, he will thus find himself in possession of that valuable habit, pronounced by the proverb to be, of itself, a great revenue: *magnum vectigal parsimonia.*[1] He will be disposed to employ his little capital to the best advantage, in articles of durable use (such as furniture and comfortable fittings up for his cottage, trees for his little plot of garden ground, and the like), rather than in what is called good cheer, and other instruments of momentary enjoyment. His affluence, the fruit of parsimony, will not be, like that which comes from a prize in the lottery, an acquisition which has been observed to prove not infrequently the ruin, instead of what is called the *making*, of the man whom it finds in the lower ranks of life: on the contrary, like substantial food, it will *stay by him*, as the phrase is, and do him good.

To aid him in his choice, a printed paper containing a set of general hints and instructions applicable to his situation in life might be presented to each contributor, at the time of his taking his little capital out of the Bank, pointing out the various modes of employing it to advantage. Composed according to the views of government, it could not, on the part of government at least, but be supposed well adapted to the purpose. *Valeat quantum valere potest.*[2] If, in but one instance out of ten, the advice thus given be pursued, it will be so much gained.[a]

The institution here proposed, would, in addition to its own proper utility, afford a support to the above proposed establishment of a corresponding system of *Poor Man's Loan Offices*: the surpluses of the affluent affording a supply, as far as it went, to the wants of the indigent in the same rank of life. But it was not from the idea of any such accidental, secondary, precarious and probably superfluous utility, that the suggestion took its rise.

One objection presents itself, which seems to have some title to an answer. The idea, it may be said, is founded on absurdity—for, in relation to every class of men, the notion of affording artificial encouragement to marriage is an absurd one:

[a] To every person liberated by the benevolent Society for the discharge of Prisoners in custody for small debts, a paper of advice and exhortation is presented at the time of his enlargement.[3]

---

[1] i.e. 'frugality is a great revenue': see Cicero, *Paradoxa Stoicorum*, VI. iii. 49.

[2] i.e. 'Let it be worth as much as it can be worth.'

[3] See *An Account of the Rise, Progress, and Present State, of the Society for the Discharge and Relief of Persons imprisoned for Small Debts throughout England*, 13th edn., London, 1796, p. 65: 'Rule VII. That at the time of discharge, a short printed EXHORTATION be given to every person released.' The exhortation itself (see pp. 77–91) underlines the importance of sobriety and industry. The Society was formed in 1772, and would intervene to settle debts of less than £10 in deserving cases, provided that the debtor in question had not been assisted by the Society on a previous occasion.

1. With regard to the species in general, radically so: as if there were not in the species a disposition adequate to the purpose of providing for its own continuance: as if a degree of attraction between the sexes adequate to the purpose was ever known to fail, or would ever be conceived to fail: as rational would it be to employ the powers of government in order to get people to eat, drink, or take their rest.

2. With regard to the proprietary, and non-productive class, it would be pernicious in the first instance, and in the long run nugatory: since in as far as any person of that class refrains from marriage, the relative quantity of wealth, the ratio of opulence to population, is increased: and therefore *vice versa*, in as far as any one of the same class engages in a prolific marriage, the ratio of opulence to population is diminished: so that by every marriage in a family of that class the family is proportionally impoverished, and some other member of it who would have engaged in marriage, had the means of supporting himself in that state been permitted to devolve upon him, kept out of it.

3. With regard to the non-proprietary, and productive class, it would be pernicious were it to be efficacious, besides being experimentally needless—since on their part the disposition to engage in matrimony is always more than sufficiently abundant, and the indigence, which is so much the object of lamentation and legislation, is the fruit of it.

These objections, some of which I have seen urged with much warmth, I leave to their own strength: for the purpose of the present proposition, it is not necessary either to confirm or combat them. The institution here proposed is not an encouragement to marriage simply speaking: the tendency of it is rather to retard than accelerate the period of marriage, to reduce rather than increase the number of marriages within a given period. It is an encouragement to happy marriages only: to marriages the fruit of which promises to live and thrive: to marriage in such circumstances, and such only, in which lasting comfort promises to be the result of it. It operates even as a discouragement, though by the gentlest means, to marriages affording prospects of the opposite nature: to marriages which threaten to be productive of distress on the part of the parents, and of imbecility and mortality on the part of the children.

Should the tendency of the institution be deemed useful, the institution itself will not be a superfluous one. The more closely we examine, in this view, into the circumstances of the Poor, the more thoroughly we shall be satisfied of two things—that the demand for that sort of service which is rendered by a Banker is still greater in the lowest ranks of life than in the higher; and, that if the poor man is to have a safe, and constant, and ready Banker, it is government that must find him one.

To the opulent a Bank is of use in two capacities: as a fence against depredation, and as a machine for saving time in the operations of telling out the money, and keeping an account of it. To these uses is added, in the instance of the Poor man, a third, and that of more importance perhaps than either—the serving as a shield to prudence, against the assaults of prodigality in the shape of present pleasure.

The difficulty of resisting the incitement to expence, afforded by the sensible presence of money, is a difficulty which, comparing man with man in an adult state, will be found to press with peculiar force against the Poor. The comparative weakness of their faculties, moral as well as intellectual, the result of the want of education, assimilates their condition in this particular to that of *minors*. The money of the Poor-man, like that of the school-boy, *burns* (as the phrase is) *in his pocket*: unable, as he is, to divest himself of the possession of it to any advantage, and unaccustomed therefore, to divest himself of the possession of it in large proportions, as rich men do of theirs, it lies perpetually within his grasp, the whole mass of it at once, ready at the call of every short-lived pleasure.

Nor are the disadvantages much inferior, which he experiences in his endeavours to secure it against the dangers that assail it from the caprice of fortune, and the improbity of man.[a]

[a] Men of the opulent classes are little aware of the obstacles which men of the labouring class experience to their wishes of placing in security the pittance which prudence would enable them to snatch from the jaws of appetite. They may *lock it up*:—but the box, if small, might itself be stolen; and if its size be adequate to the protection of it against such accidents, the purchase money of the security, lock and box together, would for a long time continue to swallow up the value of the property to be secured. He would have cent per cent[1] to pay for this security, and that too, before he had wherewithal to pay for it. If a labouring man lives *by himself*, his home remains, for the greatest part of the four and twenty hours, exposed without a guard to the attacks of depredation: if he is member of a *family*, the probity of the other members of it may not always be proof against temptation: or if proof against temptation, not exempt from *suspicion*, which, in this instance, comes to the same thing. *On his own person* (it may be said), *it will at least be secure*. No such thing. His working habiliments are in no such constant state of *soundness*: and though they were, accident or design, while seeking in the arms of sleep, at the first vacant moment, and on the first bank that presents itself, a *casual* respite from his labours, may the same moment bereave him of his portable estate. *He may deposit the money* (it may be replied) *with the little shopkeeper his neighbour*: but little shop-keepers, like great Merchants, are not always honest, nor always fortunate. Another danger too, is that with his neighbour the *shopkeeper* the treasure would always, so long as the trustee continued to fulfil his trust, *continue within the owner's reach*: at the same time

[1] i.e. one hundred per cent.

It is government, I observed, that, if the poor man is to have a Banker, must find him one. Every body is ready to be the rich man's Banker. Nothing but charity could induce the rich man's Banker to do the same office for the Poor Man: and charity has never yet shown itself in so burthensome a shape. Here and there perhaps, sits some rare personage of unsuspectable trustworthiness, and equal benevolence, in whom the poor man, if he durst look so high, might find a Banker of this uncommon sort. But the poor man dares not look so high, and the benevolence of this gratuitous Banker, were it to manifest itself, would only manifest itself to the chosen few, and to them only during its own good pleasure. The only persons who, with views other than charitable ones, could think of rendering this troublesome service to the poor man, that is to all poor men that chose to apply to them, would be persons who, frequently in fact, and almost necessarily in his view of the matter, would, in holding out their hands to receive the money, have no other design than to run away with it.

Yet further. Taking this course for the promoting of frugality, is not only taking a fit and necessary course, but it is beginning *at the right end*. The prevalence of improvidence on the part of the Poor has not unfrequently been made the theme of lamentation, nor certainly without cause: nor, under such impressions, could any endeavour be more natural, than that of cherishing the propensity to the opposite virtue. But it is to little purpose to increase propensity where power itself is wanting: it is giving bitters instead of food. The first article to look to is *power*: that created or found existing, it is then, and then only, that to give existence or strength to inclination can be of use. This creation of power is oftentimes all that is wanting to be done on the part of government: for the nature of things may furnish inclination, and enough of it: but without power, all the inclination in the world is but uneasiness in waste.

Oftentimes where inclination appears wanting, and perhaps really is wanting, it is only because opportunity is wanting—that power, and consciousness of power, without which inclination can not so much as bring itself into life:—and such is the case here.[a]

that not only it might be to be *wished* on *his* account, but *he himself* might on *his own* account very *sincerely* wish, that it were not so *perfectly*, and *readily* within his own reach on all occasions.

[a] In Scotland, the Highlands are still the seat of idleness.—Why?—Is it because a Highlander has no stomach or no hands?—no: but because land, being pre-occupied, is not to be had, nor if it were, would it produce any thing, without capital to fertilize it, in that ungenial climate.

In America, every hand is busy.—Why?—because there is land for every body, if a

Examining the institution proposed with a view to the probability of success, *and* the probable extent of its adoption, and comparing it in this point of view with that kindred, and already happily established institution of the Friendly Societies, the comparison will not show to its disadvantage. The existing institution, excellent as far as it goes, is accompanied with a circumstance that operates in limitation of its extent, in as far as it is the result of choice. Fear rather than hope, the view of pain rather than of pleasure, is there the operating motive. The contingencies *there* provided for, sickness and old age, are, one of them distant in itself, and seen at an exaggerated distance (for such are the optics of the mind), both of them such as nature does not love to look at. Here, the object in view is as inviting as the other is repulsive; and the distance, how much soever regretted, yet not only far less in itself, but capable of being lessened more and more by industry.

The contribution is, in that case, attended with this farther disadvantage: that while the privation is certain, the benefit is apt to wear the semblance of being precarious. In the event of a man's being attacked by sickness, he is indeed to receive support: but, to a man in the vigour of youth, who knows not as yet what sickness is, the danger of it is but a dream: he who hopes never to be sick, is to punish himself with present privation, in order to insure himself against this unexperienced, and consequently undervalued, misfortune.

To insure himself—did I say?—I might have said—*to insure others.*—He knows that others may be sick, for he sees them so: and it is to save *them* from sickness, whom he sees doomed to sickness, rather than himself, whom he conceives exempt from it, that he is called upon to surrender the fruits of his own labour. In the case of the Marriage-fund Bank, it is for self that the sacrifice is made, and for no one else: unless it be for one other, who is already in some measure, and in prospect still more perfectly, a second self.

If he lives long enough, indeed, he is sure enough of being old:—but is he destined to live long enough? Will the powers of enjoyment remaining to him at that age be enough to pay him for the sacrifice he

man chooses to go far enough for it, and capital, laid up by Nature, presents itself upon the land.

In Holland, though there is no land, every hand is, as yet, equally busy.—Why? because capital there is still a weed: though in what a degree that weed will continue to thrive, under the new-planted tree of French liberty, time only can show.[1]

[1] France declared war on Holland on 1 February 1793, and had occupied the country by February 1795. On 16 May 1795, by the Treaty of the Hague, Holland became virtually dependent on France, and her ally in the war against Britain.

must make of the instruments of enjoyment, at an age when the power of employing them is in all its vigour?—Every thing of that sort lies wrapt in clouds.—And at the worst, there sit the distributors of public charity, whose never-failing hand holds out to him a never-failing resource against every want of necessaries. Such are the arguments which the ingenuity of appetite is so ready to oppose to the voice of prudence, but, more especially, of that melancholy sort of prudence which has the fear of pain, rather than the hope of pleasure, for its prompter.

Yet more. In this case, the motives on the influence of which the contribution depends for its commencement, are not only of the painful kind at that period, but, on each renewal of it, they are still of the same nature, and even augmented in degree. The idea of laying the groundwork of a provision against calamity, how far soever from being of the exhilarating kind, wears at any rate a face of comfort and satisfaction on its first appearance. But as the chain of contributions lengthens, the satisfaction, which gave birth to the first link, wears off: insomuch that, little by little, the business, if it goes on at all, comes to be carried on rather by the idea of the shame and regret that would be produced by forfeiture (the sure result of interruption),[1] than by the stale prospect of the faint and distant good, by which so persevering a course of self-denial is to be crowned in future.

In the new case, it is not only pleasure that lays the first stone, but fresh pleasure is stamped upon every succeeding one. Each period of payment brings the man so much the nearer to the enjoyment, every addition to the *quantum* of payment brings the enjoyment so much nearer to the man: the satisfaction, instead of wearing off by repetition, is brightened by it. From the commencement of the process to its consummation, the consciousness of liberty never quits it. No surly monitor to pull a man by the sleeve and say, *You must come in instantly, and pay to the uttermost farthing, or the door is shut against you for ever.* A man may increase his payment, diminish it, continue it, or discontinue it, according to every variation in the

[1] Friendly Societies did possess the authority to expel members, a penalty which would involve the forfeiture of contributions. However, there appears to be no evidence that this sanction was habitually imposed for a casual interruption in contributions. George Rose, who introduced the Act of 1793 (33 Geo. III, c.54) which gave legal recognition to Friendly Societies, wrote a pamphlet giving advice on the framing of their rules, in which he addresses the issue: 'The Punishment of Expulsion, which is not taken away by the Act, should be inflicted in few Cases, and those of Enormity only, as for wilful and repeated Neglect in paying the Subscriptions, habitual Drunkenness, and the like': see *Observations on the Act for the Relief and Encouragement of Friendly Societies: to which are added, Forms of the several Instruments Necessary under the Act: together with An Abstract of the Act*, London, 1794, p. 9.

figure of convenience. Not a penny of what he has advanced is ever sunk in any case: it lies, all of it, for ever at his own command, ready at any time for the purchase of any suddenly proferred benefit, or for his protection against any extraordinary misfortune.

If then, under such disadvantages, the Friendly Society plan has taken root and flourishes, so much to the benefit of the members in particular, and of the community in general, what might not be to be expected from the proposed Marriage-Bank institution, if grafted on that of the intended Industry-Houses?

The degree of success that has attended the various societies known by the name of *Tontine Societies*[1] (I speak here not of the utility of the institution, but of the readiness shown to embark on it) might, if examined in the same view, be found to reflect additional brightness on the prospect of success in the proposed instance. But what has been already said in that view will surely be deemed sufficient.

One great advantage will hardly be denied to this plan:—Let it fail altogether, the failure does no harm. Should nothing be gained by the experiment, nothing could be lost by it. It is not often that a political measure, so promising in point of possible good, is so perfectly pure from every thing of mischief, possible as well as actual, be it in the shape of expence, or in any other shape.

3. *Collateral Use the third—Applying the system of Industry Houses, together with the Central Office, to the purpose of what may be termed a* Poor Man's Bank of Remittance.

Every thing goes on smoothly in the transactions of people in easy circumstances, that is, of the only class of persons whose case ever presents itself to view when money transactions are spoken of: every thing goes on raggedly, if at all, in the transactions of the Poor. Paper gives wings to money for the benefit of the rich: but the poor man's money is all lead. If a rich man has occasion to send a few hundred pounds, or a few thousand pounds, from one corner of the island to another, nothing can be more easy: till of late he might have done it

[1] Tontines took their name from Lorenzo Tonti (1630–95), a Neapolitan banker who settled in France, and initiated the first Tontine schemes in or about 1653 as a means of raising loans for government. Subscribers to a loan were each granted an annuity, which increased as the number of subscribers was reduced by death, until the last survivor enjoyed the whole of the income. The Tontine Societies to which Bentham refers were saving schemes aimed at the poor into which subscribers paid small instalments for a set period, at the end of which the accumulated capital was divided among the surviving subscribers. For an account of their popularity, and criticism of their organisation, see *Tontines Calculated, and their Principles and Consequences Explained, and Exemplified in the Yorkshire Tontine; with Hints for one on an improved Plan*, London, 1791, pp. 3–8.

for nothing: and he may still do it for a few pence.[1] But the poor man's pittance is immoveable. A dutiful child, who has quitted his native cottage for employment, might send (one should think), a few shillings, as he could save and spare them, to assist an aged parent in his struggles against indigence: husband for wife, wife for husband, brother for brother, might do the same kind office:—No: it is not to be done. Their lot is fixed, that of one party or both, remote from every track of regular correspondence.[a]

The system of Industry Houses, under the direction of the Central Office, might administer charity in this unexpensive, and surely, in every point of view, unexceptionable shape. The money might be deposited either in the Central Office, or in any Industry House, and on advice given, paid accordingly in any other. Printed forms, with proper blanks, might be provided: and such letters, sent open, might pass free. The same conditions which, in the instance of the proposed Banks of deposit, serve to cover the actual expence, at the same time that they protect the agents of the public against vexation (the result of wantonness, malice or negligence), would afford equally effectual security in the present instance.[b]

[a] The post takes thousands, but shillings are too heavy for it: the carriage would eat up the treasure. Nor does the post come, perhaps, within ten miles. So many times a week, perhaps, the Lord or Squire, when he happens to be in the country, dispatches a man and horse for his letters to the Post Town. But he is not always in the country, and when he is, his servant is not always, nor of course the servant of the Poor.

[b] The convenience of this mode of remittance will not, it must be confessed, be equally perfect in all situations. The Parish in which the person lives, to whom the remittance is to be made, may, if situated at the extremity of the District, be from ten (say) to 12 or 13 miles distant from the House. But, at the worst, this would be but a day's, or part of a day's, walk thither and back again, for the person by whom the money is to be received, or, if through infirmity unequal to the labour, for any more able-bodied friend whose assistance he may be able to procure: and if the day of cessation from money-getting work be taken for this charitable service, it may be rendered without expence. But, should the system of institutions here proposed be established to the whole, or to any considerable part of their extent, a general and constant intercourse between the Industry House and the several Parishes within its District would be one of the results.

In France, so lately at least as the year 1792, any body might, by means of the post, remitt money to any body, and that not only in specific pieces, payable for by weight,

[1] A stamp duty on bills payable on demand had been introduced by 23 Geo. III, c.49 (1783). From 1 August 1783, bills under £50 were charged 6d stamp duty, and bills over £50 were charged 1s. No stamp duty was payable on an order transacted with a banker residing within ten miles of the place of drawing. The rate of duty was increased in 1791 (31 Geo. III, c.25), when, for example, duty of 1s 6d was charged on bills of between £100 and £200, and duty of 2s on bills in excess of £200.

4. *Collateral use the fourth—Rendering the system of Industry Houses applicable to the purpose of a* Bank, *for receiving the contributions, and paying the allowances, of the* Friendly Societies.

A place of deposit, so well guarded against depredation in every shape, and so manifestly seen to be so, would form a very convenient receptacle for the payments made into the hands of the voluntary Societies patronized by the legislature under the name of *Friendly Societies*. Were the Governors of the Industry Houses empowered, and required to receive these moneys, in their several Districts, from such Societies as thought fit to avail themselves of the opportunity, Government warranting the trustworthiness of these its Agents as before, these public hands would naturally obtain an universal preference over all individual ones: and the security, and consequently the value, of the funds of those useful Societies would receive a proportionable encrease.

To the purpose of payment, the use of the Banks in question, thus thinly scattered over the country, would naturally be more confined: for small and frequent payments, private hands, stationed near the abodes of the respective claimants, would of course be more convenient, especially as far as the allowances in case of sickness are concerned: but, as far as concerned the fixed annuities, for distributing the funds among these several private paymasters, in

as here, but sum for sum, in any sum, however fractional. But, being made an object of revenue, the charge was enormous: no less than 5 per cent.[1] In England, even this enormity would, in a thousand instances, be a blessing. Had a poor man, in one part of England, half-a-crown to send by the post to his sick father or mother, in another part, he could not do it, if at all, for less than eight pence or a shilling according to the distance: from 30 to 40 per cent.[2] *Nonsense*! (cries the man of finance, whose dealings with money are by millions) *Nonsense!—to think of sending a half crown backwards and forwards between London and Northumberland*!—Well then:— is it nonsense in a Duke of the county to have £500 of his rents remitted to him from thence, when he has occasion for them?—Calculate, and you will find, that there are individuals in this kingdom of whose income half-a-crown forms a much larger portion than £500 does of the Duke's: and, what is more, that even a majority of the inhabitants, in this and every country, are in that case.

---

[1] According to *Almanach national de France l'an troisieme de la république françoise une et indivisible*, Paris, 1794–5, p. 532, the five per cent charge for this postal service was introduced in 1794.

[2] There were in fact several methods of transmitting small sums by post. Bentham's figures suggest that he had in mind the sending of coins by post, on which double postage was chargeable, at a rate of 8d for up to thirty miles' distance, or 1s for up to one hundred miles: see H. Robinson, *The British Post Office: A History*, Princetown, 1948, pp. 149–50.

time for payment, and not before, these public Banks might still, even as to the business of paying, have their use.

§ II. *Second Division of the Collateral uses to which the system of Industry Houses might be applied: Uses relative to the business of Travelling*

[5. & 6.] *Uses the fifth & sixth*—Poor Man's Inns *and* Carriage Stages.

Places of Call or Inns, at and by means of which, the Poor, in the course of their migrations, might, at the cheapest rate, be sure of being provided with food and lodging, and convey themselves, or be convey'd, from House to House in a manner suitable to their respective circumstances.

For such whose migration is purely voluntary, and who are able to walk, so that they require no escort, the expence of travelling may thus be altogether taken away: the expences of travellers being defray'd upon the same scale of frugality as those of inmates.[a]

[a] The degree of economy with which this business may be carried on depends, on one hand, on the expence for which a man can be maintained in full health and strength for a day, on the other hand, on the value of the work which a man of the working class, being in a state of ordinary health and strength, can without hardship be made to perform in the same compass of time. The expence I state at 3^{d}, grounding the estimate on the experiments and observations made by Count Rumford in his 3rd Essay relative to the Poor (p. 239),[1] in which the expence of a day's allowance of soup and bread consisting of 4lb 3oz, is stated at $2^{d}\frac{3}{4}$, computed according to the extraordinarily high prices, and those the London prices, of the present winter: being an allowance in point of nutrition evidently much greater, and probably at least twice as great, as the average of the allowance at which prisoners have been actually kept for many years, in remarkably good *health*, at the Pentitentiary House at Wymondham. See Account of the regime of that House in the *Annual Register* for 1788.[2]

The value of the work I set down at 1^{s} a day: being no more than the lowest wages of the commonest Day-labour any where in England.

On this footing, the average value of a man's daily earnings, in one of the Houses in question, in the instance of adults of the male sex, being in a state of ordinary health and strength, and not disabled by age, may be stated at four times the daily expence

---

[1] In fact, the calculation by Rumford which follows appears at *Essays, Political, Economical and Philosophical*, i. 245.

[2] The 'Account' is in the *Annual Register* for 1786 rather than 1788. See Sir Thomas Beevor (1726–94), 'An Account of the Origin, Progress, and Regulations, with a Description of the newly-established Bridewell, or Pentitentiary House, at *Wymondham*, in Norfolk', *Annual Register*, xxviii (1786), 87–93, especially 91, where a table of diet indicates that the prisoners received two meals a day, with breakfast always consisting of 'a penny loaf', and dinner either of another loaf, or vegetables, or soup.

To such as do require an escort, the expence will likewise be reduced in a very great degree: since the conductors, being stationed at the several Industry Houses, will have no Public-House Charges to defray. The time of the Conductor will be the only charge: and this need cost very little, since it will be extraordinary if the whole establishment does not afford one inmate capable of executing such a trust. Female conductors may be allotted to female travellers.

Asses, by far the cheapest beasts of draught and burthen, where speed is not required, might be kept at every Industry House for the conveyance of the infirm, and of young children, from House to House: and the milk of the females would be of use to some descriptions of the sick.

The descriptions of persons in whose instance an accommodation of this sort might be of use, may be distinguished into persons under engagement, and persons not under engagement.

1. Under the head of persons under engagement come:

i.[1] Soldiers.
ii. Militia men.
iii. Mariners in the King's service.
iv. Soldiers in the E. India Company service.
v. Mariners in the E. India Company service.
vi. Mariners in private service.

The migration of persons of the above descriptions, after discharge or on furlough, is, in the instance of some of them, a source of considerable expence to the public, as well as of mischief and abuse. The expence might be reduced to its narrowest possible limits, and the abuses altogether done away, by the use that might in this way be made of the Industry Houses.

i. Such of the persons in question as had money in plenty, and chose to dissipate it in the purchase of the pleasure of the moment,

of his food, leaving a clear surplus of 9^{d}. The value of the earnings of a grown person of the female sex, I set down at 6^{d}, half the value of that of a grown person of the male sex. The calculation seems rather low than high, if applied to such works of the laborious kind as are exercised in common by both sexes: and in the instance of the sedentary employment of spinning, the average earnings of 112 children, candidates for premiums, was $5^{d\frac{1}{2}}$. (See *Account of the Society for the promotion of Industry in Lindsey District*, 3rd Edition: no date but posterior to 1789, p. 89.)[2] The children, it is true, were all candidates for premiums. But the average of their ages (most of them females) was but 11 years, 11 months.

---

[1] For the sake of clarity, Bentham's Arabic numerals in this series have been rendered as Roman.

[2] For details see p. 64 n. above.

instead of applying it to purposes of permanent utility, would of course betake themselves to Public Houses, as at present.

ii. Such as were not, any more than the former, destitute of money, but chose to travel upon the most frugal plan, though at their own cost, might here find the means of doing so.

iii. Such, if any, to whom it might be deemed proper to afford, at the public expence, the means of visiting their families or other lawful connections, might, on obtaining from their proper superiors the proper warrant for this purpose, receive in this way the means in question at the least expence to the public, and without the scandal of begging, or the danger of being obliged, or fancying themselves obliged, to steal or rob, to supply the casual deficiencies of that disreputable resource.

iv. Such, to whom, though penniless, there might be no sufficient reason for affording the means of migration at the public charge, might have the opportunity, if they pleased, of gratifying their wishes in this respect, by working out their passage, paying for their entertainment in work at the established rate.

2. Travellers not under engagement.

Periodical migrations take place among persons of various descriptions, on a variety of occasions. From the Welsh part of England, and from Ireland, to the metropolis and its neighbourhood there is a regular receit, and as regular and almost as numerous a return, of useful hands. Hay-harvesting, corn-harvesting, and fruit-gathering produce an influx of Irish, chiefly of the male sex: fruit-gathering produces in like manner an occasional accession of Welsh hands, chiefly female. Of Irish hands, a similar importation is said to take place in some of the maritime counties of England situated towards Ireland.

Many of these birds of passage are said to lay up, each his little hoard, which, when the age of adventure is past, sets him down in a state of affluence in his native nest: and by exemplifying, they begin, it is said, to diffuse an improved mode of living in those less matured portions of society. To so laudable and useful a system of economy, the Industry Houses, which the itinerants would find in their way, might be useful in a double point of view: as Houses of call, they might afford personal accommodation at the cheapest rate; while, in the capacity of a Bank, whichever House happened to lie most conveniently would afford a secure receptacle for these minute accumulations.

To these periodical migrations, which take place in consequence of a regular demand for hands, afforded at particular periods, by particular branches of work, on the part of persons flocking in with correspondent regularity from remote distances in multitudes at a time, may be added the occasional migrations that take place on the part of scattered individuals at uncertain times, and in consequence of variations that are liable to take place all over the kingdom, in regard to proportion between the number of working hands and the quantum of the demand for work: an encrease in the demand, and hence in the rate of wages offered, occasioning a proportionable influx from all parts without distinction to a certain spot, till the demand is satisfied: a diminution in the demand at a certain spot, occasioning a proportionable dispersion from that spot.

I have, under another head, had occasion to speak of the use that might be made of the system of Industry Houses, together with the central office of General Inspection, as a receptacle and source of intelligence with regard to the demand for work in all its branches.[1] In the capacity of Poor Man's Intelligence-offices, they would thus convey to the ears of the industrious all over the kingdom, the information of each place at which there happens to be an extraordinary demand for work: in their capacity of Poor Man's Inns they would, in as far as the Law of Poor-Man's Settlements allows, or can be prevailed upon to allow, afford the means of supplying the demand.

The bands of domestic society would be drawn the closer by the unexampled facility thus given to travelling, in the lowest and most numerous ranks of life. A man, who began his journey penniless, might cross England from sea to sea, live comfortably all the while, and visit his friends with money in his pocket at his journey's end. After travelling one day and working another, a man might always carry out of the house at which he worked enough to maintain him in travelling for two days more. Even a woman, if she spun tolerably, might, by spinning one day, earn enough to maintain herself in travelling another day.[a] By walking in the early part of the morning from one Industry House to another to breakfast, say 12 or 15 miles (a trifle to a labouring man in good health), he might perform $\frac{1}{2}$ or $\frac{3}{4}$ of a day's work the same day, pursue his journey the next day, and so on without interruption, and every day with an additional 3ᵈ or 6ᵈ in his pocket.

In the existing order of things, nothing of all this can be done.

[a] See above, note [a].[2]

[1] In the copy, Bentham has noted in the margin at this point: 'In a paper that does not accompany the present Papers.' For a discussion of the Poor Man's Intelligence Office see 'Outline of a Work entitled Pauper Management Improved', *Annals of Agriculture*, xxx (1798), 280–1 (Bowring, viii. 398).

[2] See p. 92 n. above.

Employment, entertainment, every thing is unattainable. Demand for work may exist in abundance, but its existence is unknown, and while a man should be performing the work that he may eat and live, he must be hunting for it and starving. Be the demand for work ever so great, he may get none. Unknown he is suspected: he is regarded as a vagabond, and confounded with thieves.[a] (See *Table of Cases calling for Relief* Cols. [VI & VII.])[1]

[7. & 8.] *Collateral Uses the 7th and 8th. Making the Industry Houses serve in quality of what may be termed* Pass-Stages, *for the passing of delinquents and supposed delinquents: and for the conveyance of poor Debtors to prison under Arrest.*

In each Industry-House there might be a *Strong-Room* or two, fit for the reception of persons travelling under custody: though indeed according to the plan of construction already recommended,[b] any part of the building within the field of inspection would be strong enough for the securing even of criminals of the highest class, and of the most desperate kind.

It is scarce necessary to mention, that there should be different rooms for offenders of an infamous description, and offenders of a description not infamous: and both perfectly separated from the apartments occupied by the irreproachable inhabitants of the House.

Delinquents arrested on mesne process,[2] or transmitted for committment in execution, might thus be convey'd almost without expence from Constable to Constable, and from Industry House to

[a] The lately translated *Travels of Moritz*, the German Clergyman, in England, are curious in this view. Being on foot, his great and constant difficulty was to get houses of entertainment to take him in: though decently clad, speaking English, and travelling for pleasure with money in his pocket.[3]

[b] The plan of central Inspection.[4]

---

[1] MS 'V & VI.' See p. lvii above.

[2] Since no law-suit could proceed in the absence of the defendant, it was necessary to secure his attendance. This was achieved by a writ issued by the court, known as a judicial writ. The whole process was distinguished as the mesne, or middle, process. A writ of *capias ad respondendum*, for instance, provided for the arrest of the defendant by the Sheriff, and thereby ensured his presence in court.

[3] Karl Philipp Moritz (1756–93), German writer on aesthetics and language, visited England between 31 May and 18 July 1782, and did indeed discover travel on foot to be fraught with difficulties: see Charles P. Moritz, *Travels, Chiefly on Foot, through several parts of England, in 1782. Described in letters to a friend*, London, 1795, p. 124 (first published as *Reisen eines Deutschen in England im 1782 in Briefen an Herrn Direktor Credike*, Berlin, 1783).

[4] Bentham had originally recommended central inspection in *Panopticon: or, The Inspection-House*. For his recommendation of the principle in his poor law writings see pp. 204–5 below, and 'Outline of a Work entitled Pauper Management Improved', *Annals of Agriculture*, xxx (1798), 116–17 (Bowring, viii. 375).

Industry House, and, where extraordinary assistance was thought requisite, it might be easily provided at each House.

The same system of unexpensive receptacles might even be of use in the instance of arrested Debtors, to wit those of the poorer classes: the Debtor having his option of being convey'd to an Industry House upon his journey, instead of an Inn, or Spunging House.[1] This would be a great relief and comfort to poor Debtors, not to mention their Creditors.

It is an old saying, and hitherto but too true an one, that *Prisons pay no Debts*. It might cease to be so, were this idea adopted, and that in the instance of the greater number (since the poorest class comprises the greater number) of these, as of all other unfortunate individuals. None of the Debtors committed in the present state of things, by the Courts for the recovery of small debts, termed *Courts of Conscience*,[2] (Conscience being conceived to be listened to in *these* courts) need ever be committed to any other place: at 1^{s} a day earnings, and 3^{d} a day expence, two calendar months abode in an Industry House might cancel the largest debt. In most instances the Debtor would probably be glad to see it cancelled on these terms: and there seems no reason why the operation should not be made compulsory, especially if the insolvency, in pursuance of a power of inquiry to be given for that purpose, were adjudged to have been accompanied with blame. Hitherto it has been a principle of English Law, to make little or no distinction between blame or no blame in regard to the contracting of a debt, ability or no ability in regard to the discharge of it.[3]

What makes travelling charges in cases of the above descriptions so high, under the existing order of things, is the necessity of obtaining the requisite refreshments at Public Houses, where costly liquors must be called for, and the whole expenditure arranged upon a scale adapted to the stile of the House. By the want of rooms adapted to the purpose of safe-custody, the expence is likewise increased, in many instances, in the article of guards.

[1] i.e. a house maintained by a Bailiff or Sheriff's officer as a place of preliminary confinement for debtors.

[2] The delay and expense associated with the pursuit of small debts in the Common Law courts had led the Common Council of the City of London to establish a Court of Requests in London. The Court's jurisdiction was limited to cases of debt amounting in value to less than forty shillings, while judgement was given by a body of non-professional Commissioners. The jurisdiction of the Court was confirmed by 3 Jac. I, c.15 (1605), which instructed the Commissioners to make such orders between party and party 'as they shall find to stand with Equity and good Conscience'. During the next two hundred years many such 'courts of conscience' were established in localities outside London by special Acts of Parliament.

[3] Perhaps Bentham had in mind the fact that, at Common Law, the pleading in cases of debt was '*nil debet*', rather than 'not guilty'.

The same seats of industry and good order might be turned to further account, by being made use of as receptacles for delinquents, under sentence of fine or imprisonment for inconsiderable misdemenors, to wit either exclusively made use of, or in concurrence with the present Jails, and Houses of Correction, at the option of the convicting Magistrates: especially in cases where no blemish to reputation resulted from the offence: perfect local separation as well as visible marks of distinction being employ'd, to prevent the persons of these offenders from being mixed with the unoffending and irreproachable part of the inhabitants, or the lot of the one being confounded with that of the other.

Among persons travelling in custody, it makes little difference with regard to this purpose, for what cause: but if there be a difference, the opportunity might be embraced, with still more unquestionable advantage, in the case of the insane.

§III. *Third Division of the Collateral Uses that might be made of the system of Industry Houses: Uses of a Medical cast*

[9.][1] [*Collateral Use the ninth*—Medical Dispensaries.]

Making them answer the purpose of *Medical Dispensaries* in favour of the independent Poor, or of such descriptions of them (Labourers in Husbandry for example) to which this species of favour were thought fit to be extended:—relief being administered to each patient at his own home, unless where his own accommodation would be better consulted by his removal to the House.

If there be any description of persons to whom, either on the score of a permanent cause of insufficiency in regard to the wages of their labour (Labourers in husbandry for example), or of an extraordinary degree of pressure in regard to the burthen produced by the multitude of children, a permanent provision in the way of relief were thought fit to be made, there can surely be no shape more unexceptionable, as far as it goes, in which such relief can manifest itself:—none which keeps better time with exigence, none which in itself stands clearer from abuse, or which is so easily clearable by political arrangement, from whatever portion of abuse it may stand exposed to in its own nature.

The objections to the system of *out-allowances* in general, even in

[1] MS '1.' In this section of the essay, Bentham has enumerated the medical collateral uses independently of the earlier sections. Bentham's enumeration has been emended in order to maintain a continuous enumeration of uses throughout the essay.

kind, and that though of the properest kind, still more when in the shape of *money*, are what I have elsewhere had occasion to represent at large:[1] and that, whatever be the efficient cause of the indigence proposed to be relieved, whether the habitual insufficiency of earnings on the part of the poor family, or the extraordinary multitude of helpless members of it to be provided for.

Medical relief is not liable to any of these objections. 1. The exigence being purely casual, and peculiar to uncertain individuals, it is not taken into the account by any of the causes which concurr in determining the wages of the *class*. The wages of the class are determined not by the sick, but by those in health: not by the wages which the casual few, but by what the many, are willing to take, if offered, rather than attempt to betake themselves to some other occupation, or some other country, or cast themselves upon the parish. Relief might, therefore, in this transient and casual shape, be administered by government, without counteracting its own purpose: that is without effecting an equal reduction, or any reduction at all, in the wages which the labourer would otherwise have been able to obtain from his employer. It would therefore not be thrown away: it would rest with the poor for whom it was intended, without running through their pockets into those of the rich for whom it was not intended.

2. The sort of exigence to which it administers is not of the number of those which a man might be apt voluntarily to embrace, or negligently to give way to, in contemplation of the relief. A man might affect nakedness for a while, for the sake of getting new cloaths for nothing: he might forbear to work as much as he was able, in expectation of seeing the gap thus left in the amount of his earnings filled up by charity without work. But no man would either counterfeit, or voluntarily contract disease, for no other advantage than that of receiving medical visits and taking medicine.[a]

3. Were the Medical curator to be allowed to charge any thing to the public, either for the visits he pays, or for the medicines he administers, he would stand exposed to the temptation of multiplying both, beyond the exigency of the service. But of course, no charge on either score would be allowed. His salary would be such as he himself should have been willing to accept of, in full compensation for the whole of his time.

[a] At least in the instance of what commonly presents itself under the name of *medicine*. Of palatable articles exhibited in the way of medicine, mention will be made further on.

[1] See Essay II, §XI, pp. 57–9 above; and 'Pauper Systems Compared', pp. 154–83 below.

The medicines would be not his property but that of government: the elementary drugs bought under proper professional inspection, upon the largest and most economical scale, at the most advantageous market, and from thence dealt out to the several Industry Houses in the proportions pronounced competent, by persons standing clear of all interest in the undue augmentation of the expence, in the way either of quantity or quality.[a]

Paid in this mode, the Medical Curator might be apt to be backward (it may be said), or negligent in his attendances. But backwardness in point of attendance, whether any thing be or be not to be got by it, is a failing neither frequent in the practice, nor natural to the situation, of this most beneficent and respectable of all temporal professions: for though the pocket should fail to be enriched by visits to the poor, the stock of experience, of skill, and thence of reputation, can never miss of its encrease. Accordingly, gratuitous assistance is as notoriously abundant in the medical profession, as in others it is rare.

Whatever danger may be thought to remain on this score, a farther remedy, if thought necessary, might be the making the appointment only for a year, requiring renewal consequently from year to year.

Many, however, are the articles, it may be observed, which to their usefulness in the way of medicine against pain and disease, add the faculty of being immediately grateful to sense and productive of present pleasure. Strong broths, jellies, conserves, in short all articles coming under the well known denomination of *kitchen physic*, present themselves as coming under this description: but above all, those of which the charms have but too much attraction for persons of all classes, but more particularly, on a variety of accounts, for the class of persons here in question—inebriating liquors. Liquorishness will be apt, as in the instance of children, so in that of the uneducated poor, who are a sort of grown children, to engage them to counterfeit, or even create, a medical demand for such delicacies: false humanity, or a fondness for creating dependence, might induce the Medical Curator to give undue way to such demands.

[a] For example, a Committee of the College of Physicians,[1] whose Report on this subject, with the reasons on which it grounded itself, should be regularly made public.

---

[1] The Royal College of Physicians was founded in 1518 by a Charter of Henry VIII (1491–1547), King of England from 1509 and King of Ireland from 1541. From its inception the College was an examining body, having powers to examine and grant licences to those qualified to practise medicine, and to punish instances of malpractice. The College presented lecture series and anatomical demonstrations, and was called upon by government to advise on medical issues. From 1768 it published *Medical Transactions*, which included data and results from enquiries undertaken under its auspices.

Persons really sick might, moreover, pretend symptoms indicative of a demand for kitchen, or brandy-shop physic, without either need or even relish, at the instance, or for the benefit, of the healthy parts of their family or their friends.

But against this abuse there are three remedies: one applying to the situation of the patient, another to that of the Medical curator, a third to both together. The first consists in the taking measures, according to the nature of the case, for the depriving of their palatable qualities all medicines administered on such terms, as far as may be done without rendering them unfit for use.[a] The second consists in the throwing the light of publicity, in a state of particular intensity, upon this part of his proceedings, and in requiring the concurrence, or at least the previous privity, of his fellow-Officers to this part of his measures. The third consists in the engaging him, as far as may be without inconvenience, to see, in the instance of all medicines liable to this abuse, that the prescription be actually taken by the real patient for whom it is prescribed, and no part of it by any one else: and to enter a mark declarative of such attestation, upon the books.

I say upon the Books.—For, of the establishment of such a fund of Medical Relief throughout the kingdom, an appendage equally obvious and necessary, is the prescribing a system of Book-keeping, for composing and preserving upon record a methodical history of the proceedings of all those by whose instrumentality the relief is to be administered.

The heads under which the minutes in such a Register should be entered may be as follows: viz:

I. Application for Relief.—i. Name. ii. Age. iii. Condition in respect of marriage. iv. Abode of the party on whose behalf application is made. v. If by another person, name of that other person. vi. Year, month and day when. vii. Place where.

II. Visits made accordingly.—i. If there be more than one Medical Curator (Master & Apprentice for example), by which of them. ii. and iii. Time and place of each visit, as before. iv. Persons attendant on the Patient—or in the House at the time.

III. Symptoms apparent on each visit.

IV. i. Prescriptions determined on in consequence. ii. and iii. Time and place of administering each prescription. iv. Persons in the house with the Patient at the time.

[a] Thus if *vinous* spirits must be prescribed, *bitters* in large proportion, and those of the most unpalatable kind, might be directed to be mixed up with them, in all cases where no unsalutary effect would be to be apprehended from such admixture. Mentioning this to a friend, as what might perhaps be proper to be done, I was answered by the mention of instances in which, by his orders, it had been done.

V. Event of the assistance given—Termination of the complaint by i. Cure. ii. A Different complaint. iii. An infirmity deemed incurable—or iv. Death.

Articles of a nature to be coveted on their own account and independently of their use in the way of medicine, such as those above spoken of, besides being entered on the list of prescriptions in the Medical Register, with a Column for the computed cost of each prescription, might be entered in a book by themselves, and not issued without the signature of the Governor and Chaplain, or one of them.

Periodical returns, monthly for example, might be made to the Metropolis, from the Medical Register of each Industry House, in duplication, one to the College of Physicians, the other to the Central Poor Office.[a]

General Abstracts of these returns might be made, and published periodically, once a year or oftener, in two different points of view: the one medical, under the direction of the College; the other economical, under the direction of the Inspector General of the Poor, for the information of Parliament and the public at large. The Medical abstract would exhibit a compleat body of *Medical Transactions* for each year, in relation to the Poor throughout England: a work of which the Poor would, in quality of actual patients, be the subjects, but from which poor and rich would receive equal benefit, in their quality of frail, and but too frequently imprudent, mortals, incessantly exposed to the danger of becoming patients. An accumulating body of medical information, authentic and universal, would thus be annually poured into the treasury of useful knowledge. It is by such means, and such alone, that the progress of improvement in this most important walk of science can be made to receive its utmost degree of acceleration.

The volume of the *Medical Transactions*, as above described, for the preceding year, would constitute an indispensable article in the library of every Medical practitioner throughout the kingdom. It would be worth more than many a hundred other volumes of which

[a] The business of copying, be it observed, being performable, as far as a few copies are concerned, by a Machine, would be attended with no other expence than that of the paper, added to the prime cost of a Copying Machine (5 Guineas) for each House,[1] an article applicable to every branch of the Accounts.

[1] Bentham may be referring to the copying machine patented (No. 1244) by James Watt (1736–1819), engineer, in 1780. The copying process used specially prepared ink, which produced an impression upon a dampened sheet of tissue paper when the original and the dampened sheet were pressed together. Watt, whose designs were widely imitated, produced both a large machine for use in counting houses, and a portable model.

such libraries are composed. The obligation of buying it might be made a condition of the permission to practise in the profession, in any of its branches. The price of the book might, on those terms, be cheaper in proportion than that of any other book, and yet the sale of it be attended with a profit more than sufficient to requite the labours of the most able operator who could be employ'd in the extraction of this literary quintessence.

The light of publicity, beaming thus with unexampled intensity upon every step taken by each practitioner in the track of his art, would light up a blaze of emulation that could not but be productive of the most salutary effects. It would afford a universal and perpetual security against incapacity. Ignorance, certain of being unmasked, would not dare to offer itself.

Two very natural and obvious concomitants of the Medical branch of the Register, above proposed as proper to be kept in each Industry House, as well as to each other, would be a *Register of Health* for the District at large (as well as for the House), and a *Register of the Weather*: works which would afford joint occupation for the scientific acquirements of the Medical and Spiritual officers of the House. I need scarcely expatiate on the richness of the contribution which a compleat and constant set of Registers of these two kinds, all over England, would yield to the Medical department of science. The minutest phenomena might be noticed almost without trouble, in regard to the tract of country immediately visible from the House: and general notices might be collected in more or less abundance, and with more or less accuracy, from the whole of the District to which the House belonged.[a]

Great as the relief would be, the expence might, if established usages and dispositions afford a ground for inference, be next to nothing.

[a] Amongst other inferences of a practical tendency that might be afforded by such a Register, may be instanced the following:

1. Remarks on the influence of weather on healthiness, in the same and different situations: from whence might be deduced inferences with regard to the choice of situations for the abode of man.

2. Observations on the effects, if any, resulting to health from particular modes of culture, such as draining, irrigation, manuring with putrid fish, or other putrid manures of a particularly offensive nature &c.

3. Remarks on the influence of the rigorous observation of the Sabbath on the sufficiency of the harvest, particularly in unfavourable seasons and in parts of the country situated in an unfavourable climate.[1] Enquiry how far the reasons which

[1] Bentham has deleted the following sentence from the text at this point: 'Enquiry whether sufficient attention has been paid to the text in which the Jews are laughed to scorn for the too rigorous observation of *their* Sabbath.' The reference is to Mark 2: 24–7; and Luke 6: 1–11.

A Medical Curator, for each Industry House, is supposed at any rate: an apprentice or apprentices, in such a situation, he and the public would have the service of for nothing. The care of such part of the inhabitants of the *House* as are actually sick, and whose cases are not out of the reach of medicine, can never occupy more than a very small proportion of his time. In a well ordered Industry House, as in a well ordered Ship, the benefit of the Medical Superintendent's care will be felt much more in the shape of prevention

prescribe the suspension of such labours as are not immediately necessary to the support of life, and can be carried on as well at one time as another, extend to the case of such operations, on the success of which the support of life absolutely depends, and which, if not performed on some particular day, as weather permitts, may not be performable at all?[1] Enquiry whether an Ox or an Ass might not be suffered to continue in a pit for a whole day,[2] with less danger than a whole harvest might experience from being suffered to lie on the ground for the whole of a fine day, immediately succeeded by days, or weeks, of incessant rain. Enquiry what proportion the loss by the death of the greatest number of oxen and asses that throughout the compass of the globe have ever fallen into pits, within the compass of a period equal to that of harvest time, a loss mentioned as an instance of a damage too considerable for even the most notorious hypocrite to pretend to fancy it necessary to expose himself to, even under the Jewish Law, would be likely to have to the least loss that has ever accrued, in any year, by the suffering of the harvest to lie on the ground on Sundays, within the single Island of Great Britain, particularly the Northern part of it. Enquiry whether, even with reference to Judea, any text be to be found, by which any interruption of harvest work appears to have been either prescribed or countenanced, directly or indirectly, by the author of our religion: and whether even a positive ordinance on his part, were any such thing to be found, enjoining the suspension of those works in the hot, dry and steady climate of Judea, could justly be understood to extend to the cold, moist and uncertain climate of this our island, particularly the Northern division of it. Enquiry how far the laxity of the practice, in the instance of the works allowed under the notion of necessity, is consistent with the rigour of the practice, in regard to the disallowance of the more eminently necessary operation here in question? Whether the labours of the Cook and the Hairdresser, for example, would not bear suspension in all seasons better than those of the Husbandman in a precarious season? Whether people in general could not do without hot meat, milk and fresh fish, for example, for one day in a week, better than without hay for their cattle, or bread for themselves, bread for the whole year. Whether it be altogether consistent, or even respectful, to put up petitions for a plentiful harvest, and for fair weather, as if a grant of those blessings by supernatural means were expected, while we wilfully forbear to make use of that share of them which is actually bestowed upon us? And, in fine, whether a strict and universal proscription of all money-getting labours not of necessity, together with a heavy Sunday toll in favour of the poor cattle, might not atone for the harm, if there be any, in making hay for them on the only days on which, as it may happen, hay for them may be to be made.

[1] The remainder of this note does not appear in the copy.
[2] An echo of Luke 14: 5–6.

than of cure.[a] By far the greatest part of his time will remain applicable to the service of such of the independent Poor as shall have been marked out for this and other favours (Labourers in husbandry for example), throughout the District.

In averages and round numbers, 200 Industry Houses (say) for the 15000 Parishes, and Parish-like rateable Districts, in the 50 Counties of England and Wales:[1] this gives 75 Parish-like places to an Industry House: say 80. Ten of them, viz: the ten immediately circumjacent, may be managed in this way by the surplus time of the Medical strength attracted to the House: remain 7 such Sub-Districts, each containing its ten Parish-like places, each requiring a visiting Medical Curator to itself: such of the sick in the whole District as are removable to the Industry House with advantage, being accordingly removed to it.[b]

Situations in Medical Charities, though unpaid, are objects of competition, because by the opportunity and reputation of experience, they afford an introduction to practice: which, however, supposes them to occupy a part only of a man's time.

The medical care of the Labourers in Husbandry in ten Parish-like places, need occupy, it is conceived, but a part of a man's time, the heavy part of the business being taken off his hands by the Industry House, and he would take care that it should occupy no more than such part as should be left unoccupied by that part of his business which he depends upon for subsistence.[c]

[a] Two or three thousand persons of all ages, all of them living constantly and literally under the very eye of those to whom the care of their health is made a constant duty, maintained in frugal plenty, and cut off from all means of excess, will frequently not afford a single individual to whom the Apothecary or the Surgeon could, as such, be of any use.

[b] Many Counties, it should be remembered, perhaps most, have County Hospitals.[2] These would continue upon their present footing: operating in ease of the Industry Houses, unless in as far as it may be deemed advantageous upon the whole to melt down those establishments into the Medical establishments of the Industry Houses.

[c] The quantity of medical business in an Industry House District can not, it is evident, but admitt of a certain degree of inequality, as between district and district, according to the circumstances of each. But among Labourers in husbandry,

[1] In the margin Bentham has noted the exact figures for counties, '52', and for parish-like rateable districts, '14,649, counted from the returns': see 'Abstract of the Returns made by the Overseers of the Poor, in pursuance of An Act, passed in the Twenty-sixth Year of His present Majesty's Reign, intitulled, "An Act for obliging Overseers of the Poor to make Returns upon Oath, to certain Questions specified therein, relative to the State of the Poor"', *Commons Sessional Papers of the Eighteenth Century*, lx. 13–322.

[2] For a list of thirty provincial hospitals in existence in 1783 see B. Abel-Smith, *The Hospitals, 1800–1948: A Study in Social Administration in England and Wales*, London, 1964, p. 4.

From such a distinction a man would derive not only a general advantage, in the way of his practice, but a particular advantage, with a view to the practice of the Friendly Society men, and the opulent classes of workmen to which the members of those Societies mostly belong.

To these natural advantages, which of themselves have in parallel cases been found adequate to the purpose, might be added the privilege and reputation of having a man's whole stock of Drugs from the public stock of the Industry House, examined, selected and authenticated by the highest authority in the Medical department, as above proposed: the allowance at prime cost, and at so many months' credit: the stock thus allowed adequate to the supply not only of this gratuitous part, but of the whole, of a man's practice.[a] Solemn and written promise before hand, with or without oath, that he will not sell, or otherwise alienate from the purpose, any part of the allowance thus obtained. Upon every fresh application for further allowance, oath by affidavit, of his not having violated such his promise.[b]

The chance of succeeding to the titled and salaried Medical Curator in chief, would help to fill the list of advantages tending to engage unpaid volunteers, in the capacity of Sub-Curators, each in his Sub-District: while the natural emulation, among these constant competitors for reputation, would be a spur to exertion, and an incentive to merit in every degree and shape.

By these advantages, a sufficient number of active young men, either already practising or looking out for practice, might, it is

numbers are more equal than among manufacturers, and the *maximum*, in point of numbers, much better defined. The demand for medical attendance will likewise be much less in that healthy way of life than among manufacturers, almost all of them engaged in in-door employments, most of them in sedentary ones, many in poisonous ones, and all of them, by their habits of promiscuous intercourse, exposed to the seduction of the unhealthy vices.

[a] The drugs sold at Apothecaries Hall, in London, are rated, under favour of the value stamped upon them by the authentication, at a very advanced price.[1]

[b] There seems little room to doubt the *efficacy* of such an oath. Except the comparatively inconsiderable difference between prime cost and profit price, no advantage could, in the nature of things, be reaped by the breach of it. No other practitioner could buy from a man the reputation of using the authenticated drugs, without publishing him as a Perjurer.

[1] In 1672 the Worshipful Society of Apothecaries established a laboratory at their Hall in Blackfriars, in order to produce chemical medicines for the use of members and for sale, and thereby establish some standard of quality in an unregulated and potentially lethal market. A shop was attached to the laboratory to sell drugs wholesale and retail. A committee of the Society met monthly to oversee the making of all medicines, to inspect and approve all drugs sold in the shop, and to set prices for sale. The guaranteed purity of the drugs, in comparison with independent sources, enhanced their market value.

presumed, be induced not only to take charge of the health of the labourers in husbandry, each in a Sub-District as above described, but to carry into execution, each of them to the extent of such his practice, the general plan of registration as above proposed: receiving from the House a sufficient allowance of blank forms.[a]

The merits display'd by every such under-labourer in the vineyard of Medical charity, would, when presented in the *Medical Transactions* to every discerning hand, hold him up to universal notice: and when, under favour of the reputation thus acquired, the profitable part came to interfere with the charitable part of his practice, he would relinquish his situation in favour of a successor, who would find in it the seeds of a similar advantage.

Where a man of undisputed fitness accepts a duty with small pay, or what is still better, no pay at all, it is, under certain exceptions, not only so much the better in point of economy, but the better for the service. From his taking the situation with a salary, all you can know is, that he likes the salary: from his taking the situation without salary, what you are sure of is, that he likes the service.[b]

[10. *Collateral Use the tenth*—Lying-in Dispensary.]

The extending the assistance of the Medical Curator to the case of *Lying-in women* would go a good way towards removing a load of expence, which, falling in large masses at once, masses equal to the whole amount of a week or two's subsistence of the whole family, will be apt to press with sensible severity upon such of the poor whose

[a] Verifying, upon oath, the expenditure of such part of his above-proposed allowance of drugs as will thus have been expended in the unpaid part of his practice, this part of his drugs might, it should seem, be allowed him without payment.

Kitchen physic and liquor-shop physic, as above, not to be expended without the previous fiat, or at least the subsequent allowance, of his principal at the House, controuled as above, by the other Officers.

[b] Whenever peace is restored,[1] the laying up of so many King's ships will throw a proportionable number of medical men upon half-pay. One can scarcely conceive a better school than a large ship for a Medical Curator for the Poor. In the event of the appointment of a half-pay Navy Surgeon, or Surgeon's Mate, to the situation of Medical Curator to an Industry House, were his half-pay (during his continuance in that office) divided into two equal parts, the one sunk as a saving to the Navy Department, the other paid over to the fund (the Parochial suppose) on which the salary of the Medical Curator comes to be charged, the advantage of these savings would afford, to men of this class, an advantageous superiority in point of chance of success as candidates for the situation.

---

[1] In the copy, this note is included in the text, contrary to Bentham's clear intention.

pecuniary circumstances, or improvidence, may have precluded them from laying up a stock of savings adequate to the exigency.[a]

Should the assistance of females, on this occasion, be deemed more eligible upon the whole, in ordinary cases, at any rate the intervention of that stock of science, which, in the existing order of things, can not be expected but from the more enlightened sex, will probably be deemed of use in cases of difficulty and danger.

And howsoever it may be in regard to personal assistance, the use of the establishment in the character of a medicinal repository, where medicine is found necessary in such cases, will pass without dispute.

[11. *Collateral Use the eleventh*—Female Midwifery Lecture Establishment.]

But how great soever the disadvantages may be, which the female professors of an art so much their own may be conceived to labour under at present, those disadvantages might in great measure, if not altogether, be removed by a farther use that might be made of the Medical branch of the Industry-House establishment, at a very inconsiderable expence. I mean the making it answer the purpose of a school of instruction, upon a plan resembling that of the Sunday Schools, to female practitioners in Midwivery, actual or intended: to wit, by requiring the Medical Curator to give a course, or so many courses, of lectures in the Year, open to females only, in the House.

Supposing the effect practicable, it will hardly be denied to be desirable. The natural advantages which, in relation to this particular branch of medical practice, the female sex have over the male, the symptomatic sensations and experiences common to the one sex, and in so great a degree unintelligible and incommunicable to the other, are too evident to need insisting on: the topic of delicacy, moreover, presents another head of superior aptitude, in relation to which there is not likely to be much dispute. Natural aptitude being therefore so exclusively on the one side, how can it be otherwise than regretted that acquired aptitude should be so perfectly monopolized by the other? Nature, by her original patent, destined the monopoly of both heads of advantage, destined the monopoly of the whole

[a] The Rev$^{d.}$ Mr Davies, in his *Case of Labourers in Husbandry*, estimates it at 10^{s} a year upon an average: the man's earnings during the greatest part of the year not being more perhaps than 6^{s} or 7$^{s.}$[1]

[1] The estimates of the annual costs of childbirth, and of the weekly earnings of male labourers in husbandry, appear in Davies, *Case of Labourers in Husbandry*, p. 16 and p. 14 respectively.

practice, for the female sex: it is art, misapplied art, that has introduced interlopers from the male.

Nature (it may however be said, in the way of objection to the instruction of females, as it has been said in the way of objection to the employment of males), *Nature* (it may be said) is, in this, as in the other branches of medicine, *the best physician*: *female midwives* (it may be added), untutored as they are at present, *are the pupils of Nature*: and a doubt may be started whether the instructions of this unerring Mistress might not be as likely to be confounded as improved, by the very imperfect tincture which (it may be thought) would be the utmost that minds so little prepared by education would be able to imbibe from the principles of science.

The observation might have some weight, if, to the practice of these supposed pupils of Nature, there were nothing to object but simple ignorance. But the misfortune, in this as in so many other instances, is, that ignorance is the chosen harbour of false science: and the chief task, and chief difficulty of the true, is to clear the ground of the pernicious prejudices implanted by the impostor which assumes her name. If it be true that the well-instructed male assistant has really, upon the whole, any advantage over the uninstructed, or rather ill-instructed, female, he is perhaps less indebted for it to the good he has learnt to do, than to the mischief he has learnt to avoid doing. We hear enough of the multitudes said to be poisoned by the Physician: while nothing at all is said of the perhaps still greater multitudes, who for want, or in the absence, of the Physician, are poisoned or stifled by the Nurse.[a]

In cases of difficulty at least, men are still every where resorted to in preference. Would a man be deemed the better qualified for the business by knowing nothing about the matter?—Then why should a woman be?

[a] We learn from the Rev[d.] Mr Davies, in his *Case of the Labourers in Husbandry* (p. 16), that in his part of the Country (Barkham near Oakingham in Berkshire) a bottle of gin or brandy is a constant accompaniment, and composes the whole *Materia Medica*, of the Midwife.[1] I must leave it to the experienced among the faculty to answer whether, if the unfrequent and sparing use on such occasions, or, rather than the frequent and copious use, the total disuse, of this capital article of Pandora's box[2] could be generally brought about, lives enough might not be saved throughout the country, in the compass of the year, to afford a sufficient retribution for whatever cost or trouble would have been expended in the course of instruction here proposed.

---

[1] In calculating the expense of childbirth, Davies states that 'a bottle of gin or brandy' is 'always had' on the occasion of childbirth.

[2] In classical mythology, Pandora was the first woman. Zeus gave her a jar containing all kinds of misery and evil, which escaped and flew out over the world when she opened it.

The utmost stock of experience at present possessed by the most experienced female Midwife, uninstructed as female Midwives are, is still but the experience of that one person: the information that might thus be furnished her, is the accumulated experience of innumerable multitudes of practitioners, of her own sex as well as of the other.

That cases of difficulty and danger will sometimes occurr, and that in the instance of even the healthiest class of lying-in women (the wives of Labourers in husbandry, for example), will not be disputed. In these cases, the uninstructed female is glad, or at least ought to be glad, to call in the assistance of the scientifically-instructed male. But perhaps the case will not wait for him, and the patient dies. The expence too, even of the female practitioner's fee, is already more than the patient is well able to bear: and now the expence must at least be doubled: probably much more than doubled.

Fit or unfit, the greatest part by far of this branch of medical practice is at present, and seems by nature destined ever to be, carried on by females. Where the question *what will be done*? is decided, and decided for ever, the question *what had best be done*? is of mighty little use. Since then, the practice will at any rate be carried on by such hands, the only remaining question is, in what state, in point of qualification, is it best they should be—*ill-qualified*, as at present, or *better qualified*, as they might be made to be?

Were it thought fit that this should be among the assistances afforded at the public expence to the favoured class of the independent Poor (Labourers in husbandry, for example), and that female practitioners should, in the first instance at least, be employ'd in preference, the mode of affording the assistance would, of course, be by appointing the agent of the public, instead of leaving it to the patient, to pay the Midwife's fee. The choice of the Midwife might either be left to the patient, or particular Midwives might be selected by public authority for this purpose. The satisfaction of the Patient might be better provided for in the former mode: her safety in the other. In either case, no such practitioner ought to be paid by the public without her having given her attendance, once or oftener, at the course of lectures above proposed.

As a help to attention, and as a means of cementing still more closely the natural connection which exists in this instance between interest and duty, the pay of the midwife, coming thus as it does out of the pocket of the public, might be made more or less dependent on success. Half the fee might be deducted, in the case of the death, of either mother or child, within the month: the half or the whole of the remainder in case of the death of both within that period. Double fee for twins, and so on: and in consideration of the loss upon unsuccessful practice, the reward of successful practice might receive a small encrease. Upon this probably useful, and at any rate safe and unobjectionable footing, the business might, when thus paid for by government, on its own terms, be placed with as much facility as upon the common footing: and thus a useful custom, which could not be introduced by individuals, might, and that at the same time without any thing of compulsion, be introduced by government.[a]

Interchange of facts and instructions, in this case as in the [following]:[1] each pupil enriching the public treasury of the science by a tribute of *particulars*, such as came within her competence, and receiving from it general views, explanations and reasonings in recompense. Those who, by natural incapacity or acquired prejudice, stood precluded from comprehending *reasons*, might at any rate, like other nurses, comprehend *orders*: and thus something at least might be gained. Cases, whether of singularity or difficulty, would naturally be reported from the pupils all round, to the Lecturer, at the headquarters of science: and little marks of distinction might be conferred by proper authority, in the way of rewards, for the most curious and clearly-delivered communications.[b]

In process of time, supposing due facility afforded, and sufficient time allowed, attendance at these lectures might, in the instance not only of the government-paid Midwives (if any, as above proposed), but of all others, be made a necessary condition to the faculty of practising. Howsoever it might fare with the old stock, the minds of the rising generation of female practitioners, all over the country, would thus be radically impregnated with rational principles, and guarded against all vulgar and pernicious errors.

This establishment might, like so many of the preceding ones, be

[a] The whole business is, in its own nature, perfectly and happily exempt from every thing of fraud and abuse. The probability is not great, that a child which would not otherwise have been begotten, should be begotten merely for the advantage of sharing the perquisite with the midwife: and though such an effect were to take place, there would be no great harm in it.[2]

[b] See, in regard to rewards, the practice of the Society for the promotion of Industry at Lindsey in Lincolnshire.[3]

[1] MS 'foregoing'. Bentham's reference is to the Veterinary Lecture Establishment, p. 120 below.

[2] In the draft, Bentham has noted in the margin at this point: 'Transfer to 2. Lying-in Dispensary?' It seems clear, however, that the note belongs here.

[3] See *An Account of the Origin, Proceedings, and Intentions of the Society for the Promotion of Industry*, pp. 8–10. The most productive child in each district was awarded the title of King or Queen of Spinners, while all children who produced a sufficient quantity of material to qualify for a premium of clothing or money were awarded a medal, upon which their achievement was inscribed.

maintained without expence, should such frugality be thought eligible. Where the surplus time of the Medical Curator at the House is deemed sufficient for this purpose, the whole of his time being paid for, employ'd or not employ'd, there seems no very cogent reason why any extra payment should be made for this, any more than any other, part of the service. In default of this principal Medical Curator, the Curators of the proposed Sub-Districts, above alluded to, might be resorted to for this purpose: and the probability seems to be that among the seven, some one at least would be found, who, upon the same gratuitous terms, would be willing to add this to his other merits. But should it be either found necessary, or deemed advisable, to allow, in every district, a stipend to this useful purpose, either at government expence, or by voluntary subscription, the very moderate retribution that would be found necessary could hardly be looked upon as ill employ'd. But this matter will be more particularly considered under a succeeding head.[1]

The practitioners, by whom the benefit of the instruction (it may be said) would be reaped, these pupils of the public (it may be thought) might, without any hardship, be called upon to pay for their tutorage. But it seems questionable whether the real benefit would, any part of it, be their's: more children would not be born in consequence of this instruction than without it: the quantity of practice all together would not receive any encrease. The encrease which these female practitioners might derive at the expence of their male competitors, though probably not wholly ideal, would yet be too minute and uncertain to be taken into account in this view, especially as no determinate share of it would be seen to come home to any assignable individual: and, as between these female pupils themselves, no general encrease of skill derived from the course of instruction would, if, as proposed, the obligation of partaking of it were to include them all, afford any advantage in the way of preference to any one. The burthen of attendance—the time and expence, would, if nothing were done to relieve them from it, be all of it their's, while the benefit would fall exclusively to the share of their respective patients.

The pressure of the burthen might be pretty effectually taken off, and that at an inconsiderable expence, the relief being administered in the frugal stile of the House. A meal's meat, and the advantage of conveyance to and from the house, to those whose abodes were distant from it more than a certain number of miles, with a night's lodging, if by accident rendered necessary: these several accommodations, furnished all of them at the public expence, but in the same

[1] See pp. 122–3 below.

frugal stile, as above described,[a] would amongst them shut the door against every claim of exemption on the score of poverty. Those who disdained the acceptance of the boon, who would probably be the greater number, might find a sufficient compensation for the expence, in a distinction thus flattering to their pride.

The saving of most importance is that which regards the article of *time*. To this particular profession, supposing it the sole dependence, all days of the week are indeed alike. The laws of the Sabbath have never yet been so much as proposed to be extended to this species of work, even by the most rigid Pharisee. But, in country places, it seems difficult to conceive that the utmost mass of profit derivable from this source should in general constitute a person's sole, or even principal dependence. The whole business of a Parish, paying as midwives are paid by labourers in Husbandry, would not amount to so much as £4 a year: consequently the whole business of ten parishes (a considerable range to be filled by a single individual of the female sex, and on foot) not to so much as £40 a year.[b] On this as well as other accounts, Sunday, the day of general leisure, and of best attire, seems of all others the properest for the purpose. An exercise

[a] See the list of Collateral Uses of the *itinerary* class.[1]

[b] Number of inhabitants in England and Wales, say	9,000,000
This divided by 15,000, the number of Parochial districts—gives the average number of inhabitants in every such District	600
This, again divided, by the proportion of annual births to the existing number of inhabitants in a Country Parish (according to the printed but unpublished Population Table for Corfe Castle Parish)[2] $\frac{1}{40}$—gives the average annual number of births in a Country Parish, no more than	15
Fifteen times 5^{s} 0^{d}, the usual midwife's fee among Labourers in Husbandry (according to the Rev.^{d} Mr Davies),[3] gives the annual emolument derivable from the exercise of this profession in a Country Parish by a Midwife, supposing her employ'd by the whole Parish, but paid no otherwise than as above, no more than	£3. 15. 0
If employ'd and paid in the same way, by so many even as ten Parishes—no more than	£37. 10

[1] See p. 92 n. above.

[2] The table to which Bentham refers was compiled by William Morton Pitt (1754–1836), MP for Poole 1780–90, and Dorset 1790–1826. Morton Pitt attempted to interest fellow landowners in the problem of poverty, and made many improvements himself in local social conditions. Bentham wrote to Morton Pitt on 1 March 1796, thanking him for 'the Statistical present with which you have honoured me', almost certainly with reference to this table: see *The Correspondence of Jeremy Bentham*, vol. v, ed. A. T. Milne, London, 1981 (*CW*), p. 189. The table was published as 'Extract from an account of the population of Corfe Castle. Drawn up by the order of, and communicated by, W. M. Pitt, Esq. M.P.' in *Annals of Agriculture*, xxvi (1796), 188–93. The calculation to which Bentham refers, concerning the proportion of births to the number of inhabitants between 1766 and 1795, appears at p. 188. Bentham's notes on the table are at UC cxxxiii. 35, 57–8.

[3] See Davies, *Case of Labourers in Husbandry*, p. 16.

can not well be conceived more suitable to the day, more in harmony with the principle and essential business of it, than that of displaying to a reverential audience the causes and concomitants of the pains and dangers, which they have devoted themselves to experience and to relieve, unfolding thus, in as far as permitted to be unfolded, the mysteries of that science, which makes known, in the words of the Psalmist, 'how fearfully and wonderfully we are made'![1]

The Sermon ended, and this select part of the audience removed to some retired apartment, secured against all intrusion from the scoffing sex, then would be the time for the Medical Lecturer, after a blessing implored upon his labours by the Chaplain, to take his seat.[a]

The *Obstetrical Transactions* for the Year would form a valuable branch of the *Medical*: and, as to so much of the materials as could be collected from the female division of the practitioners, the contributions, however light they might weigh in the infancy of the institution, would become more and more valuable, in proportion as the instruction thus planted had come by degrees to take the firmer root.

Amongst so many contributors, all of them, according to the measure of their respective faculties, candidates for distinction, it would be extraordinary, if more than one, in the compass of the kingdom, should not, from time to time, by the talents display'd in her communications, establish herself, on this peculiar ground, upon a level at least with the domineering sex: and thus, by the favour of a discerning public, seat herself, in process of time, upon the heights of lucrative and honourable practice.

[12. *Collateral Use the Twelth*—Veterinary Lecture Establishment.]

A further use that might be made of the Medical strength of each Industry-House, a use of less real dignity than the foregoing, though on the other hand less exposed to silly ridicule, is that of affording a system of instruction in the *Veterinary* art or science: that useful, though inexpressively, and therefore unfortunately denominated art, which occupies itself in the cure and prevention of diseases and accidents incident to Horses, and other domestic and serviceable

[a] Religion, according to the ritual of The English Church, has already thrown her mantle over this awful period of female existence. To the '*service for Churching of Women*', in their quality of *patients*, no unsuitable supplement seems to be held out by the institution here proposed for the Instruction and *Churching* of them in quality of *Medical Assistants*.

[1] Psalm 139: 14.

animals: being, in relation to the animals over which man thinks fit and finds it practicable to exercise dominion, what the art of Medicine is in relation to man himself: in a word the *Cattle-healing* art or science, as it might be termed, if so novel a denomination were to be endured.[a]

As knowledge encreases, professions split and separate. It was not till within these three or four and fifty years, that the Surgeons of the Metropolis found means to separate themselves from the Barbers:[b] till that enlightened period, the art of saving the life of man formed a sort of appendage to the art of ridding him of his beard. At this day, the *Cattle-Healer*, though sometimes stiled the *Horse-Doctor*, is more commonly stiled the *Farrier*: Farrier, *le Ferrier*, the *Iron man*. The art of saving the lives of Horses is still but an appendage to the art of casing their heels with iron: which itself, in country places, is but an appendage to the art of working in iron in general, the art of the *Smith*.

As to horned and other Cattle, it is not yet settled, in point of *language*, that their lives are either worth saving, or capable of being saved. Yet in the market, whether the Slave trade or the Military trade be considered, there are Horses which are worth a whole company of men. £50 or £60 is a good price for a raw Negro:[1] £30, or

[a] *Veterinus*, by contraction from *veheterinus*, burthen-bearing: *veterinarius*, one who occupies himself in any way about burthen-bearing animals: *ars veterinaria*, the art which occupies itself about burthen-bearing animals. Unfortunately, the idea of *old age* is much more apt to be presented by this word than the idea which this word, employ'd thus in default of better, is intended to present: *vetus*, old; *veteran*, a man of old standing in service; *a*, the termination of the feminine gender; all this together, instead of presenting what it is intended to present, is more apt to suggest some such idea as that of the *Old man's art*, or the *Old Woman's art*, or the *art of turning men into Old women*. *Horse-Doctor*, a term in use, is well enough as far as it goes, to denote the professor of the art: bating the radical, though established, impropriety, attached to the use of such word as *Doctor*, Teacher, as if the business of the professional man in question were to teach medicine, instead of practising it: *Horse-Doctor*, that is Horse-*Instructor*, is a term applicable with more etymological propriety to the *Breakers* than to the *Healers* of Horses. *Cattle-Doctor*, if the term be in use, is still better, as being more comprehensive.

[b] Stat. 18 Geo. 2, c.15. The Surgeons and the Barbers remain still one profession in France, unless separated within this year or two.[2]

---

[1] In the minutes of the evidence taken before the Select Committee of the House of Commons appointed for the examination of witnesses on the slave trade, 2 March 1790, the price of a black slave is reported as fifty pounds or fifty guineas: see *Commons Sessional Papers of the Eighteenth Century*, lxxi. 234.

[2] The Act of 1745 to which Bentham refers separated the surgeons and barbers of London into two distinct corporations. In France, as early as April 1743, legislation of Louis XV (1710–74), King of France from 1715, separated surgery from barbering in Paris. In provincial areas of France, however, barber-surgeons continued to practise well into the nineteenth century.

some such matter, was, in the last war, and in one of the treaties produced by that war, settled to be a good compensation for a dead Hessian.[1] *Eclipse* sold for £1500: I forget what other Horse for £2,000 or £3,000:[2] and, in Bakewell's and other Academies, sheep and horned cattle have been educated, to a degree of accomplishment almost equalling that of Horses.[3] In Spain and elsewhere, many an individual, even of the Ass species, is, at the above rate, worth a multitude of men.

In short, if men are worth saving, Cattle are so too: for the life of man depends upon the lives of cattle. No man of middle age but must have witnessed times when very serious national losses, and still more serious national alarms, were produced by mortality, contagious or uncontagious, among this part of the brute creation.[a] If the Veterinary science had then existed, it might have had its use.

[a] In the Dutch Provinces on one of these occasions the value of the loss was many of their millions.[4]

---

[1] By Article 9 of a treaty of 5 February 1776 between Britain and the Hereditary Prince of Hesse Cassell, it was agreed that Britain would pay compensation for a Hessian soldier killed in the service of the Crown at the rate of levy money, or 30 crowns per head. One crown was equal to 4s. 9$\frac{3}{4}$d. sterling, so that the compensation for a dead Hessian in fact worked out at £7. 4s. 4$\frac{1}{2}$d. Bentham seems to have confused crowns with pounds. See *Commons Journals* (1774–6) xxxv. 575–6.

[2] Eclipse was a thoroughbred racehorse, bought as a yearling by William Wildman, a Smithfield cattle salesman and grazier, for 75 guineas in 1765. Before Eclipse's first competitive race in 1769, Captain Dennis O'Kelly (1720?-87), a successful gambler and officer in the Middlesex militia, purchased a half-share in the horse for 650 guineas, and on 19 April 1770 purchased the remaining half-share for a further 1,100 guineas. Rockingham, another thoroughbred racehorse, was purchased for 2,000 guineas by George, Prince of Wales (1762–1830), afterwards as George IV, King of Great Britain and Ireland from 1820 (see *Daily Universal Register*, 17 May 1786), a fact which Bentham also mentions in *Defence of Usury*, p. 92 (Bowring, iii. 15).

[3] Robert Bakewell (1725–95), celebrated agriculturalist of Dishley in Leicestershire, was an innovator in the breeding and humane care of livestock. Dishley was noted for the gentleness and obedience of its animals: see, for instance, Arthur Young, *The Farmer's Tour through the East of England. Being The Register of a Journey through various Counties of this Kingdom, to enquire into the State of Agriculture, &c.*, 4 vols., London, 1771, i. 113–14.

[4] A severe epidemic of cattle plague or rinderpest began in the Essex marches in 1745, spread quickly, affecting all but the most westerly parts of England and Wales by 1747, and was not finally eradicated until 1758. George II (1683–1760), King of Great Britain and Ireland from 1727, ordered a service of thanksgiving for the ending of the plague to be celebrated in all churches on 8 February 1759: see *Annual Register*, ii (1759), 66. There were further localized outbreaks in 1769, 1774 and 1781. The total loss of cattle from plague between 1745 and 1758 has been estimated at 507,000: see J. Broad, 'Cattle Plague in Eighteenth-Century England', *The Agricultural History Review*, xxi (1983), 105–15.

An epidemic of cattle plague broke out in the Netherlands in 1744, and was not eradicated until 1765. In 1768 the disease re-appeared, and persisted until about 1786. No exact figure for the scale of the financial losses arising from these outbreaks has been discovered, but in the province of Holland alone over 400,000 cattle succumbed to the disease between 1769 and 1784: see J.A. Faber, 'Cattle Plague in the Netherlands during the Eighteenth Century', *Mededelingen van de Landbouwhogeschool te Wageningen*, lxii (1962), 1–7.

For some time past, it has possessed a sort of existence. Imported as an exotic, smuggled over from France, it has been planted in the neighbourhood of London, where it has been flourishing or languishing for these five years. A year or two ago, the Frenchman died: and for some time it remained a question whether the science was not to die with him.[1] The case is, it is with this as with many other arts, to be extensively useful, it must be proportionably diffused. But, in this view, the lectures given under that establishment, useful as it is, and deserving of every encouragement, can do but little. Country Farriers can never, in any numbers, support the expence of an abode of some months, preceded and followed by the expence of journeys to and from so expensive an University for the higher class of Cattle Doctors.

But by the means now presented, the art may be spread all over the kingdom, as it were in an instant, almost, if not altogether, without expence to the public, and altogether without expence to the pupils.

To this purpose, as to that of the proposed Midwifery Lectures, the Medical strength attached to the House might or might not be sufficient, according to circumstances. In the instance of the Medical Curator in Chief, whose situation, as such, is an independent provision of itself, it might be made a condition to his eligibility the having qualified himself for giving lectures in this art, by going through a course of instruction at the London Academy.

This would be nothing more than a continuation, or rather development, of the studies which he must have already pursued, while bestowing, at some course of anatomical and physiological lectures, that attendance without which he would have been unfit to be received as a Candidate for the office. For, under the name of comparative anatomy, to which may be added more or less of comparative physiology, the foundations of the art of healing, as applied to the inferior animals, are always laid in those courses to a greater or less extent, though it be for the purpose of throwing light on the science in its more important application, rather than with a view to the particular and peculiar use of this collateral pursuit.[a]

[a] In the anatomical lectures of the late Dr William Hunter, the Garrick[2] of didactic

[1] The first veterinary school was founded by Claude Bourgelat (1712–99) at Lyon, France, in 1762. In 1778 a 'Hippiatric Infirmary' for the instruction of pupils in the profession was founded in London, but the venture failed. In 1791, the Odiham Society for the Improvement of Agriculture adopted the proposal of Charles Vial de Saint Bel (1753–93), a successful French veterinarian, and established the Veterinary College in London, with Saint Bel as professor. Bentham's reference to smuggling refers to the fact that Saint Bel left France for England on the pretext of buying horses for the Royal stud, but in reality to escape the Revolution. Saint Bel died in August 1793, and the College experienced considerable difficulty in finding a suitable successor, until Edward Coleman (1765–1839) was appointed in 1794.

[2] An allusion to David Garrick (1717–79), celebrated actor-manager.

The difficulty of producing such an effect, how formidable soever it may be in idea, is nothing in itself. Difficult or not in practice, whatever presents itself to the mind as new, is apt indeed at the time to present itself as difficult: the difficulty which the mind experiences in bringing itself to entertain the conception of an operation or result being, by a very natural mistake, transferred by the imagination to the operation or result itself: yet all the while, to him by whose exertions the effect is to be produced, there may be no difficulty in the case. It seems difficult to conceive, that, in the compass of a year or two, in consequence of any institution set on foot by government, Farriers in general should, all over the kingdom, come, as it were of a sudden, to understand something of this part of their business, especially in so short a space of time.—Why?—Because we have not been used to see Farriers know any thing worth mentioning of this part of their business, and because we have not been used to see any general system of instruction set on foot by authority, and going on all over the kingdom at one and the same time. But the real difficulty is nothing, in comparison of those difficulties which are got over every day, and by every body who chooses to get over them. The difficulty that attends the conception of that sort of instruction, which is given in a course of anatomical and physiological lectures, is nothing in comparison either of the difficulty of learning to understand, when spoken, a new language, or the still greater difficulty of learning to read one's own language. Yet all persons who, in a country speaking a foreign language, pass any length of time with the natives of that country, get over the former difficulty: and all children, infants of two or three years old, on whom it is thought worth while to bestow the pains of teaching them, get over the latter.

It is, in itself, not more difficult to cause lessons to be given, in 200 schools at a time, on the bodily structure and diseases of cattle, than on the structure of the language. It is consequently not more than $\frac{1}{75}$th part of the difficulty that attends the causing of lessons to be given on the structure of language, in 75 times 200 of those language-

Orators,[1] the illustrations afforded to the anatomy and physiology of the human frame by that of the inferior animals took up a portion of time on many occasions, if I do not misrecollect, not much inferior to that which was more immediately devoted to the principal object.

[1] William Hunter (1718–83), first Professor of Anatomy at the Royal Academy 1768–83, began lecturing on surgery and anatomy in 1746, and quickly established a reputation for eloquence, and for the apposite use of illustrative examples, of which he possessed an extensive knowledge. In the margin of the draft, Bentham has noted in pencil at this point: 'at whose feet I sat with eager delight in the days of youthful study'. Bentham had attended Hunter's lectures in 1778: see Bentham to Thomas Foley, 5 June 1822, *The Correspondence of Jeremy Bentham*, vol. xi, ed. C. Fuller, Oxford, 2000 (*CW*), p. 91.

teaching schools: yet this same 75 times as great difficulty (reckoning a school of this sort to a Parish and no more) is surmounted, and so constantly and universally surmounted, as never so much as to present itself under the name of difficulty.

The Parish-like places within the circuit of each Industry-House District, from 70 to 80 (say) in number, might be expected to furnish, upon an average, each of them one or more practising Farriers (Masters or Apprentices) to receive the benefit of the course of instruction thus provided for them. Title to admission, recommendation (suppose) from Resident Minister and Churchwardens. Use of the recommendation, to attract candidates:—the face of difficulty is a sort of certificate of value: an advantage thrown open to every body, and not offered particularly to any body, is apt to be prized by nobody.

Greatest distance to travel to and from the lectures, suppose 12 or 14 miles. To those who would have to come from that distance to (suppose) half that distance, a meal, afforded upon the frugal plan of the House, might either be sold upon the usual terms, or, if the expence were not grudged, allowed gratis in recompense for the trouble of journey and attendance. The sort of Farriers one is most apt to think of, on this as on other occasions, the Farriers of great Towns and wealthy neighbourhoods, would disdain the idea of this or any other eleemosynary assistance: but in poor or thinly inhabited country places, there may be those to whom an encouragement of this sort might be indispensable.

But the grand saving, the saving alike indispensable to all, is the saving in the article of time. By taking Sunday for the day, in this instance as in a former,[1] making this branch of the Industry House establishment a sort of Sunday school for Farriers, this saving will be effected without expence. And surely, after the exception of that more awful science, by which a corner of two of the veil of mystery that covers the birth of man is removed, after this single exception, the wisdom display'd by Providence in the creation could not receive a more striking illustration, nor a more useful demonstration, than that which this Veterinary course of lectures might be made to afford: nor could this branch of *Physico-theology*[a] be deemed a less suitable

[a] The title of a book giving a display of nature in a religious point of view, by the Rev[d] Dr Derham, a book which the obsoleteness of the physical part would have consigned to oblivion long ago, but for its connection with the religious.[2]

[1] i.e. the Female Midwifery Lecture Establishment: see p. 113 above.

[2] William Derham (1657–1735), Vicar of Upminster in Essex 1689, Canon of Windsor 1716, author of *Physico-Theology: or a Demonstration of the Being and Attributes of God, from his Works of Creation. Being the substance of XVI sermons Preached in St. Mary le Bow-Church, London, at the Honble Mr. Boyle's Lectures, in the years 1711 and 1712*, London, 1713. The book had reached its twelfth edition by 1754.

occupation for such a day, than the mechanical and, though certainly not irreligious, yet unreligious, exercises of spelling and writing, that form the business of those respectable institutions, the only ones known as yet by the denomination of *Sunday Schools.*[1]

The previous attendance of the pupils at divine service, might be made a condition of their admission to these lectures.

Both attendances will be so many respites from the Tippling-house: both studies so many rivals to the attractive powers of drunkenness: and the most amusing of the two (such is human weakness), the most efficaciously attractive. The common recipe for making men religious is by forcing them to be idle. By barring the door of every other place, where occupation of any kind, amusing or profitable, innocent or pernicious, is to be had, they are driven, it is supposed (as far as the driving them is practicable), into Church. What seems to have been not quite enough considered is, that close to, and at the right hand of the Church stands the Tippling-house: and that the gate of the Tippling-house is the *'great Gate'*.[a]

Interchange of facts and instructions between pupils and *teacher*, and, *in process of time*, licence for practising, in this case as in the preceding. Register of health and Mortality with regard to the Cattle of the District. In process of time, as the pupils increased in intelligence, Journals of their practice, and particular details of cases that had any thing particularly curious or instructive in them, in as far as they could be procured. Medals, or other honorary distinctions for those who, in the course of each year, had performed the most extraordinary cures, or furnished the clearest, most instructive, and most copious communications: from the sum total of these communications, *Veterinary Transactions* for each year, analogous to the *Medical* and the *Obstetrical*. Obligation on each Farrier practising as a Cattle-Doctor to purchase these Transactions as they come out, the price being reduced as low as possible. The burthen, light as it might be, might with better justice be laid upon the Parishes, by whom the real benefit of the encrease of skill that would be the natural fruit of this accumulating body of information, would be reaped, than upon the practitioners, to whom (as in the instance of the female pupils in midwifery) the benefit would be rather nominal than real, and who would already have been suffi-

[a] Mat. 7: 13, Luke 13: 24.

[1] Records of Sunday School initiatives in England begin as early as 1625 in Little Gidding, and 1699 in Bristol and the Black Country. From 1750 onwards many philanthropic clergymen and lay-men and women founded Sunday Schools for religious and secular instruction of poor children. However, Robert Raikes (1735–1811), who established four schools in Gloucestershire in the 1780s, is often regarded as the founder of Sunday Schools.

ciently loaded by the burthen of attendance. At the same time, it seems no more than natural to suppose, that some encrease of practice would be among the results of so encreasing a fund of skill and knowledge. Rising in reputation of ability, they would experience the benefit of a proportionable rise in confidence. A man would then resort to the well-instructed Cattle Doctor for advice, in many cases in which, under the present penury of intelligence, the chance of benefit would not appear adequate to the expence.

In recompense for the trouble bestowed in learning the business itself at these lectures, the obligation of serving an apprenticeship to a different business (the business of a Smith or Horse-shoer), might, it should seem, be dispensed with. Or if, in order to understand the case of a patient, and afford him what relief is to be afforded, it be really necessary the practitioners should have made shoes for him, then let the College of Physicians, before they are permitted to go on any farther in their practice, be put apprentices to Shoemakers.[a]

The expence of the institution might (it has already been observed) be rendered little or nothing. If the subsequent task of giving a course of lectures of this sort were added to the previous qualifications, by which the Medical Curator at the House might be required to purchase his appointment, the time which it drew upon him for need not amount to more than from one to two hours in a week, for a part of the year (suppose 6 or 8 months), at the season most favourable for travelling.[b]

[a] True it is, that, if I may trust the calculations of a person whose situation has afforded him considerable opportunities for observation, the complaints which bring horses under the hands of the Farrier in his capacity of *Horse-Doctor,* have for their cause in very large proportion (I fear to say how large) the bad practice of the same person in his capacity of *Horse-Shoe-Maker.* If the remark (which applies not, it must however be observed, to other cattle) be founded in fact, the connection between the Shoemaker and the Medical Curator may perhaps be not altogether so arbitrary in the instance of the horse, as in that of the human subject: although even in the latter instance, it is the unskilfulness of the Shoemaker that creates the greatest part of the business of the *Hand-and-Foot Surgeon,* the sort of Surgeon who sometimes distinguishes himself by the more learned appellation of *Chiropodist.* Be this as it may, in respect of all disorders, those of the feet excepted, the habit of making and putting on shoes well or ill, is not less barren of instruction in the instance of the Horse subject than in that of the human.

[b] A compleat course of instruction, as given at the Veterinary College, practice as well as theory included, occupies, I am aware, and even fully occupies, a period of three years. But in this period, not only several collateral branches of science, but a sort of practical apprenticeship are included. The shorter sort of course here proposed might at least serve as a useful abstract of the theory, might have the effect in some degree of enlightening the ignorance, and correcting the errors, of

The Industry House is the only place at which either the lectures could well be given, or the collection of preparations and other such treasures, which, sooner or later, would naturally form itself under such an institution, could conveniently be preserved. An habitual separation could not, without great prejudice to the service, subsist between the professional man and such his professional stock. It would be better therefore, that the Medical Curator in Chief should be relieved from the whole of the out-duty, were it necessary, than that either the task of giving these lectures, or that of giving the Midwivery lectures, should necessarily be committed to other hands.

Not that it need be apprehended, that the utmost demand that could be made upon his time by these lectures, even both sets taken together, would amount to any material encroachment upon the time demanded by the principal part of his duty, in-door and out-duty both taken into the account. Nothing is more common than for Medical men, in very extensive practice, to give lectures, not one day only in the week, as here proposed, but six days; each day on three or four subjects, much more widely distant from one another than the structure and constitution of the female subject in man, and the structure and constitution of both sexes in the inferior animals. The two *Hunters* continued, both of them, giving lectures of much greater frequency, long after they had each of them attained to the very highest and most extensive pitch of practice in their respective spheres.[1]

Should any expence, however, be deemed necessary to be attached to this object, either in the view of affording encouragement, or in the view of procuring assistance, to the Medical Curator in Chief, the circumstances of the case appear to be such as would afford the public a fair prospect of reimbursement, for a great part, if not the whole, of that expence. Call the allowance made at the public expence, for this species of Sunday School, 26 guineas a year, that is, a guinea a lecture for every Sunday in the fine-weather half of the year. Besides the Country Farriers, from whose slender circumstances no contribution might be thought fit to be called for (the time and journey being itself a contribution), there seems no reason to doubt but that, by views either of economy or of amusement, many persons might be drawn to

those who are already initiated in the practice, and, by displaying before so many eyes the utility, might pave the way for the gradual propagation of provincial establishments, upon the same scale of perfection as the metropolitan, maintained, like that as well as other schools, at the expence of the individuals by whom the more peculiar part of the benefit be reaped.

[1] John Hunter (1728–93) was the brother of William, and like him a noted lecturer on anatomy, physiology, and surgery.

these lectures, who would be perfectly able and willing to pay for it, as other pupils do at other lectures: say a guinea for the course.[a] Were the above fee shared equally between the public, at whose expence the system of instruction had been instituted, and the lecturer, on whose qualifications and exertions the degree of its utility would depend, fifty two such independent pupils would be enough to indemnify the public for its expence. And fifty two such pupils at a time seems not too great a number to expect from a District of 75 parishes, including its proportionate number of Towns.

It would rest with Government to decide, what, if any thing, should be allowed for the expence of this institution, either out of the National supplies, or by a power to the local authorities (the Country Magistrates) to raise the money by Parish rates, according to the present mode. Should that allowance prove insufficient, it would then rest with individuals in each district to supply the deficiency by voluntary contributions. Partly in the way of example, partly in the way of authority, a very slight exertion on the part of Government will sometimes suffice to set an establishment a-going, by drawing attention, and calling forth the exertions of public-spirited individuals.[b]

[a] Country Gentlemen, for instance, Clergymen whose duty would afford the time, considerable Innkeepers, and the better sort of Farmers.

[b] To these lectures on the art of preserving the several sorts of animals brought under subjection to man, might come to be added in process of time an appendix relative to the art of guarding against the ravages of such of them as continue his natural enemies: granivorous birds, granivorous insects, &c. &c., against whose attacks we should be the better able to defend ourselves, the more generally a knowledge of their natural history were diffused. A slip of the tree of knowledge being once planted by the hand of government, many are the branches which may come to be grafted on it by degrees, by the discernment and public spirit of individuals.

The spirit manifested in the treaty now on the carpet for the acquisition of John Hunter's Museum, consisting in a very considerable degree of specimens of the Anatomy of the brute creation, would be very happily seconded by the institution here proposed.[1]

---

[1] John Hunter had amassed a large collection of physiological specimens, both animal and human, which he displayed in a private museum. His will directed that the collection be offered to the British government, and that, in the event of a refusal, it should be sold to some foreign state, or in one lot by auction. In 1793 William Pitt indicated that the government would not purchase the collection, and it remained unsold but intact until 1799, when a committee of the House of Commons recommended purchase for £15,000. After purchase, the collection was offered to the Royal College of Physicians, who declined it, but it was eventually accepted by the Royal College of Surgeons in 1800. In 1813 the John Hunter Museum was moved to the new premises of the Royal College of Surgeons, in Lincoln's Inn Fields, where it remains.

§IV. *Fourth and last Division of the Collateral Uses that might be made of the system of Industry Houses: Uses of an Institutional nature*

[13. *Collateral use the thirteenth*—Militia Nursery.]

The first use I shall mention, under this head, is that of making the population of the Industry House, as far as concerns the male part of the orphans and other children brought up in it, answer the purpose of a *Nursery*, or rather, to a certain degree, a succedaneum to the *Militia*.

The sum total of national expence on this account would be comprehended in the pay of a *drill Serjeant*, maintained as part of the establishment of each House.

In regard to arms for exercise, such as had been returned as unserviceable from the army, would, for this purpose, be equal to the best.

But the expence would be but nominal: since an officer of this description, under the command of the Civil power, the Governor, supported and controuled by the Chaplain and the Surgeon, would be the cheapest as well as most serviceable hand that could be employ'd, for the maintenance of security, and the preservation of peace and good order in the House.

Suppose the training to commence at the age of 16, and finish at the age of 21. During the last three or four years of that period, each youth might, in time of peace, be expected to be in a state of much better preparation for military defence than the general run of Militia men under the present laws, when embodied for a single month only out of the twelve.[1]

For the two last years, for example, they might be liable to be called out to actual service. If youth of that age would serve, in time of war, for home service, in the proportion of one third, for example, to two thirds of men of maturer age, on the present footing, and if the whole number of youth of that age furnished by the whole establishment of Industry Houses amounted to about 10,000,[a] one third of the lottery of black lots might be struck off, and a considerable expence saved to the public at the same time.[2]

[a] At 200 Houses, 50 to an House.

---

[1] Men aged between eighteen and forty-five years of age were eligible for service in the Militia. All those selected were required to attend the beginning of the annual exercise, which consisted of twenty-eight days training, although one third of them, chosen by lot, were immediately released.

[2] The peacetime strength of the Militia was approximately 30,000, chosen by lot from lists of

Under favour of this supply, the service of married men with families, and even of married men in general, might perhaps, in a considerable degree, be dispensed with: and a branch of service which has been charged, it is to be feared, with too much reason, with being a school of idleness and bad habits, proportionably reduced in numbers.

The elder part of the Fencibles[1] of an Industry House thus trained, impregnated as they would have been from the first dawn of reason with the principles of constitutional subordination, reinforced by those of gratitude, would be a most useful instrument in the hands of the Civil Power, collected in constant readiness and sufficient numbers for all occasions, prepared to cooperate with, or supersede, according to circumstances, the regular branch of the military force.

The allotment thus proposed to be made is not of the number [of] those contrivances which, under the notion of doing away hardship, only shift it from hand to hand. It is not like *Las Casas's* idea, of saving the home slaves by importing foreign ones.[2] It would not stand exposed to the imputation of any of the slave-like hardships attendant on the practice of military conscription, as in use in the Russian and Austrian Empires, in the Prussian Monarchy, and in so many other States on the Continent of Europe.[3] Here, the service is purely home

able-bodied men drawn up by the parochial authorities. For instance, 26 Geo. III, c.107 (1786) envisaged an enrollment of 30,840, so that a total of 10,000 recruits from Bentham's industry houses would have supplied approximately one third of the total. The parliamentary estimate for the pay and clothing of 20,000 disembodied Militia for 1796, during the twenty-eight days of their training, totalled £59,624: see *Commons Journals* (1795–6) li. 291.

[1] The term 'fencibles' originated in Scotland where there was no established Militia, and Lords Lieutenants were empowered to raise troops on their own initiative for home defence. The term was also applied to the forces raised by voluntary subscriptions in the English counties after 1794 in order to supplement the Militia and undertake local service: see p. 15 n. above.

[2] Bartolomé de Las Casas (1474–1566), Dominican missionary and critic of Spanish colonialism in the New World, in 1518 denounced abuses of Spanish rule, and proposed the transportation of black slaves for use by Spanish settlers in the Americas, in order to liberate the indigenous population from maltreatment and forced labour. In response to accusations of responsibility for the inauguration of the slave trade, Las Casas repudiated his earlier suggestion, and inserted a detailed account of the injustice of African slave raids in the manuscript of *Historia de las Indias*, finished in 1561 but unpublished until 1875–6. However, Antonio de Herrera Tordesillas (1559–1625) used copies of Las Casas's manuscripts in compiling his *Historia general de los hechos de los Castellanos en las islas i tierra firme del mar oceano*, 8 vols., Madrid, 1601–15, and this work in turn was used as the source of information about Las Casas's original proposals by numerous writers in English: see, for instance, William Robertson, *The History of America*, 2 vols., London and Edinburgh, 1777, i. 225–6.

[3] In the Russian Empire recruitment to the army was through levies set each year by the Senate specifying the number of men to be raised per recruiting unit, each of which, from 1775, was composed of 500 inhabitants. Until 1793 conscripts into the Russian army were obliged to serve for life, while thereafter the term of service was twenty-five years. In addition, the conscript could be ordered to any part of the Empire, and typically never returned home once enlisted. In the German Hereditary States of the Habsburg Empire from 1781 all able-bodied males between

service, the duties occasional only, and the dangers purely contingent, depending upon a state of things than which few can either be, or appear to be, less likely to be realized. *There*, the service is home service or foreign as it may happen, the obligations, when once they have commenced, equally constant and severe, the dangers in full and continual prospect.

Here, the engagement, such as it is, would be the universal lot: it would find no body unprepared for it: expectation would, in the instance of each individual, be ready trained and shaped to it, from the first dawn of sentiment. There, it is in every instance the hard lot of the ill-fated few:[a] in many instances delay'd till the maturity of the imagination has presented it in its utmost terrors.[b] There, the expence of rearing them for the public service is thrown, without indemnity, upon the individuals, the afflicted parents: here, the return for the slight tribute of personal assistance they are thus called upon to pay to the common stock of national defence, has been already paid for, and abundantly paid for, in the way of anticipation, by that country to which they will, all of them, have been indebted for maintenance and education, and many of them for life: Military men in general, are, in the stile of French Poetry, termed *children of the*

[a] In Russia, one out of a hundred of the Male Peasants is a common levy, when a supply of recruits is to be raised in war time.[1]

[b] As in Russia, where they are neither inlisted nor selected, till called out for service. In the Prussian Monarchy (see Mirabeau), the mark is set on them from infancy:[2] a much better plan than the other, since their *education* may be, and their *expectation* can not *but* be, prepared for the mode of life to which they are devoted.

---

seventeen and forty years old were liable to conscription. After training the recruit was obliged to serve in peacetime for six weeks in the year. In the remaining Habsburg dominions, recruiting districts were, as in Russia, allotted a quota, while selection was typically carried out by the lord of the manor or his agents. In Prussia, each 'canton' of about five thousand households was responsible for the manning of an infantry regiment. Conscripts were registered at the age of ten, undertook two years' military training from the age of twenty, and thereafter were obliged to serve for two or three months each year until physically incapable of so doing.

[1] In Russia the customary peacetime levy was one man per recruiting unit of five hundred inhabitants, but during the Russo-Turkish war (1787–91) there were three levies of five men per recruiting unit, and one of four per unit.

[2] See Honoré Gabriel Riqueti (1749–91), Comte de Mirabeau, *De La Monarchie Prussienne, sous Frédéric Le Grand; avec un appendice Contenant des recherches sur la situation actuelle des principales contrées de l'Allemagne*, 4 vols., London, 1788, iii. 41–3, where Mirabeau explains that Prussian society is divided into those exempted from military service (the nobility, churchmen, practitioners of liberal arts, and large merchants and manufacturers) and those eligible for such service. With regard to the latter he writes: 'Au moment où naît un enfant mâle, le ministre qui le baptise est obligé de le faire savoir au bailli ou autre préposé royal, et il est inscrit sur le rôle militaire. Les parens sont obligés d'en répondre jusqu'à l'âge de puberté, qui est également indiqué dans l'Allemagne protestante, par l'acte religieux de l'admission à la cène. A peine cette cérémonie est-elle consomée, qu'on fait prêter au jeune homme le serment militaire, et dès-lors il est soldat.'

country:[1] these Militia boys might not unaptly be stiled *Foster Children* of their country, in the sober language of plain English prose.

What, after all, would be the hardship, if it amounted to any thing, to which the youth in question are proposed to be subjected, in return for every thing?—The same and no other, which these, in common with all other individuals capable of bearing arms, are naturally devoted to by the indispensable conditions of political existence. If some were not soldiers, it would be necessary that all should be—as all were, that were not slaves, in the times of fancied happiness and virtue—the classic times.[a]

[14. *Collateral use the fourteenth*—Marine School Establishment.]

Another use, in the *institutional* way, that might be made of a certain portion of the system of Industry Houses, is the giving a maritime turn to the education of the male part of the children. Here would be a natural Nursery for the Navy, in both its branches, private as well as public.

In these situations, *swimming* ought to be as familiar, and as early taught as running. How strange, as well as fatal, the solecism so often met with on board our ships! A seaman drowned for want of knowing how to swim![b]—it is as if a fish were to be drowned. At Paris, swimming is, (at least *was* before the commencement of the present troubles) taught by Professors, as an art. This art at least, an art possessed in perfection by the rudest savages, this art might, without raising expectation to an unreasonable pitch, be expected to be among the number of the arts taught with success at the Schools attached to the maritime class of Industry Houses.

In the Cluster of little Arts comprized in the variegated profession of a Seaman,[c] boys might here be initiated at an age too tender to

[a] In schools appropriated to the children of the opulent, I have seen the military exercises treated as play, and practised with delight and exultation.

[b] Mentioning this to Officers, I have heard instances of 5 or 6 seamen lost from this cause from on board a single ship in the course of a single voyage. I have heard the proportion of Seamen in a King's ship [able][2] to save themselves by swimming estimated at much less (I fear to say how much less) than half the number.

[c] Oakum-picking, Rope-splicing, Sail-making, Net-weaving, even Ship and Boat carpentry.

[1] A reference to the opening line of the *Marseillaise*: 'Allons les enfants de la Patrie'. The *Marseillaise* was composed in April 1792 by Claude Joseph Rouget de Lisle (1760–1836), and originally entitled 'Chant de guerre pour l'armée du Rhin'. It was taken up by a battalion of volunteers from Marseilles, who sang it as they entered Paris in July 1792, and was adopted as the French national anthem in 1795.

[2] MS 'unable' contradicts the evident sense of the passage.

admitt of their being admitted into a ship's company with advantage.

If, in any situation, the accomplishment of reading were allowed to the Foster Children of the public, it would surely not be denied in these situations, where one of the first uses to be made of it would be the initiating them into the practical part of navigation. This would be the occupation of the *maritime* Sunday-schooling. Were the vacuity of childhood to be filled up in the manner it easily might be, they might be *Able Seamen* in miniature, before they were of an age for what is meant by *service.*

It were strange indeed, if a portion only of the whole strength of these Maritime Industry Schools, nor that a very considerable one, employed partly in the catching of fish, partly in the conveyance of it coastwise, were not sufficient for the supplying of the chain of maritime Industry Houses all round, and perhaps even the next chain inland, with fish, even in a fresh state, sufficient for the sustenance of the inhabitants, with the help of a small allowance of vegetable food, such as potatoes, by way of mixture: and the measures now taking for the preservation of the animal species of food in a sound state, with no larger proportion of salt than would be required for seasoning,[1] would extend the benefit of extraordinary captures to much more inland situations, without any other additional expence than that of carriage; an operation which might even be performed daily, from House to House, upon quantities sufficient for the daily consumption of each, without any greater strength of draught than what might be attached to each House almost without expence.[a]

[a] N° of persons in a House, children included, say,	2,000
Weight of fish consumed daily at $1\frac{1}{2}$ lb. per head	3,000
N° of Asses requisite for drawing the above, each Ass drawing $\frac{1}{2}$ a ton, with an old man or woman for a drawer	3
Number of miles each Ass may draw the above load daily	15

Fish (it may be observed in the way of objection) *are not at present cheap enough to serve generally as food for persons maintained at the public charge. What is there* (it may be added) *in the proposed institution that should render it cheaper, and cheaper in so considerable degree*?—That a satisfactory answer might be given to this question, is what from a general view of the subject I have no doubt of: but to give that answer in detail, it would be necessary to enter into a particular inquiry into the state of the fishing trade all over the English Coast: a task which would probably be thought to diverge too far from the main subject, and would demand too much time, to be bestowed without some specific prospect of its being turned to account in the way of use.

Fishing, as far as it is productive, has in its application to the purpose (the purpose

[1] Bentham himself had been engaged in research on the preservation of food since 1794, including the development of his 'frigidarium' or 'cold house', intended for use in both the panopticon prison and the pauper panopticons: see UC cvi. 17–75.

Example, added to habit, to habit formed by a course of practice coeval with the first dawn of the thinking faculty, would, in infinitely the greater number of instances, banish every idea of hardship, and every sentiment of reluctance, from the situation of those who found themselves, from an age anterior to that of consent, destined to this mode of life. The exceptions would in all probability be so few, that the liberty of making a different choice would make no other gap in the proposed number than what might be filled up by volunteers from the inland country, without difficulty or inconvenience.

It may just be hinted at, as a subject for consideration, whether, from this part of the system of Industry Houses, any and what assistance might be desirable in the way of economy, whether in the article of building, or that of management, to the system of intelligence by signals.[1]

[15. *Collateral use the fifteenth*—Shipwreck Relief.]

Another use, depending on the giving a maritime turn to education, in the maritime part of the system of Industry Houses, is the establishing a connected and constant system of relief, all along the coast, against the calamity of Shipwreck.

The inhospitality of some of our Coasts is but too proverbial. By means of this branch of the Industry School Establishment, the national character might be retrieved, and the imputation of the vice be converted into the praise of the opposite virtue.

Another item would thus be added to the list of considerations that might come to concurr in recommending a departure, either in point of situation, or in point of number, from whatever arrangement of the component elements of the system of Industry Houses might, on other accounts, be thought to demand the preference. A sacrifice, in point of centrality, might thus be necessitated: and either the journeys of a portion of the inhabitants, to and from the Industry House, proportionably lengthened, or the number of the Industry-Houses proportionably encreased. But, in relation to this head, neither is perfect symmetry practicable, under such a variety of

of furnishing to the inhabitants of an Industry House the chief part of their food) two great advantages over agriculture—viz: there is no *rent* to pay: and there can never be any want of elbow room.

[1] In 1795 a series of eighty-seven signal towers were built along the coast of England, and between Admiralty House in Whitehall and the naval dockyards at Chatham and Portsmouth, to expedite the transmission of intelligence from place to place by means of semaphore signalling. Each tower was commanded by a lieutenant at a cost of 7s. 6d. per day. On 7 October 1794 Bentham wrote to his brother Samuel, remarking on 'optical experiments with a view to Telegraph' at Woolwich: see *Correspondence* (*CW*), v. 91.

antagonizing circumstances, nor, within certain limits, would aberration be productive of any sensible inconvenience. Cheapness of provisions, the consequence of the superior facility of obtaining fish, is an advantage sufficient, of itself, to outweigh a considerable mass of inconvenience. By the strength of the nearest Industry House, assistance against the calamity might be afforded on the one hand: defence against those whose inhuman rapacity might prompt them to embitter it, on the other.

A reward, for the first information of a vessel in distress.—The Governor, on receipt of such advice, to take order for the assistance and relief of the Crew, and for the salvage of the vessel and goods.[a]

Partly for this casual use, partly for the more constant service of general intelligence, a chain of Look-outs, at inconsiderable distances, might be maintained, between Industry House and Industry House, peopled by small detachments from the Industry Houses, victualled, and otherwise supplied, upon the frugal plan of the Industry House Establishment.

[16.] *Collateral use the [sixteenth]*[1] *and last*—National Musical Seminary.[2]

This use may at first glance appear frivolous enough: at least in the eyes of that sort of wisdom which regards pleasure, even in its purist and most innocent shape, as an enemy to use. But the more maturely this application is considered, the higher it will rise in the estimate of a judicious eye.

Nature, corporeal Nature, was conceived in former days to entertain an abhorrence for vacuity:[3] that incorporeal Nature does,

[a] In these situations, that foreigners might not be in want of an interpreter, preference might be given in the choice of the Chaplain and Surgeon to persons conversant in foreign languages—one, the Chaplain for instance, conversant in the Southern languages of Europe: French, Italian, Spanish, Portugueze—the other, in the Northern: German, Dutch, Danish, Swedish:—at a future period, Russian.

In these situations, by means of Seafaring men, it might likewise be easily contrived to have, amongst the ordinary class of inhabitants, individuals capable of performing the functions of interpreters for all the maritime languages.

---

[1] MS 'fifteenth'.

[2] This collateral use does not appear in the copy. From Bentham's headings it is clear that the text itself was written as part of 'Collateral Uses derivable from a system of Industry Houses', though there is evidence that Bentham may subsequently have considered incorporating it in his discussion of pauper education in 'Pauper Management Improved'. For further details see the Editorial Introduction, p. xxx & n. above.

[3] Aristotle, *Physics*, IV, 213^{b}30–216^{b}20, refuted the possibility of the existence of a void or vacuum, which was the standard view until the seventeenth century. The expression ***natura vacuum abhorret***, 'nature abhores a vacuum', appears in several writers, including François Rabelais (1494?-*c.*1553), 'Gargantua', *Œuvres complètes*, ed. M. Huchon and F. Moreau, Paris, 1994, p. 20.

is beyond dispute: the mental void, so surely as it has nothing innocent to occupy it, so surely will it be filled up by mischief: by mischief in one or other of its shapes, improbity or imprudence. Every pleasure pure from mischief is valuable then, not only on its own account, but by its rivality to mischief: as a candidate for the possession of the human breast in opposition to mischief. Above all species of mischief, drunkenness, the parent and ally of every other, drunkenness, which, bringing misery in its train, wretchedness in all its varieties, brings pleasure in its hand, furnishing sensations for every moment which it lasts, is, to untutored minds, that is to the great mass of the national mind in the present state of things, [to] the mental world, what Newton's ether is to the natural:[1] in that order of beings, to speak of no other, whatever mind has nothing else in it is full of drunkenness.[2] Music, with all its innocence, music possesses one property in common with drunkenness, the furnishing sensation for every moment: and in much greater perfection, since when the fumes are dissipated, the potion is loathed: whereas no loathing, much less the pains of body and mind that embitter the pleasures of drunkenness, ever disturbs the pure delights of music. Musical exertions may, like all other exertions, have been attended with fatigue: musical gratifications may, like all other gratifications, have terminated in satiety: but neither the one nor the other are ever followed by disgust.[a]

[a] The connection in the way of causality between things in themselves so disparate as music and virtue, has been announced by Poetry, and Reason proves it. In Poetry, the force of the connection has indeed been exaggerated: for without exaggeration, that is falsification in a certain form, there can scarce be Poetry. But here, the exaggeration has at least a platform of truth to stand upon. The proposition, that

> The man who has not music in his soul
> Is fit for treasons stratagems and spoils[3]

is, in quality of a universal proposition, the sort of proposition of which it wears the

---

[1] Since Antiquity there had existed a theory which conceived of space as completely filled with matter, the Plenum or Ether, in which atoms moved. Sir Isaac Newton (1642–1727), natural philosopher, appears to have rejected the theory in *Philosophiae Naturalis Principia Mathematica*, London, 1687, pp. 352–4, where he recorded an experiment with a pendulum which disproved the existence of the ether. However, in *Opticks: or, A Treatise of the Reflections, Refractions, Inflections and Colours of Light*, 2nd edn., London, 1718, pp. 322–8, he expressed a belief in the existence of the ether, as a medium more rare and subtle than air, through which heat was conveyed.

[2] In the margin, Bentham has noted at this point: 'Pushpin is morality in as far as it keeps out drunkenness.' Pushpin was a child's game in which each player pushed or flipped his 'pin' or counter, with the object of crossing that of his opponent.

[3] An inaccurate rendering of *The Merchant of Venice* v. i. 83:

> The man that hath no music in himself,
> Nor is not moved with concord of sweet sounds,
> Is fit for treasons, strategems, and spoils.

Music has this farther advantage of its being so intimately connected with attention, the exercise of the mind: it is the effect of attention, and the cause of attention. Skill in music, be it ever so slight, is the product of attention, and, in growing, keeps up the demand for it. But, to the mind as to the body, what gives exercise

form, happily not true. But what *is* true, is that the more occupied a man's mind is with music, and with the sentiments with which music is most accustomed to be accompanied (to say nothing of those with which it might be accompanied, especially in a place like that in question), so much the less exposed [is it] to the temptation of engaging in any such destructive enterprizes.

In as far as music is favourable to virtue merely by filling up with innocent recreation that time which might otherwise have been occupied by vice, trap-ball it may be said,[1] an exercise and strengthener of the body, or at least *chess*, an exercise and strengthener of the mind, are, it may be said, equally favourable to virtue. But, in favour of music, I am inclined to think, we may go farther, and pronounce it to have a connection with virtue peculiar to itself. The artificial notes, which music is occupied in the production of, bear for the most part a natural resemblance to the notes expressive of the social affections, of the affections which are so many modifications of benevolence: complaint, entreaty, soothing, condoleance, congratulation, co-exultation and the like. There is Music for War, it may be said, as well as for Love. True: but happily the War-music is comparatively but little in vogue: and even in War-Music, it is rather what there is of sociality in war, rather than what there is of malice and cruelty, that is expressed by it. The reciprocating and almost continual butcheries of the Grecian Republics, the proscriptions of Marius and Sylla, the executions under Alva, the burnings under Mary, the explosions at Lyons, the Noyades and Fusillades at Nantes, were not accompanied, I think, by Music.[2]

[1] Trap-ball was played with a wooden 'trap' from which a small wooden ball was projected into the air. The object of the game was to strike the ball as far as possible with a bat.

[2] The view that there was continual warfare between the city states of classical Greece was commonplace in the eighteenth century. See, for instance, David Hume, 'Of the Populousness of Antient Nations', *Political Discourses*, Edinburgh, 1752, p. 188.

Gaius Marius (*c.*157–86 BC), Roman general, politician, and rival of Lucius Cornelius Sulla Felix (138–79 BC) for supremacy in Roman politics, was driven into exile by Sulla in 88 BC, but captured Rome in the following year, and executed numerous political opponents before his death. Sulla held power in Rome as Dictator between 82 and 79 BC, during which time he initiated the *proscriptio*, whereby a list of men declared outlaws and public enemies was exhibited in the forum, their property and lives being thereby forfeited.

Fernando Alvarez de Toledo (1507–82), Third Duke of Alva, and general of Philip II (1527–98), King of Spain from 1556, commanded in the Netherlands between 1567 and 1573, where he was ruthless in the suppression of heresy, and condemned to death some 12,000 people for participation in a Protestant rebellion against Spanish rule.

During the reign of Mary I (1516–58), Queen of England and Ireland from 1553, between February 1555 and November 1558, some three hundred people in England were convicted of heresy and burned.

In France, in October 1793, the Royalist bastion of Lyon fell to a republican army. The local guillotine proved incapable of coping with the numbers of Lyonnais condemned to execution, and during December condemned men were blown into open graves by cannon fire and grape shot.

At Nantes in 1793 the representative of the National Convention, Jean Baptiste Carrier (1756–94), ordered the execution of some 1,800 people by means of two methods: the 'noyades', or death by drowning; and the 'fusillades', a wholesale execution by means of a volley of fire-arms.

gives strength: and it is on its strength that the mind depends for its capacity of giving to the motives constituted by the prospect of greater but distant pains the effect of prevailing over the motives furnished by immediate pleasure. But this connection with the exercise and invigoration of the mind is the more intimate the more it has of skill in it, the more it is cultivated as a science: in a word the more pains have been bestowed upon it. And where, if music were not learnt nothing else would be, it is not so much by being possessed that music, like any other art, is good for the mind's health, as by having been learnt. Happily, where neither opportunity nor natural faculty are altogether wanting, it is, of all species of instruction, one that presents itself the most naturally to be learnt. In the instance of the most important of the other employments of the mind, in the art of reading for example, the art in its utmost perfection is but a means to an end, or a confused variety of ends, towards which it has its way to make with great pain, to which it is indebted for whatever it has to recommend it: in this, the end as well as the means presents itself at the first step, and [both] advance together: every exertion has present enjoyment to reward and sweeten it.

A taste for music again, the more diffused it is, is not only proportionably the more productive as a source of innocent enjoyment in a community, but it is the purer, the more exempt from danger. It is a remark I remember hearing made among grave citizens, quoting their own experience and speaking of times some 50 or 60 years back, when a taste [for] music was less common than at present, that a good voice is a formidable snare to a young man in business. Why?—Because when the talent of singing is rare, it falls naturally into a connection with the habit of drinking. The fashion for drinking, being already established and predominant, draws the new formed and weaker fashion into its vortex. Melpomene becomes the waiting-maid, not to say the prostitute, of Bacchus, and dragged in chains behind his car.[1] The talent, though thus degraded, being at the same time agreeable, and by the supposition rare, is proportionably a mark of distinction. Conferring on the possessor the faculty of pleasing, it renders his company an object of courtship and competition among his fellows: he is admitted and invited into those parties where drinking is the principal enjoyment, song the accessory, and where music, instead of being its own reward, is paid for in the only universally current coin and medium of social intercourse in those societies, intoxicating liquor. From the same quarter the remark was accompanied, and contrasted, by another—that no

[1] In classical mythology, Melpomene was the muse of tragedy, and Bacchus the god of wine.

such danger had been observed to attend on a proficiency in instrumental music—why? Because there neither is nor ever was any such connection between instrumental music and drinking. Drinking leads to noise: and noise inspired by drinking falls naturally into that sort of bawling which has drinking for its theme: and so long as a man retains any sort of possession of his faculties, whatsoever be the disorder in them, he is fit for bawling at the same rate. Between instrumental music and drinking, there is rather an antipathy than an alliance: a man may play a drinking song, but the connection between the music and the drinking is no longer immediate but remote: he may attempt to play, but so long as he does so he must have his faculties in the most perfect degree at command. A musical performer may, after the performance, get drunk like another man: after the performance, but not while he performs: where intoxication commences disorder commences, and where disorder commences, there instrumental music ends.

In Italy, where Music as a study, and as a study that has descended and spread itself among the general mass of the people, is of so much older date, the connection between drinking and music, even vocal music, and in the lowest mouths, is scarce if at all discernible: devotion, love, moral sentiment, any thing rather than drinking, is the subject of song, even the most popular among songs. The favourite song of the Sicilian Mariners is an hymn to the Virgin.[1] In France too, the most popular among all songs, while France was France, the song which, by the simplicity of its charms, subdued all Europe to French Music, the Air de Marlbrook, was a little elegy, simple, almost affected, even to silliness, but without the most distant glance at drinking.[2] Among English Mariners, a song is scarce a song without gin and flip in it. Though, even in England now, at the close of the century, the proportion of drinking songs to others is sensibly less, and considerably less, than at the beginning or the middle of it.

Instrumental music is, in its own nature, of use in the ways above

[1] 'The Prayer of the Sicilian Mariners' was a popular hymn in the late eighteenth century: see Domenico Corri, *Select Collection of the Most Admired Songs, Duetts, &c. From Operas in the highest esteem, And from other Works in Italian, English, French, Scotch, Irish &c. &c.*, 4 vols., London and Edinburgh, [1795], iv. 83; and William Dechair Tattersall, *Improved Psalmody*, London, 1794, p. 67.

[2] 'La Chanson de Malbrough' was believed to have been composed after the battle of Malplaquet in 1709, when it was rumoured that the victorious commander, John Churchill (1650–1722), first Duke of Marlborough, soldier and statesman, victor of Blenheim (1704), Ramilles (1706), and Oudenarde(1708), had been killed. The song appeared in a collection of street songs, *Chansons, Vaudevilles et Ariettes Choisis par Duchemin*, undated, but probably published between 1769 and 1777, p. 10, under the title of 'La Mort de M. de Marlb'roug'. Bentham believed that he had heard the first performance of the song in England, in 1788: see Bowring, x. 184.

stated: as a source of innocent amusement, perpetual and inexhaustible, and as a species of exercise, wholesome and strengthening to the mind. These uses belong to it in its own nature: in its own nature it is on the one hand incapable of being abused, on the other hand incapable of being put to any higher use.

Vocal music, sharing with instrumental the uses above specified, stands in other respects on a very different footing in point of utility: by neglect, or perverse industry, it is capable of being the instrument of much mischief: by attention well directed, it is capable of being rendered the vehicle of every moral good. In its own nature, it is capable, in the hands of authority, of being made the receptacle and the vehicle of whatever sentiment may be thought fit to be impressed. It is an anchor with which every thing that is meant to be soon learnt, perpetually recalled, may be rivetted into the tender mind. Music, in this its most perfect form, may be made the preceptor of every duty, the guardian of every virtue. It is one of the most effective, as well as the gentlest, instruments, of the gentlest, as well as strongest, species of empire: the empire that may, and ought to be acquired by a good government over the affections of the people.

Verse, the form of speech to which vocal Music is always adapted, has already in this respect a vast advantage over prose: on which account it served, in default of printing, as a vehicle to the first histories, moral compositions, and the first laws. To the aid thus given to the retentive faculty, music makes another addition, nor that an inconsiderable one. Measure gives to composition the faculty of being retained; but it is melody only that affords the inducement and occasion to retain it. In solitude, a composition thus adorned occupies the vacant minute: in chorus, it continues its operations on the retentive faculty during the festivity of social assemblies. By the help of these aids, employ'd with due frugality, the impression made [by] a composition in the memory may be indelible.

I say, with due frugality: for, in every individual, the powers of the retentive faculty are limited: and in individuals of this description, particularly limited. The subjects, as well as melodies, of popular songs destined to this use should be selected with as much religious care as the subjects of legislation: and the stock of words, thus attempted to be made current, husbanded with a degree of frugality contrasting as much as possible with the equally nauseous and pernicious profusion displayed in the disposal of the literary matter of the laws.

The direct object of instruction in this line, the subjecting the voice to the laws of melody and harmony, will be accomplished in greater or less degree, or in some instances may fail altogether, according to the natural capacity of each pupil, and the talent of the instructor: but the indirect and collateral object, the fixing the sense in the memory, may be attained in equal degree in both cases: and thus it is the more important of the two that, in some measure or other, can not fail of being accomplished. Whether a man sings well or ill will matter but little, if by singing he has stocked his memory with useful things.[a]

Vulgar Legislation drags men to its purpose in chains, from which, thanks to the bungling of the grimgribber man at the anvil, who forges them by the hundred, the captives break loose in crowds: superior Legislation leads men by silken threads, entwined round their affections, and makes them its own for ever.

To the advantages thus derivable from musical instruction in point of innocent pleasure, rational exercise and moral instruction to the inferior classes, whose education is in view, and to the consideration of the additional use that might be derived in this way from the system of Industry Houses, with reference to the interests of that class in particular, and to those of the whole community in general, may be added a use of far inferior moment it is true, but which may present itself in more interesting colours, of greater interest to many

[a] The use of God save the King as a preservative of loyalty and domestic peace has been recently experienced on more occasions than one:[1] the melody recommending itself by beauty to the most polished ears, and by its simplicity to the rudest ear. A song of this complexion, implanted by the habit of half a century in the mass of popular sentiment, can not be refused a place in the inventory of the national blessings. Were it on this account alone, it were to be perhaps wished that George should be the name of all Kings of Great Britain to the remotest futurity, attached to the office as that of Pharaoh was in Egypt, and that of Louis had come to be in France: and that, in this view, to save the having recourse to the affected course of a change of name, as pursued in relation to the Papal throne, this name might form one of the constituent elements of the *Praenomen*,[2] in the instance of every male member of the Royal Family.

The War whoop of anarchy, the Marseillais Hymn,[3] is to my ear, I must confess, independently of all moral association, a most dismal, flat, and unpleasing ditty: and to any ear it is at any rate a long winded and complicated one. In the instance of a melody so mischievous in its application, it is a fortunate incident, if, in itself, it should be doomed neither in point of [universality],[4] nor permanence, to gain equal hold on the affections of the people.

---

[1] During the 1790s 'God save the King' was increasingly sung when the Royal Family appeared in public and on days of celebration as a demonstration of loyalty to both King and country. The anthem was sung at loyalist meetings to demonstrate antagonism to the radical political ideas associated with the French Revolution, and with the writings of Thomas Paine (1737–1809), whose effigy was frequently burned. See M. Morris, *The British Monarchy and the French Revolution*, New Haven and London, 1998, pp. 142–4, 154–9.

[2] i.e. 'Forename'.

[3] For the *Marseillaise* see p. 127 n. above.

[4] MS 'universally'.

an eye. I mean the application that might be made of it to the augmentation of innocent at least, however light and unprofitable, pleasure, on the part of the superior classes, by the bringing to light so vast a stock of natural talent as would otherwise have been lost to the musical world, and giving the choice of the whole national stock to that market where the article will find its highest value.

Though between a relish for sweet sounds and the power of producing them there is unquestionably a natural alliance, yet no two things can be more distinct in their own nature, or more perfectly susceptible of a separate existence. Many a voice, superior to any that has ever been heard in public, may therefore be this moment lying dormant for want of having been called forth to trial. The chance of uncommon excellence in this line, the certainty of that quantity of entertainment, which, out of a given number of persons, the powers of instruction may any where ensure, will add to the attractions of the scene, to that general fund of attractive force on which the goodness of the management depends, in as far as depends upon the stimulative and corrective influence of the public eye. Every Sunday, Chaunts, Anthemes and every other branch of the Choral service, augmented and improved, might, with an organ of course to guide, sweeten the exercise of devotion: every year, or Half year or Quarter, a selection of the best voices from a number of Districts all round might form a public celebrity, of which, at the same time that social entertainment would be the professed and direct object, the fixing the corrective powers of the public eye upon the good management of each establishment, in all its branches, would be the indirect, but not less certain, result.

Each building, provided with the quantity of space required for other purposes, might occasionally be adapted to the occasional purpose of these festivities, at little or no expence: and this even without taking into the account those voluntary contributions which, where amusement is the purchase, are never grudged.

The only expence worth notice is the Salary of a *Chapel Master*[a] to each House, to preside over the musical studies of the House. These, if English ground should not be found sufficiently rich in musical skill, might be had from the richer soils of Italy and Germany in any numbers, of competent skill, and, by means of a proper engagement, at a very unexpensive rate. For though the Marlboroughs and the Schomberg's of the Art,[1] when imported from

[a] In Italian, *Maestro di Capella*: in German *Capel-Meister*.

[1] An allusion to John Churchill, Duke of Marlborough, and Frederick Herman von Schönberg (1615–90), celebrated soldier, who held commissions successively in the French, Portuguese, Prussian, Dutch, and English armies.

those countries [are][1] paid, every one knows with what profusion, yet officers of competent, though inferior, rank in the service, are to be had at almost soldier's price.

It is a position that has been already laid down, that the cultivation of talents productive of no other effect than that of giving a relative advantage to the youth maintained at the public expence, over those maintained at the expence of their parents, ought not to be made an object of endeavour: since what one gains upon this plan, another must lose: and that wherever, by the hand of power, one man is made to lose, that another may gain to the same amount and no more, the community is the loser upon the whole, by the amount of the difference, in point of happiness, between justice and injustice.[2] It has been at the same time laid down, on the other hand, that where, by cultivation, a talent can be brought to light, from the exercise of which the public would reap clear accession of advantage, there the opportunity of giving the public that advantage ought not to be neglected: since the reason which in the other case prohibits the cultivation of talent does not hold.[3] But the sort of talent that depends upon voice is precisely in this latter case. The greater the number of persons in a country to whom the opportunity of instruction in the act of singing is afforded, the greater the chance of its producing a given number of singers possessed of a given degree of excellence. Each Industry House would in this way serve as a seminary to the Choir, and the Theatre. And, by so prodigious a multiplication of chances as would be the result of an addition thus ornamental to the fabric of public education, degrees of natural excellence in this line might be brought to view, far exceeding any thing that the country hath ever yet exhibited.[a]

[a] The profit that has been reaped by the public pleasures from the idea of adding this ornament to eleemosynary education, has been evidenced in the instance of the Foundling Hospital, for example, in the person of more individuals than one; and on this occasion, the names of Temple and Prentice and others may present themselves.[4] Should there be any one to whose estimation the force of the proof should fail of being adequate to the support of the structure here proposed to be raised upon it, it may be requested of him to consider how minute a portion of the public strength in this line is there exhibited, and under what disadvantage, destitute as it is of the

[1] MS 'is'. [2] See p. 55 n. above. [3] See ibid.

[4] The Foundling Hospital was founded by Thomas Coram (1668?-1751), philanthropist, and opened in Bloomsbury in 1745. Children were taught singing at the Hospital from the middle of the eighteenth century, and by 1790 singing was taught for one hour on two occasions per week. The singing of the children attracted people to the chapel services, and provided the Hospital with a source of income from the collections. Certain children, usually the blind and those with poor eyesight, were singled out for musical instruction, in order to provide them with a means of livelihood. Those trained as singers were often employed to sing at private parties. Neither Temple nor Prentice has been identified, although both were names commonly given

Let it not be imagined that there is any thing naturally rare or difficult in its own nature, in the attainment of such a share of musical instruction as would be sufficient for the purpose. The difficulty of learning to sing, even to the perfection of plain singing as well as voice will admitt, is nothing in comparison of the difficulty of learning to read, a task the accomplishment [of] which, by the frequency of its being overcome, is apt to be overlooked, but which will well appear the more formidable, and the conquest of it the more surprizing, the more clearly the subject is considered.[a]

In the same compass of time, according to the plan of instruction observed, and the qualifications of the master, nothing may be learnt, or every thing. Twelve years may be compleatly consumed in learning to read badly, practice the four rules of arithmetic, and

benefit of the stimulating powers of competition, as well in point of opportunity of instruction.

The scene exhibited by the annual meeting of the Charity Schools at St Paul's I have often heard mentioned, and never otherwise than as a highly interesting and affecting one: *heavenly* is an epithet I have heard employed by humane and pious lips.[1] Yet who does not perceive under what disadvantage, in point of instruction, the dismal ditties which constitute the vocal part of the entertainment are there squalled out, composed of insulated notes almost destitute of connection, destitute of all melody, and not so much as aiming at the attribute of harmony, which alone, in default of melody, could render them supportable.

[a] Among the London Charity Children, of whom 8 or 9000 have been seen exhibiting at a time, nothing can be more universal than the squalling Psalm tunes according to custom in one part: but, considering that time must be equally observed in both cases, the difference between learning to sing in one part and two parts is next to nothing. Divide ten boys into two bands of five each, giving to one band the upper part always to sing, and to the other always the lower; then, when they are perfect in their respective parts, join the two bands together, the junction will scarce be productive even of a momentary perplexity, the singers in each band having every one of them his fellows to guide him, and keep him to the time.

In the Churches of the Metropolis, the seat of cultivation, singing in parts is scarcely known: in the country, the seat of rudeness and simplicity, there is scarce any such thing as singing in the Churches but in parts: so little is there of natural difficulty in the case, so entirely does the difference depend upon accident and custom. In Country Congregations, where is the difficulty, what profitable time does it consume, and for whom is it too great?

An earlier commencement, or a longer continuance by a year to two of the Sunday School plan, would be found abundantly sufficient for the purpose.

---

to foundlings, since children were frequently left on the steps of the Temple Church, which was connected with the Hospital, while Prentice is an abbreviation of 'apprentice', and the governors of the Hospital would arrange to indenture children in their care at the age of fourteen.

[1] In 1704 a joint procession and service for 2,000 children selected from charity schools in London and Westminster was held in St Andrew's, Holborn. A Society of Patrons of the Anniversary of the Charity Schools was formed to organize an annual service, which was held in St Paul's Cathedral from 1782. The service in 1788 was described in the *Gentlemen's Magazine*, lviii. 558, as 'a scene inexpressibly enchanting to a benevolent mind'.

write a bad hand: twelve years, under a good plan of instruction, with an assortment of suitable masters, might suffice, where the case required it, for conducting a youth with profit through the whole circle of literary study, the arts and sciences, in addition to what requires as much labour, perhaps, as all of them together, two or three of the most useful languages. Greek is thought difficult, because rare: Hebrew more difficult, because rarer: but to Jews, Hebrew is not more difficult than English to Englishmen, or French to Frenchmen. In England, among Jews, the meanest and most ignorant is master of at least three languages: Hebrew and English two: the third either German or Portuguese.[1]

[1] There is no text corresponding to the following marginal contents paragraph, which belongs here: 'Addition: Music would be a bond of mutual harmony among the Apprentices after their emancipation. And by spreading among the body of the people the practice of Psalmody in an improved stile and with augmented numbers, would add to the inducements for frequenting divine service.'

PAUPER SYSTEMS COMPARED, OR A COMPARATIVE VIEW OF THE SEVERAL SYSTEMS ESTABLISHABLE AS WELL AS ESTABLISHED IN RELATION TO THE POOR

Systems relative to the mode of executing the task of making provision for the relief of indigence, are all reducible to one or other of [four][1] topics: 1. the *quantum*, 2. the *quality*, 3. the *place* where, and 4. the *fund*:

1. As to the quantum—in what *quantity* or proportion to the demand: whether there shall be no provision at all—an inadequate provision—or an adequate one?

2. As to the quality—or, in essence, the degree of *comfort* to be administered, whether such as to render the condition of a burthensome Pauper eligible or not in comparison of that of the self-maintaining Poor—and whether simply eligible or simply ineligible, or eligible or not according to circumstances.

3. As to the *place*—whether in private Houses, or in Houses of a public nature, appropriated to the purpose; and in the latter case, whether in Houses upon a *small* scale, such as common *Poor Houses*, or, as they are sometimes stiled, *Work houses*, or in Houses upon a *large* scale, such as those which have taken the name of Houses of Industry?

4. From what *fund*—that is, at whose expence? At the expence of what description of persons?—At the expence of the class of contributors at present charged, or at the expence of a new class of contributors?—And in the latter case, whether at the expence of the persons themselves liable to become Paupers (charged upon them at a period anterior to that of their becoming burthensome), or at the expence of any and what other description of persons?[a]

5. In any case, the question with regard to the Fund introduces another set of questions with regard to the *hands* in which the management of the Fund shall be reposed. Whether the Fund shall be *national*, for the whole country, as is the case with the Funds for National Defence, Administration of Justice, and other public exigences, or whether it shall be local, and broken down into a multitude of independent Funds, for example as many as there are Parishes in the Country, as at present: and, in either case, whether the hands

[a] Systems which endeavour to charge the expence of the provision for indigence upon the indigent themselves, that is upon those who otherwise might have been indigent, are of a preventive cast, and may be considered as systems, or schemes, for the *prevention of indigence*.[2]

---

[1] MS 'three'.

[2] Bentham appears to have written only a few fragmentary passages on this subject, under the heading 'Projects Various': see the Editorial Introduction, p. xxxvii & n. above.

intrusted with the Management shall or shall not have a personal interest in the success of it. Hence the following questions under the head of management—Management national, or local? Undivided, or divided? Management in the hands of Administration, or in Hands independent [of][1] Administration? Management—in interested,[a] or in uninterested Hands?[b]

Such are the questions, the discussion of which will occupy the ensuing pages.

CHAPTER I. SYSTEMS ENUMERATED[2]

By the Small-Establishment system, I would be understood to mean any system which would admitt of lodging the persons to be provided for at separate houses of their own choice, to the exclusion of the use of common lodging houses. The extent of an ordinary Parish, and at the utmost of a Parish of the largest rate, being the pattern kept in view in the institution of an Establishment destined to this system of management, the term Parochial, or Parish-Establishment, system, may be used as synonymous to, and explanatory of, the term Small-Establishment system.

By the Large-Establishment system, I would be understood to mean any system which, abandoning the idea of allowing separate and distinct lodging places, at the choice of the persons to be provided for, should content itself with providing Establishments in such numbers, as that when distributed over England with that rough sort of equality which the various modifications of local exigence

[a] To *farm* the Poor, as the phrase is, is to vest the management of the concerns of the Poor in interested hands. This introduces the discussion relative to the eligibility of the Farming System—for which see Ch. | |.[3]

[b] In the case of a National Joint Stock Company, establishing a Subscription Fund, with an authority extending over the whole country, the management is national—vested in independent and interested Hands. Independent with reference to Government, and interested (in proportion to the shares of the several Stock holders) with reference to success.

[1] MS 'in'.

[2] In the draft, Bentham provided a definition of the Home-Provision system, which consisted in the supply of relief in the form of 'out allowances', paid to persons who remained resident in their own dwellings, before providing definitions of the Small-Establishment and Large-Establishment systems. He appears subsequently to have decided to omit the definition of the Home-Provision system. For further details see the Editorial Introduction, p. xxxvii above.

[3] Bentham did not in the end decide to include the discussion of farming the poor in 'Pauper Systems Compared', but it is included in the present volume as Appendix B, pp. 276–89 below. For a discussion of this material, and its place in Bentham's writings on the poor laws, see the Editorial Introduction, pp. l–li above.

would admitt of, would allow an occasional journey on foot to be performed in the course of the shortest day, from the extremities of the corresponding District to the seat of the establishment, supposed to be as near to centrical as the above circumstances will admitt, on the part of a person of the labouring class, even of the tenderer sex, persons labouring under morbid infirmity, and children under 10 or 12 years of age, suppose, excepted.[a]

[a] Fifty-two being the number of Counties in England and Wales, and four Establishments, upon an average, to a County being the number proposed, as corresponding to the local extent of a District, consistent with the condition just supposed, over and above such further addition to the number of establishments as might be demanded for the extra-population of the Metropolis, and some other of the great Towns, the Large-Establishment system, as thus described, might, for the sake of contrasting it with the Parochial Establishment system, be termed the Quarter-County Establishment system.

Ten thousand moreover, or a number very near to it,[*a*] being the number of Parishes in England and Wales (Hamlets and other Divisions of Parishes out of the question), this number of Parishes would give, in round, 200 Parishes to a County, or 50 Parishes to the Quarter of a County, upon an average. Considered in this point of view, the Fifty-Parish system is another appellative that might be given to the Large-Establishment, or Quarter County, system, as contrasted with the Parochial Establishment system.

Moreover, since (confining the consideration as before to the article of extent, and setting aside the as yet unascertainable extra-allowance that might be requisite on the score of extra-population) 200, in round numbers, would be the number of Houses requisite in the whole, in an extent equal to England and Wales, upon the supposition of 4 to a County, the name of the Two-hundred-House system is another appellative by which, on some occasions, it might be convenient to characterize the Large-Establishment system. This number of Districts, supposing each District exactly square, and all of them equal, would divide all England and Wales into squares of such a magnitude that the length of each side of the square would be | | miles:[1] reducing to compleat squares the fragments of squares left in the maritime districts by the intersection of the sea.

If, on the Small-Establishment system, it were proposed that the District corresponding to each Establishment should be exactly commensurate in point of extent every where with the existing Parishes, the term correspondent to, and contrasting with, the appellation of the Two-hundred-House system, used as synonymous to the Large-Establishment system, would be Ten-thousand-House system. But since, in the system under consideration, an union of Parishes is provided for, and considered as the more common case,[2] and thereby Parishes of small dimension considered as

[*a*] 9926.

---

[1] While not supplying a figure here, in 'Outline of a Work entitled Pauper Management Improved', *Annals of Agriculture*, xxx (1798), 111 (Bowring, viii. 374), where the number of industry houses envisaged had increased to an initial 250, and an eventual 500, rather than the 200 spoken of here, Bentham indicates that the length of each side of such a square would initially be 15 miles, falling to $10\frac{2}{3}$ miles with the doubling of the number of industry houses.

[2] Pitt's Poor Bill provided that a parish could unite with another or others for the purposes of poor law administration by majority vote of the ratepayers: see *Commons Sessional Papers of the Eighteenth Century*, ciii. 169–70. Union between parishes for the purposes of poor relief, which

Of the Large-Establishment system as delineated and discriminated in the note, there is no perfectly apposite sample to my knowledge, any where in existence. Of existing Establishments, the nearest that I know of are some of the largest of the Incorporated Districts that cover a considerable part of Suffolk and Norfolk.[1] But the very largest fall considerably short, in point of extent, of a district corresponding to the sort of Establishment meant by a Large-Establishment as above explained.

single Parishes are excluded, let five, for supposition's sake, be considered as the average number of Parishes of which a District on the proposed Small-Establishment system would be composed. On this supposition, the Small-Establishment system might, by way of contrast to the Large-Establishment system, as expressed and particularized by the appellation of the Two-Hundred-House system, be termed the Two-Thousand-House system.

---

usually involved the establishment of a single workhouse for the poor of the several 'incorporated' parishes, could be achieved by Local Act of Parliament, although 9 Geo. I, c.7 (1722), and 22 Geo. III, c.83 (1782), provided for the union of parishes by vote in vestry meetings, thus circumventing the need for particular legislation.

[1] Bentham gathered information regarding houses of industry in Norfolk and Suffolk from Sir Frederick Morton Eden (1766–1809), *The State of the Poor; or, an History of the Labouring Classes in England, from the Conquest to the Present Period; In which are particularly considered, their Domestic Economy, with respect to Diet, Dress, Fuel, and Habitation; And the various Plans which, from time to time, have been proposed, and adopted, for the Relief of the Poor: together with Parochial Reports Relative to the Administration of Work-houses, and Houses of Industry; the State of Friendly Societies; and other Public Institutions; in several Agricultural, Commercial, and Manufacturing, Districts*, 3 vols., London, 1797; and from Thomas Ruggles (1737–1813), *The History of the Poor; their Rights, Duties, and the Laws respecting them. In a series of Letters*, 2 vols., London, 1793, ii. 261–80. Notes by Bentham on Ruggles's discussion of the Suffolk industry houses survive at UC cxxxiii. 42–3, 60. The largest house of industry recorded in Norfolk by Eden was at Gressinghall, established by 15 Geo. III, c.59 (1775), and opened in July 1777. It incorporated fifty parishes in the hundreds of Mitford and Launditch, and in June 1795 held 539 inhabitants. See *The State of the Poor*, ii. 453–71. The largest house of industry in Suffolk was at Bulcamp, established by 4 Geo. III, c.56 (1763), and opened in October 1766. It incorporated forty-six parishes in the hundred of Blything, and in June 1795 held 355 people. See ibid., ii. 678–84.

In a marginal note, Bentham refers to 'Shrewsbury, Isle of Wight'. The Shrewsbury house of industry was established by 24 Geo. III, sess. 2, c.15 (1784), and opened in December 1784. It incorporated six parishes, and in November 1795 held 389 people. See ibid., ii. 622, 639. The house of industry near Newport on the Isle of Wight was established by 11 Geo. III, c.43 (1771), and had a capacity for 700 persons. On 3 April 1796 it had 495 inhabitants. See ibid., ii. 233, 239.

QUANTUM

CHAPTER II.
OF THE NO-PROVISION, OR STARVATION SYSTEM[1]

The No-provision System, not having been exhibited any otherwise than in theory, not having ever been attempted to be brought into practice in this country, by any person invested with public authority, will not require any more than a slight mention. In another work it will receive full discussion.[2]

On behalf of this system, the heads of argument appear to be as follows:[3]

1. In an island inhabited by nothing but Goats, and affording pasture enough for 1000 Goats, and no more, all above the number will keep dying, were ever so many put in:[4] therefore, in an Island containing 10 millions of human creatures, and capable of containing 10 millions more, as many as would die off without assistance at the public charge ought to be left to perish by a slow death. There may be justice in the inference, but I can not find it.

2. Those who have not wherewithal to provide for the issue which are the result of the gratification of certain desires, ought to abstain from that gratification:[5] Answer.—Admitted—for arguments sake:—but what then? Because the Parents ought not to have married, ought the children to be left to starve?

[1] The folio containing the original draft of Bentham's discussion of the No-provision system is missing, but the corresponding marginal summary reads as follows: '1. No provision. 2. Limited or inadequate provision. 3. Unlimited or adequate [provision]. No provision and inadequate provision dismissed with reprobation. p. 1.' It appears that the rejection of these two systems within the space of a single folio was superseded by Bentham's composition of the more extended analyses reproduced in this and the following chapter: see the Editorial Introduction, p. xxxvii above. However, the following footnote relating to the missing folio, consisting of an 'Apology for the nomenclature', is at UC clii. 436: 'The Mercantile System and the Economical System are appellatives of novel complection invented, or at any rate employ'd, by Adam Smith. Without the necessary privilege of assigning new names to new ideas, that justly celebrated writer of political Economy would never have been able to convey the instruction for which the writer of letters and politics is indebted to him. Urged by [. . .?] I claim an equal right for a purpose of not inferior[?] importance[?]. By the simple application of an apposite expression, many a difficult problem has been solved.'

[2] See 'Fundamental Positions in regard to the making provision for the Indigent Poor', and, in particular, the observations on position 7, pp. 12–28 above.

[3] The following arguments are taken from Townsend, *A Dissertation on the Poor Laws*.

[4] See ibid., pp. 37–47. Townsend takes the story of the goats on Juan Fernandez Island from William Dampier, *A Collection of Voyages*, 4 vols., London, 1729, i. 88.

[5] See Townsend, *A Dissertation on the Poor Laws*, pp. 50–2.

3. That whatever comes to be given at the public charge will be so much thrown away: since it will only come in lieu of the same quantity of relief that would otherwise be given in the way of voluntary contribution.[1] Answer.—Three propositions here require to be proved:

i.[2] That the quantity of relief administered in the way of private charity would be equal in amount to that now given at this public charge. Of this proposition no proof has ever been offered that I know of, and I see not how any such proof can be found. Proofs to the contrary do exist: for where there has been no provision at the public charge, examples have appeared of mortality by famine—striking enough to occupy a place in History.[a] My notion is that lying altogether at the mercy of chance, there is infinity to one against the supply's being in any tolerable proportion to the demand. Toil and Famine in one house: Idleness and Superfluity in the next: such would be the distribution: the quantum regulated—in as far as it had any thing but chance to regulate it—the quantum regulated—not to the degree of exigency, but to the degree of skill in the rhetoric of the trade.

ii. Postulate the 2$^{d.}$—That the relief afforded would be distributed with equal justice: adapted with equal precision, in the sum of individual instances, to the degree of the exigency. The reverse of this proposition is what appears to me the true one.

iii. Postulate the 3$^{d.}$—That a given sum, 2 Million suppose, would be productive of less inconvenience to the aggregate of individuals of which the community is composed, if given in the way of voluntary charity, than if given in the way of compulsive charity, as at present. The reverse of this is what, upon the fullest consideration, I am most strenuously persuaded of. On the self-entitled voluntary plan, the tax in money would be nothing in comparison of the tax in time: for my own part I had rather pay double, treble, quadruple of what I pay at present, than see my time devoted, the whole of it would not be too much, to the trying of charity causes at my own expence. At present

[a] In England, before the system of public charity had taken root: Eden.[3]

In Scotland we find 80,000 dying in a year: $\frac{1}{15}$ part at least of the population of the time: Dalrymple.[4]

---

[1] See ibid., pp. 96–9.

[2] For the sake of clarity, Bentham's Arabic numerals in this series have been rendered as Roman.

[3] See Eden, *The State of the Poor*, i. 144: 'The situation of the Poor, even after the passing of the 43d of Eliz. for providing a compulsory maintenance for them, is represented, by some authors, as exceedingly deplorable; and the assessments for their relief are said to have been so low, that many perished for want.'

[4] See p. 16 n. above.

one or two Overseers serve for a whole Parish: on the No-provision plan, every man who would not treat his neighbour as no humane man would treat his goat, must be his own Overseer. I would as lief be my own hangman.

4. That whatever comes to be given at the public charge, is so much thrown away, or worse than thrown away: since whatever sum is there bestowed in extenuation of existing indigence, becomes itself productive of an equal, or rather greater, measure of future indigence.[1] Answer. True or not, according to the terms on which it is given: if gratis, yes: if on condition of working to the extent of ability, no.

How this argument can be reconciled to the one immediately preceding it, is more than I can see. Two millions given gratis, seems equally a bounty upon idleness, whether administered by private or public hands: and one capital argument against the giving it in the way of private charity is that, if thus given, it must be given gratis: for if given in the way of wages, and in return for work by private hands, charity is out of the question: it is the case of ordinary employment in the way of service or of trade.

Of these four heads of argument, the Goat-argument, and the forced-continence-preaching, or irregular-satisfaction-preaching, argument (for though there can be no doubt which was meant, the one construction seems no less pertinent than the other) might, it should seem, have as well been spared.

The fourth acts, according to my way of viewing it, with irresistible force against the Home-Provision system; as will be seen in its place: and therefore, if the propriety of a provision at the public charge be admitted, with equal force in favour of the Public-Establishment system. But this is not the conclusion that will be admitted by the advocates for the No-provision system, the system now before us.

It is in the third of these arguments that the great strength of the cause appears to be: at least in as far as the strength of a cause consists in the difficulty of confutation. Confutation in this instance would bring up details in a multitude for which at present there is no room.

If my eloquent and much respected friend,[2] with whom, in the cause of the indigent, I am thus breaking a lance, will lead on into this vantage-ground, I will follow him: for the present I demand a truce. Let it remain neutral.

[1] See Townsend, *A Dissertation on the Poor Laws*, especially pp. 6–18.

[2] i.e. Townsend. Bentham had become a close friend of Townsend after meeting him in 1781 at Bowood, the country home of William Petty (1737–1805), second Earl of Shelburne and first Marquis of Lansdowne: see *Correspondence* (*CW*), iii. 57.

5. Argument 5.—tendency to promote benevolence.

Another argument in favour of the No-provision System is drawn from the tendency attributed to it to promote benevolence.

This argument seems to have originated in a very frequent and fertile cause of error:—the want of sufficient attention to the true use of the qualities comprized under the name of *virtue*: their true place in the scale and catalogue of *ends*. The use of a virtue is to serve, sometimes as an efficient cause of happiness, sometimes as a remedy, curative or preventive, against unhappiness. This argument, instead of employing a remedy to keep out, or drive out the disease, is for introducing the disease in order to find business for the remedy. Gin drinking, sedition, war, plague, famine, and every species and cause of misery, ought, at this rate, to be left unpressed, or even planted, for the better promotion of sobriety, patriotism, courage, medicine and benevolence.

Shut up the temple of public charity to promote benevolence!—Shut up the Law-Courts then, to promote Justice. What remains to be explained, is how it is that the throwing the whole burthen of the service upon the article called *benevolence*, laying a tax to the amount of two or three million a year upon the use of it, should promote the growth of it.

One word more. There is one reason in the way of inducement for feeding the impotent part of the necessitous poor: regard for the sufferings of the necessitous. There is more than twice as much reason for furnishing it to the able-bodied: regard for the safety of the other classes. In Scotland, that is in some parts of Scotland, men do not mind being starved:—*because* (as the man said) *they are used to it.* But in England, they are not used to it, and they would not bear it. Were there no medicine—(but they would find a medicine)—they would rather be shot or hanged:—and let him that could find cause of blame in them fire the first shot.

To the estate of the rich man, that title which has lived sixty years is a good one:[1] the title of the indigent to his *minimum* has lived upwards of these two hundred years.

At present, when a street Beggar is troublesome, the answer is short—Go to your Parish.—Where could a man bid a beggar go, if there were no Parish, nor any thing to replace it?

[1] See p. 20–1 & n. above.

CHAPTER III.
OF THE LIMITED, OR INADEQUATE-PROVISION SYSTEM

The Limited, or Inadequate-provision system stands exposed to all the objections which apply to the No-Provision system: add to which, it is exposed to others that are peculiar to itself.

Take any period, 1 Jany 1800, for example: The *ne plus ultra* of allowance, three millions a year (suppose), being fixed, either that sum is adequate to the demand or it falls short of it, suppose by one million. If it is adequate, nothing is gained by the fixation: if deficient, it coincides, to the amount of the deficiency, with the No-provision system.

To whatever defects belong to the No-provision system, it adds that of inconsistency: it admitts the propriety of a provision at the public charge, and at the same time, as far as the deficiency extends, refuses to make any such provision. Admitting the necessity, it refuses to provide for it.

If the effects of compliance and non-compliance were the same, if the refusal of further relief, and the supply of further relief, were alike effectual against growing indigence, the Limited-provision system would answer its intended purpose: but if it did, it would still be bad by comparison: for the No-provision system would be still better. If the refusal of a two-penny loaf would save but a single man from starving, as well as the loaf itself, so would it five hundred thousand: were such the natural order of things, myriads might be fed for as little as units, and without a miracle.[1]

Under the existing system, either there is a just line of separation drawn between founded and unfounded claims, or there is not: in the first case, the Limited-provision system can not be fixt any where without violating against what [it] itself admitts to be the laws of humanity and justice. If no such line is drawn, [it is] required to draw it?—but, for the solution of this problem, the system in question neither furnishes, nor so much as pretends to furnish, the smallest means. No fresh test of worthiness does it so much as profess to furnish. If unworthy objects obtain relief, now that the demand and the supply are both at (suppose) three millions, so will they when, the supply remaining at three millions, the demand is got up to four.[2]

[1] An allusion to Christ's feeding of the five thousand: see Mark 6: 37–44; Luke 9: 13–17; and John 6: 10–13.

[2] In the margin, Bentham has noted at this point: 'Seeing *those only* that are alive, some think that *all* live. Having had occasion to examine into cases of indigence and to calculate the income necessary to existence, compared to the real income, others wonder how any live.' In referring

Under the Limited-provision system, as under the existing system, unworthy claims will crowd in, for what is there to hinder them? Unworthy claims will prevail, for what does it give to prevent their prevalence? The Statute which says so much money and no more shall be raised, will it give to paupers self-denial, to Overseers discernment, probity and firmness? At present some are unworthily fed, but no one starved: *then* some will be unworthily fed, and others starved.

Look over the *Table of Cases calling for Relief*:[1] see which of the Demands for relief the *Limited-provision* system can curtail. Observe whether it will prevent insanity, dismemberment, decrepitude, disease, child-bearing, orphanage, stagnation, loss of service, loss of character, foreignership, imprisonment, or destruction of fortune.

Unworthy claims will *not* crowd in, no unworthy claim either will or can be successful, if the relief, being in quality not more expensive than the poorest fare enjoy'd by self-subsisting industry, is never given but either to absolute and to incurable inability, or in return for work, to the extent of ability, previously performed. By these terms, the much-desired line is drawn, and drawn to perfection: for if a man does not comply with them he gets nothing: and if he does comply with them what he gets is his due: and at any rate no more than his due.

This boundary-line is the basis of the new plan or system, which it has been the business of the preceding essay to display:[2] but in the limited-provision system no traces of it are to be found. The Limited-provision system is farther than even the existing system from coinciding with it. The existing system swerves from it on one side, but on one side only—the side of the false indulgence:—the Limited-provision system swerves from it on both sides at once: the side of false indulgence, and the still worse side of inexorable inhumanity: the existing system is pregnant with profusion: the Limited-provision, or Inadequate-provision system, with profusion on one side, homicide on the other.

If the fabrick of felicity were to be reared by a man's shutting his eyes, and drawing a line any where, the Limited or Inadequate-provision system might soon raise it:—but happiness is not to be purchased, or wisdom display'd, at quite so cheap a rate.

to writers who had had occasion to calculate the income necessary to existence, and to compare it with the real income of labouring families, Bentham almost certainly had in mind David Davies.

[1] See p. lvii above.

[2] See 'Fundamental Positions in regard to the making provision for the Indigent Poor', pp. 8–65 above.

That limitation, and even retrenchment, are desirable, is not to be doubted: the question is, if and by what means practicable?

The answer is—if at all, by an intermediate body who will, with a part of their substance, throw themselves into the gap between the demand and the fund for supply, between the demanders and the contributors: to whom contribution will afford the means, and interest the disposition, to labour, and labour with a great part of their might, in the vineyard of the service:[1] in a word (speaking plainly and explicitly), to give application and execution to the principles just indicated. Exposed without limitation to the demands of real indigence, they may form, with the amount of their collected pecuniary force, a barrier, a rampart to the public treasury.

Without the benefit of some such new and adventitious force, to call for limitation of the Poor's fund is to call for bricks without straw.[2]—Limit the defences against the attacks [of] indigence within?—As well might you limit then, the defences against invasion from without.

[1] An echo of Matthew 20: 1. [2] See Exodus 5: 16, 18.

PLACE

CHAPTER IV.
HOME AND COMMUNITY PROVISION COMPARED

Introduction

As no more than two such objects can be conveniently compared at the same instant, I shall begin with drawing the parallel between the Home-Provision system on the one hand, and the Public-Establishment system on the other, laying out of the question in the first instance, whatever features of distinction may afterwards be traced in its two condivident branches. The parallel between the one whole and the other whole having been gone through, there will be so much the less to do in framing the estimate of the comparative eligibility as between the two branches.

In drawing a parallel between the two systems I shall consider them under the several heads of: 1. *universality of application*, 2. *economy*, 3. *moral influence*, 4. *justice*, and 5. *perfectibility*—the extent in which they are respectively capable of being applied, the degree in which they are respectively conducive to the purposes of good economy, the salutary or unsalutary influence which they are calculated to exercise in a remote way on the moral habits of the class of people to which they apply, and their tendency to give birth or admission to improvement in respect of the above, or any other beneficial qualities.

§1. *Parallel in respect of extent in point of applicability*

As to universality of application. If there be a single case of indigence, a portion ever so small of the indigent, to which the two systems are, either of them, incapable of being applied, that deficiency is of itself [enough] to put a negative, on the part of the system in question, to the capacity of serving in the character of an exclusive system. But as to the Home-Provision system, the cases to which it is inapplicable, absolutely and physically inapplicable, are not only collectively numerous and diversified, but separately extensive. They embrace a very large proportion (it were to be wished that the state of Parliamentary information would enable us to say what proportion) of the whole number of individuals in whose instance the demand for relief at any given time will be found to exist: and what is more, these are the very cases in which that demand is most urgent and irresistible. For those in whose instance, to the want of every thing else, the want of home itself is added, provision in the way of *home*-provision can not be made.[a]

[a] In this predicament stand:

1. All Idiots, Lunatics, and other persons who, labouring under mental infirmity, have neither property to pay for suitable Guardianship, nor relations who are at the same time able and [willing][1] to charge themselves with so burthensome an office.

2. All non-adults being in a state of orphanage, and left in the same destitute state in respect of Guardianship, and not yet arrived at an age to make provision for themselves by their own labour. In this helpless class, Bastards, the offspring of forbidden intercourse, a class forming of itself a legion, are more particularly exposed to be included.[a]

3. All persons disabled from providing for themselves, labouring under bodily infirmity, temporary or permanent, curable or incurable, and who, having been originally without property, or bereft of their property by the expence attendant on such their misfortune, labour under the additional misfortune of finding themselves in the same friendless state.

4. All individuals of the working classes, single or married, with or without families of helpless children, who, having been in the habit of lodging only from day to day,[b] or at most from week to week, can scarce be said to have a *home*, and who, from the operation of whatever cause, general or personal, find themselves without property as well as without work. Day-labourers in Husbandry in the retrenchment of the demand for their labour, for instance by the conversion of arable into pasture—Canal Diggers, Miners and Quarrymen, on the completion of the canal, or the working out of the Quarry or the Mine. Improvident or unfortunate Gardeners or Bricklayers in the course of a long-protracted frost. Manufacturers in the event of a general stagnation of the manufacture. Manufacturers, Handicrafts

[a] Give the numbers, Eden.[2]

[b] See Colquhoun.[3]

---

[1] MS 'unwilling' contradicts the evident sense of the passage.

[2] No overall calculation of the numbers of bastards is to be found in *The State of the Poor*, although Eden does indicate at i. 449 that, 'Of the considerable proportion of children, (more especially of bastards,) with which parishes are burthened, the Reader will find many instances in the Second Volume of this Work.' In volumes two and three Eden compiles poor relief statistics from 181 parishes and rateable districts, many of which do give some information concerning the numbers of illegitimate children being relieved. However, as Bentham himself noted in 'Observations on the Pauper Population Table hereunto annexed', *Annals of Agriculture*, xxix (1797), 409n. (Bowring, viii. 365n.), no reliable inference can be drawn from Eden since the figures are not presented in a consistent fashion, and are often incomplete.

[3] Patrick Colquhoun (1745–1820), Lord Provost of Glasgow 1782–4, was stipendiary magistrate at Worship Street, Shoreditch 1792–7, and at Queen's Square, Westminster 1797–1818. In *A Treatise on the Police of the Metropolis, Explaining the various Crimes and Misdemeanours which at Present are felt as a Pressure upon the Community; and Suggesting Remedies for their Prevention*, London, 1796, p. 39, he writes that 'a melancholy conclusion is drawn, warranted by a generally assumed fact; "that above Twenty Thousand Individuals rise every morning in this great metropolis, without knowing how, or by what means they are to be supported during the passing day, or where they are to lodge on the succeeding night."'

In the case of the Public-Establishment system, fittest or not fittest in this or that case, there is at any rate no case whatever to which it is not *capable* at least of being applied.

§2. *Parallel in respect of economy in relation to Employ*

Economy—In the case in question, the subject matter of Economy has two branches: supply of relief, and supply of employment: relief, necessary by the supposition in all cases without exception: employ, as I can not help contending, and as most may probably be brought to admitt, proper in all cases of indigence and relief except those in which no spark of ability in respect of work is to be found.[a]

and working Artists, on failure of the fashion to which they are indebted for their several employments.—Any of the above children of Industry, together with Journeymen Shop-keepers and Warehouse-keepers, on the Death, failure, retirement, or displeasure of an employer, or circle of employers, on whom they have been accustomed to place their sole dependence. Servants out of place, with or without characters, whether, in the latter case, the refusal of character has happened through the fault of the Master or their own.—King's service men of all descriptions, Seamen, Soldiers, Marines, Militia-men disbanded on the occasion of a peace, or deserted, or discharged with infamy.

[5.] All *ill-famed* hands [who], willing or unwilling, are unable to procure employment through original badness of character, or through want of character.—Thieves and other criminals after the expiration of their sentence.—Delinquents prosecuted for offences which, though of an infamous nature, do not, pending the prosecution, provide them with an abode by consigning them to prison. Thieves or other criminals known as such by reputation, though unprosecuted—or discharged upon the public by pardon, or by acquittal through a defect in the law, or want of evidence.—Habitual Beggars, Gipsies and other Vagrants, undiscovered Deserters, King's-service-men, Soldiers, Sailors, Marines and Militia men discharged with infamy—and lastly habitual Prostitutes, of themselves in the metropolis a most numerous and hapless list.

[6.] All *Strange* hands who, willing or unwilling, deserving or undeserving, find themselves destitute of employ not through want of character, but by the simple want of it.—Native Travellers whose money, and New-comers whose money and casual employ, are exhausted. Travellers or New comers as before, being foreigners as to English Law, though not in point of language or allegiance: Scotch—Irish—British Colonists. Foreigners in point of language as well as allegiance, thrown upon English ground in a homeless state, by curiosity, search after employ, exile, flight, or shipwreck.

[a] Employment will be found indispensable in every point of view: whether the interest of the party calling for relief be considered, or that of the party at whose expence it is to be administered: whether it be considered as a means of extracting a satisfaction, as far as it goes, for the burthen imposed on the one hand, or as a preservative against mischievousness and unhappiness on the other. See preceding §§ 'Fundamental Positions in regard to the subject-matter of the Poor Laws'.[1]

[1] See 'Fundamental Positions in regard to the making provision for the Indigent Poor', pp. 8–65 above, particularly pp. 44–58.

To begin with employ. Under this head, whether Country works or Town works be considered, the Home-Provision system, considered in respect of the very capacity of being made so far subservient to the purposes of economy as to afford a profit, will be found to labour under disadvantages, in many if not most cases absolutely and physically insuperable.

Whichever situation be considered, Town or Country, the following are the requisites which must concurr to render it possible to draw a profit from any species of employment that can be assigned.

1. A spot so situated with relation to the Magazine, or Magazines, from whence the raw materials are to be issued, and into which the finished work is to be returned, as that the consumption of time and, if necessary, implements of conveyance, by the journeys to and fro, shall not eat up, or cut too deep into, the saleable value of the work.

2. A place suitable in point of extent, shape, and, if it be a building, materials and structure.

3. A stock of fit materials to form the subject matter of the work.

4. A stock of machines, tools, or other implements adapted to the work.

5. A system of instruction and inspection, adapted to the purpose of securing the performance of the work in such manner as to yield a profit.[a]

[a] Howard, in one of his Tours, speaking of some prisoners whom he saw occupied in some employment of little or no profit, such as sawing wood with a blunt saw, and moving rubbish from one corner of a yard to another and back again, adds, that on enquiring of the Jailer what his object was in giving them such employment, the answer given to him was—'*to plague the prisoners*'.[1] In addition to the inhumanity of the motive (salutary as the probable effect was, in point of exercise and health) what struck me (I confess) at the time, as it appears to have struck Howard, was the apparent bad economy of the discipline: prescribing useless employment, amidst such a choice, as it might seem, of useful ones. But on this head, the error (as the Reader may perhaps by this time have anticipated) was on the side of the philanthropist, not of the man in office. Manual Labour, to yield a profit, indispensably requires an appropriated system of superintendence: and in the case in question, that system was necessarily wanting. Under the circumstances in question, the utmost possible profit could hardly afford a reasonable expectation of affording an adequate indemnification for the risk of loss, much less an adequate retribution for the time that would have been requisite to be expended by the jailer, in the new and widely distant function of the superintendent of a manufacturing concern. Thus exposed is natural sagacity to be led astray by first appearance, for want of those lights that are not to be obtained, but from minute scrutiny or apposite experience.

[1] See John Howard, *An Account of the Principal Lazarettos in Europe; with Various Papers Relative to the Plague: together with Further Observations on some Foreign Prisons and Hospitals; and Additional Remarks on the Present State of Those in Great Britain and Ireland*, Warrington, 1789, p. 147.

6. A system of security sufficient against the embezzlement of the materials and implements, and against the destruction or endamagement of them through ignorance, unskilfulness, awkwardness, negligence, or malice, to such a degree as to eat up, or cut too deep into, the profit upon the work: and in this view,

7. A system of recordation, or, to employ a more familiar though less expressive term, Book-keeping, appropriate to the business and sufficient to the purpose.[1]

The species of employment, in the instance of which all these indispensable requisites shall be found united, or can even by possibility be made to concurr, in the homes of the indigent, will surely be difficult to find, if not impossible: even in the best provided Towns: much more in thinly-peopled country places. Under the Public-Establishment system, all these requisites, without exception, *may* be made to concurr, and taking measures for providing them will be a matter of course: more especially under that branch of the Public-Establishment system which I distinguish by the name of the Large-Establishment system, and under which the difficulty of making a sufficient provision for the whole country will decrease with the extent of the several Establishments, because as the extent of each encreases, the total number of them is reduced.

It is in country places that the want of these requisites, most or all of them, may be seen to be particularly sensible: sensible in the joint proportion of the thinness of the population, and the distance from great towns: sensible, to such a degree as in most instances to oppose such a bar to profitable employment as may be seen to be found absolutely insuperable.[a]

[a] See this point illustrated in D[r] Anderson's *Interest of Great Britain in respect of her Colonies*, 1782, and *Observations on National Industry*, and *Tour to the Hebrides*.[2]

If a man has 3 or 4 miles to go backwards and forwards, several times a day, a large share of his working time is thus wasted, and in hot weather a considerable portion of his strength. In *wet* weather too, what is to become of him? If, on account of the wet, he stays at home, there is so much time lost to profit, and consumed in idleness. If he braves the wet or is caught in it, either he must sit still in his wet clothes, to his great discomfort and to the danger of his health, or be at such an expence in fire to dry them as his earnings will not afford.

[1] On the corresponding marginal contents sheet at UC cliv. 75, Bentham has noted at this point: 'Addendum.—8. Market near and certain.' However, no text on this subject has been located.

[2] See James Anderson (1739–1808), agricultural economist, *The Interest of Great Britain with Regard to her American Colonies, Considered. To which is added an Appendix, Containing the Outlines of a Plan for a General Pacification*, London, 1782, pp. 29–34; *Observations on the Means of Exciting a Spirit of National Industry; chiefly Intended to Promote the Agriculture, Manufactures, and Fisheries, of Scotland*, Edinburgh, 1777, pp. 22–3; and *An Account Of The Present State Of The Hebrides and Western Coasts of Scotland: in which An attempt is made to explain the*

Much will depend certainly upon the nature of the work: and unless all manner of works, possible as well as actual, had been examined in this view, it may seem too much to say, that there is no sort of work in relation to which, the difficulty founded on the necessity of a concurrence on the part of all the above requisites might not be surmounted.

What must not be forgotten is, that the condition requisite in order to render the Home-Provision system consistent with economy in this point of view, is—not the finding this or that species of employment that might [be] capable of being carried on with profit in such a situation—but an entire system of employment, sufficient for the whole number of the indigent, of all descriptions, for whom employment is, or will come to be wanted.

But even were all the other difficulties got rid of, that which respects the danger of waste and embezzlement seems to be of an universal nature, applying with equal force to the most thinly-peopled country places and the most populous Towns.[a]

Branches of industry there are, it is true, and those in no small extent as well as variety, that are carried on at the abodes of the working hands, abodes in many instances diffused over a space

[a] Take for instance one of the simplest species of work, spinning. The materials it requires are a stock of the filamentous substance to be spun: wool, hemp, flax, or whatever it be. The machine a spinning wheel. Let us suppose, in any district, a general resolution taken to furnish an implement of this kind, to say nothing of the rest of the stock, to every indigent hand capable of using it, to supply him with it at a home of his own, and let us observe what in point of profit would be the probable consequence. The value of what was wasted or embezzled would perhaps in general exceed the value of the work done. Call the cost of the wheel, 10[s]: the value of a day's spinning, 3[d]: though it would be some days probably, before an average individual, even among grown persons, would be able to give such a value to his day's work. Yet, on this supposition, if but one person out of 40 spoilt or sold his wheel, the whole profit upon the 40 would be gone. But among 40 persons of the description in question, it would be rather extraordinary if one out of 40 did not sell his wheel, another spoil it by awkwardness, a third by negligence, and a fourth through malice: knowing that neither of negligence [nor][1] malice there could be any proof, and confident that for the mere mischance, or even offence, of having spoilt his wheel, he would not be left to starve. Probity, prudence and care taken together, (it may be said) would be sufficient [preventatives][2] against such disasters. But it is, most commonly, only because these endowments, one or more of them, are wanting, that the necessity of relief comes to present itself.

circumstances that have hitherto repressed the industry of the Natives; and some hints are suggested for encouraging the Fisheries, and promoting other improvements in those countries. Being the substance of a report to the Lords of the Treasury of Facts collected in a Tour to the Hebrides, with large additions; together with the Evidence given before the Committee of Fisheries, London and Edinburgh, 1785, pp.xxi-xxxiv, lvi.

[1] MS 'or'.

[2] MS 'preventitions'.

extending to a considerable distance from the centre of employment in the neighbouring town. But in these instances, the hands thus employ'd are not the sort of hands on whose part the demand for employment exists on the account in question, on the score of indigence. They are trust-worthy, either by property—possessing within themselves the conditions requisite to the profitable performance of the work: or at any rate by established character: whereas among the indigent, the proportion of those who can be looked upon as trustworthy by character forms, if the observations of the experienced are to be trusted to, a very inferior minority.[a]

§3. *Parallel in respect of economy in relation to Relief*

Passing from the head of employment to that of relief, we shall find the Home-Provision system, though practicable enough, and but too practicable, yet yielding in point of economy to the Public-Establishment system—at least to that modification of it which employs large Establishments. This will appear in proportion as the enquiry is pursued through the several heads of necessaries, in respect of which relief may become necessary—to wit Lodging, Household Stock, Fewel, Food, Sick Attendance and Medicine: cloathing, of which afterwards, being for the present set aside.

1. Lodging.—Under the Public-Establishment system the expence of lodging may be altogether saved. Under the Home-Provision system every person to be relieved has, by the supposition, a private home: at which it has been shewn he can not, generally speaking, be employ'd to any profit. He must at working hours therefore, so long at least as he is not employ'd in the open air, be lodged elsewhere. But the same sufficiently sheltered place that serves a man for any

[a] From [two to one to four to one][1] was the proportion of the ill-disposed to the well-disposed in the Edinburgh Poor-houses, according to the estimate of a Dr Macfarlan, formed as he tells us after 18 years of official observation.

Supposing the observance of the rule which requires that earnings shall precede relief to be practicable at a man's own home, yet still, to enable him to comply with that condition, he must in the first instance be trusted with the uncontrouled disposal of a mass of property of perhaps a hundred times the value of the supply correspondent to a day's work.[2]

---

[1] MS '3 to one to 5 to one'. For the correct figure see p. 61 n. above.

[2] On the corresponding marginal contents sheet at UC cliv. 75, Bentham has noted at this point: 'Addend.—Time lost on the Home-Provision system in case of Out door work. 1. Winter evenings. 2. Rainy & snowy weather. Health Prejudiced in case of sedentary work—Spinning &c. Lindsey Spinning establishment.' However, no text on this subject has been located. For the employment of children in spinning at Lindsey see *An Account of the Origin, Proceedings, and Intentions of the Society for the Promotion of Industry*, pp. 2–6.

one of the daily recurrent functions, may serve him for every other: to have one room to work in, another to sleep in, and a third to eat in—to have a breakfast room, a dressing room, a powdering room, a study, a dining room, and a drawing room and a bedchamber, is matter not of necessity, but luxury. A tub served for all these purposes to Diogenes:—a lecturer in moral philosophy by profession—a man of education, a man of letters.[1]

Let it not be said that health requires three, or even two apartments for these several purposes, any more than twenty or thirty. Change of air is indeed necessary to health, but not change of space: change of air, which through ignorance or prejudice receives no attention in the private abodes of the Poor, but which would receive, of course, every necessary attention in any tolerably regulated establishment of the public kind. On shipboard, no such change of apartments can be experienced by the crew. Yet, under the command of Capt. Cook, in a vessel visiting all climates with a crew of about 170 men, for four years, not a single life was lost through disease contracted within that time.[2]

Reckoning 40^{s} a year as the average rent of a Cottage for a family of the lowest order of the working class, and five for the average number of persons of all ages lodged in such a house, 8^{s} a year is the difference made, in point of economy, between the two systems by this article alone. Supposing 500,000 to be the number of the indigent to be provided for at the public expence: £200,000 a year would be the difference to the nation under this single head.

2. Houshold stock. This is another article in respect of which, in point of economy at any rate, the advantage is manifestly as well as prodigiously in favour of the Public-Establishment system. In an establishment containing 2,000 persons of this class, the value of the Houshold Stock really necessary would be very inconsiderable. The expence of the one Boiler, for example, that would be sufficient for dressing the whole food of the Public Establishment, bears no proportion to the expence of the 400 Pots that would be necessary under the most rigid system of economy in the number of Cottages

[1] Diogenes (*c.*403–*c.*321 BC), founder of the Cynic sect in Athens, who lived a life of extreme poverty, was believed to have taken up residence in a barrel.

[2] Captain James Cook (1728–79), explorer and circumnavigator, recorded that among the several causes which kept his crew in 'uncommon good state of health' was the practice of airing the ship once or twice a week by means of purifying fires. Bentham's figure for loss through disease is not quite accurate. Cook indicated that during the voyage of 3 years 18 days he lost four men, though only one of these was from disease. See *A Voyage Towards The South Pole, and Round The World. Performed in His Majesty's Ships The Resolution and Adventure, in the Years 1772, 1773, 1774, and 1775*, 2 vols., London, 1777, ii. 289–92; and 'The Method taken for preserving the Health of the Crew of His Majesty's Ship the Resolution during her late Voyage round the World', *Royal Society Philosophical Transactions*, lxvi (1776), 402–6. On 31 May 1780 Bentham wrote to his brother, Samuel, stating that he had purchased the latter work: see *Correspondence* (*CW*), ii. 454.

requisite, according to the above supposition, for the lodging of the same number of 2,000 cottagers.[a]

3. Fewel.—Another article, of superior importance to that of Houshold Stock, and affording an advantage still more conspicuously in favour of the Large-Establishment system.

The difference in point of economy under this head results from two very distinguishable sources; partly from the reduction of fewel consequent upon the last mentioned reduction of the quantity of matter in the vessels to be heated, partly from the improved economy of which the management of fewel is susceptible. That in the common modes of employing fewel, whether for warming, for cooking, or for any other purpose, there has always been a great degree of unnecessary consumption, is a proposition of which no doubt has ever been entertained by persons possessed of any degree of chemical information. But the magnitude and proportion of this waste has never yet been so clearly explained, or so extensively known, as since the improvements made in this important article by Count Rumford.[b]

[a] The difference in point of economy under this head results partly from the retrenchment of a number of articles necessary under the most frugal plan of Home-Provision, and unnecessary under the Public-Provision system: partly from the relative difference in point of quantity of matter between large vessels and small vessels: the quantity of materials necessary to inclose a space of a given form decreasing, as the size of the vessel, that is as the quantity of space to be inclosed, encreases. It is this circumstance, for example, that contributes largely to the prodigious advantage which large Breweries and Distilleries have over small ones.

[b] N° of Poor to be provided for, as above:	500,000
N° of Families, at an average of 5:	100,000
Annual expence per family in fewel, at the highest rate (30^{s}):[a]	£150,000
" " " at the lowest rate (10^{s}):[b]	£50,000
" " " at the medium rate (20^{s}):	£100,000
In a situation where fewel was not cheaper than in London, Count Rumford used to cook a meal for 1000 for:	$4^{d}\frac{1}{2}$[1]
Expence per day at two meals for 1000:	9^{d}
For 2000, the number supposed:	1^{s}–6
Yearly expence for d°:	27–7–6
Calling the extra expence for warming alone as much more (a large allowance), total annual expence for fewel:	54–15–0
Total Expence of fewel for the 500,000 Poor in 250 Houses (54.15.0 × 250):	[13,687–10–0][2]

a Davies, p. 21.[3] *b* ibid., p. 15.

[1] See 'Certificate relative to the Expence of Fuel in the Public Kitchen of the Military Workhouse at Munich', *Essays, Political, Economical and Philosphical*, i. 432. For Rumford's account of his experiments to ascertain the degree of waste involved in customary methods of heating, and to improve the efficiency of the process, see 'Of the Management of Fire and the Economy of Fuel', ibid., ii. 1–196.

[2] MS '17,187–10–0'. Bentham's multiplication is erroneous.

[3] i.e. Davies, *The Case of Labourers in Husbandry*, p. 21.

4. Food. In relation to this article also, two distinct forms of economy present themselves: i.[1] Improvement in point of quality [by] the substitution in each place of that sort of food which is most economical upon the whole, nutritiousness and cheapness taken together, to that which habit, fashion, and local convenience have concurred in presenting, and which, under the Home-Provision system, would remain unimproveable: ii. The improvement in point of expence by the substitution of wholesale dealing to retail dealing, and, in particular, to the most [disadvantageous][2] degree of retail dealing, the purchases of the indigent. The former head, besides that it is a point not to be touched but with great delicacy and caution, is a point not easily subjected to calculation: the other has already received a calculation, or at any rate a gross estimate, from a writer of high character and accurate observation, who values it at $\frac{1}{10}$.[a]

Deduct from the expence according to the Home-Provision system, as before viz:	£100,000–0–0
The expence as above according to the Large-Establishment system:	[13,687–10]
Annual Saving under the Large-Establishment system in this article of fewel:	[86,312–10–0][3]

N.B. According to an advertisement repeatedly inserted by the Governors of the Foundling Hospital, the saving in the article of fewel employ'd in cooking, by the introduction of Count Rumford's improvements into that Hospital amounts to a $\frac{1}{3}$.[4]

Supposing the expence under the Public-Establishment system to be as great, bating these improvements, as under the Home-Provision system, viz: £100,000: the saving from the mere introduction of these improvements would be no more than £33,333.6.8: the difference between that sum and the above sum of [£86,312–10–0], may therefore serve to represent the difference in point of economy between the two systems, Count Rumford's improvements out of the question.

[a] Davies, p. 34, Kent's *Hints*, p. 277.[5]

Weekly expence in food of a family of 5:[*a*] 5^{s}.8^{d}

[*a*] Davies, 12.[6]

---

[1] For the sake of clarity, Bentham's Arabic numerals in this series have been rendered as Roman.

[2] MS 'disadvantageousness'.

[3] MS '83,813–10–0'.

[4] According to the advertisement, which consists of an extract from the report of Hannah Johnson, Matron of the Hospital, to its General Committee on 21 September 1796, regarding the refitting of the kitchen, the saving in fuel was considerably greater than is indicated by Bentham. See *Morning Chronicle*, 27 September 1796: 'The exact amount I cannot at present precisely state, but I have reason to believe that the saving at this time is not less than three chaldron out of the four used; and that a still greater saving will be made as we get more perfect in the use of the new kitchen.'

[5] Davies, *Case of Labourers in Husbandry*, p. 34, discusses the disadvantages of retail dealing with regard to the purchase of flour by the poor, and cites Nathaniel Kent (1737–1810), agriculturist and land valuer, *Hints to Gentlemen of Landed Property*, 2nd edn., London, 1776, p. 277, as estimating the extent of that disadvantage at ten per cent.

[6] Davies, *Case of Labourers in Husbandry*, p. 12. Bentham's figure is arrived at by deducting

5. Attendance. This article, though scarcely perhaps subjectable to calculation, is not to be regarded as of no account. In a private house, one bed-ridden person, to be properly taken care of, will occupy a considerable part of the time of another person in good health, who, if his (or her) ordinary employment would carry him at a distance from home, must for the time sacrifice his employment, and means of subsistence, for that purpose. But in a Hospital 20, or perhaps 50, bedridden persons at a time may be well and sufficiently taken care of by a single nurse.[1]

At the abode of the person in question, it may happen it is true, that the proper attendance may exist, and [be] capable of being bestowed without any expensive loss of time. With a labourer and his wife may lodge a decrepit parent, on whom the wife may be able to bestow the requisite attendance in the intervals of the attendance requisite for the children, and other domestic duties. But the wife may be wanting, and then, unless the labourer abandons his subsistence, how is the attendance to be bestowed? Or, what is worse, the husband may be wanting, and the wife herself obliged to go out to labour?

Thence D° of an average individual:	1. $1\frac{1}{2}$
Therefore annual expence of d° $1^{s}1^{d}\frac{1}{2} \times 52$ =	2. 18. 6
Annual expence of 500,000 Poor persons under the Home-Provision system: £2.18.6 × 500,000 =	1,462,500. 0. 0
Amount of Ten per Cent upon the above fare:	146,250. 0. 0

But Count Rumford, for a course of years, maintained in perfect health and strength many thousands of persons (in Bavaria) at an allowance of food, which even for a grown person of the male sex would not, in London, at a time still dearer than the present (Jan. 1797), cost more per day per head than | |.[2]

So much depends upon habit, and in a country so abundant in humanity as well as opulence, the practice of less favoured countries is so little susceptible of being taken as a standard without great alteration on the indulgent side, that I could never set down as *requisite* for an English stomach, even of the hardest-pinched class, less than half as much again of what is not only deemed necessary, but found sufficient for a Bavarian stomach:[a] instead therefore of | | per head per day say | |.[3]

[a] See Beevor's Dietary.[4]

the sum of one shilling for 'tea, sugar and butter' from the total expense for food given by Davies.

[1] In the margin, Bentham has noted at this point: 'Enquire of D[r] F.' The reference is probably to Dr George Fordyce (1736–1802), eminent physician and chemist, friend and correspondent of Bentham, whose daughter Mary Sophia had married Bentham's brother, Samuel, in October 1796.

[2] The relevant figure is $1\frac{1}{2}^{d}$: see p. 62 n. above.

[3] The relevant figures are $1\frac{1}{2}^{d}$ and $2\frac{1}{4}^{d}$ respectively. The note appears to be abandoned at this point.

[4] For 'Beevor's Dietary' at Wymondham Penitentiary see p. 92 n. above. Bentham's contrast between English and Bavarian stomachs appears to be based on the fact that the Munich poor managed by Rumford subsisted on one meal a day, whereas the English prisoners at Wymondham Penitentiary received two meals a day.

6. Extending the article of attendance from those on whose part the demand for relief in this stamp is created by sickness or decrepitude, to those on whose part it is created by infancy, we shall find it assume a still greater measure of importance. I will not on this occasion take upon me to inquire in what degree in such a situation the mother's human milk may admitt of a substitute in the milk of any other animal, or in any other species of food. But in regard to exercise, to say nothing of simple superintendence for the purpose of occasional notice and warning, rather than for that of continual and active exertion, whether it be for sleep or strength, whether the motion be of the oscillatory kind, as in a cradle, or of the up and down kind, as in the Mother's arms when dancing the child, the exertions of a single individual, rendered by indisposition or old age incapable of almost any other kind of exertion, might (with or without the aid of mechanism, either by generating the motion as well as regulating it, or by simply regulating a motion produced by more frugal sources of mechanical power) suffice for a very considerable number of children at once.

7. Medical relief. In relation to this article the advantage possessed by the Public-Establishment system in every respect, and in respect of economy in particular, is too evident to need insisting on. Even in towns, the time consumed in the street by the Medical Curator exceeds by many fold the time employ'd by the bedside. In Country places, especially thinly-peopled Country places, the excess is such as baffles all calculation.

The advantage of the Public-Establishment system in this respect will appear in still stronger colours, when the preventive branch of medical curation is considered: a branch of beneficence from the benefit of which the Home-Provision system stands excluded altogether. Where disease is the very cause by which the demand for relief is created, there the preventive branch of medical curation is certainly out of the question, and the establishment is in so far an Hospital. But in as far as at the origin of the demand for relief, the persons to be relieved are supposed in good health, more real good may be done in the way of prevention than in the way of cure: so that in such a situation, taking both branches together, the more good will really be done, the less appears to be done. Never was the union of medical skill with medical care exemplified with greater success than in Cook's four years' Voyage: yet there, in the way of care, scarce any thing at all was done.—Why?—because there was scarce any thing to do.[1]

[1] See p. 161 n. above.

[8.] Two heads of economy have all this while been reserved for consideration: food, and cloathing: the food account having been but partially stated, and that of cloathing not yet touched upon.

In the article of food, by way of set-off to the sources of saving above stated, the Public-Establishment system must be confessed to labour, in comparison of the Home-Provision system, under a very capital disadvantage. Under the Public-Establishment system, at least under the Large-Establishment modification of it as above explained, the allowance will be seen to extend, in the instance of every individual without exception, at least to the extent of the utmost demand that can exist on the joint score of health and strength, and probably even to the extent of the demand on the score of appetite: while under the Home-Provision system, that allowance may, in the instance of any number of individuals, fall short of the most limited demand of the two in any proportion whatever, so long as life continues.

Not that the deficiency is by any means to be carried, as to the whole amount of it, to the account of economy. In the Home-Provision system, the cause lies as we have seen already, not in the quantum of the provision under this system, but in the system itself:[1] for under this system, in a multitude of instances but too numerous, it is not in the power of the most lavish and inordinate allowance to secure the barest sufficiency of the necessaries of life: drunkenness and famine are known to be twin sisters: drunkenness, besides exhausting the fund, kills the very desire.

Cloathing is an article, though the only one, in relation to which the disadvantage lies evidently, and perhaps irremediably, on the side of the Public-Establishment system, as contrasted with the Home-Provision system. With respect to the ten per Cent advantage above mentioned, resulting from the difference between wholesale dealing and retail-dealing, no reason appears why it may not extend to this article, as well as to that of food.

This disadvantage turns upon two points: 1st. The difference, as in the article of food, in respect of the amplitude of the supply. 2nd. The dependence which this sort of article is naturally subjected to, in point of duration, on the management of the individual.

This is of the number of those cases in which, to screw the economy to the utmost pitch of perfection, the power of punishment requires the assistance of reward: because untill it be known what exertion can do, failure can not be punished. Under the Public-Establishment system, reward seems scarcely applicable to this

[1] In the margin, Bentham has noted at this point: 'See above.' The topic is in fact discussed in §4, pp. 169–71 below.

subject to any considerable advantage: under the Home-Provision system, that powerful principle of action attaches of itself, since whatever a man saves in this article, is so much bounty money he allows himself to be spent on other articles. The most vagarious Public Establishment neither would, nor, if it would, could carry this branch of economy to a pitch of perfection at all approaching to that to which it is carried by the most stupid drunkard: Raggedness and Nakedness being natural companions of Drunkenness, as well as Famine.

Upon the whole, confining the question to that branch of economy which regards the quantum, the balance of advantage must for the present, even under the best mode of conducting the Large-Establishment system that can be expected to be exemplified, be acknowledged to be doubtful in the instance of food, and clearly in disfavour of the Public-Establishment system in the article of cloathing: to supply the deficiency must be left to be paid for, in point of pecuniary economy, by the savings resulting under so many other heads of relief, and by the advantages in point of work, by these advantages in point of economy added to the advantages in point of health, strength and comfort on the one hand, humanity and decency on the other.

Privation, it appears, is the resource and sole resource of the Home-Provision system: its advantages are constituted by and measured by the degree of hunger and nakedness that prevail in it.

To this amounts so much as there is of truth in the observation frequently adduced in favour of the Home-Provision system, that the Poor at their own homes make every thing go much further than it *goes*—(to which is added, in the way of assumption, or can be *made* to go) in a Poor House:—to this much, I say, the truth of the observation amounts, and no more: for a pound of bread will not contribute more to nourishment, a coat of a given form and texture contribute more to warmth, in the one situation, than in the other.

[9.][1] *Education* is a branch of relief, peculiar to the case of the unripe branch of the community of the indigent: those whose intellectual faculties are developed, those whose affections are become sufficiently sensible to hope and fear, derived from the distant fountain of the law, may and must be trusted to the guidance of the distant finger of the law: those whose faculties have not yet attained this growth, must on some terms or other be subjected to the governance of a present guide. Under this head, the advantage, if there be any advantage, attendant on the business of education,

[1] The corresponding marginal contents sheet at UC cliv. 75 indicates that Bentham took the decision to include education as a branch of 'Economy in relation to relief' after the composition of the main body of the text.

[is][1] exclusively on the side of the Public-Establishment system: since it is only by the Public-Establishment system that any thing that can bear the name of education can be administered. Looking back to the list of those whose cases exclude the possibility of Home-Provision, we may number a variety of extensive classes of the non-adults: and even where the exertions of education are not, physically speaking, altogether inapplicable, yet morally speaking they may be pronounced scarcely applicable with any degree of advantage. Without a present guide, whose leisure admitts him to, while his mental acquirements qualify him for, the task, the animal may be reared, but the faculties of the intellectual and moral agent can not be subjected to any sort of culture.[a]

The grand, the undetermined and perhaps indeterminable, controversy concerning the comparative eligibility between what is called public and what is called private education, extends not to the present case: in this controversy, opulence is supposed on both sides: and if, among the opulent, there be one class more than another, in the instance of which the advantage appears to bear on the side of the private, or home- provision system, it is in the instance of the cases where the opulence is at the highest pitch: because in those instances a greater portion of time as well as talent can be paid for, than could be afforded in an inferior sphere of opulence.

To determine on which side the advantage lies under this head, no such task is necessary as that of devising and establishing the best plan of education adapted to the purpose. What is sufficient is, that under the Public-Establishment system that plan *may* be carried into execution, whatever it be, which in the judgment of the Guardians, of those to whom it belongs to determine, shall have been pronounced paramount, and extended all over the country—all over their sphere of superintendence; whereas, under the Home-Provision system, the execution of any regular plan whatever, good or bad, is physically impossible. Under this system, the Chapter of Education, that important chapter in the book of human nature, is one immense, unvaried, blank void, and nothing whatever can be written in it.

[a] What has been observed under the head of attendance in the case of casual infirmity, applies with little variation to the case of primæval infirmity: nor is the catalogue that has been given of the requisites necessary to the profitable management of a manufactory of goods altogether inapplicable to the formation of minds. In the division of labour, that great source of wealth and every other efficient cause of prosperity, the labour of the Instructor of Youth is not one of those branches which has least to gain by being extricated from the rest.

[1] MS 'are'.

§4. *Parallel in respect of certainty with regard to the administration of the relief*

This is a topic which applies in common to every modification of which the complex object termed *relief* is susceptible: it comes in therefore to advantage, after the view that has just been given of all those several modifications.

Under the Public-Establishment system—under the Public-Establishment system how indifferently soever administered, thus much you may be sure of—viz: that [what]ever you mean to have administered in the way of relief shall be administered in the way of relief, and in the precise shape in which you mean it should be administered. Lodging, Household Stock, Fewel, Food, Cloathing, Sick attendance, Medicine—even Education—whatsoever you mean a man shall have, in all or any of those ways, you may make sure of his having it—of his having it not only in specie, but in quantity, quality, and, if you think it worth your while, you may make sure even as to the individual article in each instance. You may say grain or potatoes, wheat or rye—beef, veal or mutton—surloin fillet, or saddle—you may choose the colour as well as the stuff of each man's cloaths—you may see each man's mess served out to him—and each man's coat fitted to his back. In respect to all these articles, you, whoever you are that are in authority, it depends upon you to know just as much, as well as just as little, as you please.

Under the Home-Provision system, it is of the very essence of the system, that in respect to every one of these particulars, it should be radically impossible for you to know any thing. What you give to a man, you give to him in trust, to lay it out in all those several ways, in such proportions as shall be most for his advantage upon the whole. But among those to whom you give it, take them by twenties at a time, there will always be a certain proportion, who, in making application for the bounty, come with a predetermined resolution to betray the trust. That proportion may be considered as varying, according to the situation, Country or Town, and according to the moral habits that happen to be prevalent in either, from one to ten of the twenty: though authors of name and experience go still further on the unfavourable side.[1] You give it to be distributed, according to occasion, among all those seven articles: but it stands preappropriated to an eighth article which you have not thought proper to comprize in the list. You give it principally for food: but it is appropriated principally to slow poison. You fancy you are feeding

[1] Bentham presumably has in mind John McFarlan: see p. 61 n. above.

him: but he stands predestined to be half-poisoned and half-starved. Double the allowance, you only accelerate his fate: the poison being the more copious, the operation is so much the more speedy. Double your anxiety and your trouble, give him the food in kind—unless you stand by to see him swallow it, he only eats so much the less. The poison is the one thing needful: the article absolutely incapable of retrenchment. Give him sixpence in money, he swallows threepence of it in slow poison, and threepence of it in food: give him sixpence in food, he sells fourpence halfpenny of it to buy his threepenny worth of poison: whereby instead of the sixpence you fancy you have secured for him, he has but three halfpence left for food. In the hand of Midas every thing turned to gold:[1] in the hand of the drunkard every thing turns to drink. In the laboratory of Midas weight was got for weight: but in the laboratory of the Pawnbroker, 50 per cent goes off in *service*.

Comparatively speaking, the Home-Provision system may do tolerably well for the strictly virtuous, for the strictly sober: but what should we say of that medicine, of which the best that could be said was, a man's stomach might bear it, provided he were in health? Men whose hearts are more expanded than their views, preoccupied by the attractive spectacle of obsequious virtue, speak of virtue, and think of indigence and virtue as if the most natural of all alliances were that between indigence and virtue: unhappily (or happily shall we say?) an alliance much more natural, and much more common, is that between indigence and vice.

There is moreover an alliance tripartite, between Drunkenness, Indigence and Idleness: indigence may enter and maintain its ground without either: but neither is apt to maintain its ground for any length of time without introducing the other, nor without introducing indigence.

Why is the Cottage supposed to be the favourite residence of Virtue, a Poor-house the abode of Vice? Because in a Poor House every thing unseemly meets the eye: in the Cottage, every thing of that sort is covered from it. It is the cottage of the favourite, not that of the obnoxious Poacher, that attracts the benevolent Patron's transient glance.

The Cottage is really the abode of virtue, in comparison of the abode that answers to it in great towns: for there are Cottages that are out of the reach of poison-shops. The Cottage, thus compared, is really the seat of virtue: but the town abode that answers to it has no name. Yet the Cottage and its anonymous counterpart divide the

[1] In classical mythology, the gods granted the request of Midas, King of Phrygia, that all he touched would be turned to gold.

population of the community in perhaps equal shares. Poetry has spread her mantle over the Cottage: and the Town Lodging has hedged itself in, and taken the benefit of that favoured name.[1]

§5. *Parallel in respect of Moral Influence*

Under the Home-Provision system, employment being, by the operation of the causes above indicated, rendered incapable of being administered with advantage, it accordingly is not administered in practice: so that this system, as far as it extends, is conducted in no other way than in that of pecuniary and gratuitous allowances, termed, in the books that have appeared on this subject, *Out-allowances.*

But from the single circumstance of their being gratuitous result, over and above the immense disadvantage in point of economy, the disadvantages of being pregnant with moral mischief and injustice: mischief to the moral habits of those to whom the relief is thus administered, injustice to those at whose expence it is administered.

Every penny thus bestowed upon an individual from whom, as under the Public-Establishment system, work in recompence might by any means have been extracted, is so much bounty-money given for idleness. It is pernicious to the individual thus treated in each individual instance: it is pernicious in the way of example to the public at large, to all individuals in a situation in life bordering upon his.

But to encourage idleness, it is not only an indisputable truth, but a truth pretty generally comprehended and acknowledged, idleness in company with indigence, is to encourage unhappiness on one side, and danger on the other. Idleness, meaning the absence of the habit of profitable labour, idleness combined with opulence, may also be combined with happiness, and with innocence: because opulence, by supplying the means of diversified enjoyment, may exempt the individual from the misery of inaction on the one hand, and the community from the danger of mischievous action on his part on the other. But idleness uncombined with opulence, especially when confirmed by education destitute of instruction, has every thing to urge it in to the road of vice and maleficence, and nothing to restrain it.

[1] Bentham probably has in mind the tradition of pastoral poetry which extended back as far as Theocritus (early 3rd century BC) and Virgil (70–19 BC), and which came into fashion again in the early part of the eighteenth century with poets such as Ambrose Philips (1675–1749), Alexander Pope (1688–1744), and James Thomson (1700–48), who extolled bucolic pleasures and rural retreats.

If then, a system were but established, under which relief might always be had in return for work, and work always be had in return for relief, it were better a penny were cast into the sea, than given:[1] unless it were in consideration either of peculiar merit or of past prosperity.[a]

But under the Public-Establishment system, a plan by which the connection between relief and employment, (all due exception being made in favour of the cases just excepted) may be rendered constant and inseparable, may most indubitably be instituted.[b]

Under the Public-Establishment system, the connection between relief and employment being rendered inseparable, as above, the more copious the relief, the better: because be it ever so copious, it is earnt by labour, and the expence of the one replaced by the produce of the other.

But under the Home-Provision system, as to every thing beyond what is necessary to ward off the danger of perishing, and the incitement to rapine and murder being warded off, the more copious the relief, the worse: the worse not only in point of economy, as before, but in point of moral influence also, as here the premium offered for idleness is so much the larger and more alluring.[c]

[a] I make these exceptions, because, as it should seem, these only save the donation from being mischievous in the way of example: *past prosperity*, because while the demands of past prosperity are greater, require a greater sum of money to produce a given measure of satisfaction, than those of habitual penury, the *causa sine qua non* of the donation, being a past event, presents a title which can not be exhibited in future instances by the indiscriminate crowd of the indigent: peculiar merit, that is meritorious exertion (since without exertion no merit), because a bounty given to meritorious exertion display'd in past instances, is, instead of being a premium for idleness, a premium offered for meritorious exertion in future instances.

[b] The Home-Provision system is therefore in this, as in every other point of view, ineligible in comparison of the Public-Establishment system, eligible only in comparison of the No-provision, or Inadequate-provision system, the total-starvation, or partial-starvation system. It is still good in comparison of these systems, because it is better that a larger multitude should be maintained in idleness, though, in respect of a considerable part of that multitude, the idleness may be attended with discomfort and danger, than that a smaller multitude should partly suffer death by famine, partly be driven to robbery and murder by the approach and apprehension of it.

[c] He has done his best, his utmost, his exertions have been as great as they could have been, you may say, and still he remains in indigence, and by his indigence has a claim to bounty. But this is what you can scarcely be said to have it in your power to know: for under a sharper spur, he might have exerted himself more: and at any rate, the gratuitous comfort given to this industrious individual invites to idleness others

[1] An echo of Mark 9: 42; and Luke 17: 2.

§6. *Parallel in respect of Justice*

The injustice inseparable from the Home-Provision system, already shown to be necessarily a system of gratuitous provision, is another point equally indisputable. For at whose expence but that of the laborious can the idle be relieved, at whose expence but that of those who do not enjoy, but in proportion to what they work, can relief without work be administered? In part (it is true) the expence is borne by property already accumulated: but as to a part, and that an inseparable one, it is borne by those also who have no other fund, for consumption or for contribution, other than the unaccumulated produce of their own daily labour. In this instance, as in any other, to confine the burthen of contribution to those who live upon the produce of accumulated property, without labour, would lead, if not of absolute necessity, at any rate without[1] the greatest care, to the destruction of all industry, as well as all property, by the system of forced equalization: and whether any plan of contribution, confined to the opulent, and at the same time exempt from so ruinous an objection, could or could not by possibility be devised, certain it is that no such plan hath as yet been either pursued or so much as proposed. There then would the process of injustice be carrying on at both ends: while on the one hand men are rewarded, if not for not working, at any rate without working, on the other hand, the working hands, if not punished in point of intention, are made to suffer as men suffer who are punished, for the benefit of those who are enabled to reap enjoyment otherwise than through work.

§7. *Parallel in respect of the facility of distinguishing just from unjust claims*

The bad economy, the immoral tendency, and the injustice wear a different complexion, and present still harder features, where, instead of being bestowed, although on such bad terms, upon real indigence, the bounty is wasted upon imposture under the mask of

that are less industrious. Give then, if you must give, rather in a shape [that] shall help him to work more, and so earn comfort by his work, [than][2] what shall prompt him to reap comfort without work.

[1] MS 'at any rate not without' contradicts the evident sense of the passage.

[2] MS 'that'.

indigence. Thus much as to the expence of affording relief, the existence of the demand for relief, the title, as it may be called, to relief being supposed. The allowance in the way of relief under each head being supposed to be determined, the comparison has hitherto been concerning the most frugal and cheapest mode of providing that allowance.

But does the demand (in the instance of the individual in question) really exist? Does it exist to the extent to which it is alledged to exist?—On the answers to these questions depends an article of economy, of greater importance than all the preceding ones put together. *Here* the question goes to the whole of the allowance—*there*, it goes only to a per centage on the amount of that allowance.

To constitute a sufficient title to relief at the expence of others, two requirements must concurr: 1. Actual deficiency in respect of the means of maintenance: 2. Inability to supply that deficiency in any honest way, from any other source.

Under this head we shall find the advantage as conspicuously in favour of the Public-Establishment system, as under any of the former heads.

Under the Public-Establishment system, under the Public-Establishment [system] how badly soever conducted, we shall find at least two checks opposed to unfounded claims: 1. Obligation, or at the worst probability of being subjected to the obligation, of performing work: 2. Obligation of residing in a spot which is not, and of living in conformity to a set of rules which are not, of a man's own choice.[a]

[a] The present topic affords an instructive instance of those inconsistencies to which human nature is perhaps never entirely exempt even in the most superior minds.

This property of sifting ill-grounded from well-grounded claims, this property which distinguishes the Public-Establishment system so much to its advantage in points so essential as those of economy, moral influence and justice, this property has scarcely yet been attributed to it to any other purpose than that of reproach. That this treatment should have been given to it by the partizans of the Home-Provision system is the less to be wondered at: in as much as in the composition of that multitude so principal a share is taken by those whose turn of mind leads them to be preoccupied and engrossed by the single object of the comfort of the individual concerned, without tracing up the operation to those still more important, but comparatively distant, effects upon the well-being of the community at large. With their view of the matter it perfectly consists that the bread of the industrious should be taken by force out of the mouth of the industrious, to be put into the mouth of the non-working or under-working classes, without necessity, without condition, and only for increase of comfort.

But what one should not so readily have expected is to see the same effect urged against the Public-Establishment system, in the way of reproach and reprobation, by those who are contending, and with no small degree of vehemence as well as eloquence, in favour of the No-provision system, and consequently against the

Under the Home-Provision system, both these checks are altogether wanting: employment is not, can not (as we have seen) be administered to any advantage: home is, by the supposition, as far as is allowed by the law of settlements (of which the object is rather to ascertain than to change the circle that circumscribes the home), *home* is so far, by the supposition, the home of a man's own choice.

Under this system, maintenance being secured to a man at any rate—to work or not to work, that, in the instance of every man who has not property of his own to maintain himself upon, is the question.[1]

adequate provision system in every possible branch of it, Home-Provision system, consequently, as well as every modification of the Public-Establishment system included. In one of the instances above spoken of it is stated in Italics, and seemingly with a view of representing it in the light of a crying grievance, that the '*Poor in the Workhouse were never suffered to eat till* they had done their task'.[2] This by a writer who, in a preceding publication on the same subject, had brought to view, in the character of a fundamental principle, a proposition which, from its reasonableness not less than from its origin, is eminently intitled to that character, the text of scripture in which it is said *He that will not work, neither shall he eat*:[3] this from a writer who, in the same unretracted publication, would not, at the public charge, suffer a single man to eat in any house, but that, even now that the system of 'compulsive charity' has taken the root that we all know of, advises even now the *abolition* of it, *in toto*, as an event that, when compared to a fixation of the expence, that is with the inadequate-provision system, would be still better for the state.[a] This from a writer who, in reprobating these instances of the Small-Establishment system, gives us to understand that the Large-Establishment system, a system which should 'receive the poor of the whole county', would be still worse, not only (again in Italics) *as holding out the terror of confinement, but as adding banishment from their friends to a loss of liberty*.[4] If inefficacy were meant as the only charge upon these exemplifications of the Public-Establishment system, so that it was in that point of view only, and not in that of hardship, that they were meant to be held up to consideration, the inconsistency vanishes: and of this construction the passages, considered in themselves, appear by no means unsusceptible.

What inclines me, however, to think that the supposed hardship not less [than][5] the inefficacy was meant to be holden up to view, is a passage in the already-quoted subsequent publication of the same author, still written in the same spirit, in which, with a degree of warmth as natural to a partizan of the Home-Provision system as it appears extraordinary in a partizan of the No-provision System, the expedient of

[a] *Dissertation*, 1786.[6]

---

[1] An echo of *Hamlet* III. i. 56.

[2] See Townsend, *Observations on Various Plans*, p. 17. The passage is not italicized in the original.

[3] See 2 Thessalonians 3: 10, cited by Townsend in *A Dissertation on the Poor Laws*, p. 82.

[4] See Townsend, *Observations on Various Plans*, p. 20. The passage is not italicized in the original.

[5] MS 'that'.

[6] See Townsend, *A Dissertation on the Poor Laws*, pp. 87–8.

With a view to this question, the individuals in question, considered in respect of their ability to work (under which head I comprise for the present purpose the consideration of the faculty of procuring work), may be distributed into two classes.

In the first may be included all those who attribute to themselves the ability of obtaining, by their labour, a supply exceeding, by an amount more or less considerable, the amount of what they would expect to receive upon occasion in the way of gratuitous allowance: in the second, all those who do not attribute to themselves that degree of ability.

In the former case, the option lies between the pleasure of enjoying and the pain of working: and a man will accordingly live at his own expence or at that of the public, according as in his breast the love of active enjoyment, or the love of ease, happens to predominate.

In the other instance, the option lies between the presence or the absence of, between a man's subjecting himself or not subjecting himself to, the pain of working. In this state of things (laying out of the question pride, and other motives of rare occurrence, which may be considered rather as *casus natura*[1] in minds so destitute of culture), if a man works, he acts without a motive: if the effect takes place, it takes place without a cause.

A state of inaction, it may be observed on the other side, a state of inaction, continued for a certain length of time, is a state of pain.—The observation is just: and accordingly, supposing a man so circumstanced (as he may be in a place of confinement) as to have no other option but between inaction and a single species of work, there is perhaps scarce that species of work that he would not sooner or later embrace in preference. But the persons in question are, by the supposition, not in any place of confinement but perfectly at large: and the option a man has lies not between inaction and the particular species of work which, if he chose it, [he][2] might earn money by

farming the Poor is introduced by a preface, terming it '*the most abominable one that ever was invented*'.[b]

Laying these two views of the matter together, the list of grievances, as given by the same writer, would, if stated together, appear extraordinary enough. One, that those who could not be maintained without compulsive charity are maintained by it, the other that those who could be maintained without compulsive charity, are not maintained by it.

[b] *Dissertation*, p. 75.[3]

---

[1] i.e. 'in the nature of an accident'.

[2] MS 'they'.

[3] i.e. Townsend, *A Dissertation on the Poor Laws*, p. 75. Bentham's reference to this as the 'subsequent publication' is mistaken: the publication of *A Dissertation on the Poor Laws* preceded that of *Observations on Various Plans* by two years.

instead of having it for nothing, but between inaction and the most pleasant of all the occupations which the fine situation he is in offers to his choice: and against his rejecting all these amusements, in favour of a species of employment which can never have presented itself to his imagination in any other character than that of a task, the chances may be reckoned nearly as infinity to one.

As in both cases therefore, the motives to usurpation exist, so in the latter case, it can only be as it were by accident, if they fail to predominate: and in such a situation, if the motives predominate, it can seldom be impracticable to find the means. At a distance from those whose duty it is to scrutinize into the title, inability, the efficient cause of title, may either be feigned *in toto*, or what is much more easy and more natural, exaggerated: or even, where the aversion to labour is strenuous, fabricated. Compleat ability would sometimes be, or appear to be, converted into total or partial inability: still oftener, partial inability improved into total. Thus thumbs have been cut off to escape from military service, and sore legs have been manufactured and kept up to constitute a beggar's stock in trade. When the claimant and the judge are constantly under the same roof, imposition for any length of time would, under a tolerable system of management, be absolutely impracticable: and bad indeed must be the management, if, in such a situation, continued imposition should present itself as otherwise than hopeless, and the anxiety inseparable from the attempt would be as unremitting as the labour shunned. Where the visit from the authoritative inspector is but occasional, and then but short, imposition may not be difficult, and the occasional anxiety may appear an easy price for the habitual exemption.

The facility of imposition under the Home-Provision system as contrasted with the Public-Establishment system will appear in colours equally strong, whether the situation of those on whom the claiming of relief, or those on whom the allowance of it depends, be considered. In the latter situation, we shall find the efficient causes operating to give birth to false indulgence numerous and strong: those which tend in privation of it, less numerous and feeble. Inconsiderate humanity, love of ease, fear of ill-will, love of power, love of popularity (and occasionally party affection and party interest) on the one side: little or no sensible check from pecuniary interest, little or no publicity, and thence little or no check from the fear of unpopularity, much less from the fear of punishment, on the other. How natural, how easy the imposition! How difficult, how laborious the detection! In the one case, how slight the damage! In the other, how fatal the consequence! A man must be more or less than man, who, with the purist intentions, does not give way to imposition, perhaps in more cases than he escapes from it. As in the dispensation of public bounties in general, so in particular in this, the only case in which bounty is enforced by necessity, all the social, all the generous propensities of man's nature, every thing gravitates to the side of erroneous indulgence: as in prosecutions, and with much more reason than in prosecutions, this side is regarded as the safe side. By undue acquittal, an enemy to the public is sent back in triumph, to recommence hostilities with the benefit of experience: by undue punishment (an event that scarce happens in any age) the cases are few in which the mistake is fatal and irreparable. Where relief or no relief is the question, in case of the allowance of an insufficiently grounded claim of relief, the damage is in many, perhaps most instances, in a manner impalpable, and the individual on whom it falls in a sensible magnitude is hardly to be found: in the case of the disallowance, the inflexible disallowance, of a founded claim, the wrong wears the face of murder, the consequence is death.

As on the side of erroneous indulgence, as there is neither private ill-will nor public disrepute to punish error, so there is scarce any publicity to indicate it. Every thing is done in a corner: in the case of simple indigence in a private room: in the case of alledged sickness, at a bedside: by the bed of indigence, in the midst of dirt, foul air, bad smells, loathsome sights and moaning, oftentimes under the terror, or even the danger, of infection: where no one visitor would go, if he could well avoid it, and where, more especially for so ungracious a purpose as that of putting a bridle on humanity, no second visitor is likely to think it worth his while to follow him.

Where error is so natural and so excusable, forbidden propensities have the freer range. The reciprocality of dependence as between the highest and the lowest orders, the result of that system of popular election which, in the degree in which it exists in this country, is attended with so many advantages, is, on the other hand, attended with some inconveniences; and that of widening the inlet to the sort of profusion here in question may be reckoned in the number. A man may have a vote, he may be the occupier of a portion of space in which a pot will boil, he may even have a 40^{s} freehold of his own,[1] and

[1] An allusion to the qualifications for the franchise in 'potwalloper' boroughs and in the English counties respectively. In the twelve 'potwalloper' boroughs, the right to vote extended to all householders not in receipt of alms or poor relief. The relatively large electorate in these boroughs led to the frequent contestation of elections, while their electorates acquired a popular reputation for venality. See J. Brooke, 'Introductory Survey', in Sir L. Namier and J. Brooke, *The History of Parliament. The House of Commons 1754–1790: Introductory Survey, Constituencies, Appendices*, 3 vols., Oxford, 1964, i. 10. In the English county constituencies, the franchise extended to the holders of freehold property valued, for the purposes of the land tax, at forty shillings a year: see ibid., i. 2.

yet find himself in a state of indigence constitutive of conferring a title, real or apparent, to relief. If a man himself be not in that predicament, or if his being in it destroys the vote, others that are, and are known to be, dear to him, may receive the bounty in his stead. For the perversion of public contributions in this way to the purposes of personal interest or affection, the Home-Provision system offers a secure and scarcely controulable facility, which under the Public-Establishment system has evidently no place.

If the loss and waste resulting on this ground from the Home-Provision system appears considerable in theory, it will not appear less considerable should the appeal be to experience: for, and what one should hardly have expected, documents are not wanting, from which the amount of the waste may be subjected in some measure to a sort of calculation. Upon the substitution of the Public-Establishment system to the Home-Provision system, a sudden diminution in the number of the claimants has been experienced. So considerable has been the amount of this diminution that, in consequence, a reduction in the expence to the amount of near 50 per cent has taken place: and this upon the average has been the degree of reduction in the instance of the districts, the only ones that have fallen under notice in this view. The result is, that as far as the districts by which the experience has been afforded [are][1] to be considered as a fair sample of the rest of the country, about half of what is thus bestowed in a year, is bestowed in waste. This being admitted, in the years 178[3], 178[4] & 178[5],[2] when in round numbers the tax borne in the shape of Poor Rates amounted to two millions, one million was bestowed to those who had no just claim: which leaves no more than a million bestowed with propriety, as far as concerns the objects, and that too subject to the reductions of which the exclusive adoption of the Public-Establishment system might, on the several grounds above stated, have been productive.[a]

[a] A respectable writer on the Poor-Laws (the Rev: Joseph Townsend in his *Observations on various plans offered to the public for the Relief of the Poor*, (1788)), has quoted from a work not named, but stated as published in 1732, instances of a variety of Parishes, 14 in number, in every one of which, upon the substitution of the Public-Establishment system to the Home-Provision system, the amount of the Poor Rates had experienced a rapid fall (the Establishments, it is to be observed, were

[1] MS 'is'.

[2] Bentham must have had in mind 1783–5, since these were the only years during the relevant decade for which official figures regarding the total expenditure on poor relief in England and Wales were available. In 1786 all Overseers were required by 26 Geo. III, c.56 to report to Parliament regarding the amount raised by the poor rates and the amount spent on poor relief in their localities during 1783–5. The average annual expenditure during the period amounted to £2,004,238. 5s. 11d. See *Commons Sessional Papers of the Eighteenth Century*, lx. 4.

An incident of a different nature, though in this respect of a similar tendency, has brought to view a reduction of the same kind. I mean the adoption of the Farming or Contract plan into this branch of public management: the agreeing with a party, usually if not always a single individual, to charge himself with the whole expence whatever it might prove, in consideration of a certain sum. But though the general tendency of this measure has [frequently][1] been observed, and observed upon with much energy, as operating on this same side, I know not that any cases have ever yet been made public, by which the amount of the effect has been indicated in any individual instance. Indeed, as so much in this case would depend upon the

small Establishments, Parochial Work-Houses).[2] The date of the opening of each Establishment is not uniformly specified: but the earliest date mentioned is 1723 or 1724, and the period at which the observation had been taken of the decrease, can not, from the date of the pamphlet, have been posterior to 1732.

Upon summing up the total of the expenditure for all those places, at the several periods preceding the opening of the respective Establishments, it appears to amount (neglecting shillings & pence) to:	£8364
D[o] at the several periods when the observation was taken of the expence under the respective Establishments:	£4271

The average of the reduction amounted therefore to within a trifle of 50 per Cent, or one half.

If there were probable reason for regarding this saving as being the result of any difference in point of economy between the management under the Home-Provision system, and the management under the Public-Establishment system in these instances, the inference which attributes the reduction to the disappearance of insufficiently-founded claims would not hold. But the probability runs conclusively the contrary way. As to the expence of relief, there is no reason for regarding it as likely to have been less per head per annum in any of these *small* establishments than the average amount under the Out-allowance System. No such saving would be to be expected, as will be seen farther on, *a priori*: and, in fact, the greatest fall was in the instance (of S[t] Albans) where the allowance was most lavish. Among the instances of other Parish Poor Houses of which the accounts have been made public, there is not perhaps a single one which does not afford one example to the contrary.

As to any profit from the work, it is equally out of the question. In the three instances, which among the 14 Establishments are the only ones in which any thing is said of earnings, these earnings do not amount to more than between $\frac{1}{4}$[d] and $\frac{1}{2}$[d]

[1] MS 'frequency'.

[2] See Townsend, *Observations on Various Plans*, pp. 15–19. The work to which Townsend refers is *An Account of Several Work-houses For Employing and Maintaining the Poor; Setting forth The Rules by which they are Governed, Their great Usefulness to the Publick, And in Particular To the Parishes where they are Erected. As also of several Charity Schools For Promoting Work, and Labour*, 2nd edn., London, 1732. Bentham's own copy of the pamphlet is in the British Library, shelf-mark C.T. 102 (4). In fact, Townsend provides figures for sixteen workhouses, which Bentham reproduced in tabular form at UC cxxxiii. 56. Bentham omits Colchester and Canterbury in his calculations, 'the dates of the periods in question not being sufficiently ascertained'.

individual, and so little upon the system, the instances being so much the less instructive, the want of them is so much the less to be regretted.[a]

§8. *Parallel in respect of Perfectibility*

The aptitude to receive improvement has, in the instance of the British Constitution, been remarked by De Lolme, as one of the most valuable, beautiful, and at the same time peculiar features of that form of Government.[1] The same property may with equal justice be stated as the peculiar attribute of the Public-Establishment system (I mean always that modification of it which I term the Large-Establishment system), in contradistinction to the Home-Provision system.

Under the Home-Provision system, every thing in the way of profitable employment being clearly out of the question, one half of the improveable matter is radically wanting: improvement is out of

per head per day: in the largest of the three, not more than £25 for the whole number of 73 persons maintained:[2]—a sum greatly short of what must have been the commercial part of the expence of the management: I mean of that part of the expence which resulted exclusively from the production of the work.

Upon an observation taken 53 or 54 years after, viz: on the occasion of the Returns made in pursuance to the Act of Parliament, the total expence of these same Establishments was found to have arisen to £18,460:[3] more than four times the expence at the time when the original fall was observed: and more than twice the expence under the Home-Provision system: but, on inquiry, the causes of so remarkable a reverse do not belong to the present purpose. The question here is concerning the effect of the institution as to the distinguishing and sifting the insufficiently-grounded from the sufficiently-grounded claims: the claims of pretended or voluntary, from those of real and unavoidable, indigence.

[a] Of the expediency of the Farming or Contract plan, considered in a general and comprehensive point of view, I shall say nothing on the present occasion. It will receive a full consideration in another place.[4]

---

[1] See Jean Louis de Lolme (1740–1806), Swiss jurist, *The Constitution of England; or an Account of the English Government; In which it is compared with the Republican Form of Government, and occasionally with the other Monarchies in Europe*, London, 1775, p. 444 (first published as *Constitution de l'Angleterre*, Amsterdam, 1771).

[2] Townsend gives figures for the earnings of paupers in three workhouses, which range from just over $\frac{1}{4}$d per day at Peterborough, to just over $\frac{1}{2}$d per day at Chatham. The number of paupers maintained in the houses ranged from thirty at Stroud in Kent, to seventy-three at Chatham. See *Observations on Various Plans*, p. 18.

[3] See ibid., pp. 16–19. The Act in pursuance of which the returns were made was 26 Geo. III, c.56: see p. 179 n. above.

[4] In the corresponding marginal contents sheet at UC cliv. 76, Bentham has noted at this point: 'Question of general expediency posted off to §. Parallel between L[arge] & S[mall] systems.' In fact, Bentham did not include an extended discussion of contract management in this section, but for such a discussion see Appendix B, pp. 276–89 below.

the question, where there neither is nor ever can be any thing to improve.

In the article of relief, there is nothing in the case that tends to render the management better in point of economy, and there are many things that tend to render it continually worse and worse. Every indulgence forms a precedent for fresh indulgence: every excess tends to produce new excess. One man gets one extra-allowance on the whisper of some special ground: the special ground is either unnoticed or forgotten, and then comes the cry on all sides: why not to us, as well as him? A man gets an allowance on the score of some temporary exigence: the exigence takes its departure, but the allowance does not follow it. In cases of this sort, of periodical allowances to individuals, there is a time when the correction of abuse would [be] a grievance still worse than the abuse. Thus again on the part of the dispensers of public bounty—A man's predecessor allow'd such and such claims—how rare is that man, who, for the crabbed, solitary satisfaction of adhering to the rigid rule of right, would expose himself to the maledictions of a surrounding multitude, contrasted with the blessing poured on the memory of his predecessor!

A single Manager, rendered profuse or negligent by ill-judged humanity, or indolence, or opulence, may be enough to spoil the industry of a whole Parish, and plant such a system of profusion as a man of firmer temper and correcter views, when such an one happens to take his place, may attempt in vain to eradicate.

The tendency on the part of the management to get worse and worse when left to itself, might afford but a slight ground of objection, if the evil either lay, or could be brought, within the reach of the public eye—of the superintending eye of government: but of this it is radically unsusceptible. By what possibility can instances of error in the system of Parish Management, scattered among a crowd of 500,000, or a million, or 1,500,000 individuals, repeated in an assemblage of 15,000 Rateable Districts, undergo revision in a Commission of the Privy Council, or of the House of Commons? They baffle observation by their minuteness, they confound the attention by their [multitude],[1] and by their nature they are incapable of a remedy. A.B. receives $1^{s} 6^{d}$ a week: C.D., 2^{s}:—I have a list of this kind actually before me—what information, what means of judging does it offer to my view? C.D.'s claim to the 2^{s} may have been no better than A.B.'s: or neither the one nor the other may have had any well-grounded claim to a single farthing: but what means have I, in my situation, so

[1] MS 'multituted'.

much as to detect the existence of the abuse, not to speak of putting a stop to the continuance or encrease of it.

Here, every thing is insulated—every thing is *particular*: every thing is out of reach, every thing is out of knowledge: and while every thing is growing worse and worse, every thing is out of the reach of cure.

Under the Public-Establishment (I mean always the Large-Establishment) system, the state of things is, in this important point of view, precisely the reverse. The accounts of from 2 or 3, to 6 or 7 Industry Houses, according to the extent and population of the County, may undergo a very minute scrutiny on the part of the leading members of the County Government. Even a mass of matter, composed of the accounts of 250 such Houses, where all the items are, according to a regular plan, thrown into the Tables and digested under heads, may not be so complex or so extensive, but that a few members of the supreme Executive and of the supreme Legislative Government, each in their respective spheres, may always be found, who shall manifest themselves both able and willing to devote a sufficient portion of time to the elaboration of an object, raised by its magnitude to a degree of importance worthy of their best exertions.

In such a comparative and synoptic view, every thing that is bad in any one establishment of the whole number will present itself as a warning, every thing that is good, as an object of imitation, in every other: each establishment will be to the rest a sort of experimental Laboratory.

The subject is not so complex, but that in each House, the management, under all the leading points of it, may easily be arranged under heads: and the list of these heads, will, with little variation, be the same in one house as in another. In a course of time, there is not a single point of bad management that will not, by a sort of mechanical process, have been weeded out of the whole system: not a single point of good management will have display'd itself in any one *House*, that will not have found its way into every other, by emulation among the subordinates, or by order of the superintending authority.

CHAPTER V.
PARALLEL BETWEEN LARGE AND SMALL-ESTABLISHMENT SYSTEMS

After the parallel thus drawn between the Home-Provision system and the Public-Establishment system, the parallel between the two modifications of the Public-Establishment system need not put us to much trouble. In speaking of the advantages of the Public over the Home system, it is to the Large-Establishment system that I have all along been obliged, in a manner, to confine my view: for in those advantages the Small-Establishment system, to judge from the samples of it which are lain in such abundance before our eyes, will scarcely be found in any degree to participate.

Employment, the first of the two grand divisions of the system of provision for the Poor, employment, the capital source of the advantage possessed by the Public-Establishment system, can scarcely be considered as a source of profit under that modification of it which we see exemplified in Small Establishments.

In relation to this article, it may be doubted whether the Small-Establishment system, taking it on the footing on which it stands in many, if not most instances, is not less favourable to good economy than even the Home-Provision system. Under the Home-Provision system, all chance of deriving a profit from this article of employment being plainly out of the question, no attempt to give birth to any such profit is made. If then, under this system, there is no profit derived from it, so neither is there any loss.

Under the Small-Establishment system, the call for employment is loud, and general, and plausible, while in all instances there exists a great difficulty, and in most instances perhaps an impossibility, of administering it with profit, or even without loss. By exertions more or less strenuous, and more or less enlightened, an appearance of profit may perhaps be produced, but covering a real loss: while the small apparent profit, by nourishing the hopes of greater, gives continuance to the loss. The circumstance that invests loss with the mask of profit is the omission of some article, or set of articles, in the account of the expenditure: articles which ought to be charged in the Trade account, because were it not for the purpose of that concern, the disbursement would not, or at least ought not to, have been made.

In the parallel between the Public-Establishment system and the Home-Provision system, a list has been given of certain requisites without which no commercial concern can be productive of profit.[1] Under the Home-Provision system, this list of requisites can not be provided at any rate. Under the Small-Establishment system, they may, in many or most instances, be provided, but the providing of them necessitates a certain degree of expence. If this expence be not covered by the receipts, instead of a profit there is a loss.

The several heads of Building, Household Stock, Fewel, Food, Sick Attendance, Medical curation and Education, I have stated, with a view to the advantages possessed by the Public-Establishment system, as compared to the Home-Provision system. Under all these heads the advantage must have appeared, from that same statement, to have been on the side of the Large-Establishment system, as compared with the Small-Establishment system: and the advantage (it may also have been observed) rises in exact proportion to the largeness of the Establishment (at least if, from the circumstance of magnitude, no disadvantage arises in a degree of importance sufficient to outweigh the mass of advantages): and that partly in a direct way, in virtue of the augmentation in the bulk of each establishment: partly in a less immediate and direct way, by the diminution in the number of the establishments.

The article of Building (the great stumbling block of establishments of this kind) is of importance sufficient to warrant a separate consideration. Under this head, the field of advantage may be subjected in some sort to calculation: it results not merely from the diminution of the ratio of the quantity of inclosing materials to the quantity of inclosed space: but likewise from the confining to one in number, under a single establishment, a point which, in case of a multiplicity of establishments, must be repeated as many times as there are establishments: for example: Resident Manager's House or Apartments, Resident Manager's Garden, Chapel, where there is one, Stabling, Waiting Rooms for Visitors and persons who come on business, and the like.[2]

A scale of the estimated rise in the expence, according to a series in which the number of Houses allotted to the reception of a given

[1] See p. 157–8 above.

[2] In the corresponding marginal contents sheet at UC cliv. 76, Bentham has noted at this point: 'Vessels.' Bentham discusses the economies of scale in relation to cooking vessels and their heating at p. 162 & n. above.

number of persons to be provided for (suppose two thousand) encreases from one to 25, is given in a note.[a]

[a] Table

Exhibiting the advantage in point of economy possessed by an Establishment on a larger scale, in comparison with a set of Establishments on a smaller scale, adapted to the reception of the same number of persons, exemplified in the instance of an Airing Yard enclosed, in a manner sufficient for safe custody, by Walling:

Suppositions

To a Poor House calculated for 80 persons, an Airing Yard of a Rood square[1] would be a competent allowance.

This then, makes a Rood square the competent allowance for every 80 persons.

According to this allowance, a House calculated for 160 persons would require a similar Walled Airing Yard or Area, the content of which should be equal to 2 square Roods.

But, it is evident that the Walling necessary to inclose two areas of a Rood each would be more in quantity than the Walling necessary to inclose a single Area equal to two Square Rood: that in the case of three such Areas of a Rood, each compared with a single Area of 3 Rood, the difference would be still greater.

In this table, the difference is exhibited in the instance of the several numbers of square Roods from 1 to 25 inclusive.

Estimate of the Expence of Boundary Walls to Square pieces of ground containing from one to twenty-five Roods (inclusive)

No. of inmates	No. of Roods	Contents in Square Feet	Side of the Square	Length of Walling	Expence in Separate Lots	Expence in consolidated lots
80	1	10890	104″4	417″4	208:13:4	208:13:4
160	2	21780	147″7	590″4	417:6:8	295:3:4
240	3	32670	180″10	723″4	[626:0:0][2]	361:13:4
320	4	43560	208″8	834″8	[834:13:4]	417:6:8
400	5	54450	233″4	933″4	[1043:6:8]	466:13:4
480	6	65340	255″7	1022″4	[1252:0:0]	511:3:4
560	7	76230	276″1	1104″4	[1460:13:4]	552:3:4
640	8	87120	295″2	1180″8	[1669:6:8]	590:6:8
720	9	98010	313″1	1252″4	[1878:0:0]	626:3:4
800	10	108900	330″0	1320″0	[2086:13:4]	660:0:0
880	11	119790	346″1	1384″4		692:3:4
960	12	130680	361″4	1445″4		722:13:4
1040	13	141570	376″3	1505″0		752:10:0
1120	14	152460	390″6	1562″0		781:0:0
1200	15	163350	404″2	1616″8		808:6:8
1280	16	174240	417″5	1669″8		834:16:8
1360	17	185130	430″3	1721″0		860:0:0
1440	18	196020	442″9	1771″0		885:10:0
1520	19	206910	454″11	1819″11		909:16:8
1600	20	217800	466″11	1867″8		933:16:8
1680	21	228690	478″3	1913″0		956:10:0
1760	22	239580	489″4	1957″4		978:13:4
1840	23	250470	500″4	2001″4		1000:13:4
1920	24	261360	511″2	2044″8		1022:6:8
2000	25	272250	520″10	2083″4	[5216:13:4]	1041:13:4

N.B. Another head of Waste.—Difference between them for the utmost number expected and the average number expected.—The oftener this is repeated, the more the waste.

[1] i.e. a superficial measure of land equal to 10,890 square feet.

[2] MS '625: 0: 0.' Bentham's error in addition was carried over to all the remaining figures in this column.

Another set of advantages which the Large-Establishment system possesses over the Small-Establishment system, are peculiar to the question as between these two branches of the Public-Establishment system since, under the Home-Provision system, the articles they turn upon have no place.

1. The first I shall mention is that which concerns the superior chance for good management, in as far as depends upon the choice of the Head Manager for each Establishment.

In the first place, whatever be the ingredients of fitness on the part of a manager for this purpose, whatsoever be the qualifications necessary to the composition of a fit manager, this much is evident: that it will be easier to find any given number of fit managers than to find any greater number: the chance of meeting with 250 such Managers will be ten times as great as the chance of meeting with 2500 such.

2. The choice of the Manager—I mean the Resident and Acting Manager—that choice on which so much depends, is another head in relation to which success can scarcely be hoped for with any reasonable prospect of *general* success, except under an establishment conducted upon a large scale.

The scale must be sufficiently large—and it can scarcely be too large—to afford the requisite facilities for obtaining a fit manager: a manager in whose instance the several known elements of official fitness may be expected to be found collected—qualifications personal as well as external—practical, if possible, as well as theoretical—intellectual as well as moral: one whose pecuniary trustworthiness shall be ensured, if not by property of his own, at any [rate][1] by the responsibility of sufficient sureties: one who, in those views of expanded benevolence which are not to be acquired but by that sort of a liberal education which places a man within the sphere of the superior ranks of life, shall possess a counterpoise to those principles of personal policy which are common to all ranks: one who, being connected, more or less, in sentiments, affections and prospects at least, if not habits, with the superior and cultivated world, shall not feel himself too low to be included within the circle of its notice.

The measure necessary to give the establishment the fairest chance for the utmost degree of prosperity of which it is susceptible will not have been taken, while any expedient remains unemploy'd which can tend to strengthen the connection between the interest of the establishment, and the interest of the person who has the

[1] MS 'right'.

conduct of it: but to the strength of this connection, a main pillar will be wanting if the profit of the manager does not both rise and fall with the pecuniary prosperity of the establishment: the rise and fall being in exact proportion, the result of a pre-established, arranged connection, not depending on the will, or subsequent determination, of third persons.

Unless the population of the establishment possesses a certain magnitude, the utmost profit that can be expected to be reaped from the labour of the working hands will not amount to an object capable of affording an inducement sufficient to engage in the service a man circumstanced as above described, connected in point of sentiments and affections with the superior ranks of life. It may not, although the profit were exempt from loss: much less after the deduction which it must sustain in point of value, by being coupled with the risk of loss.

The connection thus established between public and personal interest should extend, and that as equally as may be, to every branch of the management: lest, if any one be excepted, the current of profusion should be impelled, by the resistance it meets with in other quarters, with encreased impetus into that one.

In particular, it ought not to be confined to that branch of the supply which concerns the maintenance: partly on account of the danger, lest, in virtue of the profit to be made by the reduction of the allowance, the amount of it should fall short, either in quantity or quality, of what it ought to be: but still more on account of the danger to the reputation of the establishment, from the imputation of interested parsimony: a danger equally pregnant with bad consequences, be the imputation ever so ill grounded; and partly, because excluding from the sources of profit that which concerns the produce of the labour, would exclude the main branch of the pecuniary inducement, the only one that has no perceptible limits.

From this view of the principles to be attended to, in relation to the connection between the interest of the establishment, and the pecuniary interest of the person entrusted with the management, it appears that it is only a large establishment that is capable of affording a well-grounded prospect of engaging a fit manager: and that the larger the establishment, the better the expence of engaging such fit manager can be borne, whether it be defray'd solely out of the produce of the establishment itself, or partly derived from a distinct and independent fund. In the former case, because each establishment, being the larger, may be expected to yield the more; in the other case, because the multitude of the establishments being, in proportion to the magnitude of each, so much the less, the collateral supply demanded on this account will be so much the less.

3. The number of the Subordinates is another article in respect of which the advantage possessed by the Large-Establishment system over the Small-Establishment system, though perhaps less considerable than in the last preceding instance, is not less manifest. It results from the cutting off that source of disadvantage to which all establishments are exposed: the necessity of paying an entire hand, for a mass of business not large enough to occupy more than a portion of his time. If, for example, in each of twelve establishments, there be, over and above the quantity of business to which a single subordinate is equal, a redundancy, which, though requiring no more than the fourth part of a man's time, necessitates the maintaining of a second, in such case, in an Establishment equal to the twelve taken together, the above mentioned fragments of business being thus undissevered, and constituting altogether no more than three men's work, nine hands out of the dozen may thus be saved. In the annexed Table may be seen a calculation of the amount of the saving on this head, in a system embracing England and Wales, computed according to the different modifications of which the state of things, in this respect, may be considered as susceptible.[1]

4. The Division of Labour, viz: the labour of the working hands included under each Establishment, forms another source of advantage on the side of the Large-Establishment system, as contrasted with the Small-Establishment system. The magnitude of this source of advantage has been too well stated by Adam Smith, and is too universally acknowledged, to require discussion here.[2] As the degree of advantage depends, more or less, upon the nature of the employment, it is scarce possible, when the nature of the employment is not given, to subject it to calculation. It is scarce necessary to state that the greater [the][3] number of the hands included in the establishment, the more minute the division which the employment admitts of.

5. *The conspicuousness of the theatre of action* may be reckoned as another source of advantage peculiar to the Large-Establishment system, and accruing in direct proportion to the magnitude, and thence in the [inverse][4] proportion to the multitude, of the Establish-

[1] No such table has been located, although Bentham did provide an illustration of the savings possible in regard to salaries in 'Outline of a Work entitled Pauper Management Improved', *Annals of Agriculture*, xxx (1798), 131n. (Bowring, viii. 378n.), where he calculated the amount as £408,406. 5. 0. per year.

In the corresponding marginal contents sheet at UC cliv. 76, Bentham has noted at this point: 'Addend. Wholesale purchase. Refuse rendered valuable.' Bentham discusses economies of scale in relation to wholesale purchase in Ch. IV, p. 163 & n. above, but no discussion of refuse intended for inclusion in the present essay has been identified.

[2] See Smith, *The Wealth of Nations*, i. 13–24.

[3] MS 'of'.

[4] MS 'inversion'.

ments. This advantage is not the less important for being beyond the reach of calculation.

The importance of it will be equally incontestible, whether its influence be considered with relation to the subordinate elements of the system of management, or to the supreme: in the latter instance, on the magnitude of each establishment, as well as the moderateness of the number of the establishments, will depend its chance for rising to a place in the notice of persons at the head of things, whose time can not be afforded but for objects of the first magnitude. But upon the apparent probability of attracting the notice of men at the head of things, and along with them, of the world below, on the probability of drawing attention, whether it be in respect of honour or in respect of blame, depends every thing of self-denial, of correctness, of alacrity, of exertion, of emulation among the local subordinates of whatever classes.

In a system of Establishments, in multitude not exceeding some such number as 250, for the whole of South Britain, a system to which the attention of government would stand pledged, and through them the general attention of the discerning world below, each local Manager may consider himself as a Member of Administration, every such individual may consider himself as acting a part in the theatre of the world, and as destined, according to his deserts, to a place of ignominy or honour in the public eye.

In the narrow and sordid obscurity of an ordinary Poor house, good and bad examples are alike dead to the world above: the bad yields no warning: the good produces no imitation: peculation and hardheartedness burrow together in the gloom.

CHAPTER VI.
OBJECTIONS TO PUBLIC ESTABLISHMENTS OF THIS KIND

§1. *Pauper Interests*

Against the Public-Establishment system, as contrasted with the Home-Provision system, observations to the following effect, originating in sentiments and affections of the most respectable and honourable nature, have been brought forward in the character of objections: all of them having in view the welfare of the individuals in question, all of them grounded in some supposed prejudice or danger to the health, comfort or morals of these objects of national sollicitude.

1. That it is prejudicial to health, and therefore cruel, to shut people up in houses, especially crowded houses, such as manufactories are in general, and, in particular, manufactories instituted at the public expence for the reception of the indigent may be expected to be, in preference to the consigning them to employments such as husbandry labour, which give them for the greater part of the day the benefit of the fresh air.

2. That, in the instance of all persons in general comprized in the establishment, it is a hardship and a cruelty to sever them from their relations and family friends, a predicament in which by far the greater part of the inhabitants must necessarily be involved under the Public-Establishment system, and more especially under the Large-Establishment modification of it.

3. That the hardship acquires a character of distinct and additional severity, where Children and Parents are there torn from each other's embraces, and the closest ties, those formed by the very hand of nature, are thereby burst assunder.

4. That public receptacles of any kind, much more upon so large a scale, are incurably pregnant with perpetual and irremediable discomfort of the individuals which they inclose, by reason of the clamour, insults, indecencies, filthiness, indelicacies and other species of annoyance, which the well disposed must be continually liable to sustain at the hands of the ill disposed.

5. That Public receptacles of this kind, being intended for manufactories, will be so many schools of vice: for that manufactories are schools of vice: and the larger the scale, the more impetuous and irresistible the torrent of vice.

Of these several objections, the three first have this feature in common, that without any direct assertion, they involve, though tacitly, yet necessarily, various suppositions in regard to matters of fact of which not one is true.

i.[1] They suppose to be the result of force, what in point of fact is matter of choice.

ii. They suppose the obligation a gratuitous one, imposed without an equivalent, though in fact it is not imposed but in consideration of an equivalent.

iii. They speak of the inconvenience as if it were the peculiar lot of the indigent thus provided for at the expence of others, whereas it is equally the lot of perhaps an equal number of the superior classes, who are maintained at their own expence.

After all, there must be a subordination had amongst ends.

[1] For the sake of clarity, Bentham's Arabic numerals in this series have been rendered as Roman.

Granting these to be desirable in themselves, they must not be compelled in prejudice of others more desirable. If a set of individuals, able to maintain themselves, and accordingly maintaining themselves without assistance from the public, by the fruit of their own labour, were, without any need or application on their part, and without any benefit conferred on them in return at the expence of the public, that is, of others deriving subsistence from their labour, and for the sake of no saving to the rest of the public, or any other advantage to the rest of the public or themselves, thus dealt with, in any of these cases indeed the complaint would have some ground for it, the objection grounded on it would have some weight. But the matter of fact is otherwise.

1. Comparative Unhealthiness Denied

The objection grounded on the supposed close and unhealthy imprisonment, has the farther defect of considering, as the necessary result of the Public-Establishment system, a state of things which, whether bad or good, it has no necessary tendency to render more common to more individuals than it would be otherwise. On the contrary, it is one of the properties, and may be reckoned among the advantages of this system, that it admitts of applying to this head of inconvenience a degree of alleviation more than could otherwise be applied. Under the Public-Establishment system there is nothing to preclude a mixture of employments, the two classes of employments opposite to each other in this respect, the sedentary and the laborious, the Indoor and the Outdoor, employments: and that in proportions adjusted with a view to health, and compatible with the most perfect health. In the service of a private employer, there are circumstances which have hitherto rendered every such a mixture in a manner unexampled, and must render the introduction of it more or less difficult, if not impracticable. The object of the private employer is to get from each workman the most work that can be extracted from him by the pay afforded him, and that done in the best manner. He himself *understands* but one skill[?], *deals* but in one thing. What would be the plan of employment most conducive to his health is a subject into which he is neither qualified by medical knowledge, nor, naturally speaking, very sollicitous to enquire. The transfer of the hand from one employment to the other might occasion, or appear to occasion, some little loss, however inconsiderable, in the article of time: the dividing the practice between two species of work, and those so different, might be attended, or threaten to be attended, with some loss, however inconsiderable, in the article of dexterity.

The objection involves besides another supposition, which, as well as those we have seen, is not conformable to matter of fact. It supposes it to be in the power of government to determine the quantity of husbandry work that shall be done, by a simple addition to the number of hands labouring in that vineyard,[1] and thus to force fresh hands in any number into that branch of industry, without prejudice to the existing stock. But to pour hands into any employment, and to pour capital into that employment, are operations of very different, and indeed of directly opposite, tendency. The number of hands applicable to an employment remaining fixed, the tendency, and, if no other more powerful counteracting cause happens to operate at the same time, the certain effect, of an influx of capital, is to raise the wages of labour in that line: the quantity of capital applied to an employment remaining unencreased, the effect of an influx of fresh hands is, as certainly, to sink the wages of labour in that line. But a fact of which the existence is admitted on all sides, is the inferiority of the wages of labour [in husbandry], compared with that of labour exerted in any other line. If then, as it seems also pretty generally maintained, the wages of labour in that line are insufficient, and below what it were to be wished they were, and if, accordingly, the raising them be a fit object to government to aim at, and at the same time a practicable one, it is not by adding to a stock of hands already too great, but rather by subtracting from it, that the production of the effect should be aimed at: instead of pouring in hands into that branch of industry, the endeavour should be either to draw hands from it, or to attract capital into it, or to do both at once: at any rate to abstain from drawing capital from it by encouragements given to other branches: by encouragements given, and given at a vast expence, to the remaining modes of employing capital to a productive purpose—to manufactures, to the carrying trade, and, above all, to colonization.[2]

2. and 3. Objections grounded on the discomfort resulting from severance from local connections and blood relations considered[3]

The objection grounded on the hardship considered as attendant upon a separation of this sort turns upon the general topic, what

[1] An echo of Matthew 20: 1.

[2] In the margin, Bentham has noted at this point: 'Objection respecting the severing of relations would point, and with greater force, to the forbidding of voluntary migration to distant parts of the Kingdom, and [. . .?] Navigation and Colonization—the necessity not being so great.'

[3] In the corresponding marginal contents sheet at UC cliv. 77, Bentham has indicated that the objections discussed in this section concern the 'quality' of relief, that is, the second of the topics enumerated at the beginning of the essay (see p. 143 above) relevant to the mode of executing the task of provision for the relief of indigence. Bentham has also noted: 'Objections 2 & 3, though bad as objections, good as warning.'

proportion should the degree of comfort infused into the provision made at the public expence for the relief of the indigent, what proportion should the degree of comfort in this case, supposing the proportion to be at the command of those on whom the management depends, bear to the degree of comfort possessed by individuals in the same rank in life, maintaining themselves in a state of independence, by the fruits of their own labour.

As to this question, the following positions would probably be acceded to on all hands:

i.[1] That, as to every individual who felt in himself a persuasion that [the] future existence or non-existence of the necessity of having recourse to the public bounty depended upon his own exertions, it were to be wished that the provision at the public expence should, so long as such persuasion continued, appear less eligible to him than the provision resulting from the fruits of his own labour: and, it would probably be thought, that to every person possessing this persuasion, the prospect of the public provision could not, so long as such persuasion continued, be made to appear too ineligible.

ii. That, in the instance of every individual by whom the apprehension is entertained of the future existence of such necessity on his part, spite of every possible exertion on his part to exempt himself from such necessity, it were to be wished that such future public provision should appear to him as comfortable as possible: provided it were possible so to order matters as that this same provision should appear eligible to those who are under the apprehension of not being able to do without it, without appearing eligible to those whom the apprehension of falling under the necessity of throwing themselves upon it, would have the effect of preserving from that necessity.

iii. That, in the instance of every individual already included in the provision made on the public account, that provision could not be made too comfortable, provided the effect could be produced—in the first place without expence to the public, that is, without compelling one man to part with the fruits of his labour for the accommodation of another, labouring or not labouring—in the next place without producing, on the part of any of those in whose power it would be to purchase by their labour an exemption from that necessity, the effect of their suffering themselves to sink into that necessity, for want of that industry which otherwise they could and would have exerted: in the third place, without producing on the part of those who neither were, nor could be, included within the provision, the sentiment of

[1] For the sake of clarity, Bentham's Arabic numerals in this series have been rendered as Roman.

regret and dissatisfaction grounded on the comparison of their own condition with the condition of the persons so provided for.

Unfortunately, the incidents here stated as conditions *sine qua non* to the propriety of infusing into the public provision a degree of comfort equal to that which accompanies a state of independent labour, are such as appear, some of them, naturally repugnant and impossible. As to that which concerns the expence, though to myself it really does not appear by any means without the verge of possibility, yet the accomplishment of it can not but be confessed to be a matter of great difficulty, and, at any rate, situated as yet at an altogether indefinite distance.

In the mean time, the practical inference from the above observations, and the answer which, upon consideration of all circumstances, seems to be the proper one to give to the above general question, is that the provision afforded at the public expence ought not to have so great a proportion of comfort infused in it, as is commonly to be found in a state of laborious independence. When I say *comfort*, I mean *apparent* comfort, which, until means can be found of separating the reality from the appearance and *vice versa*, comes to the same thing as *real*.

This being premised as the general rule expressive of what ought to be made the general lot, under a public establishment of this sort, of those whose condition in life exposes them to the risk of incurring the necessity of taking the benefit of it, it remains only to consider whether, in order to preserve from so gloomy a situation as that of the apprehension of a fall from a situation of greater comfort to a situation of less comfort, perpetually hanging over a man's head, it might not be possible so to order matters as to confine the misfortune, in prospect at least, to those who should have had nothing but their own improvidence to thank for it.

For this purpose, the whole number of working hands in the community will require to be divided into two classes: the first composed of such whose earnings shall appear to admitt of a surplus sufficient to insure them against the fall in question, by the purchase of a superannuation annuity, sufficient for their maintenance according to the Home-Provision system, during the remainder of their days, and which might be distinguished by some such name as that of the extra-earning class, or self-annuitable class: the other composed of such whose earnings do not appear to admitt of any such surplus: these might be termed, for distinction's sake, the no extra-earning class, or un-annuitable class.

Were the line of separation made between the two classes with a firm and steady hand, for the latter, a superannuation annuity, sufficient for home-maintenance might, it should seem, be provided at the public charge, provided the period of commencement were a late one, suppose 65 years of age, without any very heavy national expence: while, in the instance of the self-annuitable class, either an adequate contribution on their parts should be made compulsory, or they should be left to be punished for their improvidence by the necessity of embracing the comparative discomfort of the Public-Establishment system.

It appears proper to confine this home-provision to old age for these reasons: because, in this case, the utmost amount of the expence may be foreknown and predetermined: and because, when age is the title, the title to this species of relief can scarcely be either counterfeited or fabricated.

The period of commencement should be a late one: because the assumption of it at a period but a few years too early would be productive of an immense and unnecessary expence. The age of 70 would hardly be too late. For the great object is not so much to meliorate sensations as to improve prospects: not so much the giving to the short concluding period of life a degree of comfort of which, after all, it may hardly be susceptible, as to preserve the long preceding time from being rendered gloomy by the prospect of an uncomfortable old age.

The state of inadequate superannuation, it may be said, the period at which a man's earnings become inadequate to his necessity, will be apt to take place (it may be said) in many instances, before the commencement of the relief, according to this fixation, may have taken place: and by this means, in these instances, the lapse into the uncomfortable state in question will have[1] taken place. The answer is—that at the worst, although the present inconvenience should have taken place, yet hope, the cordial of hope, the hope of returning into the much longed for state of comfortable independence, the perfect assurance of emerging in ease of life, will still remain: the comfortable state, not the uncomfortable one, will be the ultimate object of expectation, as the state which awaits a man at the end of his journey through life.

When hope has been thus kept alive, and such a foundation has been given it to rest upon, as much will have been done, it should seem, as the nature of the case calls for and admitts. The natural confidence in a man's own good fortune, that general and fortunate propensity which has been so well noticed by Adam Smith,[2] will

[1] MS 'will not have' contradicts the evident sense of the passage.

[2] See Smith, *The Wealth of Nations*, i. 124–5: 'The over-weening conceit which the greater part of men have of their own abilities, is an antient evil remarked by the philosophers and

ensure to the contingency its full value, and more than its full value. Scarce any man looks upon the age of 70 as the destined limit of his days: scarce any man will thus consider himself as doomed to end them in a Poor House.

If, among the conditions annexed to the grant of such annuity were numbered that of procuring from the local authorities a general certificate of good behaviour, this concomitant would be, it should seem, productive of advantage in more shapes than one: it could operate in restraint of general misconduct: affording a sort of security for good behaviour. And, as far as the certificate were refused, though this would not be likely to happen frequently, or through despair of obtaining it not applied [for], it would operate in alleviation of the public burthen: while, under favour of that self-confidence which is so natural to man, and still more perhaps in regard to good conduct than in regard to good fortune, it would scarcely operate in any degree to cloud the prospect of the evening of life.

A circumstance that would contribute in a great degree to diminish whatever hardship may be conceived to be attendant on the separation from Domestic connections, where that separation takes place, which will not by any means be universally the case, a circumstance that will remove in a great degree this part of the hardship attendant on the Public-Establishment system, is the provision that might be made, and, as it should seem, without any material prejudice to public economy, that the Industry Houses should not be upon so large a scale, but that the number and distribution of them might admitt of a visit, to and from in the course of a day, between the House and the most distant point of the District appertaining to it. Thus a perfect facility for occasional visits between relative and relative would be preserved.

The result of these expedients, if adopted, would be to effect a compromise between the contending systems, a sort of coalition among the opposite parties: if the name of party may be given to divisions of men grounded upon an honest and irreproachable difference of opinion, without a grain of interest, in any shape, on any side. All have reason, more or less of reason, on their side: not one, whose side of the question does not receive a strong support, as well from reason as from experience.

On these terms, a composition, it should seem, might be made between the demands of indulgent humanity and those of rigid justice: humanity, which requires that every individual shall, if

moralists of all ages. Their absurd presumption in their own good fortune, has been less taken notice of. It is, however, if possible, still more universal. There is no man living who, when in tolerable health and spirits, has not some share of it.'

possible, be made happy: justice, which requires that of two members of the community, equally innocent and equally deserving, not connected by any domestic tie, one shall not be compelled to part with the fruits of his own labour, without absolute necessity, for the benefit of another.

If not the whole system of provision for indigence, at any rate so much of it as turns upon the difference in point of comfort between Home-Provision and Public-Establishment provision, must surely be acknowledged to be the fruit of highly refined beneficence, a recently matured product:—a sort of luxury as it were, of government: a proof, and that a most honourable and happy one, of the improved state of humanity in the age. A secure provision for the indigent is to the philanthropist what a pine-apple is to the epicure:—but what shall we say to those who would bring us back to acorns?

Admitting or not admitting that a provision in the shape of a Home Provision should be made in some such terms and under some such restrictions as the above, at the public charge, for the benefit of the non-annuitable, no-surplus class, it is a question that will still remain for answer—whether, supposing no such line drawn—no such Public Provision made, the difference in point of comfort between the Home-Provision system and the Public-Establishment system be sufficient to warrant the exclusive adoption of the Home-Provision, outweighing all the articles of disadvantage we have seen.

The answer, I must confess, as far as appears to me, can be no other than in the negative.

The considerations against regarding that difference as putting a negative upon the Public-Establishment system, as contrasted with the Home-Provision system, as likewise upon the Large-Establishment system, as contrasted with the Small-Establishment system, may be summed up as follows:

i.[1] That the mischiefs depending on the tendency to slacken industry are of themselves a price too great to pay for an advantage of so refined a nature as the avoidance of that sentimental hardship.

ii. That the injustice to the more abundantly productive hands, on whom a proportionable burthen must be thrown in order to defray the expence of this favour to the less abundantly productive hands, is another price which, even if it stood alone, would be too great to pay for the advantage.

iii. That the hardship, such as it is, is of the number of those against which it is absolutely out of the power of society to insure the whole number of its members.

[1] For the sake of clarity, Bentham's Arabic numerals in this series have been rendered as Roman.

iv. That it is a hardship which can not even properly be placed to the account of indigence: since it is shared by individuals of all ranks from the lowest to the very highest, in great abundance. The condition of youth of all ranks, and of both sexes, in as far as they are consigned to the public branch of education, the condition of military men and of sea-faring men of all ranks, from the peasant to the prince, the condition of all travellers, for education or in the mercantile line, the condition of a great portion of the class of domestic servants, is exposed to it. The observation that a mischief is diffused is *good*, as far as it tends to reconcile us to what is unavoidable: *bad*, in as far as it tends to slacken, much more to discontinue, our efforts to reduce it within its narrowest limits.

v. Numerous, very numerous, too, are the instances in which the Home-Provision system itself, and that neither under the actually established modification of it, nor under any other proposed or probable modification of it, would [not] be sufficient to insure the objects from this hardship: since whatever be assumed for the efficient cause of the title to settlement, many will be the instances in which the seat of the provision, as determined by that title, will not coincide with the spot which happens to be the abode of that part of a man's relatives whose society happens to obtain his preference.

vi. That, deducting from the number of those whose claim to relief has a just foundation on the ground [of] real and unavoidable indigence, those to whom the Public-Establishment provision is no hardship, because they have no home belonging to them, and those to whom it would be no hardship, for want of sufficient experience of the opposite system, such as orphans and children taken from their Parents or other relatives at an unreflecting age, and those to whom not the Public-Establishment provision would be a hardship, but the Home-Provision, by reason of evil reputation and ill will waiting for them at their home, the number of persons thus indirectly subjected to this hardship by indigence will scarcely be found superior to that of the persons subjected to the same hardship under all degrees of opulence: and even to a superior degree of it: to a degree not softened by the proposed alleviation resulting from the facility of occasional and frequent communication.

vii. That the circumstance of consent can not be alledged as drawing a line of distinction between the two cases: since in both cases, the privation is equally voluntary, equally clear of compulsion from without: and if, in the case of the indigent, the impelling motive be of such a strength as to come under the notion of necessity, a notion exclusive of free consent, yet the benefit purchased in this case as much exceeds whatever benefit may happen to be the object of pursuit in the other, as the urgency of the motive in the former case exceeds the urgency of the motive in the other.

viii. That, if not freed from every kind of disquiet, they are at any rate freed from the burthen of the heaviest kind of care—the anxiety about subsistence.[1]

4. Objection respecting annoyances answered

With regard to quarrels and annoyances, I mean the supposed superior propensity on the part of these public receptacles to harbour such disturbances, in comparison of the separate dwellings of individuals in the same rank of life, doubts may be entertained with regard to the comparative magnitude of the grievance: but, surely, no doubts can be entertained with regard to the comparative facility of the remedy.

The quarrels and annoyances existing in a receptacle containing 2000 persons may be seen by those who visit the receptacle: the quarrels [and] annoyances existing among the same number of persons dispersed in private houses can not be seen by any body. Badly as Poor Houses in general are administered—badly as Poor Houses, under the existing system, can scarcely in general, as will be seen, but be administered, it may be questioned whether, in the metropolis for instance, the number of complaints on this score originating in the several Poor Houses, and preferred either before a Magistrate, or confined within the local jurisdiction of the House, would be found proportioned in number to the complaints of the same sort brought before the Magistracy, from the independent mass of the community.[a]

How soever the case may stand, as between the two modes of living, with regard to the natural tendency to give birth to the inconvenience, with regard to the faculty of applying a remedy there is this plain difference.—In the public mode of life there is an authority always present to compose the quarrel, to put an end to the

[a] *De non apparentibus et non existentibus eadem est ratio*, says the logician:[2]—what the eye does not see, the heart does not rue, says the proverb. The difference, in point of impression, depending upon the facility of attracting notice is a most copious, but not sufficiently heeded source of delusion.

[1] In the corresponding marginal contents sheet at UC cliv. 77, Bentham has noted at this point: 'Comforts addenda. To conditions in which it is certain, either that a man can not, or will not, voluntarily place himself, any measure of comfort may be annexed without prejudice to industry, and therefore without prejudice to economy.' No corresponding text has been identified.

[2] i.e. 'With regard to that which does not appear, and that which does not exist, the rule is the same.' This is in fact a legal rather than a logical maxim: see *Wrote v. Wigges* (1591), 4 Coke's Reports 47a.

annoyance—in the domestic mode of life, there is no such present authority.

5. Objection respecting Vice answered

The answer given to the objection respecting quarrels and annoyances will be found to apply with still superior force to the objection respecting vice. As between manufactories and the private abodes of individuals of this class, without pretending to decide the question, I will say no more than this: that doubts may be entertained concerning the supposed superior tendency of manufactories to harbour vice:[a] but doubts can not be entertained concerning the existence of means of checking vice in the instance of a public establishment of this nature, which do not exist in manufactories. In the manufactory managed on private account, the direct and only direct object of the institution is to get work done: it is no part of that object to check vice. If the person at the head of the management happens to take a fancy to check vice, he may succeed in a certain degree: if he does not, the matter must take its chance. But be his zeal ever so great, it is impossible he should ever combat vice with any thing like the degree of advantage with which it may be combated, may with great facility and absolute certainty be combated, in a public establishment carried on for the relief of dependent indigence.

In a manufactory peopled by these dependent hands, it may be ordained that no spirituous, that even no fermented, liquors be introduced within the walls: and by having but one inlet, and keeping a tolerable guard upon that inlet, the infraction of the ordinance may be rendered morally impossible. In a manufactory peopled by independent hands, the Manager may perhaps, with great difficulty, succeed in preventing the introduction of such liquors into the place of work during working hours: but in the private dwellings of the workmen, and as to hours that are not working hours, he has no means of enforcing any such decrees.

In a manufactory peopled by these dependent hands, it may be ordained that between certain ages, individuals of different sexes shall not be within sight, or even so much as hearing of each other,

[a] *Quis odit vitia, odit homines.*[1] In general, where men are found, vice will be found: where a great multitude of men, a great quantity of vice. Receptacles of men are receptacles of vice. Vice is apt to strike the eye of the observer in proportion to its *absolute* quantity: whereas it is a just subject for regret in no other proportion than that of its relative quantity.

---

[1] i.e. 'He who hates vices, hates men.' See Pliny the Younger, *Epistulae*, viii. xxii. 3, where it is rendered *qui vitia odit, homines odit.*

except at certain times and under actual inspection. In a manufactory peopled by independent hands, it may perhaps be so ordered with regard to working hours, but it can not be so ordered with regard to free hours. In the one manufactory, it might even be ordained that youth even of the same sex should not exist, either in sleeping or even waking hours, but under the inspection of a superintending eye; in the other manufactory, such an ordinance would appear as impertinent, as the execution of it would be found impracticable.

In all these instances, the remedy shows itself in a prodigiously augmented force, when the several establishments, by means of their augmented magnitude and diminished multitude, are considered as continually exposed to the superintending scrutiny of the eye of government, spurred, and at the same time guided, by the eye of the world at large.

The efficacy of the superintending authority will be found screwed up to a pitch of absolute perfection in regard to all these points—health, freedom from disturbance and annoyance, freedom from vice, when the power of the Inspection-House principle, considered in the character of an engine of management, is considered, of which presently.[1]

[1] See pp. 204–5 below.

The following seven paragraphs, headed 'Large-Community Provision—Objections 1. House of Correction', are at UC clii. 544–6. While not appearing in the appropriate marginal contents sheet for 'Pauper Systems Compared', they discuss a further objection grounded on the interests of paupers.

'The same writers who condemn Industry Houses, and that in the strongest terms, approve of Houses of correction. But what is the difference? If a House of correction is capable of being made an useful establishment, what should hinder a House of Industry from being of equal use, and the same use?

'Where is the difference between a House of correction and, one may say, every other House, at least every House in which part of the inhabitants are under age? In a cottage, in the Palace, what family can keep together, in which there are not adequate means of repressing misbehaviour on the part of the non-adult members of it? And, among adults, of repressing either misbehaviour, or what is deemed by the head of it misbehaviour, on the part of the members, or else clearing it of them? In a House of Correction, men are obliged to work. But so must they in a Poor House, in every House, or no work in any House will be done. The King, when he was a child, was not he forced to work, was not he forced to do his task?

'In a House of correction, men are forced to work by harsh means, by whipping. But the King, would not he too have been whipped, to make him perform his task, if no other means would have served?

'In a prison, any more than in a palace, who would be so weak or so cruel as to employ harsher means to produce that or any other effect, so long as milder ones would serve? Work or starve, so says the original law of nature; work or starve, so says the law of God? What law more reasonable, more gentle, yet more effectual? Where is the house, public or private, which can exist without it? In an Industry House, how can you make sure of work without it? In a House of Correction, what need or use of any other law, when you have this? As to the means of producing economy, where then is the difference, between a House of Correction [and] an Industry House, or even a private House?

'Accidental and factitious differences indeed, between the sort of establishment called an Industry House, and the sort of establishment called a House of Correction, are obvious

§2. *Rateable Interests*[1]

6. Unwieldiness

Thus much with regard [to] objections having respect to the interests of the individuals for whose benefit the system is particularly designed. There remain such objections as may point more particularly to the interest of the public at large, considered in as much as the public, in virtue of its being subjected to the pressure of the burthen, is concerned in seeing that the burthen be kept as light as may be, and consequently, that the management of the system may, in every point of view, be as economical as possible.

In the way of objection to any inference that may be drawn from the advantages above represented as being possessed, in point of economy, by the Large-Establishment system, as compared with the Small-Establishment system, it may be urged, in general terms, that in a large establishment of any kind, if there be room for frugality upon a large scale, so is there for waste upon a large scale—that the range of waste is wider than that of frugality—since frugality can do no more than save a part, while it is in the power of waste to dissipate the whole, and that, in a large establishment, waste is more reasonably to be expected than frugality, inasmuch as the difficulty of keeping under inspection and direction an assemblage of objects of any kind, men or things, apartments or stock, encreases with their magnitude and their multitude.

By way of answer to this head of objection, without staying to

enough. A House of Correction is a place to which men are consigned with a view to past transgression, for the purpose of punishment, because punishment has already been pronounced necessary. An Industry House is a House to which men are consigned not on account of any past transgression, but for a purpose opposite to that of punishment, for relief. But though for relief, not for relief alone, but for relief on the one hand, coupled with work on the other, annexed to it in the form of a condition: and how is the performance of any condition to be enforced, unless by the application, if necessary, of something which when in prospect is *compulsion*, and if applied, *punishment*. Where is the place in which compulsion of some kind or other is not necessary, and in which punishment, if necessary to produce the compulsion, must not be applied?

'Approving of a House of Correction, nothing can be more idle, nothing can be more shallow, than to disapprove of an Industry House. Paupers you have. Paupers you will always have, of all characters. Men differ from one another by indistinguishable shades. The same man is not the same at one time as at another.

'To the searcher of hearts, and to him alone, it belongs to know what each man *will* be at any given time. The sort of House for the maintenance of a person of the Pauper community, is that sort of House which shall be a House of Comfort to them, or a House of Correction, according as they behave.'

For Bentham's allusion to the law of God see Genesis 3: 19: 'In the sweat of thy face shalt thou eat bread, till thou return unto the ground'.

[1] i.e. the interests of those liable to pay the poor rate.

enquire what may be the efficacy of order as a means of conquering the difficulties of multiplicity, or of the principle of the division of labour, when applied to that particular species of labour which consists in the business of management and superintendence, it may be sufficient, in answer to an objection of so vague and general a complexion, already obviated by considerations of a more pointed and explicit nature, it may be sufficient to refer, in terms equally general, to the testimony of experience. Where manufactories are in question, and production, profitable production, is really and seriously the object, it is not the smallest establishments that are found to answer best, but the largest.

If, in great houses, the management is not in general so economical as in small houses, it is rather because the direct object is not profit, but ease and enjoyment, rather than by reason of the largeness of the House. If, in large states, the management is not in general so frugal as in small states, nor in them as in the private families of individuals, it is rather by reason of the distance between the residence of the managers in chief, and most of the objects of their management, or by reason of the comparative want of closeness of connection between the personal interest of the managing hands, and the interest of the service committed to their management, than by reason of the multiplicity of the objects in question, or even their magnitude, when not extended to such a degree as to be productive of territorial distance.

But the most decisive answer to every objection grounded in the terrors of immensity and complication depends, it must be confessed, upon an engine of management not yet display'd to public view, the Inspection-House principle. That assemblage of persons and things will hardly be complained of as too vast for comprehension, the most perfect and accurate comprehension, and all-embracing and steady and uniform comprehension, which lies spread out, in every minutest part of it spread out at the same time, under the eye of the persons of all ranks on whom the management depends, together with as many other persons to whom, in quality of occasional inspectors, with or without controuling authority over the constant and official managers, faculty of access may without inconvenience be allowed.

Be the scale of building ever so large, causes of ill health are not likely to be violent or abundant where, by the very structure of it, the persons on whom the removal of those causes depends are, all of them, and all of them at the same time, as much exposed to the action of those causes as, and that in a more perfect degree than, the meanest individual comprized within the establishment.

Be an establishment ever so large, quarrels, clamours, insults, indelicacies, indecencies, vices of any kind are not likely to abound in it, so long as matters are so ordered that there shall not be so much as a look or a gesture of any of the individuals comprized within the regimen of the establishment that may not at any time be subjected, at one and the same time, to the eye of as many persons as are meant to be occupied in the management, as well as of as many inspectors, permanent or occasional, official or un-official, as may happen to present themselves: the persons exposed to inspection being at the same [time] precluded from the faculty of making any such observation as would inform them whether, at any given moment, the persons destined to the business of inspection were actually at their post.

§3. *Both Interests*[1]

7. Experience Unfavourable

But against the comparative aptitude for good management here attributed to the Public-Establishment system (though the allegation be it always remembered is all along meant to be confined to large establishments, and those of a certain magnitude), the most specious and plausible head of objection lies yet behind:—the testimony of experience.

But experience of the past or present can afford no just inference with regard to the future, any farther than the state of things in the instant of the existing establishment is really, and not merely in appearance, parallel to what would be the state of things under a proposed future establishment. But the more detailed and exact the view we take into the objects to be compared, the more perfectly we shall perceive the parallelism to fail.

In the first place, the testimony of experience, when rightly applied, will not be found to be, in point of economy, in disfavour of the Public-Establishment system, in contradistinction to the Home-Provision system. True it is, that as far as employment is concerned, in perhaps two hundred instances for one, the Public-Establishment system, in the existing state of it in this country, is either upon as bad a footing as, or a still worse footing than, the Home-Provision system. Under the Home-Provision, no undertaking to draw profit from the labour of the persons provided for is attempted: under the Public-Establishment system, either no such attempt is made, or it is made

[1] i.e. the interests of both paupers and ratepayers.

under circumstances which render profit, meaning neat profit, impossible, and loss certain.

True it is, moreover, that as far as relief is concerned, the relief administered under the Public-Establishment system is perhaps universally more expensive, perhaps, in some instances, as far as once or twice as expensive again, not only as compared with the supply that would have been administered to them in the way of relief at the public charge, but as compared with the supply which persons in the same class of life are commonly able to afford themselves when in a state of independent labour.[1]

But so long as, in either branch of economy, a single instance of better management can be found, the two hundred, or the two thousand instances, if there were so many, would to the present purpose prove nothing. The question is not what has been done, but what can be done.[a] Bad management is possible enough, and common enough: that we all know full well: but that is not what we desire to imitate. What we want to know is whether there be a single instance of good economy: of profit drawn by public management from the labour of those from whom, without such management, no labour would have been drawn, or from whose labour, without such management, no profit would have been drawn. That single instance is what we desire to know of: because that single instance, and not one of the opposite ones, is the example we mean to follow. That single instance is the pattern of what is intended to be done: that single instance, if there be nothing peculiar, nor uncommunicable, nor recondite in the plan pursued in it, that single instance is the fair sample of what may be expected to be done.[b]

It is for want of communication—it is for want of knowing better—that existing miscarriages afford no warning, existing successes no pattern—that the miserable economy we see is every where to be found. If, in any instance, a good point or two is discoverable and discerned, what eagerness to embrace it! How it rains elogiums! 120 foot by 20 foot to do nothing at all in: another 120 foot by 20 foot

[a] If in the past managing of your affairs, said Demosthenes to the Athenians, there had been no ground for change, your present plight would be hopeless indeed.[2] Past mismanagement affords so much ground for future comfort.

[b] Note: Lincolnshire constitution.[3]

---

[1] In the margin Bentham has noted at this point, 'Note giving a view of these instances of bad management.' No corresponding text has been identified.

[2] Demosthenes (384–322 BC), Athenian orator. Bentham's rendering is a paraphrase of *First Philippic*, II, and *Third Philippic*, V.

[3] Bentham's allusion is to the management of the Society for the Promotion of Industry, in the Lindsey district of Lincolnshire, and in particular to the utilization of 'premiums' or rewards to augment the amount of work produced: see p. 64 n. above.

to pray in:[1] and the Architect referred to and applied to, to give to admiring imitators the benefit of this thrift.[2] Three meals a day in the country, while, amidst the extravagance of London, paupers are content with two: five times a week Butcher's meat,[3] when self-maintaining industry is unable to get it once: and because only 100 out of 350 are altogether idle,[4] this House too must be held out, as to the bulk of existing Houses it most deservedly may be held out, as a pattern for imitation.

Against Industry Houses in the Public-Establishment system other objections have been urged, and urged with great seriousness, such as can scarce admitt of a serious mention. In the character of arguments they are as frivolous, as in the character of matters of fact they are frequently incontestible.

Argument 1.[5] Sad profusion, and sad waste in these Houses.—Answer.—Profusion certain.—Waste admitted.—Remedy.—Put an end to the profusion, put an end to the Waste.—No—says the objector—Down with the Houses.—Answer.—And sow the land with salt, and then no more Houses, no more waste.

Argument 2. No work done in these houses.—Answer, admitted.—Work will not do itself. Effects will not come into existence without causes: actions without motives. Remedy—*no work—no eat* principle. What this means, if not seen already, see further on.[6]

Objection: Sad scolding there.—Answer. Oh lack! Oh lack!—Remedy.—Cotton in the ears. On the Inspection House plan,

[1] See Wood, *Some Account of the Shrewsbury House of Industry*, p. 38, where these figures are given as the dimensions of the chapel. The phrase, '120 foot by 20 foot to do nothing at all in', may be a reference to the dormitories, which were the same size as the chapel: see ibid., p. 54.

[2] See ibid., p. 116n.: 'Frequent applications have been made from various parts of the kingdom and from Ireland, for plans of the Shrewsbury House of Industry: it must be observed, that the building now applied to that purpose, was originally constructed for a Foundling Hospital. Very ingenious improvements have been suggested in a design by Mr. J.H. HAYCOCK, of Shrewsbury, Architect of the Salop County Hall and County Gaol; in which the disposition and dimensions of the various apartments appear to me very judicious, and the whole, to furnish every desirable convenience, at the least possible expense.' John Hiram Haycock (1759–1830).

[3] See 'Bill of Fare', ibid., p. 73.

[4] See ibid., p. 28n.: 'The average number of poor in the house is 350. The average number of *working* poor employed there, about 250'.

[5] In this and the following paragraphs, Bentham rehearses the more extensive discussion found in 'Fundamental Positions in regard to the making provision for the Indigent Poor', pp. 29–34 above.

[6] This principle, which Bentham usually termed the Earn-First Principle, is defined at UC cliii. 173: 'In every instance, where it can be practised without hardship, and where good behaviour has not been sufficiently habitual to warrant confidence, let it be a rule that the allotment of work shall have been finished before the meal which is the reward for it is administered—*Work before Pay—Service before Reward*.' See also 'Outline of a Work entitled Pauper Management Improved', *Annals of Agriculture*, xxx (1798), 150–1 (Bowring, viii. 383): 'When ability adequate to the task is certain, and laziness apprehended, no meal given, till the task by which it is earned has been *first* performed.'

Governor, Chaplain, Surgeon, the whole staff will be in the middle of it all. Are they amused by it? So may be the rest of the inhabitants.

Every thing admitted—and in ten times the degree—all, all admitted—and what then?

In a book as strong in method as it is weak in argument, Dr Macfarlane rakes together all the bad points in human nature, for the sake of giving the credit of them to these Houses:[1] Sin—Vice—Wickedness—Infirmity—every thing one would wish neither to see, nor hear of—was it all the growth or manufacture of these Houses? The tree that bore the apple Adam [ate][2] of did come up like a mushroom in the Court yard of one of these Houses?[3] [Dr Mcfarlane] is by this time, I believe, in heaven:[4] if on earth, at least if on Scotch earth, he ought to have done penance. What becomes of original Sin, if every thing one would wish not to see, or not to hear of, is to be imputed to these Houses?[5]

CHAPTER VII.
COMMUNITY PROVISION COMPARED WITH COMMUNITY AND HOME PROVISION MIXT, FOR NON-ADULTS

An essential feature of this plan[6] is the perfect command of the unripe part of the stock of hands. This renders it necessary to enter a comparative survey of the plans pursued or pursuable in relation to this part of the subject, for the purpose of stating the advantages of the system supposed by the above condition, over all others that can come in competition with it.

[1] i.e. *Inquiries concerning the Poor.*

[2] MS 'eat'.

[3] An allusion to the tree of knowledge: see Genesis 2: 9, 3: 3–7.

[4] McFarlan died in 1788.

[5] On the corresponding marginal contents sheet at UC cliv. 78, Bentham has noted, 'Points of good management stated with reference to the subject in hand, to show that they have never hitherto been completely observed', but added in pencil, 'Not written.' Bentham's original intention was to include at this point a sketch of 'Rules of Management', and UC cliv. 78 does indeed continue with a list of contents for such a sketch. However, Bentham then seems to have decided to discuss the subject of management rules in 'Pauper Management Improved', and a précis of that discussion appears in 'Outline of a Work entitled Pauper Management Improved', *Annals of Agriculture*, xxx (1798), 137–62 (Bowring, viii. 380–6).

[6] i.e. Bentham's plan to provide relief for the indigent poor of England and Wales in 200 or 250 large-scale industry houses, administered by a joint-stock company called the National Charity Company. At one stage, Bentham intended to conclude his survey of possible systems of poor relief with a proposal for the formation of the National Charity Company, and to annex a sketch of its capitalization, organization, and responsibilities, but failed to do so. The sketch was presented instead in 'Outline of a Work entitled Pauper Management Improved', *Annals of Agriculture*, xxx (1798), 90–104 (Bowring, viii. 369–72). For further details see the Editorial Introduction, pp. xxxix–xl & n. above.

Considered with relation to this branch of the subject stock of hands, the several plans or systems pursued or pursuable are reducible under three heads or divisions: 1. The Home-Provision plan, that is, in the present application, the *Home-Education* plan. [2.] The Public-Provision plan, that is the *Public-Establishment* plan, or Public-Education plan, and [3.] The *Mixt* or *Half-and-Half* Plan.

With reference to the body of the indigent at large, we have had occasion to oppose to one another the No-provision system and the Home-Provision system. With respect to this particular branch of that body, the two opposite systems coincide: Home-education is, in the rank of life in question, precisely the same thing as no education at all. Under other heads of relief, provision in some way or other must be made of necessity, or the individual perishes: therefore under those heads the No-provision system and the Home-Provision system are incompatible. But to this head, the necessity in point of existence certainly does not extend. Without culture there may be fields: without education there may be men.

At the Labouring man's house, be it cottage or town lodging, every requisite for the culture of the mind is essentially wanting: knowledge, intellectual acquirements, time,[a] and suitable *stock* always:—moral propensities but too frequently.

In the Industry House, all those requisites concurr, every one in perfection: at any rate in whatever wears the character of perfection in the eyes of those on whom the management depends: Local Governor, Directors,[1] Administration, Parliament, Public: the improvement of education will keep pace with the growth of wisdom in the age. Under Home-Education, though perfect instruction were in one Cottage, perfect ignorance would be in the next. Under Public-Education in an Inspection House, whatever be the degree of improvement, uniformity will be an attribute of it: whatsoever things are thought good for all the children, if one has them, so will all. Whatsoever good things are administered in any one such House, will be administered in all.[b]

[a] The Father's time is engrossed by labour: the Mother's partly by labour, partly by attendance on the infant children of the family.

To cultivate a young mind to perfection, nothing less than constant attendance is sufficient: if there be but one child, then the whole time of a grown person for that one. Under the Inspection-House plan, two tutors, relieving one another, may give the benefit of constant attendance to fifty or a hundred pupils, or even several hundred pupils.

[b] In this subject as in most others strange notions have been entertained:—that nothing in a mind is better than any thing: or that if something must be there that

---

[1] i.e. the Directors of the National Charity Company.

Examining the mixt, or half-and-half system, we shall find it possessing the bad properties of the Home-Education plan, frustrating the good effects of the Public-Education plan, and, in the

something will be better supplied by negligence than by design:—as if Fortune were Wisdom's surest guide.

But nothing will not keep its hold in any mind. Be it as it may with space, nature endures no vacuum in minds. The mind is that field in which so sure as man sows not wheat so sure will the Devil be to sow tares.[1]

Another strange notion, if another it may be termed, has been entertained—the notion of a repugnancy between morality and letters: as if the health of the affections and moral faculties, in this rank of life more than any other, depended upon a morbid state, or the inanition, of the intellectual.

Letters it has been said may be an instrument of fraud: so may bread, from the mouth of a cannon, be an instrument of death. So may whatever is good in physic be converted into poison. In every line use and abuse are as inseparable as they are hostile: the question in every case is which accords best with experience and probability, the use or the abuse.

Though fraud were frequent in the train of letters, even thus they might do good service. Fraud levelled against property is by accident the growth of cultivated minds: but violence is much more certainly the growth of the uncultivated. Fraud, in proportion as it spreads, takes place of violence: and to public security and tranquillity, nothing can be more advantageous than the change. Fraud confines its attack to property: violence, involving person along with property, propagates mischief in the only shape in which it is irreparable. Property may be replaced by contribution: not life or limb.

Nor can letters disseminate the poison, but they disseminate the antidote: the operation of the poison accidental and rare, that of the antidote constant and universal. The will to preserve *self* is never wanting: the will to injure others never breaks forth into action but when called forth by some extraordinary combination between opportunities and motives.

That the joint abundance of both, poison and antidote together, is more favourable to moral health than their joint scarcity, is witnessed by every page of history. Where letters are a monopoly, fraud, clad in the mantle of religion, takes the place of government, and seats herself on the throne. Where have letters been productive of most mischief, in Egypt and Hindostan, where the monopoly of a sacred language has given birth to distinction of casts, and slavery not to be eradicated but with the vitals of the religion, or in Britain, where the diffusion of letters produces now and then a forgery, of which the detection is ensured by the same cause?

Fraud not only bears its own antidote along with it, finds its antidote precedes it everywhere, but yields to another remedy—the hand of the law. Violence rises up against the remedy.

In proportion as population is thin (which is as much as to say misery and wretchedness abundant), violence prevails: in proportion as it is abundant, fraud. In antient Germany and uncolonized, that is almost uninhabited, America, one may see the Theatre of violence: in China that of fraud.[2]

---

[1] An echo of Matthew 13: 38–9.

[2] For the view that violence was widespread in ancient Germany see Tacitus, *Germania*, XIV. 4: *pigrum quin immo et iners videtur sudore adquirere quod possis sanguine parare*, i.e. 'he thinks it tame and spineless to accumulate slowly by the sweat of his brow what can be got quickly by the loss of a little blood'. For the view that violence pervailed in uncolonized America see, for

combination, giving birth to new mischiefs which neither element would have exhibited alone.

Under the half-and-half system, each child has two masters given it to serve: two independent rival masters: a task which divine concurrs with human wisdom in pronouncing an impossible one.[1] Regulated talent presiding over one half of the 24 hours: rough ignorance the remainder. The progress will be that of [Penelope's][2] web: the work of the day will be unravelled by the night.[3] Honour thy father and thy mother,[4] will be a lesson the child will be taught every seventh day: to despise, to look down upon both father and mother, is a lesson which, whether taught or no, he cannot fail to learn, if he learn any thing, the other six. To cleave to the instruction of the Cottage, or the mean town lodging, will be to hate that of the school: to hold to that of the school will be to despise that of the Lodging or the Cottage.

The loss of time would in every case be an object[ion], in some an insuperable obstacle, to the very existence of the plan. Distance to a certain amount, especially in certain weathers, takes away the possibility of daily vibration beneath a certain age. Must home be the resort not only for sleep, but meals? Thus is the time consumed in vibration doubled, trebled.

To this regular obstruction would be added casual and irregular, but altogether natural and probably frequent ones. The affections, the caprices, the little interests of the day would be perpetually renewing the desire of keeping the child at home, and if desire prevailed, the pretence for gratifying it could not, in such a case, ever be wanting.

The greater the distance, and the younger the child, the more steps required—strength consumed—danger to health from bad weather—and necessity of being kept from s[c]hool by it—necessity of a guide, or, for want of a guide, danger of its losing itself, or idling about alone or with others, instead of going to work. The child can not be punished for a fault which, if there has been any fault, may have been the Parents': At what hour was the child sent from home?

instance, Thomas Hobbes, *Leviathan* (first published in 1651), ed. R. Tuck, Cambridge, 1991, Ch. XIII, p. 89. For the view that fraud was endemic in China see, for instance, Charles Louis de Secondat, Baron de La Brède et de Montesquieu (1689–1755), *De l'esprit des loix*, 2 vols., Geneva, 1748, Bk. XIX, Ch. XX.

[1] See Matthew 6: 24; and Luke 16: 13.

[2] MS 'Penepole's'.

[3] In classical mythology Penelope was the wife of Odysseus. While faithfully awaiting his return from the seige of Troy, she was pressed to marry one of her many suitors. She resisted their demands by explaining that she could not marry until she had finished weaving a shroud for Odysseus's father, Laertes. Every night, she unravelled the work she had done during the day, in order that the shroud should never be finished.

[4] The fourth commandment: see Exodus 20: 12; Deuteronomy 5: 16; and Matthew 15: 4.

Lies, unsusceptible of detection, would be the result. Truth being at such a distance, the trouble of hunting it so great, and the chance of finding it so little, the benefit to be got from the trial of such causes would never pay the labour.

The limits to power are the limits to responsibility. The power of the public instructor being thus reduced by division, and by division with a hand stronger than his own, every thing of responsibility on his part undergoes a proportionate reduction. When the best conduct is not sufficient to success, failure, though the result of ever so bad conduct, is secure from blame. Be the scholars ever so ignorant, ever so idle, ever so disorderly, the apology is ready. *From me they get nothing but what is good, and as much of that as possible: but the good they get from me is done away by the evil they get elsewhere.* No success without exertion: no exertion without hope. In this state of things a good preceptor, were chance to place him there, would sooner or later become a bad one. Yet, were it known, a very good one, a man drawn by affection rather than emolument, would scarcely offer. Under such prospects, nothing but necessity would supply candidates.

Not only would the instruction be originally bad, but the faculty of improvement, the means of being made better, would thus be denied it. Thus crossed and counter-acted, the effects of the public plan of discipline, good or bad, would be indistinguishable. What impression it makes can not be known: for whatever may have been the impressions made there, may have been obliterated elsewhere.

Under such circumstances, the benefit of experience would be lost: even experiment would be unavailing: for no experiment is a fair one if, [of] the influencing circumstances, the greater part are under a cloud, screened from observation in the darkness of the Cottage.

The comfort and tranquillity of the scholar will be found to be but ill consulted by this imperfect schooling. With the idea of *home*, every pleasurable idea will become associated: with the idea of school, every painful one. But *school* is the only place where any thing will be so much as attempted to be taught: home the place where nothing will or can be taught, were it only for want of time. Painful ideas will therefore be associated with the idea of every thing that is taught, with the idea of every thing that is meant to be infused under the name of religion, or of virtue, or of knowledge. Can any state of things be more repugnant to the end in view?

In an ordinary school, in which the Parent not only approves of what is taught, but approves so highly that he is content to pay for it, pay even a great price for it, whatever instruction is gained, or supposed to be gained, will, if not much seconded, at any rate be praised. In this half-and-half Industry school, backwardness on the part of the Parent is supposed: and money is proposed to be given, not by the Parent, but *to* him, in the hope of conquering it.[1]

In the seminaries of the opulent the militation between the useful and the agreeable is but too natural, and, as every one knows, but too frequent. But, in the case in question, the causes of repugnancy will be infinitely stronger. In the case of the rich, the school life, to help ballance its disadvantages in respect of pleasantness, has the advantage of home in respect of the plenty and choice it affords of *play-mates*: if it be the chief scene of work, it is at the same time the scene of superior opportunities for play. But the schools in question would scarcely on any plan afford near so much time or opportunity for play, as is afforded by the existing schools of superior education: nor ought they to afford any sort of play but that best sort, which is work at the same time. Home, in the vacation hours and days, is, on the other hand, in the house of every careful parent or guardian in the cultivated ranks of life, the scene of work to a certain degree as well as school, though in part of a more or less different sort of work perhaps, and not in quite so great a quantity: but in the abodes of the labouring and indigent Poor, it can scarcely, on the half-and-half plan, be expected to be the scene of any sort of work at all. Not of bodily labour, the stock of strength being exhausted, or supposed to be exhausted, by the school task and the journey: not of mental, for want of both the inclination and the means of forwarding it.

It is to the contrast between school and home, and the frequent revival of that contrast by vacations, that the condition of the school-boy owes all its irksomeness. No home, no hardship. The mixt plan, under the semblance of lenity, conceals real rigour: the simple plan, under a semblance of rigour, contains real lenity.

The discipline of the home, were that alone the scene, the discipline of the home, being administered by unpolished hands, is a fortuitous mixture of hardness and indulgence. On the half-and-half plan, another power intervening, the distress and perplexity will be encreased. Under the unmixed plan of public discipline, causes of passion and partiality being absent, the discipline regulated in all its motions, and transparent in every part of it, disobedience hopeless,

[1] Bentham's reference is to the proposal contained in Pitt's Poor Bill to provide weekly allowances to certain parents of children unable to maintain themselves, on condition that such children attended one of the parochial schools of industry which the Bill would also establish: see *Commons Sessional Papers of the Eighteenth Century*, ciii. 164, 173.

cruelty impossible, the days of the scholar, undisturbed by contrasts, untorn by conflicts, will glide away in innocence and peace.

On the unmixt plan, were an Industry school really a scene of hardship, which, in a school on the Inspection-House principle under the Large-Establishment system would be impossible, the hardship would be no more than what a child might reasonably be expected to be reconciled to by time, or at least by the ignorance or oblivion of any better state. But on the mixt plan, the idea of hardship is perpetually refreshed.

The germ of discontent can never thus flourish among the children, without continually inoculating itself into, and exasperating the original discontent of, the Parents. The child that suffers, how justly soever at school, from the displeasure either of the masters or his fellow-scholars, will go home with his own story, full of complaints of injury. Thence come back complaints from the Parents. If these complaints are treated with neglect, there will sometimes be injustice, always the appearance of it: if they are heard, time must always be consumed in the trial, and frequently satisfaction not given after all.

How much better is prevention than litigation, not only in penal contests, but in civil ones!

It is scarce possible that the plan of management, be it ever so good, and utterly impossible if it be completely good, should not have some thing or other in it repugnant to the feelings of every parent to whom it thus presents itself: suppose it comprizable in 20 rules: 19 out of the 20 may be regarded with indifference by each: one only out of the 20 disapproved: but that one may be different in the instance of each individual: thus twenty persons may join in being dissatisfied with it, though each for a different reason. If the children are to be going backwards and forwards between school and home, every little article that seems amiss in the eyes of the parents will become the topic of perpetual discussion and disquiet: whereas if the children are kept entirely at school, the management will be viewed in the lump, and, if the child appears in good health and spirits on the few visits which the parent will have opportunity to make, he will be satisfied. The pleasure of meeting will dispell for the moment the disposition to look out for grievances, and that pleasure will not have been worn off before the time for departure is arrived.

On the half-and-half plan, the conduct to be observed by one of the conflicting authorities, the natural and the constituted, towards the other, would, on the one side, be matter of no small difficulty. On the Parent's side, it is true, the embarrassment would be but little: following the bent of untutored nature, aversion towards the rival authority would be the natural sentiment, and maledictions the natural expression of it. On the side of the instructed, the regulated and responsible minister of public authority, the facility would be very different. To inculcate disobedience or disrespect to Parents would be repugnant to religion as well as morality: to inculcate obedience and practical respect to an opposing power would be repugnant to every purpose of the institution: and, in the too frequent case of an immoral parent, to morality itself. It would be to say, and say in the same breath, nay in the same words, obey and disobey at the same time: do as I bid you, by doing as those bid you who bid you do the contrary to what I bid you. I do not ask what child, but what instructor, how deep soever his sagacity, could find a clear course to steer between such difficulties?

On the purely scholastic plan, there will be no difficulty in the case. Honour thy father and thy mother, will be among the lessons of the day: and neither contrariety nor other inconvenience can result from the inculcating of it. The Parent will be as the King: the more easy to honour, the more difficult to see. Guarded and awed by the discipline of the House, the rough or immoral Parent, coming with his best deportment and his best attire, will, in his few and short and well-watched visits, have neither audacity nor liberty to give vent to hostile sentiments, nor occasion nor time to nourish or conceive them. At the emersion of the scholar from the state of immaturity and subjection to the state of maturity and liberty, the age of legal obedience as towards Parents will be at an end: and, as to respect, the course to be taken for separating respect towards the relation from undue compliances towards the individual who may disgrace it, a task against which the scholar will have been prepared by general and guarded suggestions comprized in the instruction of the school, would find him, at his period of emancipation, of an age sufficiently matured for making such application of the suggestions as occasion may call for and prudence dictate: while the title to at least the externals of respect will by this time, on the part of the parent, have acquired an accession of strength by age. The union of respect with compassion, respect for the relation, compassion for the infirmities of the individual, will have suggested the proper medium, the proper line of deportment to be observed.

In the ground of moral infection, how wide the difference! How prodigious the advantage of the pure and simple plan!

In the half-and-half plan, association being promiscuous and inspection interrupted, if ninety-nine instead of thirty or forty out of the hundred were pure, the one scabby sheep would be sufficient to inoculate and keep up contagion in the whole flock. Under the unmixt regimen of an Inspection-Industry-House, were the whole hundred consigned to it in an infected state, the taint might soon be subdued by the never absent, never wandering eye—by the unintermitted and unfluctuating discipline of the House.

OBSERVATIONS ON THE POOR BILL

CHAPTER ONE
INTRODUCTION

If from any thing that has been said in the above preliminary view of the three contending systems[1] it should have been made appear to any reader that the Home-Provision system is ineligible in comparison of the Public-Establishment system, and that, of the two modifications of that latter system, that in which the establishments are upon a Parochial or other such small scale is ineligible in comparison of that in which the establishments are upon so large a scale as to require but four, upon an average, to a County (allowance being made of a few more to provide for the extra population of some of the largest towns), if, in a word, it should have been made appear to him that every mode of provision is ineligible other than that administered according to the Large-Establishment [system] as above described, every such reader will have already been prepared without further discussion for passing his judgment on the general complexion of the Bill.[2] If accordingly, these observations, considered [with] reference to the several possible systems in this subject contemplated in the abstract, should appear to have reason on their side, they will not have been thrown away, considered with respect to the paricular arrangements exhibited in the Bill: since the more has been said with regard to the systems in question, each considered in a mass, the less will require to be said on the subject of the particular legislative provisions by which two of these are proposed to be carried into effect, with new-devis'd extensions and improvements.

Though no determinate principle of arrangement presents itself as having been adopted for the purpose of this Bill, or at least as having been steadily pursued throughout the course of it,[a] the whole matter

[a] Before I engage in the discussion of particular clauses, I find it indispensably necessary to state an apprehension I have throughout been labouring under—the

---

[1] i.e. 'Pauper Systems Compared', pp. 141–216 above.
This paragraph was omitted from the copies of the text which Bentham circulated in February 1797, and from that edited in 1838 by Edwin Chadwick (1800–90), sanitary reformer, secretary to Bentham from 1829, Secretary of the Poor Law Commission 1834–46. For Chadwick's edition see the Editorial Introduction, pp. xlvii–xlix above.

[2] The Bill for the better Support and Maintenance of the Poor, introduced on 29 December 1796, combined the establishment of a system of parochial schools of industry with several new entitlements to home relief, all to be overseen by a new administrative structure which gave increased powers to local magistrates. The Bill was abandoned in February 1797. For further discussion see the Editorial Introduction, pp. xli–xlvii above.

of it may be conceived at least as distributable under *four* heads or compartments: *one* part taking up the Out-allowance or *Home-Provision* system, and opening new sources of relief in that shape; a *second*, taking up the Home-Provision system and the *Small-Establishment* system jointly,[a] and, in a system of working places under the names of *Schools of Industry*, establishing throughout the southern half of the Kingdom a system of employment and industrious education, of which the scene is to *shift* in a manner between the *public* school-room and the private *home*; a *third*, occupied in establishing a system of superintendence, to watch over the management of these schools of industry; and the *fourth* taken up with a set of regulations in the way of *procedure*, and a few other arrangements of a *technical* nature, such as it is commonly deemed necessary to tack to the end of statutes creative of new powers, to be exercised by particular authorities.

On looking into the portion of matter relative to the subject of *Home provision*, we shall find it distinguishable into two main divisions: the one occupied in the distribution of *occasional*, or *temporary* allowances, the other in giving commencement or facility

apprehension of doing an unintentional injustice to the Bill, by mis-stating from time to time the intended import of it. The truth is, the degree of difficulty I have experienced in the course of my endeavours to comprehend that import, has been as extreme as those endeavours have been sincere. Whatever therefore is herein advanced as conveying my own sense of the import of the Bill, must be understood to be submitted all along to correction—to whatever correction may be thought fit to be administered by stronger minds. When the examination of the Bill, considered with reference to its *matter* and general import, has been gone through, some observations may perhaps be subjoined with relation to the *form* of it, *expression* as well as *method* included: and, in the course of these observations, after stating and confessing the difficulties I have experienced, I may perhaps venture to submit a specimen of *method* and *phraseology* such as presents itself to my apprehension, as standing clear of these or any other such difficulties.[1]

[a] So termed here, in contradistinction to the *Large-Establishment* system, by which is meant that branch of the *Public-Establishment* system (as contradistinguished from the system of *Out-allowances*) according to which the establishments would, separately considered, be upon a *large* scale, such as that of a *County* Work-house, or even a system of Work-houses, of which *four* (suppose) should be allowed to a county upon an average.[2]

---

[1] Bentham's comments on the expression and form of the Bill appeared in 'Essay on the question, Who are the persons for whom the several bounties provided by this Bill are intended?', pp. 255–63 below.

[2] See 'Pauper Systems Compared', and in particular the distinction between the Large and Small-establishment systems, pp. 144–6 above. In both Bentham's draft and the copies, the footnote continues with a note not intended for publication, but for the information of those to whom the text was privately circulated: 'This refers to a paper not herewith sent but intended for publication, entitled "Comparative view of the several systems, establishable as well as established, in relation to the Poor".'

to a system of what may be termed *superannuation annuities*, humanely destined to diffuse a gleam of perpetual comfort over the evening of life.

As to the *general* principle on which this part of the Bill appears to be founded, viz: the eligibility of the *Home-provision* system, that system, taken in its general features, having been fully described in the preceding survey,[a] a simple reference to that paper will be sufficient here.[1]

On looking into the amendments applied by the *Bill* to the plan of relief afforded by that system in the *present* state of the law, we shall find them introductive of the following *extensions*:

In Sect. 2, a *supplement* is meant to be provided for whatever deficiency, in point of *earnings*, may result from any deficiency in point of *ability* with reference to work.[b] In Sect. 1, another supplement for whatever deficiency, in respect of the means of maintenance, may be produced in families by an *overcharge* of helpless *children*.[c] In Sect. 3, power is given (to whom not mentioned) to administer relief in the shape of *capital*, to be employed in the purchase of 'a Cow, or *other animal yielding profit*'.[d] In Sect. 4, a provision is made that *property*, 'visible property', though it amount to £30, or perhaps more, shall not operate in *exclusion of relief*.[e] And in Sect. 23, provision is made for conferring on the scholars of these schools, in certain cases, the benefit of *apprenticeship* at the public expence.[f]

I shall now consider the several clauses in the order in which they have just been brought to view.[g]

[a] Comparative View &c., as above mentioned.[2]

[b] This clause I shall take the liberty of distinguishing by the name of the *Under-ability*, or *Supplemental-wages* clause.

[c] This may be termed the *Family-relief*, or *Extra-children* clause.

[d] This may be termed the *Cow-money* clause.

[e] This may be termed the *Relief-extension*, or *Opulence-relief* clause.

[f] This I shall term the *Apprenticeship* clause.

[g] In the Bill itself, the sections are not numbered: it is not the usage: sections never *are* numbered, either in an *Act* (I speak of the authentic Manuscript) or in a *Bill*. I have taken upon me to number them at a venture: knowing no other means of distinguishing them in the way of *reference*. My principle of distinction has been the recurrence of the introductory surplusage, *And be it further enacted*, coupled with the consideration of those discontinuances, or breaks in the line of text, which are the mechanical result of the operations of the press.

This privation of the physical possibility of becoming the subject-matter of reference; this prolific cause and certain pledge of immensity, disorder, and

[1] The foregoing paragraph is omitted from the Bowring edition of the text.

[2] i.e. 'Pauper Systems Compared'.

CHAPTER TWO
UNDER-ABILITY, OR SUPPLEMENTAL-WAGES CLAUSE[1]

By the *under-ability*, or *supplemental-wages* clause, provision is made that *'if any poor person entitled to the benefit of this Act . . .'* (the *efficient cause of title* is not otherwise specified) 'not able to earn the full rate *or* wages . . . shall agree to work at an under-rate, the deficiency may be made up to him out of the Poor rates, *without compelling such poor person to be employ'd in any manner under the authority of this Act.*'

What sort of persons this class is intended to be composed of, is a question respecting which I must confess myself unable to satisfy myself, not being able to collect who the persons are that are *'entitled to the benefit of this Act'*:[a] thus much, however, I understand from the clause, that there *is* a class of persons, to every one of whom, upon condition of their working in *any* manner, and receiving for their work a rate *or* wages *falling short* to any amount of the *'full rate usually given in the Parish'*, *somebody* or other (I do not perfectly see who) shall have it in his power to make up the deficiency at the *public* charge.

The inability of the lowest class (I mean the worst-paid class) of working hands in this country (viz: the *labourers in husbandry*) to make such provision for the sustenance of themselves and families as

inconsistency, each in the extreme; this privation of one of the many helps to intellection, the exclusion of which is peculiar to that species of composition, in which the importance of the qualities of order, precision, and conciseness stands at the very highest pitch; this deficiency, if it be a fault, is not the particular fault of *this* Bill, or of any one concerned in it. It is the fault of *every body*, and thence of *nobody*.

[a] I have by me a dissertation of 15 or 16 pages, the result of which is that the discovery is impossible.[2]

---

[1] 'And be it further Enacted, That if any Poor Person entitled to the Benefit of this Act, in any Parish or Parishes to be united by virtue of this Act, not able to earn the full Rate or Wages usually given in such Parish or Parishes united therewith, shall contract and agree to work at any inferior Rate or Wages, which Wages shall not be sufficient for the Maintenance and Support of such Poor Person, singly or in Conjunction with his or her Family, it shall and may be lawful to make up such Deficiency (Regard being had to the Earnings of such Family, and to the Allowance (if any) then payable to him, her, or them, from any Parochial Fund which may be established by virtue of this Act in such Parish) out of the Rates made for the Relief of the Poor, without compelling such poor Person to be employed in any Manner under the Authority of this Act: Provided always, That the Parish so advancing any Money to any Persons not having any lawful Settlement therein, shall be reimbursed the same, in the Manner and in the Cases specified in the Schedhule hereunto annexed.' See *Commons Sessional Papers of the Eighteenth Century*, ciii. 164.

[2] i.e. 'Essay on the question, Who are the persons for whom the several bounties provided by this Bill are intended?', pp. 255–63 below.

shall be *constantly* adequate to the purpose—that is, under every variation which the *ability* as to *work*, the *faculty* of *obtaining* work, and the *magnitude* of the *burden* resulting from the *condition* and *multitude* of the *infants* and other *helpless* branches of the family, are susceptible of, is a point which, I *fear*, has been but too incontestibly established.[a] To this inconvenience, such remedies as in the course of the preceding observations presented themselves as the proper, and only proper remedies, have already been pointed out.[1] The remedies proposed by the Bill in general, and the part now in question in particular, must be confessed to be of a different stamp.

As to the casual *inadequacy* of the *earnings* of the individual, compared with the *demand* for *subsistence* on the part of that same individual, two expedients have presented themselves: one is, to *fix* the rate of *wages*, and thereby of earnings: viz: of the rate to be paid to individual labourers by *individual* employers: the other is, leaving the rate indefinite, to make up the deficiency, whatsoever in each individual instance it may happen to amount to, at the *public* charge.

The fixation of the rate of wages is an operation which, on different occasions, has been *proposed*, and in some instances even *practised*, with opposite views: to *prevent* what has been looked upon as *excess*, and to *cure* what has been looked upon as *defect*.[2] It is with the *latter* view that it has lately been proposed with reference to the case now before us.[3]

Against the fixation of wages with a view to prevent *deficiency*, there is however, this objection: viz: that thereby you *exclude* from

[a] Particularly in *The Case of Labourers in Husbandry*, by the Rev. David Davies, 1795, 4to.

---

[1] See 'Collatoral Uses derivable from a system of Industry Houses', particularly pp. 69–78 and 98–108, and 'Pauper Systems Compared', particularly pp. 192–3 and 195–7.

[2] Statutory regulation of wages dated back to the Statute of Labourers of 1350 (25 Edw. III, Stat.1), which, in the face of severe labour shortages, established maximum daily rates of pay for servants and agricultural labourers. During a later period of price inflation, 13 Ric. II, c.8 (1389) empowered Justices of the Peace to adjust such rates from year to year 'according to the Dearth of Victuals', while 5 Eliz. I, c.4 (1562) greatly extended the number of trades so regulated. In Bentham's own time, statutes continued to regulate the wages of specific trades, sometimes to decrease wages and sometimes to increase them. For instance, 8 Geo. III, c.17 (1768) established maximum daily rates for tailors in London in order to restrain a perceived rise in their wage rate, while 13 Geo. III, c.68 (1773), which empowered the London magistrates to determine the daily rate payable to local silk weavers, resulted from an appeal to Parliament by the silk weavers themselves, and led to a general increase in their wages.

[3] On 9 December 1795 Samuel Whitbread (1764–1815), MP for Bedford 1790–1815, introduced a Bill to amend the Statute of Artificers of 1562 (5 Eliz. I, c.4) by allowing Justices of the Peace at Quarter Sessions to establish minimum as well as maximum rates of pay for agricultural labourers. In the debate on the second reading of Whitbread's Bill on 12 February 1796, the measure was defeated, having been strongly opposed by Pitt, who promised to bring forward an alternative measure of reform in the near future. For further details see the Editorial Introduction, pp. xiii–xiv above.

employment many persons who might otherwise have obtained it: you *aggravate* the distress of the *very persons*, or at least of a considerable proportion of the persons, whose condition you propose to *meliorate*. What you *can* do (let it be admitted) is so to order matters in behalf of the object of your benevolence, that *if* he receives *any* thing he shall *not* receive *less* than what you *wish* him to receive: but what you can *not* do, is so to order matters as that, under *these* circumstances, he shall receive anything *at all*. To *give* him that sufficient rate of wages is an obligation *not* imposed upon *any* employer whatsoever: it is therefore an expence to which *no* employer, who does not think he shall find his account in it, will ever think of subjecting himself.

In a word, a regulation fixing the rate of wages so as to prevent its falling *below* a certain rate, is, in effect, a regulation of the *prohibitive* kind, excluding from employment all such hands the value of whose labour does not rise to a *level* with that rate: a prohibition enforced by a specific and unavoidable penalty: and that penalty is the *difference* (whatever it may be in each case) between the *highest* sum which the labour of the *workman* is *worth*, and the *lowest* sum which the *employer* is *allowed* to give.

True it is, that upon a *minuter* scrutiny, the exclusion will not be found altogether *so* universal as at *first* glance it might appear. In some instances (partly from motives of a *personal* nature, under the difficulty of getting another hand, but at an extra price, partly from motives of *compassion*, rather than have an industrious workman destitute) an employer, who otherwise might have got the labour of the *feeble hand*[a] in question at an under rate, proportioned to his diminution in point of ability, will pay him that *full* and intended *legal* rate, which, with reference to that ability, will be an *extra* rate. But the effect of the principle, thus operating in limitation of the exclusion, has its bounds. An employer *may* give 9s. a week, for example, to a labourer whose labour is worth but *8*s. or *7*s., but he will *not* give the 9s. to a labourer whose labour is worth but *3*s. or *4*s. He will rather give, for his nine shillings-worth of labour, *10*s., or *11*s., or *12*s., to *one* workman in full ability (importing him, if necessary, from another Parish) than 27s. among *three* labourers, whose labour taken all together is worth no more than the nine shillings.

Besides the *general* danger (the danger of idleness) inseparable from the *Home-Provision* system, a *particular* source of danger seems to be opened by the particular wording of *this* clause. By his character

[a] See the annexed Table of Cases calling for Relief.[1]

[1] See p. lvii above.

for idleness or negligence, a man, though in respect of *bodily* ability not *unequal*, perhaps, to the *fullest* rate of earnings, shall have so ordered matters that no *master* will employ him but at a rate more or less *inferior* to that rate. In that case, it will be perfectly true that, to use the words of the Bill, he is '*not able to earn the full rate or wages usually given*': for, whatever may have been the *original cause* of the inability, the *existence* of it is not the less real. So far then, as this cause of inability extends, that is, so far as the class of the *idle*, the *negligent*, and the *dissolute* extends (a multitude, the encrease of which seems but too much to be apprehended from the operation of this clause), the effect of it seems to be, the putting the *idle* and *negligent* exactly upon a footing, in point of prosperity and reward, with the *diligent* and *industrious*.

If conjecture may be allowed, the circumstance that gave rise to this clause, in the breasts of those who framed it, seems to have been the humane consideration that, when a man does his *utmost*, it is *hard* to leave him in a worse condition than his neighbours, on account of an infirmity which is his *misfortune* merely, not his *fault*. But the extreme difficulty of forming, in each individual instance, a well-grounded judgment (to whomsoever it belongs to form it) on the question *fault or no fault*, and, if fault, in what degree, may by this time perhaps, have been perceived. But *fault will* not be, *ought* not to be, imputed without special and full proof: and perhaps the blameable conduct, the blameable cause of the inability, the *bad character* in which the inability to obtain the ordinary rate of wages originated, this cause, though continuing and operating in full force, is susceptible of no *proof* but what is confined to a period long since *past*. This being the case, and supposing all possible ability, as well as integrity on the part of those by whom the claim to this bounty is to be determined, I must confess, I do not see how it can be otherwise than a *frequent*, not to say *general*, case, that *idleness* should, upon the establishment of this clause, find itself in as *good* plight as *industry*.

Under this difficulty of drawing the line, an expedient which, I must confess, I expected to have found adopted, was the *confining* the *title* to some such *efficient cause* or causes as should be out of the reach of *counterfeiting* as well as of fabrication. *Old age* stands in this respect on the *highest* ground in point of eligibility: after that come specific modifications of infirmity, such as loss of limbs, loss of the use of limbs, rupture, epilepsy, nervous afflictions: complaints which, according to the greater or less *difficulty* of *ascertaining* the *matter of fact*, will constitute so many efficient causes of inability, more or less clearly and certainly *exempt from blame*, more or less exempt from the danger of opening an inlet to *abuse*.

Whether all the precautions that *could* be taken, all the precautions which the nature of the case admits of, would be sufficient to confine the mischief within any tolerable bounds, is what I cannot but entertain some doubts of: but, at any rate, so long as no such checks are applied, the danger from this clause, supposing it to stand, seems very serious. For, how opposite soever the views and intentions of the contrivers in the two cases, the *equalization-system*, as applied to *wages*, seems hardly less threatening to *industry*, and thence to *property* (to say nothing of the *expence*), than, as applied to *property*, it would be to *property*, and thence to *industry*.

Against these and all other dangers of abuse, the dependence for a remedy and safeguard is, of course, on the wisdom and integrity of those into whose hands the *execution* of the Act may come from time to time to fall: but (not to mention how multifarious the ingredients *sine quibus non* of the mixed mass called *wisdom* are) *wisdom* may be wanting in *one* quarter, *integrity* in *another*, *both* together in a *third*, and after all, we know not *who* they are: besides that, as we have seen, the cases are various, and of frequent occurrence, where the union of *both* qualities, and *both* in the highest degree, would be of no avail. To oppose *all new* powers, on no distincter ground than that *all* powers are open to abuse, would be the effusion of *undistinguishing* imbecility, or of political *jealousy* run mad. But when a system of provision is on the carpet, involving in its essence a system of powers *peculiarly open to abuse*, the danger may at least operate as a motive for *inquiry*, whether there may not be found some *other* system less obnoxious to abuse.

What, in such case, shall be deemed this '*full rate or wages*', which is to be made up at all events, is another point that seems as necessary as it may be found *difficult* to be settled. In the compass of *England and Wales* some hundred thousands a year may be at stake upon this single point. 1. Is it the '*full rate or wages*' of the *highest-paid* species of labour in the district in question?—Certainly not in *every* case. 2. Is it the '*full rate or wages*' of the highest-paid species of labour, where the employment of the *individual* in question happens to be of that species?—If so, we may have bad *shipwrights* pensioned at 9s. a-week, or a guinea (according as day work or piece work is taken for the standard), or bad *mathematical-instrument*-makers at half as much.—*This* therefore was not intended. 3. Is it the '*full rate or wages*' according to an *average* taken of the earnings of *all* the species of employment exercised within the District *put together*? This, requiring a vast previous assemblage of *highly interesting* but hitherto *uncollected* documents, is what, for that as well as other reasons, can hardly have been intended. 4. Is it the *'full rate or wages' earnt* in the species of employment *most abundant* in the district, as the words *'usually given'* might seem to import?—I should suppose—nor *that* neither. 5. Is it the *'full rate or wages'* earnt in the *lowest* (meaning the *lowest-paid*) species of employment therein exercised?—This, I should *rather* think, is what is meant, or at least upon this view of the diversity *would* be meant, because this construction would be the *least dangerous*:—but this is not any where *expressed*.

Take even the *lowest-paid* species of employment, the *quantum* of the earnings will be found to admitt of great variation in *great towns* (the metropolis for example) compared with *distant country* places. There are country places in which it is not higher than 1s. a-day: in London and the neighbourhood it can hardly be reckoned lower than 2s. With all this enormous difference in the *habitual* rate of *supply*, the *necessary* means of living are scarcely cheaper anywhere than in London. Are so many thousands of bad workmen then, with or without families, to receive near £32 a year as a *minimum*, when less than £16 a year is proved by experience to be enough for good ones? And who will stay in the country at *single* allowance, if he can secure *double* allowance, only by coming up to London, which, partly by a *late* Act, partly by this *intended* Act, everybody is enabled to do without disturbance?[1]

An answer is—that, as at *present* and in practice, *necessity* is *measured* for the purpose of *relief*, so in future, and *under this Act*, will *wages* be measured for the same purpose. The reply is—*no such thing*. As far as the intended law is *obey'd*, as far as it produces the effect it aims at, the measure at *present* used for this purpose will *not* be employed, but *laid aside*. Under the *existing* order of things, the relief granted is measured by and adjusted to what, in the breasts of those to whom it belongs to judge, *is* the proper *quantum* of the demand on the score of indigence. But this mode of measurement is precisely that which will *not* satisfy the liberality of the framer of this Act: for this is what the Act declares, if it declares anything. *Full* is a word not only of precision, but of *energy*: the *'full rate'*, that and nothing less, is the rate without which the legislator has declared he will not *in future* be satisfied: and whosoever presumes to give less

[1] The 'late Act' to which Bentham refers was 35 Geo. III, c.101 (1795), which amended the law of settlement to prevent the removal from a parish of any person until they actually applied for relief and thus became a charge upon the poor rates. Pitt's Bill itself further provided, 'That no Poor Person whatever shall be liable to be removed from the Parish . . . as actually chargeable by Reason of any Relief or Allowance granted to such Person under the Authority of this Act, on account of any temporary Disability or Sickness of such Person, or of any of his or her Family, or on account of the Number of his or her Children in respect of whom he or she shall be entitled to or shall receive any Allowance by virtue of this Act.' See *Commons Sessional Papers of the Eighteenth Century*, ciii. 165.

than that full rate, *disobeys*. That such disobedience would not be uncommon, is what I will not say either I should *hope*, or I should *fear*, but what at any rate I should *expect*. But where would be the expediency of that law, of which the sole trust were to lie in the disobedience it might excite? Meantime disobedience, eligible or ineligible, pardonable or unpardonable, will not be *universal*. *Five* standards (as we have seen) for the measurement of the bounty, five standards, rising one above another in liberality, lie, in every parish, open to a man's choice. In each instance, be his *inclinations* what they may, be his temper what it may, ever so *weak*, ever so *lavish*, ever so *heedless*, within the prodigious scale raised up by these five standards, a man may, without much straining, find a warrant in this part of the intended Act: but at any rate, to one or other of them he *must* conform himself if he pays any regard to the Act. Five standards, the lowest of them little less than sufficient, as we have seen, to double the Poor-Rates, overwhelm the metropolis, and depopulate whatever part of the country is not covered by a town.

CHAPTER THREE
FAMILY-RELIEF, OR EXTRA-CHILDREN CLAUSE[1]

In this clause (§1) two classes of persons are instituted, who on the condition of their respectively having a certain number of children, 'parts' of their respective '*families, and unable to maintain themselves*', shall be entitled to a weekly allowance. Considered in respect to its *quantum*, this allowance is *not* to amount, at any rate, to *less* than a shilling a week for each *extra child*, and it may amount to ever so much *more*. Considered in respect to its *duration*, it is to continue

[1] 'And be it Enacted, by the King's Most Excellent Majesty, by and with the Advice and Consent of the Lords Spiritual and Temporal, and Commons, in this present Parliament assembled, and by the Authority of the same, That from and after the Time herein appointed for the Commencement of this Act, any Father entitled to the Benefit thereof, according to the Provisions hereinafter mentioned, and having more than Two Children, Part of his Family, and unable to maintain themselves and any Widow, being so entitled and having more than One such Child, shall have such Weekly Allowances from the Parish or Parishes, to be united by virtue of this Act, where he or she shall reside, in respect of any such Child or Children of such Father beyond the Number of Two, and in respect of any such Child or Children of such Widow beyond the Number of One, to such Amount, not less than One Shilling for each such Child, as shall be ordered and directed in Conformity to the Provisions of this Act; and that such Allowances so made shall continue, in respect of such Child or Children above the Number of Two and One, respectively, as aforesaid, until such Child or Children in respect of whom such Allowances are made, can and shall maintain themselves by their Labour, if such Child or Children shall so long remain Part of their Father's and Mother's Family as aforesaid.' See *Commons Sessional Papers of the Eighteenth Century*, ciii. 163–4.

not only till each such extra child shall be *able* to maintain itself by its own labour, but till it *actually shall* maintain itself by its own labour—'*can* and *shall* maintain themselves by their labour' says the Act.

1. Measuring the extent of this clause, we shall find it, I much fear, at once too *ample* and too *narrow*: too ample to be reconcileable to the interests of private industry or of public economy, too narrow to cover the extent of the *demand* for the relief which [it] itself provides.

To judge of the demand, in point of *necessity* and *utility*, for the *bounties* given by this clause, let us observe upon what footing the *title* to *relief* stands under the *existing* order of things. At present, supposing the *discretion* properly and successfully exercised, *demand* and *supply* are proportioned to each other: from those who have *not* wherewithal to maintain themselves and families, be those families ever so *small*, relief will *not* be *with-holden*: to those who *have* wherewithal to maintain themselves and families, be those families ever so *large*, relief will *not* be *given*. Under this clause, a family may labour under the severest *distress*, and derive *no* benefit from the intended Act: a family may wallow in abundance, and derive an enormous pension from it.

To entitle the head of the family to the allowance, to the pension, or congeries of pensions, thus provided, it is not necessary that the family *taken together* should be unable otherwise to maintain itself; it is sufficient if the *extra children*, the children exisiting in an extra number, should, *separately* taken, be unable to maintain themselves. The heads of families in question, as described are: 1. A *Father* having more than *two* children unable to maintain themselves, and 2. A *Widow* having more than *one* such child. As to the difference made here between *Fathers* and *Widows*, that in general the *ability* of the *male* sex in this respect will be greater than that of the *female*, is not to be disputed, but will it in *every* instance be exactly in that proportion? May not there be some instances in which a *woman* with a *good* trade will be better able to maintain *two* children, than a *man* to maintain the *same number* with a *bad* one? May not the instances be *many*, in which a *man*, with or without a *wife*, shall be better able to maintain *three* children, than a *Widow* to maintain *two*? And may not there be instances, where a Widow with *two* children shall be better able to maintain herself and family, than a Widow left pregnant for instance, with *one* child in arms, or in a state requiring still more attendance, may be able to maintain herself and *that one*?

Doubts remain with regard to the *import*, that are material to the *effect*. This inability, with regard to the maintaining themselves, is it *sufficient* if it extend to the *supernumerary* children, or *must* it extend to all the children? And in either case is it *sufficient* if it be *partial*, or *must* it be *entire*?

2. As to the *quantum* of the pension.—Under the *existing* system, if 6d. a week, for example, per child, be *requisite* and *sufficient* to make up for the deficiency of earnings, 6d. a week *may*, without any further addition, be allowed. Under *this* Bill, a shilling a week, requisite or not requisite, *must*, if *anything*, be allowed: shillings in any number *may* be allowed: and that more than one *should* in *general*, or at least *frequently*, be allowed, seems to be intended: for that *less* than a shilling, requisite or not requisite, should not in *any* case be allowed, is *expressly* stipulated. A shilling a-week is £2–12s. a year: 6d. a week is £1–6s.: 9d. a week is £1–19s.: 3d. a week is 13s. Thirty-nine shillings, almost £2 a year, or even six-and-twenty, or even 13s. a year, repeated upon forty or fifty thousand children, amounts to no small sum. Granting (what is a good deal to grant) that less than the shilling a week can not in *any situation*, or at *any age*, be made to suffice for the maintenance of *any* child, what can not *possibly* be granted, is that this deficiency in the amount of earnings can not exist in the shape of any *less* sum than the *entire amount* of the sum necessary for a child's maintenance. In situations where money is oftener reckoned by millions and thousands than by pounds and shillings, the saving that might be made upon a pitiful shilling a week is apt to appear as nothing: but where a penny comes so often to be repeated, an error to the amount of a few pence in this *low* pension-list, may amount to a source of profusion not only more abundant in *quantity*, but much less warranted by use, as well as much more pregnant with *mischief*, than even the *High* Pension-list, which is the object of so much jealousy, as well as so much envy.[1]

3. The *duration* of the allowance presents another topic of observation. The continuance is to be untill the children in question 'actually *shall maintain themselves by their labour*': while their earning any thing will depend of course upon the head of the family. So long as the head of the family, through wilfulness, or negligence, or indolence, shall keep the children either in *idleness*, or employ'd in *labour* which, however useful to the family, *can not*, or *need* not, be brought to account in the shape of a *fixed sum*, so long the allowance, excessive or moderate, is to continue.

The maintenance, it may be said, will be afforded, and that in the fixed shape in question, by the wages which the child will receive for the work which the head of the family must send the child to perform at the school of Industry, on pain of receiving none of the *benefits of*

[1] In the margin, Bentham has written at this point, 'note calculating the amount', but no note to this effect has been identified.

the Act. It *may* be so—however, it *may* be *otherwise*. The children may, some or all of them, be under the age (5 years is the age at which this schooling is to commence (§20)).[1] In a thinly-peopled part of the country, the burthen of the school, with its *schoolmaster* and *schoolmistress*, and *warehouse* and *warehouse-keeper*, will, if the parish be *single*, be by far too heavy for it: if several parishes are put together, the school, put it *where* you will, will, by its distance, be rendered inaccessible to a great part of its scholars.—The pensions are to commence in *July* next (§§ 1, 67).[2] Not a school can be begun to be built, till at the *end* of a *chain* of administrative operations, such as in known instances has taken up *years*, and of which the first *link* cannot take place till *after Michaelmas* (§10),[3] and it is 'in aid of the *fund* for the support of the *school*' (§20), and *not* in aid of this *pension-fund*, that the earnings, whenever they *do* take place, are, after all, to be applied.

A circumstance that renders the danger the more formidable is, that the *two* currents of profusion—the allowance on the score of *extra children*, and the allowance on the score of *supplemental wages*, may, for anything that appears to the contrary, mingle *together*, and flow with *united force*. First comes the *pay* of the *idler* made up to an *equality* with the *earnings* of the *industrious*: then come the *extra children* of the idler, to be put, in whatsoever number, upon the *pension-list*. 'Regard' (it is provided) 'shall be had to the earnings of the *family*.' Regard (it is provided) shall be had to the allowance from a fund, not named, but which appears to be what I call the *super-annuation* fund:[4] but of any *regard which may be had* to any such allowance as that on the score of *extra children*, no mention is to be found: no deduction is, therefore, *intended* to be made on any such score.

The over-narrowness of the provision with reference to its evident object, the *scantiness* of it in a particular point of view, comes now to be considered. To characterize the *head* of a family, on whose labour the subsistence of the family is considered as depending, '*Father*', if of the male sex, '*Widow*', if of the female, are the only terms employ'd. But there are *other* relations, which are either *charged* by *law*, or at least apt to be *engaged* by *shame* or *affection*, in the maintenance, or at any rate in the *guardianship*, of their infant or *other helpless* relatives. Within this sphere of duty, perfect or imperfect (for I will not plunge

[1] See *Commons Sessional Papers of the Eighteenth Century*, ciii. 173.

[2] See p. 228 n. above and *Commons Sessional Papers of the Eighteenth Century*, ciii. 193 respectively.

[3] See ibid., 167.

[4] i.e. the parochial subscription funds proposed by Pitt's Bill to provide benefits in sickness and old age: see *Commons Sessional Papers of the Eighteenth Century*, ciii. 165–6.

into discussions of *positive* law for the purpose of drawing the line), *Grandfather* and *Grandmother*, *Brother* and *Sister*, *Uncle* and *Aunt*, may, at any rate, be considered as comprized. In whatever point of view the matter be considered, if the claims of the *two* relations *specified* are to be regarded as *strong enough* with reference to the intended bounty, those of the six relations *not specified* present themselves as *still stronger*. In the instance of these comparatively distant relatives, if *bound* by law, the *burthen* of the *obligation* (unaccompanied as it is in their case with those matrimonial comforts which constitute the equivalent for parental burthens), is so much the *harder*: if *not bound*, the act of *taking* up the burthen is so much the more *meritorious*, and stands so much the more in need of foreign inducements to give it birth.

To give *consistency* to the provision by the *supply* of these *omissions*, is a task which, though certainly *not impracticable*, would be found *not unaccompanied with difficulty*: and if the *expediency* of the provision, considered in substance, be liable to *doubts*, this *difficulty* will add *force* to them. *Complication* is of *itself* an evil, and *such* an evil as requires no inconsiderable mass of *benefit* to *outweigh* it.

CHAPTER FOUR
COW-MONEY CLAUSE[1]

I now come to the Cow-money clause. The *benevolence* which suggested this clause is expressed in the most conspicuous characters: on the question of *policy*, the following observations have presented themselves.

Hitherto, the danger of profusion has confined itself to *income*: it now threatens *capital*. In the *preceding* clauses, the allowances authorized, how much soever too ample, continued to be, as they are under the existing system, in the first instance occasional only, at the worst gradual, accommodated, as to their rate of efflux, to the influx of the fund, from which alone they could be derived. Here, *capital* is given, under the very *name* of capital, and as a substitute to income. The pension *during pleasure* is virtually converted into a

[1] 'And be it further Enacted, That if it shall appear that any Person entitled to the Benefit of this Act, and wanting Relief for him or herself, or his or her Family, would be enabled, by the Advance of Money for purchasing a Cow or other Animal yielding Profit, to maintain him or herself, and his or her Family without farther Parochial Relief, it shall be lawful to order the Payment of such Money in Advance as will be necesary for the Purchase of such Cow or other Animal, out of the Rates made for the Relief of the Poor, in the Manner and according to the Form No. | | in the Schedule hereunto annexed, and subject to the Conditions therein directed to be expressed in such Order.' See *Commons Sessional Papers of the Eighteenth Century*, ciii. 164–5.

pension *for years* or *during life*, and that pension *at the same instant* bought out by a *gross* sum, leaving the demand for a *fresh* pension to recur at any time, to be again bought off, and so *toties quoties*.[1] The spiggot was *there* opened, *here* the bung-hole.

It would be *something* in the way of security, though surely not much, if the Cow were but safely housed in the stable of the indigent, to whom the possession of her is to be an inexhaustible spring of affluence. But even *this* security, slender as it is, is not provided. The capital to be advanced is to be advanced—not in the shape of the *Cow*, but in the shape of *hard money*, with which the object of this extraordinary bounty is left perfectly at liberty to lay in a fund, either of *milk* or *gin*, according to his taste.

The Cow *dies*—or is *stolen*—or, what is much more likely, is *supposed* to be stolen, being clandestinely *sold* to an obliging purchaser at a distance—what is to be done? '*Want of relief*' warranted the *first* cow: the same cause will necessitate a *second*. Limit who can the succeeding *series* of cows. The disappearance of the *first* cow (it may be said) will excite *suspicion*: the disappearance of a second cow will *strengthen the suspicion*:—true, but upon a mere suspicion, without *proof*, will a family be left to *starve*? The utmost security then amounts to *this*—that to a certain number of successive pensions thus *bought out*, will succeed a pension which will *not* be bought out.[a]

By donations or loans of this sort, made by gentlemen of high account to deserving individuals, selected from such of their tenants or dependants as have been fortunate enough to be comprized within the circle of their notice, *good* is said to have been done in certain instances.—I make no doubt of it. Milk is a wholesome, as well as pleasant beverage: milk is particularly good for children. Thirty pounds, twenty pounds, or even ten pounds, can not but form a

[a] The quantum of the capital thus to be hazarded is no light matter. A friend of mine, who at this present time happens to be looking out for a Cow, assures me he can hear of no animal of that kind, to be sold for less than £30, that can be depended upon for giving milk sufficient to pay for her keep—for '*yielding profit*', to use the expression in the Bill. The *time*, it is true, is a dear one, and the *place*, the vicinity of the metropolis. But to this purpose, within what may be termed the *vicinity* of the metropolis, a circle of at least 20 miles radius must surely be comprized. A Cow which is worth £30 in the heart of this southern division of the two united Kingdoms, can hardly be worth less than £15 at the very furthest extremity: because a difference much less than that of £15 a head, would, upon a very moderate number of Cows, abundantly pay for the expence of driving them up to London from even the most distant part of England. This £30 price (let us hope) will not *always* continue. But at the most favourable season, should it fall to £20, the reduction will be full as much, I fear, as can reasonably be expected.

[1] i.e. 'as often as the occasion demands'.

very comfortable accession to the property of an individual of the labouring class, especially to an individual who happens at the time to be suffering under the pressure of indigence. When, at his *own* expence, a man administers charity in so large a mass, it would be extraordinary indeed if he did not pay a *considerable* attention to the propriety of the application of it: and, should the *object* prove *less deserving* than was supposed, or the *benefit* less *permanent* than was hoped, there is at least no *immediately perceptible* harm done to any *assignable* individual. But, while the hands by which the bounty is to be dealt out remain in the clouds, or were they even lying upon the table, it seems rather too much to expect *equal* attention, or even in general *sufficient* attention, where the *praise* and the *thanks* are reaped by the hands which thus disseminate the bounty, while the *burthen* of it rests on the shoulders of *third persons*.

Over and above the general love of *popularity*, motives of a more personal nature may intervene, and that most naturally and frequently, to no such light amount. A man, to all appearance wanting 'relief' for '*him* . . . self, or *his* . . . family', and who, to all appearance, 'would be enabled, by the advance of money for purchasing a Cow . . . to maintain him . . . self and his . . . family without farther Parochial relief', may, besides being, to all appearance, a very industrious and deserving man, have the good fortune to possess a *vote*. No matter what the situation, high or low—Parliamentary, or having nothing to do with Parliament: for a county, for a borough, or for one of those situations which gives votes for boroughs.[1] If he *himself* does not possess the vote, his father, or his son, or his brother, or the father or brother of his wife or sweetheart may, which may come to much the same thing. To any man thus circumstanced (and the multitude of men thus circumstanced is not likely to be small) this *Cow-money* clause will be a matter of particular convenience. To give the value of a dinner for such a purpose might be an act of imprudence as well as a matter of expence, and, as experience has shown, might be fatal to the cause.[2] A bounty for good votes, a bounty to the amount of £10, as

[1] For the franchise in the county constituencies see p. 178n. above. The franchise varied considerably between borough constituencies, extending most broadly to resident householders not receiving relief, but restricted elsewhere, for instance, to householders paying poor rates, to freemen of the borough, or to members of the corporation. See Namier and Brooke, *The History of Parliament. The House of Commons 1754–90*, i. 12–50.

[2] The 'treating' of electors was common practice in eighteenth-century elections. However, the buying and selling of votes was illegal, and successful candidates who distributed their largesse without sufficient subtlety were liable to be unseated on petition to the House of Commons, and on occasion even prosecuted and imprisoned. For one such instance, relating to the election in the borough of Hindon in 1774, see 'Trials of R. Smith and T.B. Hollis esq.', in T.B. Howell, *A Complete Collection of State Trials and Proceedings for High Treason and Other Crimes and Misdemeanours from the Earliest Period to the Year 1783*, 21 vols., London, 1816, xx. 1226–86.

we have seen, or £20, or £30, might, under favour of this clause, be given with the most perfect safety, and without a farthing of expence.

It is the *profusion*, I must confess, that frightens me: the topic of *corruption* I leave to purer and more brilliant pens. Figures of arithmetic, and not of speech, are the figures that govern me. Standing even upon this frigid ground, I can see no bounds, I must confess, to the profusion, where, the incentives remaining in full force, the main checks, all the checks which preserve any tolerable uniformity of operation, are thus to be taken away.

Even the *shape* of the bounty seems, to my unfortunate apprehension, as objectionable as the *quantum* of it. If the £10, or the £20, or the £30, *must* be given, I had rather have seen the disposal of it left altogether to the dispensing hand, than clogged with the condition, enforced or not enforced, of converting it into a *Cow*.

1. A resource which is to supply a *permanent* deficiency *should* be as permanent as that deficiency. Here the deficiency is deemed *permanent*, since an *occasional* or *temporary* allowance is deemed inadequate to the supply of it. The probable remainder of the life of a Cow already in a condition to yield an annuity in the shape of milk is limited, sickness and casualties apart, to about 8 years: after which she may sell for about half price.

2. A resource which is to supply a permanent deficiency should, in the variations, if any, to which the amount of it is subjected or exposed, *keep pace* with any variation in the deficiency; or, if that can not be, should remain *constant* and *unvariable*, so as to afford a solid ground of dependence without any *partial*, much less *total*, cessation during the period that the demand continues in *unabated* force. But the annuity paid by a Cow undergoes a necessary suspension, frequently of four months continuance, never of less than two months, average, say, three months—a quarter of a year.

3. A supply, allotted as a resource to indigence, should be of a nature rather to *strengthen* by *exercise*, than to *weaken* by *omission* or disuse, the spirit and habit of *industry*. A *dairy* of Cows *would* do this. Attendance upon a *single* Cow is a species of industry, if industry it can be called, which is, of anything that *can* bear that name, the nearest of kin to idleness.

4. In the *general* account of the national well-being, nothing is gained, but a good deal lost, if *Paul* be *stript* of as much as is *bestowed* on *Peter*. Setting aside the accidental faculty of profiting by the too little known opportunities afforded by husbandry in its highest and freshest state of improvement, to the maintenance of a Cow, the possession of *land* will be indispensable. This land must either be land in separate *ownership*, or land in the state of *waste and common*

land. Of land in *separate ownership*, about three acres is looked upon as necessary to the constant maintenance of a Cow. Those three acres, how are they to be had? Are they to be *bought* and *given* along with the Cow? This the clause does not go so far as to say. Are they to be *hired*, and the *rent paid* for them, not to mention Cow-house and Dairy, for which articles shifts, it may be said, will be made? Nor *this* neither. The Cow, then, is to be turned upon the *Common*. But no sooner is the Cow upon the *Common*, than the expiration of the annuity, of at least by far the greatest part of it, 5, 6, or 7 eighths, is certain and near at hand. In the existing state of population on the one hand, and husbandry on the other, it is a point pretty well ascertained: a Common *will* afford *airing ground* to a milch cow, but it will *not* afford *maintenance*. It *will* keep the *animal* alive: but it will *not* keep alive in her the capacity of yielding milk in a quantity amounting to a resource. While the *annuity* is thus sinking, so is the value of the *capital* itself. After a year's existence upon a common, a well-fed cow, turned out in the increasing vigour of her youth, will, instead of *gaining*, have *lost* in value.

But before the Cow was turned upon the Common, the Common was *already* overcharged. The Common which is *not* already in this state, will, I believe, be difficult to find. The *accession* of this new mouth will not *add* to the quantity of the *pasture*. So much therefore, as the owner of *this* Cow *gets*, so much do the owners of *other* Cows *lose*.

Capital therefore, cannot be given in this shape, without being paid for at least *twice over*, even laying out of the question the certain and enormous depretiation in value: once by the amount of the purchase-money, again by the amount of the *annuity* or *rent-charge*, thrown, by the depretiation of the amount of the pasture, upon the *other* Commoners: a depretiation *equal* at least to the utmost gain accruing to the *Commoner* thus *favoured*. If ten pound then be the money *paid*, and ten pound be the value of the Cow to the individual on whom she is bestowed, £20 at least would be the loss to the remainder of the *community*, the receiver of the bounty deducted, £10 the *clear* loss to the *whole* community, the receiver of the bounty included.[1]

[1] Chadwick's edition of 'Observations on the Poor Bill', p. 20 (Bowring, viii. 449), includes at this point the following two paragraphs, written by Bentham in February 1796, in criticism of the 'Cow Money Clause' as contained in an early draft of the Poor Bill which Bentham had received from William Wilberforce (1759–1833), politician and philanthropist, MP for Hull 1780–4, Yorkshire 1784–1812, and Bramber 1812–25: 'By donations in any shape you may take a few favoured individuals out of the class of poor, and place them in the class of people of easy circumstances. But this, which is only the system of monastic charity upon a great scale, giving the beef whole instead of dealing it out in broth, is limited in its extent as well as pernicious in its effects, and in relieving present indigence, sows the seed of future.

'The system to be sought for is a system which shall make the supply of means keep pace with that of wants, and that by a pre-established chain of causes and effects, whatever be the

Consistency may be another point to be considered. While the Bill, with this clause in it for the *surcharging* of Common Land is depending, another Bill is depending, or at least in contemplation, the professed and sole object of which is the *diminution* of the *quantity* of the Land thus circumstanced.[1] The principle in the one case is, that the existence of Land in this state is *advantageous* to the community: in the other case, that it is *dis*advantageous. An option between these two conflicting measures seems very requisite to be made.

The tendency of the *General Enclosure Bill* seems alike favourable to the interests of the *rich* and *poor*. It does, perhaps without much seeking, all that *can* be done of what appears to be *sought* to be done by the *present Bill*. Its most direct and prominent object is the giving facility to the *wealthy* towards the augmentation of their wealth. But at the same instant it effects with equal certainty an object of still higher account, the raising of the wages of labour in favour of a class among the poor, and that the only one, in which the wages of labour have been shown to be in many cases unavoidably inadequate to the purpose of maintenance.

I confine myself to the Cow, because the Cow alone occupies the foreground. There are indeed other animals in the offscape: but the species is undiscernible: and I have already plunged but too deep into the details of husbandry.[2] I should incline to the *Sow*: as absorbing less capital, as giving more exercise to industry, and affording a resource less precarious in its nature: but there are those that will tell

rapidity or anomality of the progression. This problem has been the object of a good deal of reflection, embracing the subject in all its relations and dependencies, and the solution of it is supposed to be effected.'

There is no evidence that Bentham intended to include these paragraphs in the final text.

[1] The General Enclosure Bill, introduced into the House of Commons on 23 February 1796 by Sir John Sinclair (1754–1835), MP for Caithness 1780–4, 1790–6, 1802–6, 1807–11, Lostwithiel 1784–90, and Petersfield 1796–1802, President of the Board of Agriculture 1793–8, 1806–13, sought to enable landowners to enclose, divide, and cultivate waste and common land without the trouble and expense of a private Act of Parliament. The Bill made considerable progress in the House of Commons, but was supported only half-heartedly by Pitt in the face of opposition from both the Church and the legal profession, and was lost when the House was dissolved on 20 May 1796. A similar Bill, reintroduced into the House of Commons by Sinclair on 9 May 1797, was passed on 7 July 1797, but was rejected by the House of Lords on second reading. After a further unsuccessful attempt in 1798, a much diluted measure finally became law in 1801 as 'An Act for consolidating in one Act certain Provisions usually inserted in Acts of Inclosure; and for facilitating the Mode of proving the several Facts usually required on the passing of such Acts' (41 Geo. III, c.109).

[2] In the margin of one of the copies of the text (see UC cliii. 462), Bentham has noted at this point: 'This is only to show that no limitations of the application of the money can answer their intended purpose, and that they can only do mischief. This was argued, in the unpublished book entitled *Panopticon*, against the Old Penitentiary Act.' See *Panopticon: or, The Inspection-House*, i. 50–9 (Bowring, iv. 49–51), where Bentham argued against the restrictions laid down in 19 Geo. III, c.74 (1779) on choice of trades to be undertaken by prisoners. *Panopticon: or, The Inspection-House* had been first printed in Dublin and London in 1791, and circulated privately.

me, that in the government of the *Dairy* swine are dependent upon Cows: nor will the expansive beneficence of the author of this clause content itself with so inferior a resource. Looking beyond the sow, I see every thing or nothing. A rattle-snake is *'yielding profit'* to the hand that shows it, and no *common* is surcharged by it.[1]

The resource presented by a *loom* is a *permanent* one: it *may* be *rendered* an *unfluctuating* one. A loom eats nothing: is not apt to be sick: does not sink in value by under-feeding: has no legs to be driven away upon, and is not exposed to sudden death .... The working of one loom need not hinder the working of another ....

A loom is but one example of a machine.... But, protesting against the donation of capital in any shape, protesting against the *principle*, I will not dive further into the mode.[a]

CHAPTER FIVE
RELIEF-EXTENSION, OR OPULENCE-RELIEF CLAUSE[2]

We come now to the *Relief-Extension* clause:—or *Opulence-Relief* clause. In reading the above system of donations, a natural, and, I am apt to think, a scarcely avoidable, supposition, is, that it is for the

[a] Some five-and-twenty years ago I remember seeing in Elmsley's window, fresh imported from Germany, a book with this title—*Means of Enriching States*, by an Aulic Counsellor to one of the Margraves.[3] It was seized with an avidity proportioned to the importance of the discovery. *The secret had been tried, and had succeeded.* It consisted in stocking your farms *well* with Cows.—But the difficulty was to *get* the Cows.

[1] Bentham is probably alluding to advertisements which appeared in the press in the latter part of 1796 headed 'Wonderful production of nature. *Just arrived from America.* A Live Rattle Snake.' The curious were invited to showings of the snake at an admission fee of one shilling, or sixpence for servants and children. See, for instance, *Oracle and Public Advertiser*, 25 October 1796; and *Morning Post and Fashionable World*, 4 November 1796.

[2] 'And be it further Enacted, That no Person shall be excluded from Parochial Relief, or any of the Benefits of this Act, on account of the Possession of any Tenement or Cottage, with its Appurtenances, whatever may be his or her Estate or Interest therein, or on Account of any other visible Property, not exceeding in the Whole the Value of Thirty Pounds, which shall consist either of Tools or Implements of Trade, or Household Furniture, Wearing Apparel, or other Necessaries suitable to the Condition of such Poor Person; but that every Person in the Situation and Condition before mentioned, and not able from other Circumstances, to maintain him or herself, or his or her Family, shall be entitled to all the Benefits of this Act, as fully and effectually as if such Person was not possessed of such Property as aforesaid.' See *Commons Sessional Papers of the Eighteenth Century*, ciii. 165.

[3] Peter Elmsley (1736–1802), bookseller. Bentham is probably referring to the writings of Sigmund Franz von Hasslang (1740–1803), Bavarian diplomat, but the work with the title mentioned, *Abhandlung von der Bereicherung eines Landes durch den Flor, und die Aufnahme des Handlungs-Geschäftes mittelst nützlicher Fabricken, und Manufacturen, welche an dem Höchster-freulichen Namensfeste*, Munich, 1773, in fact discusses the cotton industry. It is more likely that Bentham had in mind Hasslang's work on the influence of agriculture on the happiness of states, *Abhandlung von dem Einflusse eines wohlgeordneten Ackerbaues in die Glückseligkeit eines Staats*, Munich, 1771.

indigent, and the indigent *only*, that they could have been intended: whether they are *really* confined to the indigent, whether the field opened to them be not so ample as to comprize what, in the instance of people of the *working* class, may be stiled *opulence*, is a question on which it will rest with the reader to decide.

The proviso is '*that no person shall be excluded from Parochial relief, or any of the benefits of this Act, on account of the possession of any tenement or cottage, with its appurtenances, whatever may be his or her estate or interest therein, or on account of any visible property, not exceeding in the whole the value of thirty pounds, which shall consist either of tools or implements of trade, or household furniture, wearing apparel, or other necessaries suitable to the condition of such poor person*'.

Under these words, what seems tolerably clear is—that a man may be worth thirty pounds of '*visible* property' (to say nothing of concealed or non-apparent property), and still come with as irrecusable a claim to the above list of pensions and donations, as if he had not property to the value of a single farthing:—what to myself (I must confess) *is not* by any means clear, is—to what *higher* pitch the opulence may rise, without striking the proprietor's name out of the book of indigence.

Let us consider it, in the first place, as *not* exceeding the thirty pounds. A document naturally enough to be wished for, by one who would wish to form a just estimate of the effect of this clause, is a comparative statement, setting forth, on one hand the number, actual or probable, of individuals whose property *rises* to the *height* of this *minimum*, on the other hand the number of those whose property *falls short* of it. Should the indigent list, as thus defined, be found, as I cannot help vehemently suspecting it would be found, to include a vast majority of the good people of England, 5, 6, or 7 millions for example, the system of *Home-Provision*, as thus explained, would be found (I much fear) to amount to a plan for *throwing the parish upon the parish*.

The nature of the process by which the *mass* of national wealth is *accumulated* was (I doubt [not]) not sufficiently considered in the formation of this Bill. To judge by *this* clause in particular, it looks as if certain hypotheses, somewhat of kin to the following, had been assumed:—that Wealth is the gift of nature, not the fruit of industry:—that every human creature, male as well as female, comes into the world with £30 in its pocket:—and that this sum is what it belongs to the government to guarantee to every man the undiminished possession of, against misfortune and improvidence, as it guarantees to him the possession of his two arms and his two legs against the attacks of injury.

The apprehension of doing undesigned injustice to the intentions of the Bill, is an apprehension that pursues me through the whole tenor of it: but really I know of no means of coming at the *intention* of an instrument, unless it be through the *words*. Judging of it then from the words, thirty pounds is the mass of property, which *every* person *without exception* may, it is supposed, possess, and yet be in a state of indigence: in a state so low, so much below the natural state of man in this respect, as to require a defalcation—a *forced* defalcation—to be made from the property of *others*, for the purpose of raising him to that lowest level, below which the state of man ought not to be suffered to continue. This *minimum*, the guarantee we see thus made of it, is not confined to *families collectively taken*—it is not confined to heads of families—it extends to *every* human being whatsoever—*having* a family or *having none*—living *under the head of a family*, or living *by himself*. A head of a family may have his *own* thirty pounds—he may have ten children, each possessed of its thirty pounds—£330 may be the amount of the family estate—and all the while the family be hanging on the parish.

If consistency be an object in legislation, it may be worth while to compare this intended *Pauper-relief* Act with the *Pauper Law Relief Act* of Geo. I.,[1] which exempts, or seeks to exempt, persons whose circumstances fall below a certain pitch of supposed indigence, from the sort of general outlawry in which that proportion of the people stands involved, against which the weight of the expence, howsoever heaped together, has shut the doors of justice. £5 is the sum assigned in *that* case: £30 (not to say £300) is the sum assigned in the present case. According to this proportion, it will be matter of some curiosity to observe, how much easier a man will find it to get *other* people's money than his *own*: and how many there will be in possession of the *former* faculty, while they stand excluded from the *latter*.

That it is by no means clear, that under this clause the specified sum of £30 is the highest which a man might retain of his *own*, while he was maintained at the charge of *others*, has been already hinted: and the more closely the clause is scrutinized into, the greater the difficulty of ascertaining the real limit will appear.

My doubt is, in the first place, whether, in the computation of the visible property, the moveable is, or is not, to be added to the immoveable:—whether the words '*in the whole*' are meant to be confined to the '*other visible property*', or to be extended to the

[1] The Act in question was in fact 2 Geo. II, c.28 (1729), which empowered judges to assign counsel and appoint attornies who would be obliged to defend, without charging a fee, any person imprisoned on a charge relating to the excise who swore an affidavit to the effect 'that he is not worth, over and above his wearing Apparel, the Sum of five Pounds'.

'*tenement or cottage*'. That they were *not* meant to extend to the tenement or cottage, and that therefore a man may, without standing excluded from any of these bounties, be possessed of £30 worth of visible *moveable* property, in addition to the fee simple of a cottage, may be thus argued.

From the word 'appurtenances', it may be inferred that the cottage may have more or less land annexed to it, especially when it is considered that, under the *Cow-money clause*, it is intended a man shall keep a Cow. But, even without land, 40s., or even 50s. a year, is but an ordinary rent, but an ordinary annual value, for a cottage: and as in the instance of immoveable property, small concerns (coming within the reach of a greater proportion of purchasers) are apt to sell for more years' purchase than *large* ones, 20 years' purchase upon 40s. a year, that is £40, may be taken for rather a low estimate. Allow but the £30 for the value of the dwelling, this will not leave a farthing for the furniture, tools, cloaths, and other necessaries. It does not seem to accord with the views manifested in this Bill, that the property of the cottage a man lives in, altogether unaccompanied with every other kind of necessary, should debar him altogether from a part in the bounty so liberally bestowed, when the annual value of the House is no more than the ordinary rent of the abodes of the *worst paid* class of labourers.

But, if the value of the cottage is *not* to be *included* in the £30, it is then to be *added* to the £30: £40 worth of immoveable property, upon a low estimate, may thus be added to £30 of moveable property, and the possessor not excluded by this £70 from the right of obtaining Cows, supplemental wages, and pensions, on the plea of indigence.

The pursuit of the strict rules of grammar might raise up other difficulties in abundance, on the ground of this *single* clause: but this specimen may suffice.

The more conspicuous the spirit of humanity that shines through every clause, the more sincerely one regrets to see it in such straits. What seems to have led the author of the Bill into the difficulty in the present instance, is the often painted, and always melancholy, picture, of an industrious family reduced by blameless misfortune from a state of comfort and independence, to a state, perhaps of *confinement*, at any rate of wretched dependence, from which a small relief, if administered in time, might have rescued them: dependence on scanty, and, in point of quantity, precarious charity: confinement to the idleness, and discomfort, and ignominy of an ordinary Poor-house—*Come in and give up your all, or stay out and starve*: such is the harsh, though unavoidable alternative, presented by Poor-house charity in the existing state of things: an alternative the more excruciating, when the *all* thus to be given up for a mess of pottage[1] is, as it sometimes will be found to be, the sad remnant of fallen opulence, sufficient at one time to place its possessor above the necessity of manual labour.

This is one of the many cases in which compassion is as laudable as, in a feeling heart, it is unavoidable. But compassion is one thing, relief, efficacious and unmischievous relief, a very different thing: the one may be *always* bestowed, and in any quantity: the other should never be attempted to be bestowed, especially at the *expence* of the community, and upon a scale extending over the *whole* community, till after the strictest and most comprehensive inquiry, whether the undertaking lies within the sphere of practicability, and whether the removal of the evil, if possible, be not inseparably connected with the introduction of still heavier and more extensive, though less prominent and immediate, evils. We commiserate *Darius*, we commiserate *Lear*:[2]—but it is not in the power of *Parishes* to give Kingdoms. To banish not only *indigence* but *dependence*, it would be necessary to banish not only *misfortune* but *improvidence*. To guarantee to every man a *subsistence* is *practicable*, and *practiced*: to guarantee to every man the perpetuity of his station in the scale of opulence would be altogether *im*practicable, the very *attempt mischievous*, and *perseverance, ruinous*.

What seems not to have been sufficiently considered is, that betwixt the *absolute refusal of relief*, and the exaction of the *absolute surrender of permanent property* in return for *transient relief*, there is a *medium*—which is, the granting the relief, to the extent of the property, on the footing of a *loan*. This middle course, the only feasible one, the only unpernicious one, *is* practicable, for it is *practiced*. A mode of practising it, and practising it without expence, forms one leading feature of the *Large-Establishment* system, in the shape and magnitude herein above supposed.[3]

Meantime, although it were regarded as an established point, that Cottages, any more than Kingdoms, can not, by the hand of *public* charity, be secured against decline, let us not conclude that the misfortune is altogether beyond the reach of remedy. It is in this quarter of the region of distress that we may behold a part of the extensive field in which *private* charity, as well as domestic friendship, may exercise and feast itself without prejudice either to *industry* or *justice*. Nor let it remain unheeded, that so long as there is *property*,

[1] An allusion to Esau's sale of his birthright to Jacob: see Genesis 25: 29–34.

[2] Darius III (*c.*380–330 BC), King of Persia from 336 BC, lost his kingdom to Alexander the Great (356–323 BC), King of Macedonia from 336 BC, before being murdered by disaffected followers. For King Lear see p. 6 n. above.

[3] See 'Collateral Uses derivable from a system of Industry Houses', pp. 73–6 above.

or even established *character*, with but a *tolerable* prospect of *repayment*, if no assisting hand can be obtained, either from domestic connection, from neighbourly intimacy, from special patronage, or from wide-spreading though private charity, the presumption, though not absolutely conclusive, is at any rate not weak, that not only extraordinary merit, but ordinary good conduct, has been wanting, and that the pangs of falling prosperity are but the just and *useful* punishment of improbity or improvidence.

CHAPTER SIX
APPRENTICESHIP CLAUSE[1]

By this clause every child of a certain description is declared to be *intitled* to be put out as an apprentice or hired servant with certain advantages, not specified.

This clause being but a *frame*, and the picture not hung up (but why not hung up?), a criticism on the picture may appear chargeable with precipitation.

Reasoning under this disadvantage, what occurs to me on the subject is as follows—

In the matter of apprenticeship, three points may be distinguished: the legal subjection during the continuance of the relation thus contracted:—the exclusive privileges attached to that relation by a particular law, in a numerous class of instances:—and the comparative rank in life it confers in a still more extensive class of instances, as compared with the condition of an unprivileged hand occupied in ordinary labour.

1. Of the utility of the legal subordination my conception is the same with that which stands apparent on the face of the Bill. Conceiving of it as calculated to operate in a certain degree as a *source of instruction*, and, in a yet higher degree, in the still more important function of a *security for good behaviour*, every accession to the number of the instances of its existence presents itself to me in the shape of a public benefit.

2. As an instrument of monopoly in trade, I know of but one opinion relative to it: oppression, in the instance of the individuals

[1] 'And be it further Enacted, That every Child who shall at any Time have received Employment by virtue of this Act, and shall obtain a Certificate of his or her good Behaviour, during the Time of such Employment, according to the Form No. | | in the Schedule hereunto annexed, shall be entitled to be put out as Apprentices, or hired Servants, in the Manner, and with such Advantages, as are specified in the Forms No. | | and No. | | in the Schedule annexed, or to that or the like Effect.' See *Commons Sessional Papers of the Eighteenth Century*, ciii. 174.

excluded from the occupation thus engrossed:—excessive earnings, in the instance of the partakers of the privilege:—whence the alternation of penury with excessive plenty, in a rank of life where sensual excesses supply the demand for occupation in a vacant mind:—enhancement of prices in every article connected with the subject matter of the monopoly:—such appear to be the consequences to the several parties interested—individuals excluded—individuals favoured—and the community at large.

3. As a source of exaltation, so long as the superiority it confers is confined to that which is the natural result of the improvement and augmentation of natural powers, the situation presents nothing but what appears to be the unavoidable consequence of any such improvement—a consequence beneficial perhaps, in some points of view—pernicious in none: but so far from being either necessary or useful, it seems pernicious, to wit on the accounts just mentioned, if in any respect it be the result of coercive law. But, this property is what may be attributed to it in either of two cases: if a man be excluded from the situation by a direct prohibition to engage in it: or if public money be employ'd to pay a man for helping a boy to get into it: in the one case, the coercion takes the shape of restraint; in the other, of compulsion: in the one case, the monopoly is a direct one; in the other case an indirect one, produced by an addition made to the general mass of taxes.

Considered as confined to the lowest, that is the *lowest-paid*, class of working hands, I see an uncertain chance of improvement, in point of morality, to be bought at a certain expence. I am not disposed to under-rate morality—but in the present instance I am not able to obtain what to me appears a requisite assurance that the chance purchased will be worth the price. In the instance of each apprentice thus taken in consideration of so much public money, there are two points, in regard to each of which I want sufficient means of assuring myself: that an apprentice would not have been taken without the money, and that the portion of morality paid for by the money will be worth it. In the first case, the business seems exposed to the following dilemma: if the fee be small, it will not be sufficient to turn the scale: it will produce no more apprenticeships than would have been produced without it: if it be large, it opens a proportionably wide door to profusion and abuse. In the second case, the fee, large or small, holds out to improper hands a temptation, which without it does not exist. He who takes the apprentice without money, can propose [to] himself no other advantage than what is to be derived from the service (and thence the instruction, employment and morality of the apprentice). He who takes the apprentice with and for money, may have employment for the money without having any for the apprentice.

All this while, let it not be forgotten—there are existing laws under which the taking of apprentices in the employment in question, without money, is compellable, and which are more or less enforced.[1] Hence a source of complaint, and jealousy, and injustice, real or imagined, while one man in a parish is compelled to do for nothing that which another man is paid for.

Under these doubts, though really they are but doubts with regard to the value of the purchase, the *vis inertiae*[2] would, I think, if it depended on me, be sufficient to keep the money in my pocket: especially while there are so many purchases to be made with it, the value of which is beyond doubt: among which the purchase of so much security in respect of property, as is constituted by the leaving the money in the pockets of the contributors, ought not to be forgotten.

To judge of the clear benefit resulting from this or that application of a sum of money, *compare* the gross benefit with the mischief of the most mischievous tax: for instance, the taxes operating in prohibition of justice. This test, I consider as a principle in finance, and it is, for aught I know, a new one. Of the expenditure that will abide it, the utility ought, it should seem, to stand pretty clear of doubt.

If the occupations into which it is proposed to force hands by public money be of the extra-paid class, the question of the expediency of the provision presents itself under a different shape. If the individual thus forced into apprenticeship in this class by dint of the fee, be one more than would have existed in the class without the fee, this addition, as far as its influence extends, goes to the opening of the monopoly, and tends accordingly, though in a microscopic degree, to the diminution of the mischiefs of it. If, on the contrary, he makes no addition to the number of the sharers in the monopoly, but only occupies the place of some other individual, who, but for the fee would have occupied it, then no effect is produced, but the throwing away of so much money.

Reasons for apprehending that the addition, upon the whole, may

[1] By 43 Eliz. I, c.2 (1601), churchwardens or overseers, with the assent of two Justices of the Peace, were empowered to bind children whose parents were unable to support them as aprentices 'where they shall see convenient'. The provision was repeated by 8 & 9 Will. III, c.30 (1697), which also provided, 'That where any poor Children shall be appointed to be bound Apprentices, pursuant to the said Act, the Person or Persons, to whom they are so appointed to be bound, shall receive and provide for them, according to the Indenture signed and confirmed by the two Justices of the Peace', and rendered the refusal to receive such an apprentice punishable by a fine of ten pounds for each offence. Further legislative refinements were made by 18 Geo. III, c.47 (1778) and 32 Geo. III, c.57 (1792).

[2] i.e. 'the force of inactivity'.

be rather apparent than real, are not wanting. This expedient, for forcing hands into the class of employment in question, has no tendency to increase the quantity of employment in the species of employments belonging to that class: its real tendency is of the opposite kind:—to send hands to the employment, not employment to the hands. But, taking the whole mass of employment of the species in question in the lump, while the demand for the work, for the produce of the employment, is not increased, no fresh hand can be forced in to the employment in question without forcibly keeping an equal number out of it.

The individual who would thus have been kept out, in any instance, by force of the bounty, the individual who, but for this bounty, would have been received into this extra-paid and superior class, is more likely to be one belonging to that same class, than one belonging to the inferior class. For no reason can be assigned why the superior class should not, in the way of natural encrease, be as capable of keeping up its numbers as the inferior class: and the offspring of the superior class has better opportunity of an introduction into his own superior class, than is likely to fall to the share of a member of the inferior class. If this then be the case, it seems to follow that as often as the child of the labourer or impoverished tradesman thus receives a lift, the consequence is that some other child of a tradesman, by finding the condition of the tradesman shut against him, must receive a fall.

Let me not be understood as pleading in favour of any forced system of casts: all I contend for is a system of equal and unexpensive liberty. Where no partitions are set up or kept up by the hand of law, good fortune and merit on the one hand, ill fortune and improvidence on the other, will keep up every facility of mixture which the interests of *hope* and *industry* can require.

The conclusion seems to be, that in this instance as in the other, no advantage is near so certain as the expence.

If the bargain, natural advantages and bounty taken together, be worth making, candidates for a share in it are not likely, on either part, on the part of Master or Apprentice, to be wanting. The individuals it lies open to are 'every child who shall *at any time* have received employment by virtue of this Act, and shall obtain a certificate of his or her good behaviour during the time of such employment, according to the Form No. ( ) in the schedule . . . annexed'. If then five pound, for example, be the apprentice fee, five pound may be the price of a day's service. While a Patron exists in whose judgment a douceur of this kind, whatever be the amount of it, may be worth the acceptance of an obsequious Client, howsoever it be with other manufactures, the manufacture of apprentices need not stagnate. Whether an article of this sort be worth throwing into any such fund as the Election fund,[1] is a question that must wait its answer till the picture above spoken of has been inserted into its as yet vacant frame.

The facility thus provided might have been regarded and intended in either of two lights: in the light of a distinction or reward, or in the light of a general benefit. In either case it may have been regarded as an instrument of morality: though exercising its operation at a different period in the two cases: in the one case, at the period previous to the apprentice-contract, acting upon the individuals concerned in the quality of candidates for the advantage: in the other case, at the period subsequent to the formation of the contract, acting upon them in the quality of persons subject to the powers conferred by the contract.

In which of these two lights it was considered is what I do not clearly see: the question is not altogether immaterial: for the purposes do not exactly harmonize: at least in the quantity of expence they call for, there is a considerable difference: in the one way the magnitude of the benefit is in the direct ratio, in the other in the inverse ratio, of the numbers on whom it is conferred. The facility of admission being so great, it follows that unless the facility were the result of inadvertence, the direct benefit, rather than the indirect one resulting from the operation of the distinction in the character of a reward, [was][2] the object principally in view: for the certificate of general good behaviour, being a matter of course, unless where some very flagrant and special instance of ill-behaviour can be proved, can scarcely be considered as drawing any other than an accidental line.

The difference between the quantity of money that may be requisite in the two cases is such as may render this point, minute as it may seem, worth settling. Call the average number of Parishes in an *Union*, five: this, for the 10,000 Parishes in England (Wales included), makes 2000 unions. Annual average number of boys and girls capable of being put out apprentices in each union suppose, ten: 20,000 in the whole. Annual total amount of Apprentice Fees at £5, £100,000: at £10, £200,000.

Suppose distinction and reward to be the object, rather than immediate and universal benefit, then instead of the five, one

[1] The Treasury habitually assisted in the financing of government candidates in elections, using secret service funds drawn from the King's private account, expenditure from which was not accountable to Parliament. Bentham's point is that the judicious disbursement of apprenticeship bounties could be used as an additional source of patronage to gain votes for government candidates.

[2] MS 'were'.

apprenticeship for each sex in the course of the year will (let us say) suffice: in this way the expence would be reduced from the £100,000 or the £200,000, to £20,000 or £40,000.

The refusal of the certificate will be a stigma: fewer or more, what is to become of the individuals thus stigmatized?—Who will give them employment? Who will have anything to do with them that can help it, they who have been thus pronounced unfit either for apprenticeship or service? These, for whose good behaviour security is most wanted, these are they in whose instance the security is refused. Once more, what should we say to that *Pharmacopoeia*,[1] which for those who are in good health should provide *aurum potabile*,[2] and other expensive drugs, but for those who are sick, nothing, whether *found* sick, or *made* sick by it, as here?

The considerations thus brought under review will be apt to appear minute, and somewhat vague: but that the utility of a provision should turn upon considerations to which those epithets are applicable, and that too a provision by which public money is scattered without being weighed or counted, is not that a circumstance sufficient of itself to present the provision in a questionable shape?

Is the supposition above made of the ten apprenticeable youths per union to be regarded as a reasonable one? This is but one out of a multitude of arithmetical questions, all equally pertinent, which may have presented themselves in crowds under this, as well as every other, of the clauses touched upon. For all such questions, I must confess myself to have but one answer—utter ignorance.—The blame, however, if I may venture to say as much, lies not with this humble comment, but with the text, which, while heaping up so immense a mass of bounty, knows nothing of the numbers of those by the number of which that bounty is to be multiplied, nor consequently of the expence.[3]

[1] i.e. 'Book of medicines'.

[2] i.e. 'drinkable gold', a suspension of particles of gold in volatile oil, used as a cordial.

[3] Bentham originally intended to insert at this point the following remarks, at UC cliii. 428, on the effect of Pitt's Bill on the operation of the law of settlements: 'That which is not only reasonable but carries its reason on the face of it, needs no comment: and with this remark I dismiss the three sections (§§ 5, 6, & 7) which relate to settlements.

'One word only.—The laying a few Parishes together to compose a District diminishes, as far as the union extends, the danger and expence of litigation on the question of settlement: and this seems to be among the benefits in view. But the superiority of the Large-Establishment system over the Small-Establishment system in this particular is as the magnitude of the districts in the one case is to the magnitude of the Districts in the other: or in other words, inversely as the multitude. If in the [one] case the District[s] are ten times as large as in the other, the Large-Establishment system would, in this particular, be ten times as good as the one intended by the Bill.'

For the sections of the Bill to which Bentham refers see *Commons Sessional Papers of the Eighteenth Century*, ciii. 165.

CHAPTER SEVEN
EXPENCE BEFORE SUPPLY

But for all those bounties a fund, it may be said, is provided—and that an ample one: the fund arising from the whole stock of as yet unemploy'd ability, now for the first time to be turned to use.

To this I feel myself compelled to make two answers: one is, that the system of employment will produce nothing: another is, that at the time these draughts are made on it, it will not have been so much as brought into existence.

On the first of these points I shall have occasion to touch separately:[1] the other is more particularly to the purpose here.

The impediments to the coincidence in point of time between profit [and] relief employment, and thence all profit to be drawn from employment on the one hand, and relief and the distribution of the bounties on the other, are these:—

1st. That the distribution of the bounties is to commence at the very commencement of the Act, viz: on the 10th of July in the present year.[2] But (by § 10)[3] it is not till after the 29th of September following, that the first link in the long and complicated chain of causes and effects, on which the commencement of the means of employment is to depend, can be begun upon: a work which, where it finds willingness on the part of the great variety of persons whose co-operation is necessary, can scarcely do otherwise than take up years: and which in those districts in which there is any want of such necessary co-operation, will, so long as such want continues, not be begun upon at all.

Mean time the distribution of the bounties is running on full swing: for immediately *'from and after the commencement of the Act'* as aforesaid, it begins as soon as 'any Father' is 'entitled to the benefit thereof according to the provisions hereinafter-mentioned.'[4]

For the purpose of entitling a man to the benefit of the Act there is nothing any where specified, from the beginning to the end of the act, unless it be the qualification of wanting relief, the qualification spoken of in the 16th section:[5] nor yet to disentitle a man, but the act of refusing employment or instruction, the disqualification

[1] Bentham does not appear to have drafted a discussion of this issue for inclusion in this essay. However, his reference may be to the comparison between the profitability of employment in small and large establishments in 'Pauper Systems Compared', pp. 184–5 above.

[2] i.e. 1797. See *Commons Sessional Papers of the Eighteenth Century*, ciii. 193.

[3] See ibid., 167.

[4] See ibid., 164. There are minor inaccuracies in the rendering of the passage.

[5] See ibid., 171.

specified in §21.[1] On such refusal a man is made to stand precluded not only from the 'benefit of the Act', in short, not at all from the benefit of the Act by name, but from relief itself, from every species and degree of relief whatever.

But till a man has made the refusal in question the disqualification does not take place, and till tender shall have been made refusal can not have taken place. But tender of employment can not be made till the means of employment exist, that is, till the establishment for affording employment has been set upon its legs. The only assignable disqualification then can not take place, in any district, till nobody can say when: while the only assignable qualification, the wanting relief, exists in itself already: and exists in the shape of a qualification under the Act, as soon as the Act itself comes into existence: that is, on the 10th of July next.

[2nd.] Another circumstance that stands in the way of the coincidence between disbursement and supply is the impracticability of performing the condition on which the bounties are made to depend: viz: the acceptance of the instruction and employment: an impracticability that will be found to take place in many cases. That the children are not to be lodged in the schools in which they are to work seems pretty clear: that the adults are to be lodged in any such common habitation does not appear. The districts, though not upon anything like what I have termed the Large-Establishment scale, will, so it seems, consist of a considerable number of parishes laid together. The greater the number of parishes [that] may come to be laid together, the greater the distance between the school, wheresoever situated, and the houses of the greatest part of the number of the scholars, who are to be of all ages from 5 years upwards. Here then comes a sort of dilemma. If the district is small, the expence necessitated by those parts of the establishment of which the expence is incapable of diminution (Manager's House—Manager's Salary—Ware-house—Ware-house keeper's salary—and so forth) will be so great as to cut out every possible profit that could be made out of the earnings of so small a number of working hands. If the district is large, whether from the proportion of the time consumed in the journey to and fro, or from inability to perform it, or inability on the part of the Parents or Managers to enforce the performance of it, the labour of a greater part of the intended scholars will be out of the reach of being collected.

The exclusion thus put by distance in the instance of infancy is coextensive, it is evident, with the inability, whatever be the source.

[1] See ibid., 174.

But wherever the performance of the condition meant to be annexed to the *receipt* of the bounty is, or is deemed, impracticable, and that without any supposed fault on the part of the intended object of the bounty, the condition sinks of course, and the bounty stands alone.

After what has been said on topics of so much more weight, a hint of this topic will probably be deemed sufficient: to follow it up and apply it in the way of calculation would be matter of some difficulty, and occupy more space than can be allotted to it here.

3rd. A third reason is that from the mode of payment a large proportion of the hands must be fully paid, while their work is worth nothing, so far from being worth enough to pay for its own charges. The mode of payment prescribed, and prescribed without limitation or exception, is payment by the piece. I do not say that this is not the best mode of payment in many instances, perhaps in by far the greatest number of instances. But in some instances it is impracticable, because the degree of advance made in quantity of work done is unsusceptible of mensuration: in other instances it is apt to be disadvantageous, on account of the difficulty of ascertaining the goodness and quality of what is done, and in proportion to the difficulty of ascertaining quality, will be the certainty of bad work: and work may in many instances be so bad, as not only to afford no profit, but to destroy the value of the materials. But in all instances, there will be a certain period, the period of instruction, during which with all imaginable diligence and honesty on the part of the workmen, the work will be worth nothing. But while the work is acquiring its value, the workman must live, and will be made to live. Accordingly, by § 19, should the sum allotted for the 'support and maintenance' of the family, whether under the name of wages, earnings or allowances, prove deficient, the deficiency is to be made up.[1] Payment by time instead of the piece will there take place, in the first instance through necessity: and, having taken root, the interest which idleness will give a man in its continuance will render it not very easy to eradicate. I do not dispute but that it may in most instances be eradicated, under a proper system of regulations and inducements adapted to the nature of the case: all I mean is, that I see no great probability of the growth of any such good economy, under the auspices, or rather the rod, of a system of legislation which after enacting that, practicable or not practicable, the working hands, that they may do so much the more work, shall be paid according to what they do, enacts in the same breath that they shall go on for an

[1] See ibid., 172–3.

indefinite time receiving whatsoever may be thought proper to allow them under the name of maintenance, although what they do shall continue to be worth nothing: and this without so much as the inconvenience of quitting their own homes.

Had the application been left to individual discretion, a hint, so good as a hint, and coming from so high a quarter, might, as a hint, have been of no small use: but, the precept being thus peremptory and unbending, its tendency would rather be to bring the principle into discredit, than to promote the use of it.

The grant of this indulgence is limited, it is true, to the case of a man's being 'a person entitled to the benefit of this Act',[1] but how this point is to be ascertained is a matter which I am much inclined to believe will be found beyond the comprehension of those who are to judge—it most certainly is beyond mine:—and, in the mean time, the family must not be left to starve.

CHAPTER EIGHT
HOME PROVISION: CONCLUSION

Thus stands the account of the mischief, the apprehension of which has been excited by the view of the destined amendments to the existing system of *Out-allowances*. What possible good can arise out of those amendments in any instance, I must confess myself unable to conceive. Under the existing system, indigence does actually receive *such*, and, taken in the lump, at least as *much*, relief as is *necessary*. The plan of *distribution* remaining untouched, what was the task that *could* remain for these amendments? Either to do *nothing*, or to administer relief where it is *not* necessary.

Against the system of *Out-allowances*, setting aside those objections on the score of economy and industry, which have been urged by way of objection to the system itself,[2] the great and general complaint, as far as I have had occasion to observe, is—not that it *is insufficient*, but that it *should* be *necessary*:—that so many industrious hands should be continually *thrown upon the Parish* (as the phrase is), who ought (as certainly they ought, *if possible*) to be enabled to maintain themselves without being subjected to any such degrading obligation. But the *keeping* them *from* thus falling upon the parish, is what the Bill neither *does*, nor so much as *professes* to do: so far from it, as far as it does anything, it *throws* them there: it throws

[1] See ibid., 172.
[2] See 'Pauper Systems Compared', Ch. IV, pp. 154–83 above.

them in greater *numbers*: it throws them with greater weight. The *grievance* is that the industrious *poor* should be so liable to be *indigent*: that *independent* hands should be so liable to fall into *dependence*. Whether the *cure* be possible, is another question: but be that as it may, the Bill does not attempt it.

What I had all along been considering as a point understood to have been established, was the inferiority of the wages of *husbandry* as compared with those of other labour.—What I had in consequence understood to have been the object of the Bill, as far as *Out-allowances* are concerned, was to confine the bounty to the class which presents this title to it. But unless the benefit of the *Cow-money* clause be thus confined (which it can only be by *forced implication*, for there are no words of *limitation* to perform the office), I can see no branch of the bounty to which *working hands* in *general* have not a claim as irrecusable: *all* are equally *invited*, none *excepted*: manufacturers, handicraftsmen, even domestic servants.

If *necessity* (it may be said) be *equal, no matter what the class*. True, but in any other class necessity is *not* equal: at the same time that in *every* class, *the full rate or wages*, whatever be the *class* and whatever be the *rate*, the full rate or *wages*, be the work worth *any* thing or *nothing*, is guaranteed by the Bill to every hand without exception, which, with ever so little good-will or fruit, will set itself to work. The bounties it provides are bestowed (for anything that appears) not only upon the *worst-paid* classes, but upon *every better-paid* class, up to the *best* paid: and upon these, the *quantum* of the bounty it bestows is not a quantity limited by that which is *necessary*, but a *superfluous* quantity, rising up to the height of the highest pitch of superfluity which the earnings of the *best-paid* class are capable of furnishing. It relieves them—not according to the measure of their necessities, nor according to the quantity of relief they really want: but according to the '*full rate or wages usually given*'—*given* one knows not to *whom*, unless to *them*—in a word, according to the means they have had in their hands of placing *themselves* above the necessity and above the bounty.[1]

Under this Act, if the words of it be a sufficient warrant, the Vice-Roy or Ambassador, reduced by super annuation or other causes, from so many thousand a year to half the number, may come to the Parish of St James,[2] and addressing himself to (I don't know very well

[1] In the margin, Bentham has noted at this point: 'This to relieve the driness of the discussion, in case of publication.' Chadwick's edition omits the remainder of this Chapter.

[2] Bentham's hypothetically indigent ambassador would apply for relief to the parish of St James, Westminster, since it contained within its boundaries St James's Palace, the principal Royal residence in London, to the Court of which foreign ambassadors were accredited.

who) say, in the words of §2,[1] *Here am I, a 'poor person', for I have nothing of my own, and at this present moment I am 'not able to earn the full rate or wages usually given in' (this) 'Parish . . . to persons of my class.'—Take notice then, that I have 'contracted and agreed' with (such an one, suppose the Minister) 'to work' in the manner I have been used to work, and at an 'inferior rate or wages': viz: at half price:—which said inferior rate or wages is 'not sufficient for the maintenance and support of' (me, the said) 'poor person, with' (my) 'family', in as much as I am not able thereat to support myself and my said family in the same manner as I did support myself and them, when, being 'able to earn', I did earn 'my said full rate or wages'. 'Make up' therefore, to me, the said poor person, 'such deficiency . . . out of the rates made for the relief of the Poor', and that 'without compelling' (me, the said) 'poor person' to be employ'd in any manner under 'the authority of this Act'.*—Let me not be mistaken—I do not mean to say, that this notice, how well soever settled by Counsel, and how nicely soever adjusted to the tenor of the Act, would be successful—I do not mean to say that either the intended Warden of the Poor, or the two intended Justices of the District, would concurr in making an order upon the Parish to 'make up this deficiency'.[2] I do not mean to say, but that even supposing any such application made, something would interpose to save the Country from the success of it. But that something is general reason, the expounder and corrector-general of this and other acts: not any particular reason that could present itself to a man in the course of any search he might make for reasons, among '*the benefits of this Act*'.

[1] See *Commons Sessional Papers of the Eighteenth Century*, ciii. 164.

[2] For the roles of the proposed Wardens of the Poor, and of Justices of the Peace, see ibid., ciii. 167, 170–1.

APPENDIX TO OBSERVATIONS ON THE POOR BILL

ESSAY ON THE QUESTION, WHO ARE THE PERSONS FOR WHOM THE SEVERAL BOUNTIES PROVIDED BY THIS BILL ARE INTENDED?

When a mass of bounties so various and so vast in its magnitude, and in its apparent burthensomeness to the public thus formidable, is provided, a natural question is, who are the persons who are destined to partake of it? This answer, I must confess myself unable to give: had I been able, it is the answer I should have given, not this essay, or rather, as the question would have been needless, the question would not have been started.

The benefits of the Act:—This word *benefit*, as employ'd with reference either to the Act in general, or to some part of its contents, occurs (either in the singular or the plural) in 9 sections: in five of them (1, 2, 3, 19, 20)[1] in the singular: on which five occasions such of the effects of the Act as are considered as being of a beneficial nature are considered as comprizing one entire, undistributed, undiversified mass of benefit: in two others in the plural (§4, 17):[2] and in the two remaining ones the benefits spoken of are spoken of as resulting from particular provisions therein mentioned, and not as resulting from the entire body of the Act.[3] In neither of these two sections therefore, is to be found *the* benefit of the Act.

The first time the phrase occurs, which is at the very opening of the Act, a sort of promise is made to give the elucidation here sought:—'*any father entitled to the benefit thereof* (viz: of this Act) 'according to the provisions hereinafter mentioned'. The accomplishment of this promise, if it be one, is unfortunately forgotten. Provisions there are enough which speak of this benefit, which allude to it, which, like this provision, speak of it as indicated, but there are none that indicate it.

Had the task been mine, having settled with myself who the persons were whom it was my view to benefit, my first care, I must

[1] See *Commons Sessional Papers of the Eighteenth Century*, ciii. 164, 172, 173.

[2] See ibid., 165, 172.

[3] i.e. §§ 8 and 9 (according to Bentham's enumeration), in which particular benefits arising from subscription to parochial funds for the 'Relief of Sick, Infirm and Aged Subscribers' are introduced. See ibid., 166, 167.

confess, would have been either to have found, or to have made for them, a *name*. This name, and no other, is the name I should have called them by, as often as occasion recurred for speaking of them.

Having fixed a name for them, little should I think of discarding that name for any circumlocution, much less a circumlocution so enigmatical as that contained in the words, *the persons entitled to the benefit of this Act*: a designation of this sort may be pleasant in a riddle, but whether pleasant or no, is certainly not profitable in an Act of Parliament.

If it seemed to me a fit occasion for a riddle, I should at any rate think it incumbent on me to give the key to it: and how little soever conformable it be to the usage of riddles, the key should go along with the riddle in the first instance. I would say, *the persons entitled to the benefits of this Act—are such and such persons*. But it is evident how much better it would be to say simply *such and such persons*—at once, leaving the benefit to speak for itself. To state who the persons are, who are intended to be *bound* by an Act, is matter of equal necessity and facility: because when new obligations are meant to be imposed, if nobody is bound by them, nothing is done. But to state and discriminate who the parties intended to reap benefit from it are, is perhaps never a necessary task, and would seldom be found an altogether easy one. The very existence of benefit in any shape may be problematical: and supposing it ever so undisputed, the wider it is in its extent, and the more pregnant in its consequences, the more difficult it is to trace. Should the benefits of this Act prove such as [the] benevolence of the authors of it have been expecting to see, and such as the author of this essay on it would most sincerely wish to see, result from it, the more rich the benefit, the more difficult to discriminate. Of this Act it might truly be said, as is said by the poet of I forget what else,

Aeque pauperibus prodest, locupletibus aeque,
Aeque neglectum pueris senibusque nocebit.[1]

So diversified, so extensive, so lasting, so prolific the benefit, it would be difficult to say whether rich or poor, old or young, possessed the largest share in it.

But little as it seems necessary in the text of an Act to make mention of its benefits, what seems indispensably necessary is to state, and that in the clearest terms, who the persons are who may be considered as entitled to such of the benefits, or supposed benefits, of it, for which there is any thing to be done: in other words, how a man may know whether he is or is not entitled to whatever he may be

[1] i.e. 'It benefits the poor and rich equally, but, if neglected, will harm equally boys and old men.' Horace, *Epistulae*, I. i. 25–6. Horace's subject here is philosophy.

disposed to claim under the notion of its being a benefit: and consequently, if, for that purpose, any thing is to be done, what that is which becomes thus requisite to be done.

The necessity of being thus explicit will appear the more indispensable, when it is considered out of what description of persons those for whom the most immediate and largest share of the benefit appears to be intended are to come: the class of all others to and for whom information of every kind is most wanting, and most necessary. In such mouths a most natural, and surely not altogether an unreasonable, question is—If the writer knew which of us he meant, why did he not tell us: and if he did not, could he expect that we should?

Whichever situation in life be considered, that of the Poor, who are to receive the main benefit of the Act, or that of the Magistrates, who are to dispense them, of this, as of every other Act, all and singular the benefits depend upon its being understood; and its being understood depends upon its being intelligible.[1]

Whatever is given in such abundance by the Act—Head-money for children—supplemental wages—Cow-money—is expressly confined to those who are entitled to the benefit of the Act.—Who are they? I don't know. Where is it said who the persons are that are to be considered as entitled to this benefit? No where.

In five of the sections, as hath been already instanced (§§ 1, 2, 3, 19, and 20), the beneficial result of the Act is spoken of as one undiversified, indivisible, or at least undivided, mass: and then the persons in question, the persons alluded to, are spoken of as entitled to *it*, *videlicet* to the whole of it, insomuch that [anybody][2] who has any part of it can have, or at least is intended to have, the whole of it.

In two other sections (4 and 17) benefits in a countless, or at least uncounted, multitude, are spoken of as flowing from the Act: and now a man may have some of them without having others. By §4, 'no person shall be excluded from Parochial Relief or any of the benefits of this Act', on any of the accounts there specified.

In §17, employment and instruction, two most desirable benefits, are destined for certain persons. But, to come in for his share of those

[1] In the margin, Bentham has noted in pencil at this point: 'Reference to Abbot's Report.' Bentham's step-brother Charles Abbot (1757–1829), first Baron Colchester, MP for Helston 1795–1802, Woodstock 1802–6, and Oxford University 1806–16, Speaker of the House of Commons 1802–16, was a consistent critic of both the lack of clarity in statute law, and the failure to disseminate new statutes sufficiently widely. In 1796 he drafted the reports of two Select Committees which investigated the issue. See 'Report from the Committee upon Temporary Laws, Expired or Expiring', *Commons Sessional Papers of the Eighteenth Century*, xcviii. 307–412; and 'Report from the Committee for Promulgation of the Statutes', ibid., cv. 1–71.

[2] MS 'nobody'.

benefits, it is expressly provided that a man must be 'entitled to all the benefits of this Act'. Before he can have these two, or either of them, he must make out his title to every other. Before he can obtain the smallest particle either of employment or of instruction, this vacant, this neglected, this altogether unfurnished mind, must possess a degree of instruction—I fear to state it—a degree of instruction—with respect I speak it, such as does not appear to be possessed by even the legislator himself—a degree of instruction (I much fear) beyond the power of any man that lives—he must have comprehended the Act —comprehended it in all its parts—traced it through all its consequences—investigated and catalogued without exception '*all*' its '*benefits*': and this as an operation preliminary to the enquiry whether it be his good fortune to be *entitled* to any the smallest share in so rich a prize.

I will endeavour, to the best of my ability, to make out this list of benefits.

I. Articles which in themselves would appear to be intitled to be comprehended under the list of benefits, though not expressly characterized by that appellation, but rather expressly excluded out of it.

1. Benefit of receiving head-money for supernumerary children.

2. Benefit of receiving supplemental wages at the public charge, in addition to such wages as individuals will give.

3. Benefit of receiving Cow-money, money to buy a cow (§3). This however, is expressly mentioned as neither constituting the benefit of the Act, nor so much as any part of it: since the being 'entitled to the benefit of the Act' is mentioned as one of two conditions which must concurr in order to give a man his chance for receiving this species of bounty. The same observation is equally applicable to both these other clauses.[1]

In one sentence our inquirer might be tempted, for a moment, to fancy himself on the point of possessing the object of his wishes,—but disappointment would be the termination of his hopes. In Section [4],[2] after providing that 'no person shall be excluded from parochial relief, or any of the benefits of this Act, on account of the possession of' certain property therein described, it goes on and adds, 'but that every person in the situation and condition before-mentioned, and not able, from other circumstances, to maintain him or herself, or his

[1] No manuscript source has been identified for the following two paragraphs, although the pagination of the manuscript indicates that one folio is missing here. The gap is filled by the corresponding section of the printed text at Bowring, viii. 458–9.

[2] Bowring '68'. According to Bentham's usual numeration of the sections of the Bill in this text, the reference should be to §4. For further details see the Editorial Introduction, pp. xlii, xlviii–xlix above.

or her family, shall be entitled to all the benefits of this Act'. Absolutely? If this be the case, then, the problem is solved. Is it then *absolutely*? Alas! no: but *comparatively* only: § [4]:[1] 'as fully and effectually as if such person was not possessed of such property as aforesaid'. Property, or no property, so the property be not above the mark, a man will be equally entitled to these benefits: but still the question remains unanswered, *What must I do to be entitled*?

If this concluding reference had not put out the light which for a moment appeared to show itself, the introductory one would have done the business,—would have been sufficient to render the obscurity equally impenetrable. To be entitled to all the benefits of the Act, it is necessary a man should be in the situation and condition above-mentioned: and in travelling over the three preceding sections to see what that situation and condition is, it appears to be the situation and condition of him who is entitled to the benefit of the Act.

Who then, is a person entitled to the benefit of the Act?—Who?—Why a person entitled to the benefit of the Act.—What is to accommodate?—Answer—'to accommodate'.

In one place (§16)[2] a juncture of time is mentioned in which a certain class of persons therein specified may receive certain advantages therein specified, and a sort of person therein also specified '*shall*' (it is said) with the consent of two other persons therein specified ('two Justices of the Peace in the district') 'take order for' the administering to them these benefits. This, though something like light, and the most like it of any thing that is to be found in the whole compass of the Bill, is not, however, *that* light. The advantages there spoken of are special in their nature, the description of them being contained in, and confined within, that single clause; neither are they spoken of under the name of *benefits*. They are benefits, if to be instructed and employ'd and maintained are benefits: but they are not therein spoken of under the name of benefits: much less as the benefits comprizing *the* benefit of the Act.

If they were, we might cry with Hiero, εὕρηκα![3] we have found it: for to these benefits the statement of the title is as explicit as could be wished.—Who are the persons intitled to these benefits?—Answer.—*All persons wanting relief*? If these were the same persons as those alluded to by the expression, any person entitled to the benefit of this Act, with what advantage, in point of brevity as well as

[1] Bowring '68'.

[2] See *Commons Sessional Papers of the Eighteenth Century*, ciii. 171.

[3] The ejaculation was actually made by Archimedes (*c.*287–211 or 212 BC), mathematician and inventor, on discovering a method for determining the proportions of gold and silver in a wreath made for his employer Hieron II, King of Syracuse 271–216 BC: see Vitruvius, *De architectura*, IX. pref. 9–12.

precision, might this former expression have been substituted to this latter!

If then it be really the case, that by the words '*every person entitled to the benefit of this Act*' is meant neither more nor less than '*all persons wanting relief*', the secret is out, the mystery is unravelled. But if all persons wanting relief are really to be admitted, why are they to be thus muffled up?—why all this pains to put them in masquerade? Throwing away the surplusage about *benefits* and *titles*, why not say simply—*all persons wanting relief*—or even more simply still—*all persons*:—since, if relief is to be had in such quantity and on such terms, it may be difficult to say who it is that will *not* be '*wanting*' it. The adjunct *wanting relief*, may be the more easily spared, and added to the heap of discarded surplusage, inasmuch as if a man wants relief it is intended he should have it, and if he does not want it, he won't ask for it.

Unfortunately we are still at sea. The hope of a safe landing, though after so much buffeting from clause to clause, is still delirious. The want of relief is not sufficient to entitle a man to the benefit after all: for in the 19th section, the case is put of a man wanting relief, and it is, if not expressly stated, yet necessarily implied, that a man may want relief and yet not be a person entitled to the benefit of the Act—'in case' (says the Bill) 'the person wanting relief shall be a person entitled to the benefit of the Act': so that now we are as much at a loss as ever.

Moreover, in §3, the being 'entitled to the benefit of this Act' is one thing, and the 'wanting relief', another: for both conditions, it is there expressly provided, must concurr, before a man can be admitted to receive the bounty there provided—viz: money to buy a Cow.

Another thing to be collected from that same clause concerning the benefit of this Act, is that the receiving money to buy a cow neither constitutes the benefit of this Act, nor so much as any part of it: since the benefit of this Act is a distinct thing which a man must absolutely be entitled to, before he can take his chance for receiving this money for the purchase of a Cow.

Should any one, in the course of his pursuit after the true intent and meaning of the Bill, be led to take any such stride as from that 16th section to the 21st, he will there find it written, that in regard to Relief, if that be the benefit, or among the benefits of the Act, in order to be entitled to this benefit, for such it will not be denied to be, whatever becomes of the benefits of the Act, it is not altogether sufficient to be a person, nor yet to be a person wanting relief, for that there is a sort of person who, be his want what it may, is not to be considered as 'entitled to any relief from any Parish or united Parishes': 'No poor person, who shall refuse any work offered to him or her under the authority of this Act, which he or she is able to execute, or to receive instructions for executing such work, or who shall not, on request made, according to the directions of this Act, permit all or any [of his or her Family, who capable of working, or of being instructed to work, and cannot otherwise support themselves, to be employed under the Authority of this Act, shall be entitled to any Relief from any Parish or United Parishes.]'[1]

Here, if any where, one should have thought, was the place for speaking of the *benefits of this Act*: in which case, if we had not learnt in direct terms who *are* entitled to those benefits, we should at any rate have learnt who are *not*, which is one step towards it. Instead of that, we have the very general and extensive word *relief*. Thus much the mention of the word *relief* will be apt to do—to bring to a man's view the benefits of the Act: but this is raising doubts, not solving them. Is *relief* precisely the same thing with the benefit of this Act? It covers a great deal of the same ground certainly: but, if tried in the geometrical way of superposition, we should find it, in some parts of its extent perhaps, over-hanging the benefit, in other parts, at any rate, falling short of it. The advantage of being put out apprentice can hardly be termed relief, and yet this, as often as the Act has more benefits than one belonging to it, is surely one of the number. Instruction, if instruction be a benefit, is another of the benefits of the Act: yet this is certainly not comprehended under relief, for it is expressly put in contradistinction to it: no instruction, no relief: and so with regard to employment. Besides, in the Cow-money clause (§3), as we have already seen, the benefit of the Act is one thing, relief another thing: the benefit is a sort of thing he must be *entitled to*, the relief a sort of thing he must *want*, in order to take his chance for getting the Cow-money. Yet, while it falls thus short of the full measure of the benefit or benefits of the Act, it extends, or at least wears the appearance of extending, beyond the Act, for it extends to whatever relief can be found to be provided by all the existing Poor Laws put together. This sends our inquirer upon the hunt over the whole body of the Poor Laws, for the purpose of picking up the several crumbs of relief, the several constituent elements of the general mass of relief provided by those laws, for the purpose of taking measure of the aggregate, and comparing it with the aggregate mass of the benefit or benefits provided by this Act.

It may here occurr, that in proportion as the difficulty of finding out receivers for the bounty encreases, the above-mentioned arguments

[1] The portion of this extract from the Bill left incomplete in Bentham's MS is supplied from *Commons Sessional Papers of the Eighteenth Century*, ciii. 174.

that turn upon the alarming magnitude of the bounty will be losing their force: and that if, after all, no claimants for it should be to be found, the mischief of which so much has been said in this comment will be as ideal as the benefit of which so much is said in the Act. But, not to mention that the benefit of a Parliamentary revisal is yet in store, let it not be thought that because the Draftsman has not perfectly succeeded in finding out the objects of his bounty, there will not be others who will find them for him. Hunger, says the proverb, will break through stone walls: it will find still less difficulty in making its way through mists: and whether it be from humanity (for humanity, howsoever misguided, ought not to be robbed of its name), whether it be from humanity, or from some of the less pure motives above hinted at, the efforts of those who may conceive themselves invited to put in their claim to the bounty, are not likely to pass every where unseconded, by the corresponding efforts of those who may conceive themselves called upon to dispense it. In a word, the obscurity may plague the Justice, but it will not prevent the mischief. Obscurity is the source of every mischief: it is a remedy to none.

The conclusion is that I am altogether ignorant who they are who [are][1] entitled to the benefits of the Act—nor how to find them: after drawing thus amply upon my own industry and the reader's patience, I can not tell—I really do not know: and in this I am altogether positive. Should any body else be more fortunate—it is not easy to be more diligent—any one of the million, for example, who have been set a-gaping for these benefits—let him accept my congratulations and my envy—I envy him and give him joy.

A defect, if defect there be, a defect which though in stile, goes to the vitals of the matter, and taints it through its whole extent, might it seemed, if any thing could, engage the reader to committ himself for a few paces into the muddy and thorny roads of verbal criticism.

With this single dissertation, the reader is now let off: [to] want of the necessary time, despair of attention, despair of fruit, he is indebted for his dismission, even at this late period: certainly not, by any means, to any want of matter in the text. | |[2] is the number of pages here bestowed on it, considered in this technical point of view. Considered in the same point of view, the same or thereabouts is the number of volumes that might have been bestowed on it, and with about equal cause. The same is about the number of volumes that may at any time be bestowed with about equal cause, on almost every law, while the form in which laws have hitherto been expressed

[1] MS 'is'.
[2] This essay occupies sixteen pages of MS.

continues to be observed. Reform in the mode of composing the laws, reform in the laws considered as laws, is reform in the instrument—in the very instrument by which all the work is done. Reform in the Poor Laws, or in any other branch of the laws, is but a reform in this or that branch of the work. *Sedeant sedeant*—Let them sit and sit and sit again.—Bad instruments can make nothing but bad works. Reform in the instrument, how remote soever in apparent use, is, in fact, prior in importance and in necessity to any reform that can be conceived to be called for in this or that corner of the field of legislative labour.

APPENDICES

APPENDIX A
NEIGHBOUR'S-FARE PRINCIPLE DEFENDED[1]

This rule may be stated as the Sheet-Anchor of public charity. Without it no tolerable economy, no real justice. Above a million a year at least depends upon it: and the pecuniary part is perhaps the smallest part of its importance. It may be termed the *Magna Charta*[2] of national charity. No rational economy can rationally be expected from that manager, who, when the matter has been thus stated to him, should persist in stating it as a grievance, and as a matter of charge against the Management of an Industy House, that a man had rather live out of it than in it.

Applied to treatment, as to any thing else, *good* and *bad* are terms of comparison: they suppose a standard. In the present instance, every

[1] The Neighbour's-Fare Principle is defined as follows at UC cliii. 189: 'Considering that the rendering the condition of those who are maintained at the charge of others more eligible than the condition of those who are maintained at their own charge is not consistent, either with justice, or with general industry, or with public economy, and that the gratification, derived from the several means of sustenance, depends not upon the expensiveness of them, but upon habit, expectation, and the health of mind and body with which the use of them is attended, let it be treasured up, as a maxim not to be departed from, that while the quantity of every article is sufficient in every instance to ward off every uneasiness resulting from the want of a sufficiency to supply for the demands of nature, the quality, so it be not prejudicial to health, shall in every instance be of the least *expensive* kind that can any where be found. In a word, *Charity maintenance*, maintenance at the charge of others, *should not, on the whole or in any article, be made more expensive than self-maintenance.*

'Names for the corresponding principle—1. Home-fare principle. 2. Equal-treatment principle.'

See also 'Outline of a Work entitled Pauper Management Improved', *Annals of Agriculture*, xxx (1798), 156 (Bowring, viii. 384): 'Charity-maintenance—maintenance at the expense of others, should not be made more desirable than *self*-maintenance.'

Bentham cancelled the following text at UC cliii. 174, which was originally intended to precede the material reproduced below: 'Who is my neighbour? Neither the question nor this application of it is new. It is with a view to charity that it was started on the first occasion on which we hear of it. It is with a view to the same purpose that I repeat it. It was then started and answered, with a view to the choice of objects for relief. It is now started for the first time that I know of with any determinate view, with a view to the quantum of relief: with a view to the construction of a standard for dealing out the dole of charity.

'The burthensome Poor are the spoilt children of the rich.

'The self-maintaining Poor are forced to cater for themselves.

'The burthensome poor have the affluent for their caterers.

'The standard by which their portion is measured out to them is a standard laid down by affluence.'

For 'the first occasion on which we hear of it' see Luke 10: 29–37.

[2] The 'Great Charter' of liberties conceded on 19 June 1215 by King John (1167?-1216), King of England from 1199.

thing depends upon the choice of the standard: upon the assumption of the only true one. The standard presented by economy, justice, industry, morality and genuine humanity, is in this case the fare of the lowest paid, and therefore worst-faring class of independent, self-maintaining, self-subsisting hands.

The standard set up by misadvised humanity, deaf to the laws of justice, economy, industry, morality and genuine humanity, is a sort of vague, obscure image of the sort of treatment which a man himself conceives he could put up with in such a case. No standard was ever more erroneous: none more variable: the error varies and rises, as the individual rises in rank and opulence. The Poor have one standard, the substantial Tradesman another: but even that of the substantial Tradesman (the ordinary judge in causes of this sort) is much too high. The true standard would be that which would be set by a Jury of a man's peers, just able to maintain themselves, each man by the sweat of his own brow, and none of them exposed, (if so the case would be) to fall into that situation in which it would be a man's interest to wish the fare as luxurious as possible. When I say peers, I do not mean Peers of the Realm, but peers of the pauper whose claim is before the Court. To be judged by his own true peers, by his own next neighbours in rank and fortune, such in this case is man's right, such ought to be his obligation. Unfortunately for the country, unfortunately for the interests of justice, industry, economy, temperance, morality and genuine humanity, it is by Peers of the Realm, and their neighbours in Council, or in Parliament, that the standard comes to be fixed.

Being favoured by a friend in office with the accounts of an establishment of considerable magnitude for the maintenenace of persons of this, the lowest class, I was looking over some of the articles with him, while the soup I was about to give him was putting upon the table. Pre-apprized of his opinion, that the expenditure, taken in the lump, was such as might bear retrenchment, I thought myself tolerably secure from disagreement, in pointing out by way of confirmation, as an example tolerably in point, an annual charge for pepper to the amount of £18 in money. *Pepper* (said my guest)—*after a pause for reflection—Pepper,* repeated he, and with genuine not affected gravity—No I would not grudge them a little pepper. *Pepper, let me tell you,* (the approach of the soup was by that time become sensible) *pepper is no uncomfortable thing for a poor man to have a little of in his soup.* I had begun starting the question how our forefathers managed, in regard to soup and comfort, before the communication was opened with the pepper countries:—but the soup, with or without pepper in it, was by that time on the table. My Right Honourable and truly honourable friend, who is little expecting to see the laws of hospitality thus violated in his person, will in consideration of the occasion and the motive, smile forgiveness upon this treachery; on similar consideration, the traitor, in the name of the country, forgives *him*.

I took care to specify freedom from interest in the event as a qualification not to be dispensed with on the part of the Jury above supposed: and certainly not without good cause.

Some years ago, a tenant of mine, a Butcher in a country town, and who happened at the time to be Overseer came to me in a state of alarm: the inhabitants of the Work-house, so called *ut lucus a non lucendo*,[1] were up in arms against him—For what offence?—*Feeding them with sheep's heads*. What, according to the conception of those gentlemen in low life, was the proper destination of the species of offal in question, whether to feed the men that worked for them, or to feed dogs with, or Scotch members, the informant did not state. A few days after, I happened to be dining with a gentleman of the latter description. At the dinner—a first dinner and an excellent one, what I stuck to as the best dish was this very species of offal, which had given so much offence to my fellow parishioners. From the documents communicated by the Rev. Mr Davies, I have the satisfaction of finding that, even in England, there are parts of the country in which there are persons to whom the dish is no such object of aversion.[2] But the people he speaks of are hard-working people—labourers in husbandry, who think themselves but too happy if now and then, once in a week or so, they can, at their own expence, give themselves such a treat. For all this, I would not answer for their not proscribing sheep's heads with as much rigour as the Butcher's boarders did, were they in quality of the Jury above supposed, to have to sit for the purpose of settling the dinner for the first day of their dining with the Parish.

I forget on what occasion, a friend of mine, on giving me an account of an exhibition of Charity Children,[3] was mentioning as a treat that was given to them in the course of it, a portion of Cake and Wine. On the mention of this part of the celebrity, observations, not altogether of the approving cast, could not but present themselves.—A new and dangerous taste infused into those children of indigence, a taste for luxuries unsuited to their condition, and high above their reach.—Hence, within themselves, the seeds sown of the sense of privation, regret and discontent—towards their superiors in opulence, and

[1] i.e. 'as a grove from not being light': see Quintilian, *Institutio Oratoria*, I. vi. 34. The pun is lost in translation, but Bentham is referring to the naming of objects from qualities they do not possess, his point being that in the workhouse very little work was done.

[2] See *Case of Labourers in Husbandry*, p. 12, where the account of meat consumed by a labouring family includes 'a few sheep's heads'.

[3] See p. 139 n. above.

those in authority over them—the seeds of jealousy, envy and ill-will.—Fermented liquors, the grand source of vice and misery—more prolific than all others put together, held up to their longing eyes, and held up by authority, in the character of a bounty and a reward: held up a chosen instrument of gratification, a fit object of desire. In a word, this glass of wine, I could not but confess—it showed as the cup of Circe to my eyes.[1] I hazarded but little of all this: for it was soon apparent that that little was too much. The right of the dear sweet innocents had been proclaimed a heavenly one. It was a fond Father I had to deal with—with a fond Mother by his side: and one of them had no aversion to a glass of wine. Benevolence and beneficence were familiar to my friend: theoretical and rigid enquiries into the principles of public economy were not equally so. I was glad to make my escape as quick as I could: with the loss of I know not how much of my character for common humanity and good nature.

The substantial Tradesman's standard is not the true standard (I have said) any more than the Peer's. Witness the Dietary of the Shrewsbury House of Industry:[2] one of the very best patterns of economy in this line that the country has hitherto afforded. Three meals a day: while men in the highest ranks of life content themselves with *two*, not to mention that Homer's heroes grew into heroes upon *one*. Butcher's meat five days out of the seven: their providitors, conceiving by the force of sympathy the hardship it must be to fast (for not eating Butcher's meat is fasting) even for a single day, nor yet unmindful of the propriety of keeping up a distinction between the receivers and dispensers of public charity, ordained a two days' fast by way of compromise. Five days out of the seven, Butchers meat at the expence of others: while one day in the week so many are glad to get it, and not one day in the week so many are able to get it, of those whose existence rests on no other fund than the produce of their own labour. Such has been the course of these too generous dispensers of their own, as well as the public, bounty, boasting, and in print, of their economy for these ten years: boasting with almost universal applause, and certainly, when comparisons are made, not without prodigious reason. But such economy would require yet to undergo no inconsiderable change, to bring it to the standard either of true economy or justice.

Is not this enough? Turn then to the union of St George's and St Andrew's. There is a place to look to if you would wish to see Paupers living in high state: there you may see to what lengths that

[1] In classical mythology, Circe, a sorceress who lived on the island of Aeaea, transformed Odysseus's crew into swine by administering to them a magic potion.

[2] See the 'Bill of Fare' in Wood, *Some Account of the Shrewsbury House of Industry*, p. 73.

indulgence *may* run and *does* run where the true and only true standard, the neighbour's-fare principle, is lost sight of.

Charity-fed idlers refusing the cloaths provided for them[1]—why?—because they have cloaths of their own that they like better.

Charity-fed idlers with a train of servants to attend them: beggary and impudence enthroned: industry and independence ministering unto them. *Maitre d'hotel* under the name of Master: Housekeeper, under the name of Mistress, each a servant to themselves:[2] Treasurer to the Household:[3] Cobbler at a salary: Taylor and mantua-maker paid by the piece: Yeoman of the pantry, or pantry Assistant, one: House-maids, 5: *Valet de Chambre* one, under the official stile of Barber: House-Porters, one: Hall-keeper, one: Cook, one: Scullion, one, Messenger, one, Butlers two: stiled cellarmen, one Upper and one Under: Coal-Cellar man, one: Laundry Maids, 12: Chairmen, one or more pair, number not mentioned: All at separate salaries.[4] Each with their appropriate functions: each one adept in that branch of Servant Hall science, which in technical language is called the *knowledge of his place*: each, like a Senator in his Curule Chair,[5] nobly determined not to budge an inch from it. The House Maid who cleans the Committee Room disdaining the Hall: the Hall-cleaner the Kitchen: the Kitchen-cleaner the Pantry: the Pantry-cleaner the Stairs.

The officer who, upon occasion, turns a cock,[6] or is supposed to turn it, is a separate officer: the Footmen either want science for it, or disdain it. How the spit can have been turned must be left to conjecture. I find no officer to turn it. Perhaps, like the King's, it required a Member of Parliament:[7] and the last incumbent had lately accepted the Chiltern Hundreds.[8]

[1] See *Rules, Orders, and Regulations, for the Government of the Workhouse belonging to that Part of the Parish of St. Andrew, Holborn, which lies above the bars, In the County of Middlesex, and the Parish of St. George The Martyr, In the said County*, [London], 1791, p. 36n.: 'Many Paupers in the House will not wear Parish clothing'.

[2] The salaries of the Master and Matron are set out at ibid., p. 42; for the attendance of a maid on each see ibid., p. 43.

[3] Possibly the Clerk of the House: see ibid., p. 42.

[4] See the tables of '*Money Paid by the Master to the Nurses and others* Monthly, which is charged in his weekly Bills' and '*Money paid by the Master* Weekly, *and charged in his Bills*', ibid., pp. 43–4.

[5] A folding stool, inlaid with ivory, which was the chair of office of the higher magistrates of ancient Rome.

[6] See *Rules, Orders, and Regulations*, p. 44.

[7] Bentham's source for this allusion was Edmund Burke's speech in the House of Commons on 11 February 1780, presenting a 'Plan for the better Security of the Independence of Parliament and the Oeconomical Reformation of the Civil and Other Establishments'. Burke relates that the efforts of William Talbot (1710–82), first Earl Talbot, Lord Steward of the Household, to reduce the charges associated with the King's kitchen had foundered '*because the turnspit in the king's kitchen was a member of parliament*'. See *The Writings and Speeches of Edmund Burke*, vol. iii, ed. W.M. Elofson, Oxford, 1996, p. 512. No Member of Parliament who held the office of turnspit in the King's kitchen has been identified.

[8] Appointment to the sinecure Stewardship of the Hundreds of Stoke, Desborough, and

Reading over the Red book of the establishment,[1] I am led to fancy myself in Hindostan: where no man who smokes [a] pipe ever lights one: one man fills a pipe, and another lights it. No: I am at the Opera: where four Footmen with laced liveries form part of the establishment of a Woodcutter. In Hindostan, gentlemen have indeed more servants than are quite necesary: but beggars, at any rate, do without them. In Hindostan, the world is somewhat broad at the base: but it is not turned topsy-turvy, as at St George's and St Andrew's.

Oakhum Overlooker one: Oakhum Boiler as many.[2] These appear to be a sort of Chief Justices in Eyre[3] or Chancellors of the Dutchy:[4] for though there is an Oakhum-picking and boiling Room with Coals for it,[5] and perhaps it should seem in order that there may be coals for it, of Oakhum picked or boiled no traces are to be found. For to him who boils Oakhum, it is too much to look at it.

Not a trace of work done by any body, unless it be at I know not what silk Mills: and there, instead of being paid for the work, the establishment pays for doing it: 50 children at the silk Mills with 2^{s} a week each.[6] 50 young gentlemen and ladies whose work is worth 2^{s} less than nothing.

Reader—Oh, but you mistake the matter. These servants are not hired on purpose: they are the Paupers themselves in masquerade: what you take seriously is but a jest.

Burnham in Buckinghamshire, a non-political office of profit under the Crown, was used as a means of resignation from the House of Commons.

[1] An allusion to the *Royal Kalendar*, first published in 1767, which listed holders of Royal appointments.

[2] See *Rules, Orders, and Regulations*, p. 43.

[3] The Royal forests possessed their own peculiar body of law and peculiar courts from the time of William I (1027?-87), King of England from 1066. From 1238, two Chief Justices in Eyre of the Forests were appointed with jurisdiction over forest courts north and south of the Trent respectively, but discharged their duties through deputies so that the offices had largely become sinecures by the end of the fourteenth century. Bentham's immediate source was Burke's speech on economical reform of 11 February 1780, where Burke described the offices as 'a useless piece of antiquity' and proposed their abolition: see *The Writings and Speeches of Edmund Burke*, iii. 507. The offices were eventually abolished by 57 Geo. III, c.61 (1817).

[4] The Chancellor of the Duchy of Lancaster was an official of the Crown as owner of the Duchy, who formally presided over the Duchy Court of Lancaster, which had jurisdiction over all matters of equity relating to lands held of the Crown in the right of the Duchy, and matters of revenue relating to the Duchy. In presenting the Chancellor of the Duchy as the holder of an expensive sinecure, Bentham again draws on Burke's speech on economical reform of 11 February 1780, which attacks the replication of the administrative and juridical functions of the Crown in the separate jurisdictions of the Principality of Wales, the Duchies of Lancaster and Cornwall, and the Counties Palatinate of Chester and Lancaster, on the ground that 'every one of these principalities has the apparatus of a kingdom, for the jurisdiction over a few private estates; and the formality and charge of the exchequer of Great Britain, for collecting the rents of a country squire': see *The Writings and Speeches of Edmund Burke*, iii. 498.

[5] See *Rules, Orders, and Regulations*, p. 33.

[6] See the table of '*The Number of Poor supported and relieved Yearly*', ibid., p. 40.

Author. If it be, it is a very expensive one: for jest or earnest, they are all paid. What they were before they were put into these stations does not seem of very material account: the material thing is that they occupy them and are paid for it: paid for it exclusive of their board, or their board wages. Thomas what are you about?—Nothing, Sir. John what are you doing?—Helping Thomas. This dialogue gives the classification. The Johns and the Thomases, divide this flock: the bulk of it Thomases: the flower of it Johns.

To some eyes this may seem profusion: no—it is frugality. Under this management, even under this management, the yearly expence per head, if the statement given of it is to be believed, (common expenses excluded) is but £6:[1] in St Martin's it is more than double.[a]

I must be allowed to mention on this occasion—though not on any but with respect—the Revd Mr Davies. I have much to answer for to that gentleman. Valuable, highly valuable, are the documents for which we are indebted to him. He gave them for one purpose: I have employed them for a very different—perhaps an opposite one. How insufficient the pittance, cries he, which the industrious, the self-subsisting poor, have to live upon. More therefore, says he, ought to be given to them. Agreed, say I, as far as it is possible without prejudice to justice or to industry. But is it possible? Meantime I draw this conclusion—more, at any rate, ought not to be given to the burthensome poor—to those who, with or without necessity casting themselves upon the public charity, are subsisted not at their own, but at the public charge. Thus different therefore, at least, though certainly not repugnant, are our views. His, to augment the portion of the self-subsisting poor: mine, to reduce to that standard the portion of allowance made to the burthensome poor. Observe then the difference between the two schemes: the one, wearing the face of indulgence on the surface of it: but at bottom neither useful nor practicable: the other, wearing rigour on the surface: but at bottom, practicable, useful, and the only one that is so.

It is with difficulty the self-subsisting Poor can get even small Beer: many even go without it altogether. Well: and are they at all the worse for the want of it? In point of health and strength at least, no man can say yes, they are. Very well then, if it is not necessary to the self-maintaining and labouring class, still less is it to the burthensome and

[a] £12.10.6. Eden II. 444.[2] The difference of the years is indeed to be taken into the account. In St George's and St Andrew's 1790: in St Martin's a year composed of the years 1795 & 1796.

---

[1] See ibid., p. 37.
[2] i.e. Eden, *The State of the Poor*, ii. 444.

unlabouring class of Poor. Out then with small beer: away with it. Strike the article of small beer then out of the list of fancied necessaries.

What then, cries my humane and reverend antagonist—would you grudge a man, an industrious man—a man who strains every nerve to procure subsistence for himself and family—would you grudge such a man a little small beer?[1] Heaven forbid—nor Tokay neither if it were possible for him to have it, I mean for all to have it who have the same pretensions to it: and to have it without prejudice either to his own industry, or to the justice due to others.—But it is possible? There lies the difficulty: the unfortunate, insuperable difficulty. Of those to whom you were to give the small beer, one would sell it to buy strong—another would make ground from it to plant[?] his inquiry in to get bread by, or meat to add to it: both will proportionally shrink from work, or at least make others shrink from it by their example.

Ask Mr Wood else: to whom the public are indebted for the elegant and instructive account of the Shrewsbury House of Industry.[2] House-room is more necessary than beer:—What, would you grudge a man a house to shelter from the inclemency of the weather? Do so and he comes upon the Parish to be fed as well as housed. This argument had rendered it a practice to pay rents (p. 16. ed. 1791). What was the consequence? In how many instances was this rent allowance consistent with either economy, industry or justice?—Not '*in one out of fifty*':[3] and the proof of it was, that when the rent allowance was taken away, instead of throwing themselves on public charity for either food or lodging, they lived more comfortably than before. Economy, now becoming necessary to them, was found practicable, and practised.

Ye who feel the error, blush not to avow it. It scarce needs, it scarce admitts of, an apology. Few errors have been more pernicious in their effects: none ever was, none ever can be more respectable in its source. It flows from the most amiable of the virtues, and religion herself has spread her mouth over it.

The golden rule—*whatsoever ye would that man do unto you, that do ye also unto them*,[4] a mine not less of prudence than of beneficence, is a mine of which the stores have scarce yet been sufficiently explored. Yet even this, with all its expansion, has its bounds. Justice confines it in one quarter: Possibility, in another. The Sheriff ought not to

[1] See *Case of Labourers in Husbandry*, p. 38: 'Time was when *small beer* was reckoned one of the necesaries of life, even in poor families: and it seems to have been designed by Providence for the common drink of the people of this country, being deemed a preservative against some of its worst diseases.'

[2] i.e. Wood, *Some Account of the Shrewsbury House of Industry*.

[3] ibid., p. 16.

[4] See Matthew 7: 12; Luke 6: 31.

change places with the Assassin: the Peer can not feed Paupers as he would wish, or as he has been wont to feed himself. Both pray for, both ought to have secured to them, their daily bread:[1] but the daily bread of the one is not the daily bread of the other.

But Generous as the error is, it is not less truly an error, nor a less pernicious one: nor of this, any more than other errors, let it be forgotten—that 'when the error has been pointed out, the apology is gone'.

This is not, this surely is not of the number of those transgressions, against which guiltlessness should be numbered among the qualifications for throwing the first stone.[2] If it was, few hands would be more eminently incompetent than the one now so busy in the task.

Mark well the principle then—*neighbour's-fare*. The name given to it is proverbial—familiar—even to vulgarity.—It must be so to be useful.—Wide waft it, ye winds—God speed it among the throng.

I am fighting some of my best and most respected friends—I know it but too well—I cast myself on their forgiveness.—Will this obtain it?—I am fighting myself likewise.

What has been said of Dr Johnson on the ground of infidelity,[3] may not be inapplicable to myself on the ground of false tenderness. The stronger my propensity to yield to it, the more strenuous my efforts to subdue it.

[1] See Matthew 6: 11; Luke 11: 3.

[2] An echo of John 8: 7.

[3] Bentham's reference is to Samuel Johnson (1709–84), lexicographer. The allusion has not been traced.

APPENDIX B
FARMING DEFENDED[1]

But this is farming the Poor (says an Objector)—*and farming the Poor* is—every thing that is 'abominable'.[2]

To this, my answers are two. One is, that even under the existing system, farming is, in every instance in which it is practised, the very best species of management that can be practised:—the other is, that whatever objections it may be exposed to, as practised under the existing system, under the system here proposed it would stand altogether clear of them.

That it possesses one advantage—economy—is agreed on all hands. To counterpoise this argument, something in the way of argument might rationally be expected:—no such thing. Led away by prejudice, the result of passion—though a passion of a most laudable and purest kind—men talk, on this as on so many other subjects, as sheep walk. Farming is a species of usury—what can I, what can *I*, say more?[a]

Not only public economy, but justice, private industry, and most of the virtues of humble life turn (it has surely been said often enough) upon the efficacy of the means employ'd for separating unfounded from founded claims. What I have taken the liberty to term the *neighbour's-fare* principle is, once more, the most powerful, and, where coupled with the *Earn-first* principle, the infallible, and only infallible, as well as only permanent, test, which the nature of things affords for effecting this separation.[3] The farming principle, as employ'd in the existing order of things, is, in the existing order of things, the most effectual course that can be taken for ensuring the application of one or both those fundamental principles, according to the circumstances of the case.

That it is equally favourable to the comfort, real or apparent, of the individuals to be provided for, might be too much to say: but that, in respect of whatever degree of comfort is not incompatible with the

[a] See *Defence of Usury*.

[1] For the relationship between this discussion and Bentham's other poor law writings see the Editorial Introduction, pp. xl–xli and l–li above.

[2] The objector Bentham has in mind is Joseph Townsend: see *Dissertation on the Poor Laws*, p. 75.

[3] For definitions of the Neighbour's-Fare Principle and the Earn-First Principle see p. 207 n. and p. 267 n. above respectively.

pursuit of the still superior objects of attention so often spoken of, it possesses an advantage not possessed by the ordinary or uninterested mode of management, may safely be affirmed.

The jealousy and suspicion so apt to be awakened in every feeling breast by the spectacle of an arrangement in appearance so unpromising to the comfort of the persons who are the subject of it—the prevalence of this very jealousy and suspicion affords a security, and that of the strongest kind, against the existence of those very abuses on the existence of which the foundation for these tutelary affections depends. I do really take it for an indisputable truth, and a truth that is one of the corner stones of political science—the more strictly we are watched, the better we behave. Management on the interested plan acts as a stimulant on the superintending eye: management on the uninterested plan, as a relaxant. The Farmer of the Poor will always be watched: and every selfish and dissocial principle will, in his instance, fight with a muffle on it. All superintending ears are open to hear complaints against him: and therefore all interested tongues are upon the watch to find matter for such complaints. The Overseer of the Poor will, comparatively speaking, not be watched at all. Is he accused of cruelty?—his answer is ready.—What should make me cruel?—what have I to get by it?—little perhaps, besides the gratification of the dissocial passions:—for avarice there is, perhaps, but little place: but indolence, peevishness, pride, party enmity unchecked by sensibility, have full swing. See how it stands in point of fact. Complaints loud enough to terminate in prosecutions have, in the instance of Overseers, been not altogether unfrequent, and, it may be added, in general but too just: of a prosecution against a Farmer of the Poor I know not that I ever met with an example. The Court of the public eye is his Court, and (being though not so learned nor quite so temperate as other Courts, yet rather more expeditious in the proceedings, and less fettered by irrational rules of evidence) keeps him in order, without troubling the King's Bench or the Old Bailey.

We ought not to imagine—though men talk as if they did imagine—that the checks which have been provided in the case of Overseers are wanting in the case of Farmers: that the Pauper, for instance, who is heard by a Magistrate in his complaints against an Overseer for neglect or cruelty, can not be heard against a Farmer.[1] The same checks exist in the one case as in the other:

[1] The manner in which farmers of the poor treated their charges was open only to limited inspection. The preamble of 22 Geo. III., c.83 (1782) criticized the 'Want of due Inspection and Controul over the Persons who have engaged in those Contracts' (to maintain and employ the poor of particular parishes), and noted that the poor 'instead of finding Protection and Relief, have been much oppressed thereby'. In consequence, the Act limited the term of any such

with this difference, that in the one case they find the hand that should administer them naturally backward, in the other as naturally alert.

Dr Burn, in one of his books, has drawn a hobgoblin, and written under it Farmer of the Poor.[1] This picture has from that time to the present stood in the place of argument.

Adam Smith has drawn his hobgoblin, and written under it *Farmer General.*[2] Had Adam Smith's book contained nothing of any greater depth or truth than this picture, it would not have been what we see it. It was a picture from the French: who after bespattering the most frugal Collectors of the Revenue under the old system, cut their throats under the new one.[3] It may be questioned whether, even in the article of diminution of hardship, the contributors have been gainers by the change.

I don't know whether it was before or after Smith's book came out that I too must be drawing my hobgoblin. Like Smith's the colours of it [were][4] French: Montesquieu could not have done it better: for it was all epigram: consequently all false: and the stings were picked up here and there from Montesquieu.[5] Such was my hobgoblin picture: but after it had undergone its probation on the shelf for more than Horace's term of nine years,[6] instead of publishing it, as Burn and Smith did their's, I threw it into the fire.

contract to twelve months, and gave power to two Justices of the Peace, upon proof of abuse, to dissolve the contract. Eden noted that in Sedburgh the Justices refused to authorize the contract for farming the poor 'upon the Contractor's not allowing them sufficient victuals': see *The State of the Poor*, ii. 90.

[1] See Richard Burn (1709–85), legal writer, *The Justice of the Peace, and Parish Officer*, 10th edn., 4 vols., London, 1766, iii. 439: 'the overseers in many places having found out a method of contracting with some obnoxious person, of savage disposition, for the maintenance of their poor: not with any intention of the poor being better provided for, but to hang over them *in terrorem*, if they will not be satisfied with the pittance which the overseers think fit to allow them'.

[2] See *The Wealth of Nations*, ii. 902–5, where Smith, with specific reference to France, attacks the practice of farming out the collection of public revenues, and the leasing from 1697 of the collection of indirect taxation to sixty financiers, known collectively as 'Farmers General', each appointed by the King for six years, and paid an agreed sum in advance for each year.

[3] The harshness with which the Famers General exacted their collections, and their ostentatious wealth, made them the target of severe criticism before the French Revolution: see for instance Victor Riqueti, Marquis de Mirabeau, *Théorie de L'Impôt*, Avignon, 1761, pp. 73–91; and L.S. Mercier, *Tableau de Paris*, 12 vols., Amsterdam, 1782–3, ii. 123. In 1790 the farming of indirect taxes was abolished, and in February 1793 the National Convention launched an enquiry into the abuses of the tax farmers. On 8 May 1794 twenty-seven Farmers General and other financiers were guillotined in Paris, having been condemned on charges of fraud and counter-revolutionary conspiracy.

[4] MS 'was'.

[5] See Montesquieu, *De l'esprit des loix*, Bk. XIII, Ch. XIX, where the raising of revenue by direct taxes is compared with tax farming, to the disadvantage of the latter.

[6] See Horace, *Ars poetica*, 388: *nonumque prematur in annum*, i.e. 'let it be suppressed for nine years'.

Shutting up Burn, Montesquieu and Smith, and looking a little more closely into the book of human nature, I found out at last that a species of management, the characteristic property of which is to afford at the same time the strongest stimulant to what is good in management, and the strongest check to what is bad, is, instead of being the worst species of management, in most cases the only good one.[a]

The pleasant thing is to observe the champion of the No-provision system, joining the cry against the Farmer: seeing the monster down, he too must have a kick at him. A harder kick is not often given:—an 'expedient . . . the most abominable that ever was invented.'[b] What then?—Giving them too little, if that were really the effect—giving them somewhat less than the two shillings mentioned in the way of example, is it more abominable than the giving them nothing at all? No matter—the temptation was irresistible—there stood the caitiff in the pillory—the instrument, and fortunately the obnoxious instrument, of that other abominable system which keeps the poor from starving. When a mobbing scene is begun, with what different views of things may different individuals join in it. Those who put the Farmer into the pillory did so for not giving enough. Monster! heart-of-stone! cries the reformer who is for giving nothing.

One property it would not have been easy to deny to the monster: the property of keeping out of the temple of Charity unworthy claimants, themselves being judges: and my friend in the same breath admitts it. Laying every thing together, his quarrel with the existing order of things, in a word with the adequate-provision system, turns upon one or two grievances, according as the abominable expedient is or is not employ'd: the one is that relief is administered where it is necessary: the two are—that it *is*

[a] The strong tincture of envy, which enters into the composition of the suspicion with which the hands through which money passes are regarded, is one main cause of the delusion. A penny peculated makes more sensation than a pound wasted: hence it is that pound-folly is so frequent an accompaniment to penny-wisdom. Hence it is that all the artillery of reform are pointed at corruption: whereas the mischief which the departments of administration [are][1] exposed to from corruption is as nothing in comparison of what they suffer from inability and that indiscipline which is the prolific cause of it.

Pure or impure, interested management will not endure hands that are unequal to their task: incapable, even to drivelling, uninterested management will not rid itself of them, so long as they are thought pure.

[b] *Dissertation*, p. 75.[2]

---

[1] MS 'is'.

[2] i.e. Townsend, *Dissertation on the Poor Laws*, p. 75.

administered where it is *necessary*, and that it is *not* administered where it is *not* necessary.[a]

'But then is not this' (cries my friend) 'a partial, impolitic,

[a] Yes—that I will—rather than think the instruction should be lost, I will turn informer, and tell tales.

Partaking not many years ago of the hospitality of my friend,[1] and begging leave to put myself to school to him in this branch of public economy, I was taken by him to two places.[2] In both the management struck me as good, preeminently good; and it was for this reason that he showed them to me. But there are degrees of good: and without thinking of system, for my mind was then blank paper upon the subject, one of them struck me as still better than the other. Which then, was this best of two good establishments?—It was the den of one of those monsters, and a monster, whether placed or no I forget, but at any rate valued and countenanced, by my friend. The man without interest had an electrical machine (I do not say a bad implement) but at any rate, as an implement, for sifting out the bad claims, from the good.[3] The monster had no machine. Was the monster any thing else than a kind, as well as a thrifty, manager, any thing different but what, in such a situation, one would wish a man to be?

I could no more believe it than I could doubt of my friend's being a good manager, a good husband, a good father or a good master. Allowing for the difference of situations, the evidence (the *evidentia rei*)[4] was precisely the same in both cases: a neat habitation—cheerful accents and contented countenances. Having at that time a dawn of a situation similar to that which the course of events has at length brought within reach,[5] I looked at the monster with longing eyes. But he seemed too valuable to be willingly parted with: and the consideration where I found him, and by whose means I found him, that and that only—stopped my mouth. Next to the having my friend for an associate, this was the man (I thought) I should like to have as a subordinate.

How to reconcile then what I *saw* with what I *read*?—the inconsistency is apparent,

---

[1] i.e. Townsend.

[2] The corresponding marginal summary at UC cli. 5 states: 'Head and the Bradford man.' Head has not been identified. Eden recorded that since 1784 the general Overseer of the Poor in Bradford, Wiltshire, had been a Mr Rainey, at a salary of £100 a year, of which he accepted only £60. However, in Bentham's view, while Rainey was thus 'uninterested', the master of the workhouse in Bradford received £10 a year, and was 'allowed 2d. out of every shilling which the Poor earn', which rendered him an 'interested' man. (See *The State of the Poor*, iii. 783–5.) It is therefore not clear whether Bentham's 'Bradford man' is the interested or uninterested manager in the following discussion.

[3] The electrical machine to which Bentham refers may have been the portable electrostatic generator for which Edward Nairne (1726–1806), instrument maker, was granted a patent (No. 1318/1782) on 5 February 1782, and which was supplied as part of a medical electrical kit with special conductors to draw sparks from, or to give shocks to, the patient: see *The Description and Use of Nairne's Patent Electrical Machine; with the addition of some Philosophical Experiments and Medical Observations*, London, 1783. No reference to such a machine's use to detect fraudulent claims to relief has been discovered, although the exposure of supposedly useless limbs to electric shocks would presumably have rendered such imposition less tempting.

[4] i.e. 'the evidence of the matter'.

[5] i.e. the establishment of Bentham's proposed panopticon prison house. Pitt had approved Bentham's plan as early as July 1793, but attempts to execute it had been beset by difficulties. At the time of writing, early in 1797, Bentham was confident that the prison would finally be built in Tothill Fields, Westminster.

oppressive repeal of a bad law, without reducing the tax?—for it continues to encrease, and without making a better provision for those among the Poor who are most worthy of attention'[1]—Thus far the oppugner of the Farming expedient.

As to the partiality—we have seen what it amounts to—keeping in the worthy—shutting out those who, themselves being judges, are unworthy. As to the words '*impolicy*' and '*oppression*', if they mean any thing distinct from partiality, I really don't know very well what to make of them. If the badness of the law consists in oppressiveness, the repeal of it, as far as it goes, should, one would imagine, be not oppressive, but disoppressive. As little do I know what to make of the non-reduction of the tax. What is 'confessed', and that immediately before, is 'that many are thereby deterred from making application for relief, who would otherwise have been a burthen on the public.'[2] How this should take place without reducing the taxes in question, and reducing them as far as it takes place, is more than I can see. The '*for it continues to encrease*', would be good logic if the 'abominable' expedient were employ'd every where: but it is not in perhaps one place out of twenty. Who are meant by those among the Poor 'who are most worthy of attention', and what better provision is the want of which, by this champion of the No-provision system, here spoken of as if it were a grievance, are two other points that seem to stand in need of explanation. According to my view of the matter, those who are most worthy, not to say the only persons worthy of attention in the way in question—in the way of relief at the public charge—are those who can not do without it. These, I presume, will not be deterred from applying to the monster by any picture that can be drawn of him: they will take a peep at him at any rate, to see whether he be like his picture. They will therefore apply for relief, and they will get it: for there must be, not one monster, but a neighbourhood of monsters, the whole body of Magistrates included, if any of those, who want relief and ask for it, starve.

'Partial, impolitic, oppressive repeal of a bad law'?—shall this be our account of the Farming System? No: but (speaking roundly, and bating shades of improvement) let us say rather—a repeal of what

but not real. My friend had taken his theory from theory. The general horror had been imbibed from general horror: and the particular example on the other side did not seem sufficient to countervail the general voice. What was taken for granted was the general rule: what was visible passed for no more than an exception.

[1] See Townsend, *Dissertation on the Poor Laws*, p. 76. There are minor inaccuracies in the rendering of the passage.

[2] Ibid. There are minor inaccuracies in the rendering of the passage.

there is bad, in a law of mixed complection—preserving there what is good in it.

But (says somebody) all this is personal and *verbal: all it proves is, that your friend's acknowledged eloquence happened on the occasion in question to want a dash of logic to correct it.*—No such thing:—it goes to the throat of the cause:—for on this side, let me see that man that can argue better. What he gives are sounds and pictures: and by whom has any thing else been given?—by whom can anything else be given?

When the engagement of the Manager is upon the farming plan, the connection between duty and interest, between the interest of the public and the interest of this individual, is in his instance as strong as possible. In respect of relief, it is the interest of the public that those who are a burthen upon it should be subsisted at as small an expence as possible: both on account of the expence, that the burthen on the public may be as small as possible, and on account of the example, that as few individuals as possible may be disposed to relax their own industry and throw themselves on the industry of others. This is the interest of the public, and the Farmer's interest is the same.

In respect of work, it is the interest of the public that as much be done, that is work to as much value by every such individual by whose work it is to be assisted in bearing the burthen, as possible: and that both for the sake of lightening the burthen, and, in the way of example, for the sake of showing that relief is not, by those who can work, to be had but in return for work. Such, as to this point, is the interest of the public: and the interest of the farming Manager is the same.

Objection. But it is not the interest of the community (says somebody) that a Pauper (who is as much a member of the community as any body else) should be either starved, or worked to death, or even to ill health:—and may not this be the interest of the Farming Manager: or (what would come to the same thing) be conceived by him to be his interest?—and is not this a sufficient reason for not having any thing to do with him, while others who have no such interest in opposition to humanity are to be had?

Answer. Although this were his interest, it would be no objection so long as there are powers sufficient to restrain him from giving way to this sinister part, the only sinister part, of his interest. So long as I can profit by a workman without injuring him either in his life or health, I am disposed to make what profit by him I can:—admitted—but does it follow that I should be equally disposed to pursue my profit, where I can not pursue it without doing him some such cruel injury?—Were I thus naturally disposed to pursue it, is there nothing external to restrain me? No law? No Magistracy? No means of preferring complaint? No ears open to receive it?

What is the money that a Farmer of the Poor could get by murdering one of his Wards in this manner, in comparison of the money that the eldest son of a rich Father would get by murdering his Father? But what are the opportunities in the one case, in comparison of the opportunities in the other?—Yet in how many instances since trials have reached the public eye through the medium of the press have the annals of the country been stained by parricide?

But it is not his interest, not even his pecuniary interest, to be guilty of any such abuse: it would not be, although there were no such thing as justice in the land. If I work my servant to death, I lose his service: if I work him into ill health without killing him, I hurt myself so much the more: it costs me at least as much, commonly more, to keep him, while I get less by him, if any thing, while he is kept. If again, I starve him to death, he is again lost to me: if I starve him into ill health, I must be a nice calculator and a nice manager indeed, if I can contrive to save as much by what I subtract from his food, as I lose by what is lost in the value of the work. Talent infinitely less would enable me to get much more without either guilt or infamy.

If I am paid by the head, as many as I lose, whether by over-working, by starving, or by negligence, so many the fewer am I paid for: what I gain is a few pence, once paid: what I lose is an annuity, perhaps for life.

If I am paid by the lump, then indeed, by starving or working them to death, I may save the expence of maintenance, at no other loss than the value of their labour: and therefore in this case, if there be neither conscience in my breast nor law in the country, I may be a gainer in respect of all such, the value of whose labour can not be made equal to the expence of keeping them alive. But in this case, the lease must be a very long one, a longer [one] than in such cases [has][1] ever perhaps been made, or I am still a loser: for as often as the lease comes to be renewed, people will make a pause: they will not, upon the renewal, pay me as much for those that are dead, as they would have done had they been alive.

Consider now how the matter stands, between the Farmer and another Manager, as to other points of ill usage, as to those species of ill usage which can have nothing but ill humour or indolence for their efficient cause, and by which nothing, not even for the moment, is to be gained. As to all these points, we shall see that interested

[1] MS 'as'.

management has much the advantage of uninterested: that the connection between interest and duty in the Farmer's case has a degree of strength which it has not in the other. The interest which the Farming Manager has in the health, strength and life of the persons committed to his charge, is what we have just seen: the other sort of Manager has no such special interest. He may have that general sort of interest which the principle of common humanity affords: but what should make the Farming Manager have less of it? Is a man less likely to be humane for his having a particular interest in being so?

As to negligence, indolence and so forth, these may exist on the part of the uninterested Managers, these may exist on the part of the Farming Manager—these may exist any where. But for the main purposes, viz: the purposes of keeping the people alive, and getting what work out of them can be got, the Farming Manager has an interest in looking after them, and that a strong and never-failing one: whereas the salary-paid sort of Manager (setting aside that general sort of interest which is common to both) has no special interest in the matter to any purpose at all.

Call them cattle—suppose them treated on no better footing than that of Cattle. I farm them. So long as I continue to farm them they are at any rate *my* Cattle. I look after them with not more attention, be it admitted, yet at any rate with not less attention than I do after my horse. I am a Farmer, keeping for my own use that species of Cattle. By whom then are they likely to be best taken care of? By myself, to whose share the loss by their death or sickness falls, or by the prentice, or fine gentleman, or fine gentleman's footman, who has them of me, and whips and spurs them on terms which ease him of the loss?[1]

But supposing the farming mode of management were a bad one under the existing order of things (the contrary of which has, I think, been proved), it would not the less be a good one under the system which is here proposed.

Under the existing order of things, the Farming Manager is always a man in a low sphere of life—a man of narrow education—a man who is not in the habit of looking up to that part of the world by which humanity, and the reputation of humanity, is most prized. He is, I say, that low and unpolished sort of man; for where the work is so much and the scale so small, terms capable of engaging a higher sort of man can not be afforded. Under the proposed system, the scale being beyond example large, the Managers in chief proportionably few,

[1] Bentham's allusion is to the 'roundsman' or 'billet' system, whereby the able-bodied poor without work were allotted to employers, with the parish providing part or all of their wages.

terms adequate to the engagement of a manager of the highest class of those who are not above the business of management may be, and, as proposed and insisted, should be afforded, and a proportionable scrutiny made into the fitness of the Candidates. Such a scrutiny, instituted or not by the Directors of the proposed company,[1] would at any rate be instituted and kept up by the public at large.[a]

Under the proposed system, the public is fixed upon the management—this, and a number of subordinate checks afford a safeguard in this case which is altogether wanting in the other. Under the existing order of things, no accounts kept, not so much as one, or if kept not published—or if published, scarce any body in the Parish, nobody out of it, would bestow a look upon them. Here every tittle of the management registered, published, pried into: the Parishes have their motives for looking into it: the Directors theirs: the Stockholders theirs: not to mention Administration, Parliament and the public at large. All lying within compass: an annual Volume of no more than 200 to 250 Folio Pages: and this not to be read over as a treatise, but to be turned to only as a Dictionary.

Farming is but one of a set of institutions which, with or without design, have been attended, or been supposed to be attended, with the effect of rendering the condition of a pauper, in reality or appearance, less eligible than that of a self-maintaining hand: and thence of deterring men from the act of investing themselves with this condition.

One is, the substitution of the Public-Establishment provision to Home-Provision: the general utility of this in other respects, and its

[a] The inconveniences which have created so general a dislike to the practice of farming the Poor are:

The districts in which the practice has obtained being small districts, the number of poor consequently small, the profit to be made from the undertaking proportionably small, and the term for which the establishments have been put out to farm short (in general only from year to year, the duration of the Overseers' time in their office), it has never been worth the acceptance of any man of education or fortune. The persons to whom it has been confined have been persons of the meanest order, in whose instance, for want of education, no refined sentiments of humanity, nor so much as any extensive and liberal knowledge of economical management, could be to be expected.

If they happened to be of a humane turn of mind by nature, yet, by reason of the shortness of their term, it was not worth their while, nor, for want of capital, in their power, to make any considerable profit by giving an advantageous direction to the sum of labour at their command. Parsimony therefore, was their chief, if not sole, resource: their profit would arise, if at all, from the smallness of the allowance they made, not from the amplitude of the produce to which they gave birth.

[1] i.e. the National Charity Company: see p. 208 n. above.

particular efficacy with regard to the particular point here in question, have been exhibited on a former occasion.[a]

Another is the introduction of Farming management, of which we have been just speaking.

A third is, the institution of badging, of which it remains to speak.

The introduction of the neighbour's-fare principle is another institution, the operation of which could not fail to act in the same direction, and with a very powerful addition of force.[1]

The introduction of the no-work no-eat principle would afford another and very powerful addition of repulsive power.[2]

The expedient of a Badge has experienced violent censure: it is a degradation of the human character: it is stamping infamy upon misfortune: it is confounding innocence with guilt.

Answer. Degrading a man is turning a man down from the class in which you find him, into another class which is below it. The Badge marks the class in which it finds him: and there it leaves him. Degradation changes the class: badging indicates it only, indicates it as being what it is, leaving it unchanged. It indicates him, it is true, as belonging to the lowest class:—true: but why?—because he does belong to it. At this rate a Coronet upon the Crest of a Baron is a degradation: why?—because it shows him to be below a Viscount.

If the mark for a Pauper were the same as that for a felon, then indeed, the affixing it would be stamping constant infamy upon what would oftentimes be mere misfortune: then indeed it would be confounding innocence with guilt. The mark branded upon the body of a felon certifies him to be a delinquent, and a delinquent of that class of delinquency which is termed felony.[3] The mark termed a Badge, and tacked to the garment of a Pauper, does not certify him to be a delinquent in any shape. What it does certify is that he is Poor: and so he is: that he is a burthen upon others: and so he is.

Under the existing system, the condition of a Pauper is in most

[a] Ch. iv.[4]

---

[1] See p. 267 n. above.

[2] i.e. the 'earn-first principle': see p. 207 n. above.

[3] 4 Hen. VII, c.13 (1487) enacted that persons not in holy orders would be allowed the benefit of clergy only once, and to this end prescribed that lay persons found guilty of felonies and granted clergy should be branded on the brawn of the thumb, with a letter indicating the nature of their offence, for instance with an 'M' for murder, and a 'T' for theft. Although the denial of the granting of clergy for a second offence was never regularly enforced, the branding of felons who had taken the benefit of clergy continued to be standard practice. In 1699, 10 & 11 Will. III, c.23 enacted that such felons should be branded not upon the thumb but on the left cheek, but this Act was repealed in 1706 by 5 Anne, c.6, after which the site of branding returned to the thumb.

[4] i.e. 'Pauper Systems Compared', Ch. IV, pp. 154–83 above.

instances that of an idler; under every system, it must be that of an hanger-on: what good purpose it can answer that the condition of the idler should be exhibited as upon a level with that of the man of industry—the condition of a hanger-on, upon a level with the condition of those on whom he hangs, is more than I can see: what harm it can do that the condition of the idle should be exhibited as below the level of the condition of the man of industry—the condition of a hanger-on as below the condition of those on whom he hangs, is more than I can see. The good that it can do, is what I do see. It consists in rendering the condition of the man of industry in appearance more eligible than that of the man of no-industry: it consequently tends to dispose men to embrace the former condition in preference to the latter.

Rank is relative: you can not raise one of two contiguous ranks, but you depress the other: you can not depress the one, but you raise the other. Poverty you have on both sides: poverty you have at any rate. How do you like it best?—with or without industry—take your choice.

By all this, I do not mean to say, that under the proposed system I would make a point of affixing a badge:—it would not be necessary: the cloathing best adapted to other purposes, would have the effect of operating as a distinction, with or without that view. What I mean to say, is that should that same effect follow from that or any other operation, with or without that view, so much the better: and that the principle upon which the effect is grounded is a principle not to be censured but adopted with applause.

When a man is thus deterred—be it by the substitution of the Public-Establishment system to the Home-Provision system—be it by the introduction of Farming management—be it by the execution of the law which prescribes badging[1]—be it by the introduction of so severe a measure as that of the neighbour's-fare principle, or the industry-enforcing principle—what becomes of him?—Does he sit down and starve?—No: he betakes himself to industry. If, upon a trial, he finds himself unable to derive a subsistence from that source,

[1] i.e. 8 & 9 Will. III, c.30 (1697), 'An Act for supplying some Defects in the Laws for the Relief of the Poor of this Kingdom', which directed that all persons in receipt of poor relief should 'upon the Shoulder of the Right Sleeve of the uppermost garment . . . in an open and visible Manner, wear such Badge or Mark as is herein after mentioned and expressed, that is to say, a large Roman P. together with the first Letter of the Name of the Parish or Place whereof such poor Person is an Inhabitant, cut either in red or blue Cloth'. Refusal to wear the badge was punishable by the withdrawal of relief, whipping, and confinement in a House of Correction for up to twenty-one days, while Overseers who allowed relief to unbadged persons were liable to a fine of twenty shillings. The Act was never widely enforced, and by the time Bentham was writing had become something of a dead letter.

does he *then* sit down and starve?—No—he comes back again to the Poor House. But is his condition, when he is in it, as eligible as it would be if he were out of it?—enquires the man of relentless humanity, determined, in the teeth of possibility, to bring happiness to a level? No certainly; it would be—or at least would appear to be, a good deal happier, if a pension were given to him to live upon where he likes best. A pension is a good thing: and it were a good state of things, if all of us could have pensions. But still there remains this difficulty.—When all are to receive pensions, who is there to pay them? When all are receivers, who are payers?

Men's faculties are of two kinds: passive and active. It is only through the passive that impressions from without can make their way through to the active: but so sure as an impression is made on the passive, so sure, under certain circumstances, does it pass on, and make its way to the active, and, according to its nature, apply restraint or impulse to the active. The short-sighted eye of false humanity is arrested at the first of these stages: strength will not permitt, it can travel no farther: and this short-sightedness, this inadvertence, is the source of all its errors. It considers man only in as far as he is a passible being: whereas he is never a passible being without becoming proportionably an agible one. Turning to the delinquent, false humanity says to itself—No: He shall not suffer—what follows?—that because this one guilty man is not to suffer, many that are innocent suffer a great deal more. Turning to the indigent idler, it says to him—Take that my poor fellow, and be happy.—What follows—that by being thus made happy for the moment, he is engaged or confirmed in a life of idleness, which is a life of wretchedness: a life in which the industrious are thenceforward compelled by law to fix him at their own charge. What then does this philanthropist, man of charity, of generosity, of fine feelings—by whom men of equal humanity but superior discernment are to be scorned for the hardness of their hearts? On one hand, by affording momentary enjoyment, he fixes permanent misery: on the other hand, to purchase a momentary gratification for himself, he imposes a permanent tax, and we all know but too well how heavy an one, upon his neighbours.[a]

[a] Let not the order of things, or of reasonings, be misconceived. It was not to recommend the farming system that I set about giving this statement of what ought to be the condition of the dependent Poor: it was as a means of fixing that which ought to be the condition of the dependent Poor, that I set about enquiring into the propriety of the farming system. So soon as any body shall have shown me, either that such ought not to be the condition of the dependent Poor, or that the Farming system of management is not the system of management best adapted to the fixing

them in that condition, my recommendation of the farming system is at an end. Should the farming system be adopted, it will be of use that the reasons that plead in favour of it should have presented themselves and been made public before hand, and not be suspected of having been thought of afterwards.

The relative order in which two sets of considerations have happened to present themselves to the mind of A or B, is a question than which, with a view to the justness of those reflections in themselves, nothing can be more frivolous: but it is upon these points, in themselves so frivolous, that the judgment of the bulk of mankind is but too apt to depend: to judge whether a reason is good in itself requires more time than a man chooses to spare, and commonly more talent than he is master of: but to judge of it by that most irrelevant and indeterminable of all criteria, the supposed motives of him by whom the reason is held up to view, requires neither time nor talent, nor any thing else but the giving the rein to a man's affections: if I happen to be in a good humour with a man, I call his motives good, and I give him credit for the goodness of his reasons: if in a bad humour, I call his motives bad, and, as for his reasons, I won't hear them.

INDEX OF SUBJECTS

Note. The following is a unified index which refers to the texts of all the works included in this volume, without identifying the particular work in question.

References to Bentham's notes and to editorial footnotes are given by means of the page number(s) followed by the letter 'n.'.

The symbol 'v.' is used to indicate 'as distinct from' or 'as opposed to'. Other abbreviations for frequently occurring words and phrases are as follows:

h.p.s.	Home-Provision system
i.h.	Industry house(s)
p.e.s.	Public-Establishment system

INDEX OF NAMES

Note. The following is an index of names of persons and places appearing in the introduction, text, and notes; the last (whether Bentham's or the editor's) are indicated by 'n.' Under Bentham's name only references to his other works are indicated.